中南财经政法大学2021年研究生教学教改项目"经济文本翻译"特色教材项目研究成果

经济文本翻译教程

主　编　袁奇
副主编　田川　周敏

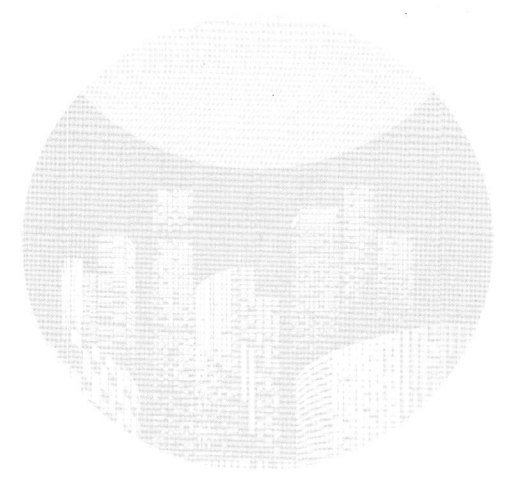

A COURSEBOOK ON TRANSLATION
OF ECONOMIC TEXTS

武汉大学出版社

图书在版编目(CIP)数据

经济文本翻译教程:汉、英/袁奇主编.—武汉:武汉大学出版社,2021.6
ISBN 978-7-307-22178-9

Ⅰ.经… Ⅱ.袁… Ⅲ.经济—英语—翻译—高等学校—教材 Ⅳ.F0

中国版本图书馆 CIP 数据核字(2021)第 047123 号

责任编辑:罗晓华　　责任校对:汪欣怡　　版式设计:韩闻锦

出版发行：**武汉大学出版社**　（430072　武昌　珞珈山）
（电子邮箱：cbs22@whu.edu.cn　网址：www.wdp.com.cn）
印刷：湖北金海印务有限公司
开本：787×1092　1/16　印张：18.5　字数：416 千字　插页：1
版次：2021 年 6 月第 1 版　　2021 年 6 月第 1 次印刷
ISBN 978-7-307-22178-9　　定价：52.00 元

版权所有,不得翻印;凡购我社的图书,如有质量问题,请与当地图书销售部门联系调换

前　言

在社会经济发展中，经济文本扮演着重要的角色，已经成为许多人工作和生活中不可或缺的一部分。随着我国经济与世界经济的接轨，经济文本翻译的重要性日趋明显。本教材中的经济文本泛指人们在进行经济研究、从事经济活动、讨论经济话题时所使用的文本，具有丰富的内涵和形式。经济文本涉及的领域极其广泛，几乎包括了经济活动的所有领域。而且，经济文本涵盖的文本类型不一，形式多样，特征各异。一份经济调查报告，一篇经济学的学术论文，或者是在一个经济工作会议上的演讲稿，都可以被看作经济文本。本教材中主要探讨的经济文本包括经济新闻报道、经济研究与调查报告、经济学论文、经济学教材、经济学经典文献、经济会议演讲发言、经济会议联合公报、经济发展计划、经济合同相关法律法规等。

本教材是中南财经政法大学翻译硕士（MTI）"经济文本翻译"课程教学改革探索和实践积累的成果，旨在帮助学生顺利翻译经济活动相关的英语文献和资料。编者认为，MTI的教学工作有其独特的性质和特点，更偏向于实践性，让学生通过大量的翻译练习来学习翻译技巧和提高翻译水平。因此，针对MTI专业课程的翻译教材应该注重满足学习者的实际需求，从解决现实翻译问题出发。本教材是基于以上认识编写完成的，旨在系统介绍经济文本翻译的基础知识、各类经济文本的语言特点及翻译技巧。通过选择实际工作中会经常接触到的经济文本形式和真实的翻译案例，重点讲解在翻译中经常碰到的各种问题及其解决方法，帮助学生尽快了解各种类型经济文本的翻译，以适应实际工作的需要。本教材主要适用于高等院校翻译专业的本科生或者研究生，可用作其经济翻译类课程的教材，也可作为经济翻译相关工作者的自学教材。

本教材共分十章，每章内容由四个部分组成。第一部分"经济文本分析"，主要介绍本单元所涉及文本的语言风格和特点。第二部分是"翻译知识讲解"，主要介绍本单元所涉及的翻译策略、方法和技巧。第三部分是"常用词汇与表达"，主要介绍本单元所涉及的常见专有名词、专业术语和特殊表达式。第四部分是"译文赏析"，主要通过对具体翻译案例的分析进行讲解。另外，每章最前面设计了"思考题"，主要用于课程导入，引出本章话题。每章最后设计了"翻译练习"，包括词组翻译、句子翻译和语篇翻译，目的在于巩固本单元所学知识。书后附有每章的练习参考译文，便于学生核对和自主学习。

本教材是中南财经政法大学2021年研究生教学教改项目"经济文本翻译"特色教材项目的研究成果，出版得到了该项目经费资助，我们对学校的大力支持表示感谢。其次，感谢参与本教材编写与审校的老师和同学：周艳芳、潘晓妃、霍世莹、毕淑婷、陈孖婧、吴越、叶冉、王同宇、钟佩殷、张思颖、张丹丹、廖薇、胡思雨、吴晓敏、周小芳。此外，本教材在编写过程中参考了国内外的相关书刊并引用了部分资料，在此向有关作者和单位表示诚挚的感谢。

由于编者水平有限，编写中肯定存在不少疏漏和欠妥之处，欢迎同行专家和广大读者多多批评指正。

编者

2021 年 2 月

目　　录

第一章　经济文本翻译导论 ··· 1
　第一节　经济文本分析 ··· 1
　第二节　翻译知识讲解 ··· 7
　第三节　常用词汇与表达 ·· 12
　第四节　译文赏析 ·· 13

第二章　经济新闻报道翻译 ·· 22
　第一节　经济新闻报道文本分析 ·································· 22
　第二节　翻译知识讲解 ·· 28
　第三节　常用词汇与表达 ·· 32
　第四节　译文赏析 ·· 33

第三章　经济研究与调查报告翻译 ·································· 45
　第一节　经济研究与调查报告文本分析 ···························· 45
　第二节　翻译知识讲解 ·· 51
　第三节　常用词汇与表达 ·· 62
　第四节　译文赏析 ·· 63

第四章　经济学论文翻译 ·· 78
　第一节　经济学论文文本分析 ···································· 78
　第二节　翻译知识讲解 ·· 83
　第三节　常用词汇与表达 ·· 92
　第四节　译文赏析 ·· 93

第五章　经济学教材翻译 ··· 102
　第一节　经济学教材文本分析 ··································· 102
　第二节　翻译知识讲解 ··· 108
　第三节　常用词汇与表达 ······································· 111
　第四节　译文赏析 ··· 112

第六章　经济学经典文献翻译 123
第一节　经济学经典文献文本分析 123
第二节　翻译知识讲解 126
第三节　常用词汇与表达 138
第四节　译文赏析 139

第七章　经济会议演讲发言翻译 153
第一节　经济会议演讲文本分析 153
第二节　翻译知识讲解 155
第三节　常用词汇与表达 158
第四节　译文赏析 158

第八章　经济会议联合公报翻译 172
第一节　经济会议联合公报文本分析 172
第二节　翻译知识讲解 176
第三节　常用词汇与表达 183
第四节　译文赏析 184

第九章　经济发展计划翻译 197
第一节　经济发展计划文本分析 197
第二节　翻译知识讲解 201
第三节　常用词汇与表达 208
第四节　译文赏析 210

第十章　经济合同相关法律法规翻译 224
第一节　经济合同相关法律法规分析 224
第二节　翻译知识讲解 235
第三节　常用词汇与表达 245
第四节　译文赏析 247

翻译练习参考译文 259

第一章 经济文本翻译导论

> **☞思考题**
> 1. 经济文本包括哪些具体形式？
> 2. 经济文本具有什么语言特征？
> 3. 经济文本翻译要注意哪些问题？

第一节 经济文本分析

一、经济文本的定义与内涵

在社会经济发展中，经济文本扮演着重要的角色，已经成为许多人工作和生活中不可或缺的一部分。本教材中的经济文本泛指人们在进行经济研究、从事经济活动、讨论经济话题时所使用的文本，具有丰富的内涵和形式。一份经济调查报告，一篇经济学的学术论文，或者是一个经济工作会议上的演讲稿，都可以被看作经济文本。

例1

原文：在地缘政治紧张、中国经济增速放缓和A股市场表现不佳等大背景下，2018年至2019年上半年，证券行业的周期性特征有所显现，行业集中度进一步提升，"马太效应"凸显。证券公司积极持续探索转型之路，在组织架构、风险管控、业务创新、激励机制、人力资源等方面修炼内功，寻找新的业务模式和增长引擎。根据中国证券业协会各家证券公司经审计的年报数据汇总，经营业绩方面，2018年证券行业实现营业收入和净利润分别为人民币2633亿元和人民币624亿元(母公司财务报表口径，下同)，较2017年分别下滑了16%和44%；资产规模方面，2018年131家证券公司资产总额为人民币6.3万亿元，较2017年全年增加2%；净资产为人民币1.9万亿元，较上年增加2%。收入结构方面，2018年证券公司各业务条线收入均有不同程度的回落，整体结构与上年基本保持一致。其中，自营业务全年实现收益(公允价值变动损益与投资收益合计)人民币867亿元，较2017年相比减少了15%，但仍保持了最大收入来源。经纪业务收入受市场交易量和佣金费率持续下滑的影响，收入较上年下降22%。投行业务的收入亦下降28%，主要是由于股权融资规模下降。在去通道、限杠杆和提升主动管理能力等一系列资管新规的要求下，资管业务收入占比较上一年略有上升，但绝对额下降约11%。

（毕马威中国，《2019年中国证券业调查报告》）

译文：Against a backdrop of geopolitical uncertainty, slowing domestic economic growth and a weak A-share market, Chinese mainland securities industry, reflected a cyclical nature through 2018 to the first half of 2019 and demonstrated the "Matthew Effect", which can be observed by the industry's increasing market concentration. Despite the slowing growth, securities companies are actively trying to evolve in terms of organizational structure, risk management, business innovation, incentive systems and human resources in order to create new business models and drive growth. According to the audited annual reports of securities companies in China released by the Securities Association of China (SAC), the securities industry realised operating income of RMB 263.3 billion and net profits of RMB 62.4 billion (based on financial statements at the parent company level) in 2018, which represented year-on-year declines of 16 percent and 44 percent, respectively. The total assets of the 131 securities companies that were counted stood at RMB 6.3 trillion, representing a year-on-year increase of 2 percent; net assets amounted to RMB 1.9 trillion, which constituted a year-on-year increase of 2 percent. In 2018, income composition remained in line with the previous year, although the income level from various segments declined in varying degrees. During the year, the proprietary trading segment remained the most significant source of income. This segment realised RMB 86.7 billion in income (including profits or losses arising from changes in fair values and investment income), down 15 percent from 2017. The brokerage segment's operating income decreased by 22 percent compared with the previous year, and was the result of declining transaction volumes and lower commission rates. The investment banking segment's income also declined 28 percent year-on-year. This decrease was primarily caused by reduced equity financing. As a result of new asset management regulations that reduced funding channel operations, implemented deleveraging measures and enhanced active management capabilities, the share of the industry's total operating income increased slightly in 2018, yet the amount was down by 11 percent.

例2

原文：20世纪中叶以来，"消费"一词成为西方发达国家的核心话语之一，世人已认同用"消费社会"来标识当代西方社会，"消费主义"也成为西方发达国家占主导地位的生活方式和消费价值观。在我国，一方面，由于经济发展和西方价值观的影响，"消费主义"的生活方式和价值观念影响日深，渐成时尚，抗衡极具诱惑力的西方"消费主义"的挑战，向我们提出了建构具有中国特色的新型消费观的要求；另一方面，全球性的金融危机又将鼓励消费，提升国民的消费能力、消费意愿的目标摆在我们面前，它又要求我们建构的消费观必须是具有时代感的、健康适度的积极消费观。现实和未来要求我们重新审视我国当前社会的消费方式和消费观念，在鼓励提倡消费和批判消费主义的两难选择面前寻求平衡点。于是，探求在人的需求满足与环境保护之间、不同社会消费群体之间、人的物质享受与精神境界提高之间相协调的和谐消费观，就成为具有重大理论价值和实践意义的课题。

译文：Since the middle of the twentieth century, "consumption" has become a key word in the vocabulary of industrialized countries. As a symbol of Western society, nowadays "consumerism" is the dominating life style and values in these counties. In China it is also very influential. In order to face the challenge of this Western concept and, at the same time, stimulate China's domestic consumption under the background of the financial crisis, it's of great significance to construct a new moderate consumption concept that combines the merits of both Western and Chinese features. In view of the present situation and future development, it's necessary for us to reconsider Chinese people's spending patterns and styles, so as to keep a balance between encouraging and restricting consumption. Therefore, it's a very meaningful task to build up a harmonious consumption concept which aims to protect natural environment while satisfying different people's needs, balancing material comforts and spiritual improvement.

例3

原文：尊敬的祖马总统，尊敬的特梅尔总统，尊敬的普京总统，尊敬的莫迪总理，女士们，先生们，朋友们：很高兴同各位同事再次相聚。首先，我谨代表中国政府和中国人民，对大家出席金砖国家领导人厦门会晤表示热烈的欢迎。我期待着同各位同事一道，围绕"深化金砖伙伴关系，开辟更加光明未来"的会晤主题，回顾总结金砖合作，勾画未来发展蓝图，开启合作新航程。金砖合作已经走过10年光辉历程。我们五国虽然山海相隔，但怀着合作共赢的共同目标走到了一起。中国古人说："交得其道，千里同好，固于胶漆，坚于金石。"金砖合作之所以得到快速发展，关键在于找准了合作之道。这就是互尊互助，携手走适合本国国情的发展道路；秉持开放包容、合作共赢的精神，持之以恒推进经济、政治、人文合作；倡导国际公平正义，同其他新兴市场国家和发展中国家和衷共济，共同营造良好外部环境。事实证明，金砖合作契合我们五国发展共同需要，顺应历史大势。尽管我们五国国情不同，但我们对伙伴关系、繁荣发展的追求是共同的，这使我们能够超越差异和分歧，努力实现互利共赢。当前，世界格局发生了许多深刻复杂变化。在这一背景下，金砖合作显得更加重要。五国人民希望我们携手促进发展，提高人民福祉。国际社会期待我们维护世界和平，推动共同发展。我们应该再接再厉，全面深化金砖伙伴关系，开启金砖合作第二个"金色十年"。

（习近平，《深化金砖伙伴关系　开辟更加光明未来》，新华网，2017年9月4日）

译文：Your Excellency President Jacob Zuma, Your Excellency President Michel Temer, Your Excellency President Vladimir Putin, Your Excellency Prime Minister Narendra Modi, Ladies and Gentlemen, Dear Friends, I am delighted to meet with my colleagues again. I wish to begin by extending, on behalf of the Chinese government and people, a warm welcome to you all. Welcome to the BRICS Xiamen Summit. With the focus on the theme of the summit: "Stronger Partnership for a Brighter Future", I look forward to working with you to take stock of BRICS cooperation, map out a blueprint for its future development and set sail on a new journey of cooperation. BRICS cooperation has traversed a glorious journey of one decade. Though separated by mountains and oceans, our five countries have been closely bound by a shared commitment to win-win cooperation. As an ancient Chinese saying goes, "A partnership forged with the right approach defies geographical distance; it is thicker than glue and stronger than metal and stone." We owe the rapid development of BRICS cooperation to our adoption of a right approach. Guided by this approach, we have respected and supported each other in following the path of development suited to our respective national conditions; we have pushed forward economic, political and people-to-people cooperation in an open, inclusive and win-win spirit; and we have worked in unison with other emerging market and developing countries to uphold international justice and equity and foster a sound external environment. Past progress shows that BRICS cooperation has met our common need for development and is in keeping with the trend of history. Though we have different national conditions, we share the commitment to pursuing development and prosperity through partnership. This has enabled us to rise above differences and seek win-win results. As the world undergoes profound and complex changes, BRICS cooperation has become more important. Our people expect us to jointly boost development and improve their well-being. The international community expects us to make contribution to world peace and common development. We must redouble our efforts to comprehensively deepen BRICS partnership and usher in the second "Golden Decade" of BRICS cooperation.

经济文本涉及的领域极其广泛，几乎包括了经济研究和经济生活的所有领域。本教材中主要探讨的经济文本包括经济新闻报道、经济研究与调查报告、经济学论文、经济学教材、经济学经典文献、经济会议演讲发言稿、经济会议联合公报、经济发展计划、经济合同相关法律法规等。而且，经济文本涵盖的文本类型不一，形式多样，特征各异。

例如前文中的例1节选自毕马威中国发表的《2019年中国证券业调查报告》，原文是一篇关于中国证券行业最新发展趋势的调查报告，其中包括丰富翔实的数据，以及关于数据增加、减少等变化的表述。其次，文中还有一些关于证券公司业务的四字结构表达，如"组织架构、风险管控、业务创新、激励机制、人力资源"等。此外，文中还提到了政府对证券行业监管政策方面的内容，如"去通道、限杠杆和提升主动管理能力等一系列资管新规"。

前文中的例2节选自论文《论多重视域中的和谐消费观》，原文是一篇关于中国居民消费研究的经济学学术论文，文中主要采用第一人称，如"全球性的金融危机又将鼓励消费，提升国民的消费能力、消费意愿的目标摆在我们面前，它又要求我们建构的消费观必须是具有时代感的、健康适度的积极消费观"一句中的"摆在我们面前""要求我们"等。此外，文中还出现了许多关于国民消费的经济学专业术语，如"消费主义""消费能力""消费意愿""消费方式""消费观念"和"消费群体"等。

前文中的例3节选自习近平主席在金砖国家领导人厦门会晤上的致辞，既涉及政治合作问题也涉及经济发展问题，所以也可以被看作一个经济文本。致辞使用的是第一人称，而且原文中出现了一些世界各国领导人姓名的专有名词，如"祖马总统""特梅尔总统""普京总统""莫迪总理"。用了一些典型的外交辞令，如"我谨代表中国政府和中国人民，对大家出席金砖国家领导人厦门会晤表示热烈的欢迎"。文中还出现了中国领导人致辞时常用的方式，即引经据典，引用古文，如"中国古人说：'交得其道，千里同好，固于胶漆，坚于金石'"。

通过以上对比分析我们可以看出，尽管前文3个例子都属于经济文本，但是其风格特色各异，表达方式不同，具体内容有别，因此在对其进行翻译时，要求译者采用不同的翻译理论、翻译原则、翻译策略和技巧。

二、经济文本与管理文本的区别

要理解经济文本与管理文本的区别，首先要了解经济学与管理学的区别。从本质上说，经济学研究的是经济运行的基本规律，而管理学研究的是在现有经济运行条件下，如何实现效率的最大化。经济学往往从政府层面来研究政府如何克制企业垄断、提升市场竞争、优化资源配置，主要是解释问题的因果逻辑，为政府制定政策改善社会福利提供依据。而管理学是研究企业如何提升自身战略垄断力即核心竞争力，学习解决问题的策略和艺术，提供打击竞争对手、赢得顾客的手段。

经济和管理既有相似性，又有异质相异性，它们既有联系，也有区别。其相似性在于：两者的行为主体都是人或组织，基本原理和规律常常一致。其相异性在于：经济研究和经济实践更倾向于宏观方面，通常是整体的概念；而管理研究和管理实践更倾向于微观方面，通常是个体的概念；经济是人类社会活动的一个方面，而社会各个方面都需要进行管理。一些规律既适用于经济，也适用于管理。经济和管理互相影响，管理行为会影响到经济状况，经济行为也会改变管理行为。总体上看，经济和管理之间相互联系、相互区别、相互影响。经济学专业主要有国际经济与贸易、金融学、经济学、财政学（含税务）等。管理学专业主要有工商管理、会计学、市场营销学、工业工程、信息管理与信息系统等。

如前文所述，本教材中的"经济文本"泛指人们在进行经济研究、从事经济活动、讨论经济话题时所使用的文本。相对而言,"管理文本"则泛指人们在进行管理学研究、从事管理活动、讨论管理学话题时所使用的文本,其同样具有丰富的内涵和形式,例如管理学的学术论文、公司章程等管理文件和规定等都可以被视为管理文本。

三、经济文本与经济文书的区别

"经济文本(economic texts)"与"经济文书(economic documents)"这两个概念很容易被混为一谈。从本质上说,"经济文书"是经济应用文的通称,是法人单位或个人在经济活动和经济交往过程中反映经济情况,处理经济事务,研究、解决经济实际问题的一种具有特定格式的专业应用文体。可以这样说,"经济文书"是"经济文本"的重要组成部分,而"经济文本"所涵盖的内容更加宽泛。

根据应用文写作的基本规律,经济文书可以被细分为三类:通用经济文书(general economic documents)、专用经济文书(specific economic documents)和经济诉讼文书(economic litigation documents)。

1. 通用经济文书是各类机关团体、企事业单位和个人普遍使用的经济文书的统称。包括经济公务文书(在处理公务时所使用的、具有特定实用价值和一定惯用体式的文书)、经济事务文书(如经济工作计划、经济工作总结、经济调查报告等)和经济研究文书(如经济学论文、经济工作研究等)。

2. 专用经济文书是指在经济活动中,为处理经济事务、协调经济活动、传递经济信息而经常使用的具有固定格式的专用文书。如经济合同、经济活动分析报告、经济预/决策报告、可行性研究报告和工商、税务、证券、保险等经济部门经常使用的各类专项报告等。

3. 经济诉讼文书是指在各类诉讼或非诉讼法律事务中,由司法机关或当事人根据有关法律,按照法定的程序、手续而制作的具有法律效力或法律意义的文书。如经济诉状、经济答辩状、经济公证文书等。

四、经济文本的总体特征

经济文本以经济学为基础,以经济研究和经济实践活动为主要内容,有着鲜明的特征,其总体特点概况起来有以下几个方面:

(一)专业性

经济文本往往跟经济学某一特定领域的知识相关,同时以某一特定的经济活动为主要内容,以推动经济活动开展、提高经济效益为根本目的。因此经济文本往往具有一定的专业性。

(二)规范性

经济文本在语言运用方面往往有其特定的、惯用的和固定的表达方式,尤其是涉及经济学专业术语的使用,必须讲求规范性和正确性。部分经济文本的行文格式要求极为规范，甚至是有具体的统一规定，这样做的目的在于方便读者阅读、理解和接受，同时也能够提高经济工作的质量和效率。

（三）政策性

经济与政治有着密切联系，两者是辩证统一的。经济决定政治，任何社会的政治都是由该社会的经济关系和经济制度决定的。政治对经济有巨大的反作用，影响或制约经济的发展。有了正确的政治领导、正确的政治路线和方针政策，经济建设才能取得成功。在经济文本中，时常可以见到关于经济政策制定、调整、实施和评价等方面的内容。

（四）客观性

经济文本往往用来描述和评价经济行为主体的运行情况，必须能够客观、科学地反映出真实的经济规律和经济数据，所以其内容应该是客观真实、准确可靠的。

（五）修辞性

经济文本中注重使用学术性强的"规范"经济语言来表达，以体现出规范性和客观性的特点，但经济语言也具有生动性和灵活性的一面。在经济文本中，作者通过运用各种修辞手法，能够使经济学中艰涩难懂的理论和观点更好地被大众理解和接受，从而达到其经济目的或政治目的。

第二节　翻译知识讲解

在经济全球化的大背景下，世界各国与中国在经济方面联系紧密，对于中国来说，与其他国家及时准确地进行经济信息沟通显得越来越重要。当前对经济文本翻译的市场需求在不断增加，经济文本翻译的实际应用价值和理论研究价值日益凸显，引起了翻译界的广泛关注。

一、经济文本翻译的基本原则

翻译原则是指在翻译活动中必须遵循的准则。虽然各种文体的翻译都必须遵循"忠实"和"通顺"的原则，但不同文体的翻译也都有各自的侧重点。经济文本除了具有其语言语种在表达上的特点之外，还具有鲜明的特色，例如经济文本有多种不同的具体形式，文中运用大量专业术语和特定表达式等。因此翻译经济文本时，译者应从词汇、句子、语篇等层面，充分了解各类经济文本的特点，并根据其特点灵活处理，选取适当的翻译策略、方法与技巧，力求词汇翻译准确、句子翻译通顺、语篇翻译连贯的效果，从而增强译文的可读性，这样才能保证产出高质量的译文。总体来看，经济文本翻译应遵循以下几条原则：

（一）充分了解原文含义

由于经济文本往往是关于某一个经济学领域或者某一类经济活动的论述，其内容专业性较强，没有相关专业知识的人可能无法理解。加之经济文本在表达时也经常交替使用直接和间接的表达方式，有时使用词语的字面意义(denotation)，有时使用词语的内涵意义(connotation)，如果不结合具体语境，很难理解其真实含义。因此翻译经济文本时，首先要正确地理解原文，充分地理解作者的写作意图和文章的中心思想，然后从整个语篇着眼，不必拘泥于个别词句，灵活地运用各种翻译技巧，流畅地表达出原文的真实含义。

(二)准确再现原文信息

经济文本中经常采用大量的数据，例如关于国家宏观经济发展态势的数据，或证券市场大盘分析以及个别公司股价高低变化的描述，其目的在于运用客观数据来描述和反映真实的经济状况。在翻译此类经济文本时，译者应注意精确地表达原文中出现的数据，从而准确再现原文信息。

(三)充分体现专业特色

在经济文本翻译过程中，译者应该针对某一经济学领域或者某一类经济活动的特点，运用相关的专业知识、恰当的翻译策略及技巧进行翻译，向译文读者传递等值的专业信息。在翻译过程中，译者要能够正确地使用专业术语、专业缩略词及专业新词等。各种类型的经济文本专业特色鲜明、特点各异，这在译文中也要有所体现。

(四)严格遵循习惯用法

在经济文本中有一些惯用的表达方式，有约定俗成的译法，译者在经济文本翻译过程中，对此类译法要严格遵循。当这些译文经过了实践和时间的检验，已被广为接受和使用时尤其如此，这时无须再根据译者个人的理解和习惯推陈出新，以免产生混乱，甚至造成误解。例如一些经济学理论和概念的名称最好是参考相关的专业词典，因为其名称的译法已经是约定俗成的了，不可随意更改。此外，对一些常见经济学专业术语、人名、地名、机构名等专有名词的翻译，译者可参考权威的平行文本，选择正确的翻译方法。

(五)力求保留原文风格

有些经济文本具有鲜明而独特的风格，例如经济合同的语言严谨刻板，而经济新闻报道的语言相对活泼。经济文本的文体风格和语言特点是为了更好地实现其表达效果而设定的，它们也是原文信息的重要组成部分。因此在翻译经济文本时，除了要将原文的含义表达得清楚明白，译者还应使译文的语言风格与原文相一致。

二、经济文本翻译的重点与难点

在经济文本翻译中，存在一些关键问题，能否处理好此类问题将在很大程度上影响译文的质量。总体来看，经济文本翻译中有以下重点与难点问题：

(一)专业术语的翻译

由于经济文本往往是关于某一个经济学领域或者某一类经济活动的论述，其内容专业性较强，没有相关专业知识的人可能无法理解。加之经济文本在表达时也经常交替使用直接和间接的表达方式，有时使用词语的字面意义，有时使用词语的内涵意义，如果不结合具体语境，很难理解其真实含义。

例1

原文：Britain has enjoyed a strong inflow of foreign direct investment. It has consistently attracted more capital than any other European country.

译文：英国拥有强劲的外国直接投资注入，它对外资的吸引力一直高于其他的欧洲国家。

分析：此句中的"foreign direct investment（FDI）"的意思是"an investment made by a firm or individual in one country into business interests located in another country"，可译为"外国直接投资"或"外商直接投资"。而如果将其译为"对外直接投资"就使得投资的去向发生改变，不符合其本来的词义。

（二）专有名词的翻译

经济文本经常出现大量的专有名词，包括人名、地名、机构名等。在翻译的过程中，译者的难点之一就是对专有名词译法的词汇选择问题。而面对这样的问题，译者需要特别注意，必须通过查阅专业词典或者查看相关书籍等方法来解决。如果凭借直觉望文生义，容易给出错误的译文。例如"The 22th APEC Economic Leaders' Meeting"的准确译法是"亚太经合组织第二十二次领导人非正式会议"，如果按照英文字面意义译为"第二十二届亚太经合组织经济领导人会议"，就似是而非了。

（三）文化负载词的翻译

文化负载词（culture-loaded words）是语言词汇系统中反映该语言国家独特文化的一类词汇，能够体现有别于其他国家的独特社会生活方式，但也给文化沟通和翻译带来了一些障碍。文化负载词的翻译一直是翻译中的难点之一。经济文本中为了更加形象生动地表达经济现象和经济规律，有时会运用大量的文化负载词。因此，如何准确翻译文化负载词便成为经济文本翻译迫切需要解决的一个问题。例如"房奴（house poor）""地下钱庄（illegal private banks）""网红经济（Internet celebrity economy）"等词汇都是被新创造出来的，用于描述真实经济生活中存在的客观情况。为了让这些具有中国特色的概念能够更好地得到传播，译者在翻译时一定要考虑到其译文能否为外国人所理解和接受。

（四）数据及其单位的翻译

经济文本中经常出现关于数据的表达，使用数据描述经济状况。中文的数据表达方式和英文的数据表达方式有所不同，数据后面所接的单位名词也不完全一致。因此在翻译经济文本时，译者需要熟悉两种语言之间数据及其单位的不同表达方式，了解其单位转换的方法。中英文数字单位有部分能够对应，例如"百"（hundred）、"千"（thousand）、"百万"（million），但除此以外的单位都没有一一对应的词汇。译者在翻译数字时，往往需要用这三个词语作为基准，以就近原则进行换算。例如中文的"一亿"可译为"100个百万"(100 million),或者"0.1个十亿"(0.1 billion)。又如"一万"需要翻译成"10个一千"(10 thousand)。除了纯粹数字表达方式的转换外,经济文本中经常会见到数字和单位名词同时出现,这就要求译者了解中英计量单位名词的差异及其换算方式。例如表示长度或距离时,英文中特有的词汇有"码(yard)""英寸(inch)""英尺(foot)""英里(mile)"等单位名词;表示重量时,英文有"磅(pound)""盎司(ounce)"等词汇。翻译时,译者需先进行单位之间的换算,再进行翻译。例如可将中文的"一斤"译为英文的"0.5个公斤(0.5 kilogram)"。

(五)长句的翻译

由于英语和汉语是两种不同的语言,英语是注重"形合"的语言,而汉语是注重"意合"的语言,很多英语长句是通过联系词连接在一起的,而汉语则是靠语义过渡的,所以在将英文长句翻译成中文时,可以将其拆分成几个短句再翻译,通过中文内在的语义逻辑很自然地将它们联系起来。

例 2

原文:Nowadays the need to upgrade and augment the capital start will become more pressing as Chinese companies increasingly face fierce competition in both domestic and foreign markets.

译文:目前中国企业在国内外市场面临越来越激烈的竞争,优化股本结构和扩大股本总量的需求将变得更加紧迫。

分析:这句话的原文是一个长句,其中有一个"as"引导的从句,这符合英语中注重"形合"的表达习惯,但是翻译成中文时不必将"as"译出,而是根据"意合"的表达习惯,将其切分为两个短句,运用两部分之间的内在逻辑联系表达其含义。

(六)修辞手法的翻译

经济文本中时常可见修辞手法的运用,在翻译时译者首先要正确地理解原文,充分地理解作者的写作意图和文章的中心思想,然后从整个语篇着眼,不必拘泥于个别词句,灵活地运用各种翻译技巧,准确地表达出原文的真实含义。

例 3

原文:This country's infrastructure, energy, transport, telecommunication and water supply is inadequate. For instance, its energy production chronically lags behind total industrial output. In addition, international infrastructure statistics place it near a bottom of the world ranking.

译文:该国的基础设施、能源、交通、电信和水供应不足。例如其能源生产长期滞后于工业总产出。此外,国际基础设施统计数据显示,该国在世界排名中几乎垫底。

分析:这句话描述的是一个国家经济基础设施建设的情况,原文中的"chronically"有"长期地;慢性地;习惯性地"等含义,根据上下文,此处译为"长期",表示该状态已经持续很长时间。"place it near a bottom of the world ranking"使用了比喻的修辞手法，表示该国在际基础设施统计数据中的排名比较靠后，翻译此句时，应首先正确理解"it"的所指对象，然后灵活地翻译"place ... near a bottom..."，使用中文中表达该含义时惯用的表达方式。

三、经济文本翻译对译者知识、能力与素质的要求

经济文本翻译属于应用翻译范畴，经济文本具有专业性较强的特点，翻译难度较大，对译者水平也有较高的要求。总体来看，译者需要做到以下六点：

（一）提高自身的政策水平

经济文本常常涉及国际和国内的经济政策。译者如果掌握了各种经济方针政策，理解了各种经济现象，在翻译经济文本时，就能做到认识清、反应快、判断准。

（二）打好扎实的双语语言基础

翻译是一种语言文字工作，在此过程中，译者首先需要运用其源语语言知识对原文进行分析和理解，然后运用译语语言知识将译文通顺流畅地表达出来。如果译者没有扎实的双语语言基本功，便无法正确地、充分地理解原文，更不用说完成高质量的译文了。

（三）熟练掌握经济文本翻译理论和翻译技巧

翻译理论对翻译实践具有重要的指导作用。熟练掌握翻译理论往往是找到正确的翻译原则、翻译策略、翻译方法和翻译技巧的基础，对提高翻译实践效率具有重大的意义。此外，译者还应该通过不断进行经济文本翻译实践活动，巩固所掌握的翻译理论知识，提高自己的翻译能力和水平。

（四）努力掌握相关的经济专业知识

经济文本的长句较多，专业性较强，不够通俗易懂，如果缺乏一定的语言水平和背景知识很难读懂该类文本。经济方面的专业知识以及经济领域的实践经验对于经济文本的翻译是至关重要的。

（五）注意培养与写作有关的各种能力

在经济文本翻译时，译文的质量与译者的写作能力密切相关。因此，译者平时需要注意培养资料搜索能力、逻辑思维能力、布局谋篇能力、文字表达能力，把握各种经济文本的文体格式规范，掌握恰当的表述方法。

（六）树立良好的治学方法和职业道德

翻译本身就是一项复杂而细致的工作，需要译者具有极大的毅力和耐心。经济文本翻译工作作为中外经济交流的纽带和桥梁，肩负着重大的历史使命。因此，译者必须养成实事求是、严谨认真的治学方法。此外，翻译职业工作者还应具有精益求精、对客户负责的职业道德。在翻译过程中，对原文的理解不能似懂非懂，对译文的表达不能含糊其辞。如果对原文存在任何理解困难或对译文存在任何表达困难，译者都应尽力查阅有关资料，或向专业人士请教，切不可企图蒙混过关。

第三节　常用词汇与表达

原文	译文
中国梦	Chinese Dream
新常态	New Normal
生态文明	Eco-civilization
简政放权	To Streamline Administration and Delegate Power
精准扶贫	Targeted Poverty Alleviation
"一带一路"倡议	the "Belt and Road" Initiative
自由贸易区	Free Trade Zone
亚洲基础设施投资银行（亚投行）	Asian Infrastructure Investment Bank（AIIB）
"双创"（大众创业，万众创新）	"Mass Entrepreneurship and Innovation"
"互联网+"	"Internet Plus"
"中国制造 2025"	"Made in China 2025"
供给侧结构改革	Supply-side Structural Reform
人民币国际化	Renminbi's Internalization
金融互联互通	Financial Connectivity
雄安新区	Xiong'an New Area
包容性增长	Inclusive Growth
量化宽松	Quantitative Easing（QE）
英国脱欧	Brexit
特别提款权	Special Drawing Rights（SDR）
全球通胀	Global Inflation
全球治理体系	Global Governance System
大数据	Big Data
云计算	Cloud Computing
区块链	Blockchain
网红经济	Internet Celebrity Economy

第四节 译文赏析

原文	译文
TRADE TENSIONS, GLOBAL VALUE CHAINS, AND SPILLOVERS **Executive Summary** 　　Europe is deeply integrated into global value chains, and recent trade tensions raise the question of how European economies would be affected by the introduction of tariffs or other trade barriers. About 70 percent of total European exports are linked to forward and backward supply chains. Therefore, shocks affecting existing trade flows between the major trade hubs—the United States, China, and Germany—could affect European economies through those supply chains.	贸易局势紧张、全球价值链及溢出效应[1] 执行摘要[2] 　　欧洲现已深入参与到全球价值链中,最近的贸易紧张局势引发了关于关税和其他贸易壁垒会如何影响欧洲经济的一系列问题。欧洲出口总额的70%都与供应链的前向和后向相联系[3]。因此,影响主要贸易中心——美国、中国和德国——现存贸易流通的冲击也会通过供应链影响欧洲经济。
This paper estimates the impact of trade shocks and growth spillovers using value-added measures to get a more accurate picture of the associated costs across European countries. By measuring the impact of trade shocks through the lens of value-added exports instead of gross exports, we get a better understanding of how trade tensions weigh on activity. This distinction is particularly important for Europe, which has the largest difference between these measures as a result of extensive cross-border supply chains, both within and outside the region.	本文[4]使用附加值估算来预估贸易冲击和增长溢出效应的影响,以便更准确地了解欧洲各国的相关成本[5]。通过附加值出口而不是总出口来衡量贸易冲击的影响,我们能够更好地了解贸易紧张局势对经济活动的影响。由于欧洲区域含有对内对外的跨境供应链数量庞大,不同预估方式的结果差异巨大,所以这两种预估方式的区别对衡量欧洲经济极为重要。
These are our main findings: 　　The distribution across countries of export losses in Europe from tariff shocks is significantly different when measured according to value added versus gross trade. Through a simple accounting exercise based on input-output tables, we estimate the possible impact of a scenario in which the United States imposes a 25 percent tariff on imports of cars and car parts. Our findings suggest that about half of the impact is transmitted directly to the affected sector-country and the rest via supply chains. Most important, the negative impact would spread across more countries when measured using value-added indicators than when using gross exports, and the order of the export losses does not necessarily reflect the order of gross exports.	主要发现[6]: 　　根据附加值与总贸易额来衡量,欧洲各国出口损失与受关税冲击的分布差别很大。根据投入产出表的简单会计计算,我们预估了美国对于汽车及汽车零部件所施加的25%关税情形可能产生的影响。研究结果表明[4],大约一半的相关产业国家受到直接影响,其余部分则通过供应链传递。最重要的是,相较于使用总出口指标来衡量,当使用附加值指标时,负面影响将扩散到更多国家,而出口损失的顺序不一定反映总出口的顺序。

续表

原文	译文
The importance of Germany as the core hub country in Europe's trade is smaller when measured in value-added terms; the importance of the United States and China is relatively greater when measured that way. Germany's importance for its European trading partners in the real effective exchange rate (REER) is about 10 percent lower in value-added terms than in terms of gross exports. In contrast, the importance of the United States and China in European countries' REER is appreciably larger in value-added terms. Relatedly, when we simulate the impact of a 5 percent general tariff on all US imports (with retaliation from the rest of the countries), the average reduction in the demand for Europe's value-added output would be 50 percent higher when measured in value-added terms than if estimated in gross terms.	当以附加值来衡量时,作为欧洲贸易核心枢纽国家的德国重要性就变低了,美国和中国的重要性相对较高。在附加值方面,德国对其欧洲贸易伙伴实际有效汇率(REER)[7]的重要性比在总出口方面低约10%。相比之下,在附加值方面美国和中国在欧洲国家实际有效汇率的重要性明显较大。相应地,当我们假设5%的一般性关税对所有美国进口产品的影响(从其他国家的报复)时,按附加值衡量欧洲增值产出需求的平均减少量比按总额衡量要高50%。
Growth spillovers from the United States and China to European economies are sizable; the effects are larger for economies more exposed to them in terms of value-added exports. Spillover effects from German growth shocks on European countries are estimated to be much smaller. This likely reflects the German economy's smaller size relative to the United States and China and Germany's openness, which makes it less likely to be an independent source of large shocks. Our analysis, however, does not rule out the role of Germany as a transmitter of shocks originating elsewhere or its potentially larger spillovers if its growth becomes more driven by domestic demand.	美国和中国对欧洲经济的增长溢出效应相当可观;对于在附加值出口方面更容易受到影响的经济体而言,这两国影响更大。而德国增长冲击对欧洲国家的溢出效应估计要小得多。这可能反映出了德国经济相对于美国和中国的体量较小,以及德国的开放程度,这使得它不太可能单独成为大规模冲击的根源。然而,我们的分析并不会排除德国的作用,因为它既有可能传播来自其他地方的贸易冲击,又有可能受到国内需求的驱动产生更大的溢出效应[8]。
The conclusions of this paper could be helpful for policymakers. The findings of this paper could help quantify more precisely the impact of growing trade tensions. Understanding how trade shocks propagate through global value chains could also help policymakers calibrate countercyclical measures as needed and target social policies aimed at the citizens most likely to be affected.	本文的结论可能对政策制定者有所帮助。本文的发现有助于更准确地量化日益扩大的贸易紧张局势影响。了解贸易冲击如何通过全球价值链传播,也可以帮助政策制定者根据需要调整反周期措施[7],并针对最有可能受影响的公民制定社会政策。

难点 1

原文：TRADE TENSIONS, GLOBAL VALUE CHAINS, AND SPILLOVERS

译文：贸易局势紧张、全球价值链及溢出效应

分析：本文出自国际货币基金组织 2019 年发布的一份经济报告，主要探讨了现阶段欧洲经济贸易局势，并从增值措施来预估贸易冲击和增长溢出效应的影响，分析主要贸易中心，包括美国、中国、德国，现存贸易流通冲击是如何通过供应链影响欧洲经济的。该报告标题为"TRADE TENSIONS, GLOBAL VALUE CHAINS, AND SPILLOVERS"，其中并未出现"report"之类的词语，不过为了让读者更清楚地了解原文的题材，译者在翻译时可以进行增译，使用"关于……的报告"之类的表达。此外，原文中出现的是三个名词短语，译文也按照其字面意思进行了翻译，但将"Trade Tensions"译为"贸易局势紧张"不如译为"贸易紧张局势"，因为后者从词语结构上更符合原文中名词短语的表达。因此标题可以改译为"关于贸易紧张局势、全球价值链及溢出效应的报告"。

难点 2

原文：Executive Summary

译文：执行摘要

分析："Executive Summary"是一个在多种经济文本中使用频率很高的英文术语，如商务计划书、经济报告、投标书等。目前对于该词的中文译法可以见到的多达十几种，如"执行总结""执行摘要""综合经营报告""实施总结"等。要找到其最佳的汉语翻译，就要分析清楚该词语本身的意思。"Executive Summary"作为一份文件的一个部分，是原文件的浓缩，将整个文件的主要内容用非常简短的文字表达出来，不必涉及具体的细节。其读者通常为决策者，其目的在于使人通过阅读这一小部分便可了解全文的基本内容，据此在短时间内决定是否要进一步通读全文，并对有关事项作出决策。据此可以看出，"Executive Summary"所起到的作用就是"内容摘要"的作用，但如果要将"Executive"一词体现出来，将"Executive Summary"译为"执行摘要"也无可厚非。

难点 3

原文：About 70 percent of total European exports are linked to **forward and backward supply chains**.

译文：欧洲出口总额的 70% 都与**供应链的前向和后向**相联系。

分析：翻译中要准确地理解和表达专业概念。译者在这里将原文中的"forward and backward supply chains"译为"供应链的前向和后向"欠妥。"forward supply chains"和"backward supply chains"是供应链管理相关的概念，供应链可以分为"前向供应链"和"后向供应链"。以本企业为中心，"前向供应链"偏向供应链的上游，包含了设计、原材料、

生产制造等职能;"后向供应链"则偏向供应链的下游,是关于分销(批发和零售)、广告营销和接触消费者等。因此,此句可改译为:"欧洲出口总额的70%都与其前向供应链和后向供应链有关。"

难点 4

原文:this paper;Our findings suggest

译文:本文;研究结果表明

分析:在经济报告的写作中有一些惯用的表达方式,有约定俗成的译法,译者在翻译时遵循此类译法。例如将"this paper"译为"本文",将"Our findings suggest"译为"研究结果表明",这样读起来能使人感到该文本的"专业性"。

难点 5

原文:This paper estimates the impact of trade shocks and growth spillovers using value-added measures **to get a more accurate picture** of the associated costs across European countries.

译文:本文使用附加值估算来预估贸易冲击和增长溢出效应的影响,以便**更准确地了解**欧洲各国的相关成本。

分析:原文中有一处运用了比喻的修辞手法,使用"to get a more accurate picture"表达"更准确地了解"这一含义,这是英文中常用的一种表达方式,但是如果中文直译为"看见一幅更清晰的图画"则不妥。因此,译者没有刻意追求修辞手法上和原文对等,而是灵活地选择更清楚地表达原文的主要意思,这符合经济文本以传递信息为主要目的之特点。

难点 6

原文:These are our main findings

译文:主要发现

分析:原文是一篇经济报告,主要目的在于反映真实的经济状况,因此其语言比较平实、严谨、客观,文章的结构条理清楚。在译文中,译者通过偏"直译"的方法再现了原文中的基本信息,在一些中英表达有差异的地方又灵活地对译文做了调整。例如将"These are our main findings"译为"主要发现",这样处理简洁明了,比较好地再现了原文平实、简洁的文体风格。

难点 7

原文:real effective exchange rate(REER);countercyclical measures

译文:实际有效汇率;反周期措施

分析：原文是一篇关于国际经济、国际贸易的报告，其中用到了很多专业术语，如"global value chains""trade tensions""spillovers""real effective exchange rate（REER）""countercyclical measures"等，要将其正确翻译首先要理解其含义，上文中的专业术语翻译从总体上看基本准确。

难点8

原文：Our analysis, however, does not rule out the role of Germany as a transmitter of shocks originating elsewhere or its potentially larger spillovers if its growth becomes more driven by domestic demand.

译文：然而，我们的分析并不会排除德国的作用，因为它既有可能**传播来自其他地方的贸易冲击**，又有可能**受到国内需求的驱动产生更大的溢出效应**。

改译：然而，我们的分析并不排除德国**作为其他国家贸易冲击的传导者**的作用，也不排除如果**德国的增长更多地受到国内需求的驱动**，德国可能会产生更大的溢出效应。

分析：翻译中要注意长句的理解和翻译。这个句子相对较长，含义较复杂，主要表达两层意思：第一，德国有可能传导来自其他国家或地区的冲击；第二，德国可能因为其经济增长被内需驱动而具有潜在的、更大的溢出效应。原译文基本再现了句子主要意思，但是有表达不够准确恰当之处。例如将"transmitter"译为"传播者"不如译为"传导者"贴合语境；译文中的"受到国内需求的驱动产生更大的溢出效应"没有准确清楚地体现"德国经济增长受到内需驱动"这层意思。

翻 译 练 习

一、词组翻译

环境友好型社会
南水北调工程
西气东输工程
最低生活保障金
经济适用房
外汇储备
金融衍生工具
带薪休假
龙头企业
技术密集型产业
catering culture

trade barrier

investment portfolio

emerging economies

economies of scale

disposable income

credit rating

listed company

urbanization

regional economic integration

二、句子翻译

（一）汉译英

1. 根据建设社会主义市场经济体制的要求，我们将继续全方位地对外开放。我们要进一步理顺改革、发展和稳定三者之间的关系，培育统一开放、竞争有序的市场体系。

2. 许多中国公司相信"薄利多销"，而这种战略的假定前提是低价格将会加快周转速度，最终创造更高的利润。尽管低价战略被广泛使用，一些公司仍然在采用高价战略，其出发点在于利用中国的传统智慧："便宜无好货"和"一分钱一分货"。

3. 农业是扩内需调结构的重要领域，更是安天下稳民心的产业。要坚持把解决好"三农"问题放在全部工作的重中之重，以保障国家粮食安全和促进农民增收为核心，推进农业现代化。

4. 今后一个时期，我们将着重解决好现有"三个1亿人"问题，促进约1亿农业转移人口落户城镇，改造约1亿人居住的城镇棚户区和城中村，引导约1亿人在中西部地区就近城镇化。

5. 我们要健全城乡发展一体化体制机制，坚持走以人为本、四化同步、优化布局、生态文明、传承文化的新型城镇化道路。

（二）英译汉

1. Foreign direct investment continues to flow into China and the current account and trade balance continue to post surplus throughout the forecast.

2. While the deregulation of economy and the restructuring of the state-owned enterprise sector are under way, the central government will continue to bear the pressure of subsidizing state companies, food prices and wide variety of public utilities for a few more years to come.

3. Both domestic saving and foreign direct investment will be key in building a necessary infrastructure which in turn will help sustain economic growth.

4. In the long run, we expect China to further liberalize its economy by cutting tariffs and opening up the services and financial sectors to foreigners as well as to reduce its presence in state

owned banks and enterprises.

5. This continued liberalization of economy coupled with high level of domestic savings and steady foreign direct investment and strong exports will keep the economic growth to 8 to 9 percentage.

三、语篇翻译

(一) 汉译英

随着经济的发展和社会文明程度的进一步提高,毋庸置疑,广播电视的舆论宣传作用也日益凸显。随着全球化浪潮席卷世界媒介产业,近年来,我国的电视事业发展非常迅猛,卫视、地面频道成倍增加。媒介的主动权经历着从卖方市场向买方市场转移的过程。媒介管理者们都面临着日益严峻的市场竞争。激烈的竞争必然是无法避免的。在这样的竞争中,如何办好节目、拓展自己生存与发展的空间是湖北广电总台的当务之急。如何运用科学的营销手段,为现代化的广播电视媒体扩展传播张力、提高引导能力、注入发展活力、增添竞争实力,从而在不断市场化的媒体竞争中脱颖而出,是我们广播电视工作者面临的严峻考验。传媒产业正以令人惊讶的速度高速成长,2008年尽管受到了汶川地震、经济危机等外部不利条件的影响,但全国全年广播电影电视总收入(含财政补助收入)为1667.21亿元,比上一年增长了20.49%。其中,广播电视产业收入1350.04亿元,比上一年增长了19.54%,增速较前两年有所提升。各省、自治区、直辖市广播电视产业发展基本保持稳定,收入稳中有升。湖北是文化大省,辖省会及16个风格各异,人杰地灵的市、州、林区,70多个风景如画、各具特色的县。设在武汉的省级广播电视播出机构就有包括卫星广播电视在内的18个专业频道,如综艺、经济、影视、体育、教育等。置身于九省通衢、南北交会的荆楚大地,该如何发挥我们的媒体优势呢?知己知彼,下好营销这盘棋,乃是我们不容忽视的战略要务。

(二) 英译汉

There is no such thing as an inexpensive war. First, there is the human cost in loss of life and in the physical and psychological maiming of healthy people. While the personal cost of such loss is immeasurable, the economic cost to society can be estimated. This measure was first proposed by a French economist, Jean-Baptiste Say, in 1803. He asserted the principle that war costs more than its direct expenses, for it also costs what its casualties (military and civilian) would have earned throughout their lifetimes if they had never participated in war.

Second, war has economic costs arising from the destruction of buildings, productive farmlands and forests, public services such as waterworks, electricity-generating and distribution systems, roads, bridges, harbors, and airfields, and all manner of personal and corporate property such as homes, possessions, factories, machinery, vehicles, and aircraft. War, therefore, destroys physical capital that has been created by previous economic activity.

Reconstruction after war is a particular economic burden because the finance, imported capital goods, and labor used in reconstruction merely restore the losses a country has sustained, rather than adding to the stock of capital available to its economy. Thus, even if it manages to restore all its physical losses, it uses scarce resources that would otherwise have been available for extending and improving economic activity. As most wars since 1945 have occurred in the Third World, some of the world's poorest countries have suffered the most from the economic losses of war.

War also costs a great deal in goods and services to create the weapons of war and to supply the people engaged in the war effort. The diversion of these goods and services—which range from the metals and chemicals transformed into weapons to the food, clothing, and shelter for the armed forces—reduces current civilian consumption, which lowers the population's living standards. Metal used to make a tank cannot be used to build bridges, fuel used to transport military supplies cannot be used on school buses, and cement used to construct ammunition dumps cannot be used in house construction. This constitutes the opportunity cost of war—that is, the extent to which the economy foregoes the opportunity to commit these resources to alternative peaceful uses.

The opportunity cost of war is also felt in the future. In addition to allocating resources to consumption (the satisfaction of current needs), an economy allocates resources to investment (the new factories and machinery that produce tomorrow's goods and services). Resources diverted to war cannot be used to create new productive capacity for future consumption, and this reduces the living standards of the population below what they otherwise would have been in the future.

In summary, the total costs of war include the cost of the foregone use of the economic resources used up in the conflict. These include the cost of the foregone lifetime earnings of those killed in the war, the cost of lifetime medical care for those permanently incapacitated by the war, the cost of replacing the physical capital destroyed or damaged by the war, the cost of supplying the armed forces with the weapons of war, the cost of sustaining the armed forces and those in support functions (including their pay and pensions), and the losses to the economy caused by the diversion of resources from peaceful investment in future economic capacity.

◎ 参考文献

[1] 方梦之. 应用翻译研究：原理、策略与技巧[M]. 上海：上海外语教育出版社，2013.

[2] 李长栓. 非文学翻译理论与实践[M]. 北京：中国对外翻译出版公司，2012.

[3] 李明. 商务英语翻译(英译汉)[M]. 北京：高等教育出版社，2011.

[4] 徐珺. 商务翻译多维研究[M]. 北京：对外经贸大学出版社，2020.

[5] 袁洪，王济华. 商务翻译实务[M]. 北京：对外经贸大学出版社，2018.

[6] 曾利沙. 商务翻译研究新探[M]. 北京：外语教学与研究出版社，2017.

第二章 经济新闻报道翻译

> ☞**思考题**
> 1. 经济新闻有哪些典型特征？在翻译中是如何体现的？
> 2. 经济新闻中有哪些常见的词汇与表达？
> 3. 经济新闻常用的翻译策略和技巧有哪些？

第一节 经济新闻报道文本分析

一、经济新闻概述

处在信息时代，人们越来越关注是否能及时获得各类信息。新闻指的就是对最新的事实进行及时描述与报道，并通过简明而准确的语言、具体而形象的手法，向最广泛的公众传递相关的信息。新闻具有真实性、及时性、公开性等特点。新闻的特质决定了新闻语言具有准确、简明、具体、生动等特征。与其他新闻相比，经济新闻报道不仅要对经济现象进行专业、客观的描述，一般还会分析经济形势，预测经济发展趋势。本章将介绍经济新闻的基本结构以及经济新闻的总体特征，从而指导经济新闻的翻译，给经济新闻的翻译带来启示。

（一）经济新闻的基本结构

经济新闻的基本结构是指新闻中新闻材料安排结合的方式，主要的结构类型有"倒金字塔式""金字塔式""提要式""总分式"。其中"倒金字塔式"是经济新闻中比较常见的结构。"倒金字塔式"就是把新闻中重要的材料放在导语中，次重要的材料放在稍后的段落，从导语到结尾，新闻材料的重要性呈递减趋势的一种消息结构。"倒金字塔式"的新闻，一般由标题、导语、主体和结尾四部分构成，其中最重要的是标题。一个好的标题可以吸引读者眼球，概括全文。

（二）经济新闻的总体特征

1. 经济新闻具有共识性

共识是人们在社会交往实践中，对社会生活中的事实、价值、观念、规则、利益等所达成的共同性认识。经济新闻中的共识性指的是经济新闻读者所具备的共识经验,包括行话和专业术语。行话一般是指特定专业人士之间为了方便沟通而使用的用语,在新闻中,例如 breaking news(突发新闻)、censor(审查新闻稿件)、circulation(发行量/部)、clipping(剪报)、columns(专栏)、columnist(专栏作家)等都是常见的新闻行话。而经济新闻最大的语言特征就是使用专业术语,并且许多常用词被赋予特殊的含义,例如 long(多头)、short(空头)、call(看涨)、put(看跌)等。经济新闻中形容词大多通俗、形象,例如股市中的"熊市"和"牛市",如果没有这些专业"前提共识",就可能无法读懂某些专业信息,因此译者必须掌握相关的专业知识与词汇。

2. 经济新闻具有专业性

经济新闻具有专业性。经济新闻报道中的信息具有客观性,客观性是对客观经济现象和经济事件的准确描述,因此在客观信息框架下通常会有经济领域的专业知识,并且为了使新闻具体化、专业化,会频繁使用具体数字作为例证,并且使用经济术语。因此,经济新闻通常具有专业的风格。

例 1

央行开展 2000 亿逆回购 机构:资金面或阶段性缓和

资金面方面,8 月 25 日央行公开市场加大资金净投放力度,银行间市场短期资金供给进一步转松,隔夜回购加权利率大幅下行逾 40bp 下破 2%报在 1.92%附近。

另据 Wind 数据显示,本周(8 月 22 日至 28 日)央行公开市场有 6100 亿元逆回购到期,其中周一至周五分别到期 500 亿元、1000 亿元、1500 亿元、1600 亿元、1500 亿元,无正回购和央票到期。此外,8 月 26 日有 1500 亿元中期借贷便利(MLF)到期。此前央行已经对 8 月到期的两笔 MLF 一次性续做。

(中国新闻网,2020 年 8 月 26 日)

上面这则关于逆回购的新闻是典型的经济新闻风格。这则新闻中有很多权威的统计数据。关于一周内到期的具体数字以及下跌率的统计,使得这则新闻具有专业性,让读者信服。从例子中可以看出采用专业术语和准确的统计数字使经济新闻报道具有专业风格。

例 2

Huawei's Revenue Growth Slows as US Tightens Sanctions

Huawei said on Friday that revenues in the first nine months of the year were rmb671.3bn ($100.5bn). That translates into a 3.7 per cent year-on-year increase in the July to September period, a drop from the 27 per cent growth recorded in the third quarter of 2019. The company had a compound annual revenue growth rate of 21 per cent for the past five full years.

(*Financial Times* 中文网,2020 年 10 月 23 日)

上面这则新闻选自 *Financial Times* 中文网,可以看出无论是中文新闻还是英文新闻,具体数据都是体现专业性的重要部分。

3. 经济新闻具有实用性

在经济新闻中,除了专业性,另一个独特之处就在于经济新闻强调信息的实用性,这也使之与娱乐新闻、故事性报道、采访新闻等其他类型的新闻形成了显著的差异。经济新闻的实用性体现在它所提供的实用信息对人们的消费心理和行为、社会的整体经济管理、政府的政策制定等产生的巨大影响。

例 3

央行：中国货币政策将以更大确定性应对各种不确定性

中新社北京 8 月 25 日电（记者 魏晞） 中国人民银行货币政策司司长孙国峰 25 日在国务院政策例行吹风会上说，疫情带来的不确定性增加，中国金融市场情绪难免受到一些影响，货币政策需要有更大的确定性来应对各种不确定性。

孙国峰强调，中国货币政策将保持三个不变：稳健货币政策的取向不变；保持灵活适度的操作要求不变，既不让市场缺钱，也不让市场的钱溢出来；坚持正常货币政策的决心不变。

（中国新闻网，2020 年 8 月 27 日）

从新闻内容来看，央行关于中国货币政策的三个不变，能在疫情期间给受影响的工业企业以及个人带来安心的信号。经济新闻的报道不仅具有专业性，同时其内容大多具有实用性，不管是企业还是个人都能从经济新闻中获取自己所需要了解的信息。

二、经济新闻的语言特征

虽然中英经济新闻文本在总体上具有共同的经济新闻特点，但如果仔细观察中英文经济新闻，会发现两者之间仍存在一定的差异。认识两者之间的差异有助于译者在翻译中采取适当的策略，翻译出符合目标受众阅读习惯的目标文本。

（一）中文经济新闻的语言特征分析

中文经济新闻大多属于典型的硬新闻，具有准确、简洁、清晰、语言凝练等新闻体特征，经济新闻通常用准确的文字描述事件，不含糊，不夸张，忠实地将信息传达给读者。经济新闻中充斥着专业术语和概念，必须对其加以解释，让普通读者了解这些概念，这样才能体现经济新闻信息沟通这一主要目的。另外，受限于新闻的篇幅，经济新闻一般语言简练、内容充实。

1. 中文经济新闻的词汇分析

经济新闻是专业性很强的新闻，因此经济新闻中的用词应该准确、严谨。经济新闻中常见金融、保险或房地产等领域的大量术语和行话。有些术语出现频率很高，普通读者也很熟悉。例如"收益（returns）"或"利率（interest rates）"。但是也有一些具有中国特色的热词，热词是时代变迁和社会进步的缩影，也是社会发展的一面镜子。近年来，中国在政治、经济、文化等方面取得了长足的进步，涌现出一批热词。这些出现在经济新闻中的热词既是世界了解中国社会热点的重要途径,也是翻译的难点。例如"'一带一路'倡议",需要专业术语进行翻译,译为"the 'Belt and Road' Initiative"。再如"留守儿童""钉子户"等。这类词汇对于中国人来说非常熟悉,但是西方国家对这些现象比较陌生,因此在经济新闻英译的过程中,需要加以解释。"留守儿童"可以处理为"left-behind children, a group of children which are commonly seen in some parts of remote countryside areas"。而"钉子户"可以处理为"nail household, person or household who refuses to move and bargains for unreasonably high compensation when the land is requisitioned for a construction project"。除了热词之外,还有一些专有名词有其规范的翻译,如"北京市委"(Beijing Municipal Committee of the CPC)、"河北省委(Hebei Provincial Committee of the CPC)"。经济新闻词汇的另一大特点是数据的频繁使用,经济报道离不开指标和效益的支撑,而这些只有通过数据才能准确地描述,这既是中文经济新闻的词汇特点,也是英文经济新闻的词汇特点。

2. 中文经济新闻的句法分析

英文经济新闻喜欢在主句之后使用一个或多个从句来扩充句子结构,呈现尽可能多的经济信息,相比之下,中文经济新闻句子结构松散,喜欢使用短句。因此中文新闻的主要线索往往有两至三句话。

例 4

中国央行 50 亿元支持银行发行永续债补充资本

中国央行 27 日开展了央行票据互换(CBS)操作,操作量为 50 亿元人民币。此举将支持银行发行永续债补充资本,提高银行永续债的市场流动性,增强金融服务实体经济的能力。

(中国新闻网,2014 年 9 月 24 日)

可以看出这两个小短句都是值得被关注的重要信息,第一句话是主要信息,第二句话作为信息的补充是次要信息,两句话均简明扼要、条理清晰。另外,不同于英文经济新闻,中文经济新闻中一般会将新闻来源放置在开头的位置,而英文经济新闻的新闻来源一般出现在文末。

例 5

美国商务部经济分析局 30 日公布,今年第二季度美国国内生产总值(GDP)同比大幅增长 4%,印证了各界对美国经济正在反弹的预期。(《人民日报》,2014 年 7 月 31 日)

例 6

The U. S. economy rebounded sharply in the second quarter, expanding at its fastest pace in 2½ years, the government said Friday. (*USA TODAY*, Sep. 26, 2014)

中文的表达习惯一般是先叙述不重要的事情,而把重要的事情放在最后叙述,因此

"美国商务部经济分析局"作为新闻来源的这一不重要的因素在中文经济新闻中的开头,而英文经济新闻中"the government said"放置到了文末。

3. 中文经济新闻的语篇分析

在经济新闻的语篇方面,一般有两种主体结构,一种是采用倒金字塔结构,首先提供最重要的信息,然后依次提供次要信息等,一般英文经济新闻的语篇中多用此结构。而中文经济新闻多采用时间顺序结构,根据新闻事件的时间顺序来构建。新闻要素通常按照 Who, When, What 和 Where 来排列。

例 7

广西自贸试验区钦州港片区:打造中国—东盟合作示范区

中共广西钦州市委书记、中国(广西)自由贸易试验区钦州港片区工委书记许永锞 28 日用一份"数字报告",交出了广西自贸试验区钦州港片区成立一年来的"答卷"。

拥有 1400 年历史的钦州是古代海上丝绸之路的始发港之一,在中国宋代就设有"博易场"。彼时的"博易场"是专门设在西南边境地带,与西南少数民族地区和东南亚各国的交易市场。也是从那时起,钦州开启了最早的国际贸易,与东南亚国家进行自由贸易往来。

2019 年 8 月,广西自贸试验区获批成立,实施范围 119.99 平方公里,涵盖南宁、钦州、崇左三个片区。其中,钦州港片区是广西三个片区中唯一临海、面积最大的片区,占广西自贸试验区面积近一半,新一轮对东南亚的"博易"就此展开。

(中国新闻网,2020 年 8 月 28 日)

可以看出,此例新闻报道中先介绍钦州的历史,再引出 2019 年 8 月自贸试验区的设立,通过对新闻的顺序报道,给读者造成一种悬念,这与英文新闻恰恰相反,英文经济新闻一般会将最重要的信息放在最前面。除此之外,中英经济新闻中语篇中普遍存在各种明喻、暗喻和隐喻的修辞,例如 lucky dog—幸运儿,削足适履—act in a Procrustean way。还有此例中的"答卷"也是一种暗喻。

(二)英文经济新闻的语言特征分析

1. 英文经济新闻的词汇分析

(1)用词专业,常出现经济术语

经济新闻中常出现一些涉及经济领域的专业知识,且由于新闻文体严肃性和准确性的要求,因此经济术语就经常出现在英语经济新闻中,如 meltdown(崩盘),speculation(投机),depreciation(货币贬值),deflation(通货紧缩)等。

(2)常使用缩写

在英文经济新闻中出现的主体通常都不是某个人而是某个国际组织或集团。由于这些国际组织或集团的名字过长,因此为了节约空间和满足新闻文体简洁性的需要,常使用缩写,如 WTO,IMF,UN。此外,一些经济指标也常用缩写来表达,如 GDP,CPI,PPI。

(3)常使用新造词

随着经济、社会的不断发展,出现了越来越多的新事物,经济新闻中的词汇也在不断更新补充。例如 webisode 指在网络上发行的网络剧或网络视频短片,此外,seckill 则是由 second 和 kill 组合,指电商中常出现的秒杀活动。

2. 英文经济新闻的句法分析

(1)文章版面资源有限,篇幅较短,而输出信息大,因此常常出现复杂句

例 8

One has to do with its long running feud with regulators in New York, who in February demanded data about New Yorkers who are listing properties for short-term rental on the site, in violation of local laws. (*The Economist*, Oct. 10th, 2019)

(2)常出现主从句时态不一致

例 9

Whereas Uber has yet to turn a profit (and, sceptics say, never will), Airbnb says it is already profitable(to be precise, EBITAD-positive)and has been since 2017, when it is thought to have earned ＄93m on revenues of ＄2.6bn. (*The Economist*, Oct. 10th, 2019)

(3)直接引语和间接引语常出现在文中,使文章更有说服力

例 10

It says it has collected more than ＄1bn in hotel and tourism taxes in America alone and is "on track to become the world's largest single collector of these taxes". (*The Economist*, Oct. 10th, 2019)

(4)既具有商务文体逻辑连贯、简明清晰的特点,又具有文学文体擅长形象联想的特点

例 11

Having been in roadshow mode for several months, Mr. Chesky has polished answers for everything up his sleeve. Not that there is much room up the former bodybuilder's sleeve: his rippling physique sometimes strain the buttons of his shirt. (*The Economist*, Oct. 10th, 2019)

3. 英文经济新闻的语篇分析

在篇章层面,英文经济新闻主要采用"倒金字塔体"的写作模式。倒金字塔体就是把新闻的主要内容放在新闻文本的开头,让读者立刻看到新闻的主要内容。"倒金字塔体"的新闻一般由标题、导语、主体和结尾四部分构成,其中最重要的是标题。一个好的标题可以吸引读者眼球,概括全文。

第二节 翻译知识讲解

对经济新闻来说，要保证译文在目的语环境中能够达到和原文一致的效果，使其在特定的环境中发挥特定的作用，译文必须能够符合译入语的表达习惯，使受众易于理解和接受。为了使译文能够符合目的语的规范以及相应的文化背景，在对经济新闻进行翻译的过程中，译者要摆脱原文的束缚，对其进行灵活的翻译，本篇将介绍多种不同的翻译方法并结合实例对其进行讲解。

一、经济新闻中的标题翻译

新闻标题在新闻全文中发挥着很大作用，一个好的新闻标题可以概括全文、吸引读者。对于新闻标题的翻译主要有以下几种技巧：增词，词性转换，双关语和省译。

1. 增词

经济新闻标题一般比较短，有的甚至只有一两个词，在翻译成汉语时，需要增加字词，读者才能明白。例如"Obama's Middle Class Problem: Deeper Job Losses"译为"奥巴马面临的中产问题：失业率上升"。又如"Chalk and Cheese"也使用了增词的方法，译为"优步与爱彼迎：风马牛不相及"。

2. 词性转换

根据经济新闻文体的特点，英语原文标题一般用名词或非谓语动词短语代替句子，达到简洁的目的，在翻译成汉语时，要进行词性转换，使其符合中文读者习惯。例如"HP Innovation, One Pricey Giant Screen at a Time"译为"惠普开展创新，同时推出一款高价特大屏"。

3. 双关语

英语经济新闻标题利用词语的多义性，使用双关语，言此及彼，表达多层意思。但在汉译时，为了最大限度地实现充分性，只能选择其主要含义，舍弃次要意思。例如"Aussie Beer Drinking Market Goes Flat, Slumping to 65-Year Low"译为"澳洲啤酒市场不景气，下滑到65年以来低点"。在此标题中，原文"goes flat"是双关语，既主要指市场不景气，又含有啤酒漏气的意思，读来生动贴切。但在翻译时，只能择其主要意思。

4. 省译

经济新闻标题中的省译是指译者在翻译时，在不遗漏原文信息的情况下选择需要的重要信息进行翻译，对于那些冗余或对译语读者价值不大的信息应予以省略。例如"Misogyny, not prurience"译为"不近女色"。此英文标题出现了重复性孪生词，misogyny是名词，表示厌恶女人；prurience意为好色、渴望，因此not prurience表示不好色。当体现同一意义时，在翻译时就应当适当进行省略，以免造成译文的冗余。

再如"发改委下调国内油价 十年来首迎五连跌"译为"China Cuts Retail Oil Prices"。此标题有两层信息。一是宣布中国下调油价，二是这次下调油价是过去十年间油价连续第五次下跌。因此,在翻译中可以选择性翻译对目标读者更有价值的信息。同时,译文还省略了中国政府特有的部门的名称。中文简称"发改委"很短,但其官方译名的英文却相当长且对英语读者的价值不大,因此可以选择省略。

二、经济新闻中的直译

经济新闻中的直译要求译文忠实于原文,经济新闻是信息型文本,经常出现经济术语以及统计数据等,因此经济新闻的专业性较强,经济新闻中直译忠实的程度和形式要求较高。客观公正地传递信息是经济新闻译者必须遵守的原则。

例1

原文:At the end of February 2020, financial markets entered a risk-off phase with significantly increased volatility across markets. Equity markets began declining rapidly, losing around 30% of market value in a matter of weeks, with the speed of the sell-off exceeding that of the global financial crisis of 2008-2009(GFC).

(世界经济论坛,2020年4月)

译文:2020年2月底,金融市场进入风险规避阶段,市场波动性明显增强。股市开始迅速下跌,在短短几周内损失了约30%的市值,抛售速度超过了2008—2009年全球金融危机时期。

分析:在经济新闻的翻译中,时间或数字的微小偏差都会给读者传递错误的信息,甚至造成巨大的经济损失。此例中,"At the end of February 2020"和"2008-2009(GFC)"需要准确翻译为"2020年2月底"以及"2008—2009年全球金融危机时期",即使是文中"around 30%"的模糊表述,也要如实翻译为"约30%",以保持与原文的高度一致。

直译是既要保持原文内容,又要保持原文形式的翻译方法,为了忠实地传达出原新闻的含义,有时有必要遵照原文语言结构。英文经济新闻中的专业术语大部分有固定表达,若随意更改会对目的语读者造成歧义。因此,组织、机构等专有名词一般都采用直译。

例2

原文:NEW YORK AND WASHINGTON, D.C.
The Fed Intervenes in Short-term Money Markets for the First Time in a Decade
(*The Economist*, Sep. 21st, 2019)

译文:纽约及华盛顿特区
美联储在十年来首次干预短期货币市场

分析:原文中的"The Fed"全称为"The Federal Reserve System",中文意思为"美国联邦储备系统",但是为了保持表达的简洁性,同时和原文保持一致,可以省译为"美联储",这也是人们习惯的表达方式。可以看出此例中有新闻副标题,这在《经济学人》中是比较常见的,翻译时不仅要注意"Washington, D.C.(华盛顿特区)"这类专有名词的准确翻译，同时也应该注意形式上的对等。

三、经济新闻中的增译

经济新闻中的增译是指译者在翻译时应当充分考虑译文读者的背景知识、阅读习惯以及译文语境等因素，以增强译文的可读性为目的，适当地增加或省略原文信息，使译文在译语文化和使用译文的交际环境中有意义。翻译是一种跨文化交际，不可避免地涉及文化差异，为了使不熟悉源语文化的目的语读者更好地理解新闻内容，在经济新闻报道的翻译中，译者可以通过解释性的细节内容来扩充文本。增译就是指在原文的基础上增加信息，以帮助读者更好地理解文本。

例 3

原文：记者昨天从公安部获悉，最高法、最高检、公安部联合发布通知，对生产、销售"地沟油"的 7 种情况明确了定罪量刑标准，根据通知，涉及"地沟油"犯罪的，最高可判死刑。

（中国广播网，2012 年 2 月 24 日）

译文：Producers and sellers of "gutter oil", or illegally recycled cooking oil, could face the death penalty, the Ministry of Public Security reaffirmed on Thursday.

分析："地沟油"一词对于英文读者来说可能并不熟悉，因此译文中对"gutter oil（地沟油）"进行了解释（"illegally recycled cooking oil"），帮助目的语读者更好地理解。

例 4

原文：And consumers will not sign up to an upstart system before merchants adopt it—which merchants won't do until it has been embraced by a critical mass of customers.

(*The Economist*, March 21st, 2020)

译文：同时，新的支付方式系统也难成气候——除非商家采用新支付系统，顾客绝不会主动要求更换支付方式；但是如果大批顾客不愿意采用新支付方式，商家也不会主动更换。

分析：此处可以看出译文在保留原文信息的同时，还增加了总结句"新的支付方式系统也难成气候"紧跟破折号进行解释说明。中文中常见总分的句式结构，这样的结构往往能让读者清晰明了、理解深刻。因此此处的增译是为了符合中文的表达习惯。

例 5

原文：昨晚，中石化发布公告，披露了其子公司中石化销售公司完整版的引资名单，共有 25 家（组）投资者最终入围。25 家（组）投资者将共计斥资 1070.94 亿元人民币认购中石化销售公司 29.99%的股权。

（新华网，2014 年 9 月 15 日）

译文：China's top oil refiner Sinopec announced on Sunday that it will sell a 29.99-percent stake in its sales branch to 25 domestic and foreign companies. Those companies will jointly invest 107.1 billion yuan (about 17.4 billion U.S. dollars) in Sinopec's sales subsidiary, according to the announcement.

分析：可以看到，在将中国的经济新闻翻译成英文时，补充了所涉及企业的介绍性信息，这在翻译中是很有必要的，同时适当增译一些背景资料，补充货币信息，从而提高目标文本的可读性。

四、经济新闻中的分译

分译是根据行文要求，将一句话译为几句，常见的做法是将原文的某一部分抽出来，单独译成一句，适用于经济新闻中长句、复杂句的翻译。

例6

原文：The agencies said that they will make sure borrowers have access to the information they need to responsibly repay their loans, to protections that will be treated fairly and to assurances that servicers will be held accountable for their behavior.

译文：这些机构表示它们将保证借款者有机会获得偿还贷款所需的信息，获得公平待遇的庇佑，并且保证服务机构会为自身行为负责。

分析：根据句意将原句拆分为三个小句，每一句以介词"to"为分割线，将定语从句翻译为前置定语。这样翻译实现了从主语突出到主题突出的语言转换，符合汉语表达习惯。同时将长句拆分使得译文清晰明了，不会显得冗长繁复。

例7

原文：China Railway International USA, a consortium led by China's national railroad, will provide an initial capital investment of $100m for the line, which will first run from Las Vegas to the town of Victorville, about 80 miles from Los Angeles, and which officials hope will later connect to the city's downtown.

(*The Economist*, June 11, 2016)

译文：由中国国家铁路领导的公司，中国铁路国际(美国)有限公司，将为该条线路提供初始资金1亿美元的投资，该线路最先由拉斯维加斯运行至距洛杉矶约80英里的维克多维尔镇，而官方希望以后能运行至市中心。

分析：先找出本句的主干，即："China Railway International USA will provide an initial capital investment for the line."然后该句用了一个插入语来进一步解释中国铁路国际(美国)有限公司是由中国国家铁路领导的公司，在汉语的表达习惯里很少插入一个成分来做解释说明，故而译者在这里将说明部分提到了句首。其次，该句还用了一个定语从句来修饰"the line"，如果把用来修饰"the line"的定语从句放在前面来翻译，会导致该句头重脚轻,所以在这里把它拆分成两个小句用来避免这个情况。最后要弄明白"and which officials hope will later connect to the city's downtown"这句话也是用来修饰"the line"的,不能就近理解成修饰"Los Angeles",造成误译。

五、经济新闻中的重组

重组即打破英语原句的语序,按照汉语的逻辑顺序或者时间顺序重组句子的翻译方法。

例8

原文:Wal-Mart said Tuesday that its operating income sank 8.8 percent in the most recent quarter as the big-box behemoth shoulders the cost of a wage increase for its workers and investments in boosting its e-commerce business. (*Washington Post*, Nov. 17, 2015)

译文:商业巨头沃尔玛星期二表示,由于员工工资上涨增加了成本,并投入资金发展了电商业务,所以最近一季度的营业额下降了8.8%。

分析:"as"引导了原因状语从句,在翻译成中文时,要打破原句的语序,将原因放在前面,后果放在后面,这样更符合中文表达习惯。

第三节　常用词汇与表达

原文	译文
做市商	jobber broker
收盘	close
杠杆理论	leverage theory
指令经济	command economy
国家发展计划委员会	State Development Planning Commission
中心地段	downtown area
知识产权	intellectual property
双赢	win-win
分支机构	affiliated organizations
非公经济	non-public sector of the economy
打工族	job-seekers
股票热	stock rash
摇钱树	cash cow
工厂规模	plant size

续表

原文	译文
弧弹性	arc elasticity
IPO	首次公开募股
QE	量化宽松政策
resilient growth	弹性增长
primary market	一级市场
capital market	资本市场
equity capital market	股权资本市场
meltdown	崩盘
GDP	国内生产总值
asset-light	轻资产
step up	加速
sell off	抛售

第四节 译文赏析

一、汉译英

原文	译文
促进经济增长 积极的财政政策更加积极有为	**Proactive Fiscal Policy to Lift Growth**
根据2020年《政府工作报告》，积极的财政政策要更加积极有为。中央政府将通过增加财政赤字规模，以及增加对地方政府的转移支付，来扩大投资，保持经济平稳增长。	China will adopt a more proactive fiscal policy by expanding central government budget deficit and increasing fund transfers to local governments to boost investment and maintain stable economic growth, according to the 2020 *Government Work Report*[1].
今年中央政府拟安排财政赤字约3.76万亿元，财政赤字规模比去年增加1万亿元。今年赤字率拟按3.6%以上安排，去年这一数字为2.8%。	The central government has planned a fiscal budget deficit of about 3.76 trillion yuan this year, an increase of 1 trillion yuan from last year. The deficit-to-GDP ratio is projected at more than 3.6 percent, compared with 2.8 percent last year[2].
同时，我国将发行1万亿元抗疫特别国债，以减轻新冠肺炎疫情的影响。	In addition, China will issue 1 trillion yuan of special central government bonds to mitigate the COVID-19 epidemic effect[3].

续表

原文	译文
5月22日，第十三届全国人大三次会议开幕，国务院总理李克强向大会作《政府工作报告》时说，抗疫特别国债和增加的财政赤字全部转给地方。	The proceeds of the special treasury notes and the increased fiscal deficit will all be transferred to local governments, Premier Li Keqiang said on Friday while delivering the *Government Work Report* during the opening of the third session of the 13th National People's Congress.
第十三届全国人大三次会议开幕式后，财政部部长刘昆告诉记者，在今年的一般预算安排上，中央财政对地方的转移支付增加了12.8%，以支持基础设施投资，应对疫情对经济的影响。	The central government will also increase funds transferred to local governments by 12.8 percent to support infrastructure investment and counter economic fallout, Finance Minister Liu Kun told reporters after the opening of the NPC session[4].
刘昆说，受新冠肺炎疫情的影响，今年财政收入下降。今年的转移支付增加比例在近年来是最高的，以保障就业和民生。	It will be the highest growth rate till date in the transfer of payments to local governments and is aimed at safeguarding employment and people's livelihoods, as fiscal income is projected to decrease this year due to the COVID-19 epidemic, said Liu[5].
他说，地方财政减收增支的规模在8000亿元到9000亿元，一些地方面临较大压力。	He said that local governments' fiscal income is projected to reduce by 800 billion yuan to 900 billion yuan this year and some regions may face severe pressure.
同时，今年拟安排地方政府专项债券3.75万亿元，比去年有所增加，以促进投资，支撑经济增长。	Meanwhile, the government has also raised the quota for local government special bonds to 3.75 trillion yuan to boost investment and shore up economic growth.
恒大研究院前首席宏观经济研究员罗志恒表示，如果将增加的中央政府预算赤字、特别国债和地方政府专项债券的发行计算在内，中国的财政刺激方案总额可能达到8.5万亿元。	China's fiscal stimulus package could reach a total of 8.5 trillion yuan if the expanded central government budget deficit, the issuance of the special treasury notes and the local government special bonds are included, said Luo Zhiheng, former chief macroeconomic researcher at the Evergrande Research Institute[6].
他说，这一政策立场表明，财政政策在抵消经济风险方面发挥了主导作用，并将有助于实现政府提出的"六保"，包括保障就业和民生。	The policy stance is an indication that fiscal policy has played a lead role in offsetting the economic risks and will help realize the "six priorities" laid out by the government, including safeguarding employment and people's livelihoods, Luo said[7].
财政部中国财政科学研究院院长刘尚希在接受《中国日报》采访时表示，1万亿元特别国债的资金可能来自一些目标商业银行。	Liu Shangxi, head of the Chinese Academy of Fiscal Sciences under the Finance Ministry, told *China Daily* that the funds for the 1 trillion-yuan special treasuries may come from some targeted commercial banks.

续表

原文	译文
全国政协委员刘尚希说，目前的市场流动性足以支持增发特别国债，特别国债的发行应避免负面作用，如利率增长。	Liu, who is a member of the National Committee of the Chinese People's Political Consultative Conference said that the current market liquidity is sufficient to support the new issuance and the issuance should avoid side-effects, such as growth in interest rates.
中央财经领导小组办公室前副主任杨伟民表示，增加的财政赤字将用于保障就业和民生，特别是在市县级政府，这是一种创新的财政方法。	Yang Weimin, former deputy head of the Office of the Central Commission for Financial and Economic Affairs, said the expanded fiscal deficit will be used to safeguard employment and livelihoods, especially in the city-and county-level governments, which is an innovative fiscal method.
十三届全国人大常委会委员杨伟民说，需要采取更多的货币政策来配合财政刺激措施，比如进一步鼓励商业银行降低贷款成本，尤其是小微企业贷款成本。	More monetary actions are needed to coordinate with the fiscal stimulus measures, such as further encouraging commercial banks to reduce the cost of loans, especially for small businesses, said Yang, a member of the Standing Committee of the 13th CPPCC National Committee[8].

来源：《中国日报》(*China Daily*)

难点 1

原文：根据 2020 年《政府工作报告》，**积极的财政政策要更加积极有为**。中央政府将通过增加财政赤字规模，以及增加对地方政府的转移支付，来扩大投资，保持经济平稳增长。

译文：China will adopt a **more proactive fiscal policy** by expanding central government budget deficit and increasing fund transfers to local governments to boost investment and maintain stable economic growth, according to the 2020 *Government Work Report*.

分析：这段话中"积极的财政政策要更加积极有为"如果直译的话很容易造成冗余表达，因此在英译时，将中文的两句话合译为一句话，并且调整了语序，将"according to the 2020 *Government Work Report*"放在最后，使译文更符合英文读者的阅读习惯。

难点 2

原文：今年**赤字率**拟按 3.6% 以上安排，去年这一数字为 2.8%。

译文：**The deficit-to-GDP** ratio is projected at more than 3.6 percent, compared with 2.8 percent last year.

分析：本篇新闻中有许多关于财政赤字以及赤字率的表达。赤字率表示的是一定时期内财政赤字额与同期国内生产总值之间的比例关系。财政赤字是指财政支出超过财政收入的部分。

赤字率=(政府开支−政府收入)/GDP×100%

赤字率：the deficit-to-GDP ratio

财政赤字：the budgetary deficit

难点 3

原文：同时，我国将发行 1 万亿元**抗疫特别国债**，以减轻新冠肺炎疫情的影响。

译文：In addition, China will issue 1 trillion yuan of **special central government bonds** to mitigate the COVID-19 epidemic effect.

分析：这句话中的"抗疫特别国债"省译为"国债"，因为"抗疫特别国债"和后面的"以减轻新冠肺炎疫情的影响"语义重复，因而可以省译。

抗疫特别国债：special central government bonds

地方政府专项债券：local government special bonds

专项债券发行 the issuance of special bonds

难点 4

原文：第十三届全国人大三次会议开幕式后，财政部部长刘昆告诉记者，在今年的一般预算安排上，中央财政对地方的转移支付增加了 12.8%，以支持基础设施投资，**应对疫情对经济的影响**。

译文：The central government will also increase funds transferred to local governments by 12.8 percent to support infrastructure investment and **counter economic fallout**, Finance Minister Liu Kun told reporters after the opening of the NPC session.

分析：这句中，"应对疫情对经济的影响"译成英文巧妙地转化为"counter economic fallout"，此处是典型的意译，避免了直译的生硬。

中央财政对地方的转移支付：the central government will also increase funds transferred to local governments

[**拓展表达**] 中央对地方均衡性转移支付：the central government's transfer payments to local governments for equalizing access to basic public services

难点 5

原文：刘昆说，受新冠肺炎疫情的影响，今年财政收入下降。今年的转移支付增加比例在**近年来**是最高的，以保障就业和民生。

译文：It will be the highest growth rate **till date** in the transfer of payments to local governments and is aimed at safeguarding employment and people's livelihoods, as fiscal income **is projected to** decrease this year due to the COVID-19 epidemic, said Liu.

分析："近年来"此处的英文表达为"till date",属于比较少见的用法,可以积累一下。另外,"is projected to"原意是指"计划于;预计",在此处可以表示将会发生、必然发生的含义。

难点 6

原文:恒大研究院前首席宏观经济研究员罗志恒表示,如果将增加的中央政府预算赤字、特别国债和地方政府专项债券的发行计算在内,中国的财政刺激方案总额可能达到8.5万亿元。

译文:China's fiscal stimulus package could reach a total of 8.5 trillion yuan if the expanded central government budget deficit, the issuance of the special treasury notes and the local government special bonds are included, said Luo Zhiheng, former chief macroeconomic researcher at the Evergrande Research Institute.

分析:这句话的翻译是典型的语序调整法,对比中文和英文可以发现,原文的语序在译文中有很大的调整,说话人放在句末,其头衔紧跟其后,与中文表达习惯不太一致。且虚拟语气的语序也有所改变。语序调整是新闻翻译中常见的翻译方法,是为了更符合目的语读者的阅读习惯。

难点 7

原文:他说,这一政策立场表明,财政政策在抵消经济风险方面发挥了主导作用,并将有助于实现政府提出的**"六保"**,包括保障就业和民生。

译文:The policy stance is an indication that fiscal policy has played a lead role in offsetting the economic risks and will help realize the **"six priorities"** laid out by the government, including safeguarding employment and people's livelihoods, Luo said.

分析:此处的"六保"是采用的意译的处理方式,"six priorities"可以理解为六大优先事项,十分贴切。

难点 8

原文:十三届全国人大常委会委员杨伟民说,需要采取更多的货币政策来配合财政刺激措施,比如进一步鼓励商业银行降低贷款成本,尤其是小微企业贷款成本。

译文:More monetary actions are needed to coordinate with the fiscal stimulus measures, such as further encouraging commercial banks to reduce the cost of loans, especially for small businesses, said Yang, a member of the Standing Committee of the 13th CPPCC National Committee.

分析:此处译文将主语放置到句末,并且采用了一个无灵主语句来代替原文,使得句子更加客观地道,更符合英文新闻的表达习惯。

二、英译汉

原文	译文
Chalk and Cheese As Airbnb prepares to go public, it is keen to point out how it differs from Uber. They are the two most prominent examples of what used to be called the "sharing economy". Founded in 2008 and 2009, respectively, Airbnb and Uber pioneered asset-light platforms to bring together providers and consumers of particular services—accommodation for the first, transport for second. Both firms became bywords for entire categories: startups now claim to be Airbnb for dogs or Uber for doctors. But Uber's stockmarket flotation in May did not go well. Its share price has fallen by nearly 35% since its listing (and that of its rival Lyft, which went public in March, by 50%). As Airbnb prepares to go public next year, its boss, Brian Chesky, has been making the case for his company, both to the press and behind closed doors. He is keen to get across that, sharing-economy heritage notwithstanding, Airbnb is no Uber.	优步与爱彼迎：风马牛不相及[1] 准备上市的爱彼迎急于指出自己与优步的不同。它们是原来所谓的"共享经济"的两个最突出的例子。爱彼迎和优步分别成立于2008年和2009年，它们率先推出了轻资产平台，将特定服务的供应商和消费者聚集在一起——爱彼迎是住宿，优步是出行[2]。两家公司都成了整个类别的代名词：创业公司如今都自称宠物服务业的爱彼迎或医疗业的优步[3]。但优步在5月上市的结果并不理想，其股价至今已下跌了近35%（优步的竞争对手Lyft自3月上市后股价已下跌了50%）。爱彼迎准备于明年上市，无论是在媒体面前还是关起门来，其老板布莱恩·切斯基（Brian Chesky）一直在力撑自家公司上市。他热切地想要传达一个观点：尽管两家公司都有共享经济的血脉，但爱彼迎并非优步。
Mr Chesky founded the firm with his friends Joe Gebbia and Nate Blecharczyk, after he and Mr Gebbia, both unemployed designers, began renting out an airbed in their San Francisco apartment to make extra money. He originally thought it would be a side-hustle while he started a social-media startup. As is often the way, the side-hustle turned out to be the better idea. After an initial focus on renting spare beds in cities during conferences, when hotel rooms were scarce, the startup expanded into rental of entire properties. In 2009 Airbed and Breakfast became Airbnb. Since then more than 500m stays have been booked through its platform, which now offers more than 7m properties (including 4,900 castles and 2,400 tree-houses) in over 100,000 cities. Each night, around 2m people around the world stay in an Airbnb.	切斯基和同为设计师的朋友乔·吉比亚（Joe Gebbia）曾一度失业，靠出租两人旧金山公寓里的气垫床来赚外快，后来他们和另一位朋友内特·布莱沙奇克（Nate Blecharczyk）共同创立了爱彼迎。切斯基最初以为这只是他创办社交媒体公司时的副业。结果和很多时候一样，副业往往更有前途。一开始，这家创业公司主要是在大型会议期间酒店房间稀缺时出租市内房屋里的空床，后来扩展到出租整套物业。2009年，他们的Airbed and Breakfast（气垫床和早餐）服务正式更名为爱彼迎（Airbnb）。自那之后，通过其平台预订住宿已超过5亿次，现在平台上有超过700万个房源（包括4900座城堡和2400个树屋），分布在10万多个城市。每天晚上，全球约有200万人住在通过爱彼迎租赁的物业中。

续表

原文	译文
Having been in roadshow mode for several months, Mr Chesky has polished answers for everything up his sleeve. Not that there is much room up the former bodybuilder's sleeve: his rippling physique sometimes strain the buttons of his shirt. Oof! He cleanly dispatches a question in a television interview about safety and hidden cameras, then flips it around into an opportunity talk up Airbnb Plus, a premium tier of properties that are even more closely vetted. Pow! He bats away the notion that he is worried about Marriott, a hotel giant that is launching a rival to Airbnb called "Homes & Villas", instead seeing it as an endorsement of his model. Indeed, Airbnb is punching back, letting hotels list rooms on its site and investing in properties custom-built for Airbnb rental.	切斯基进入路演模式已经有几个月了，他的锦囊里准备好了针对各种问题的答案。这倒不是说他身上有很多塞锦囊的空间：这位前健美运动员身上的肌肉凹凸有致，衬衫的纽扣有时要崩开了。厉害呀！他在一次电视采访中干脆利落地打发了一个关于安全和隐蔽摄像头的问题，接着又把这个问题化解成一个讨论爱彼迎Plus（受到更严格审查的优质物业）的机会。帅啊！他否认自己因为万豪而忧心——这家酒店巨头正在推出与爱彼迎竞争的"Homes & Villas"住宅短租服务——反而说这是对自己模式的认可。实际上，爱彼迎正在大力回击，让酒店把客房挂在它的网站上，并投资为爱彼迎出租量身定制的物业。
The firm has grand designs to move beyond accommodation, and provide the entire trip: where to go, what to do and how to get there, not just where to stay. It intends to team up with airlines to "elevate" the experience of air travel. As part of this effort earlier this year Airbnb hired Fred Reid, the founding chief executive of Virgin America, though Mr Chesky is cagey about details. Already, users of the Airbnb Luxe service (where those castles, and other fancy venues, are listed) are assigned a "trip designer" to help them arrange transport, restaurants and other perks. Indeed, Airbnb's main growth plans hinge on offering users not just a bed but an experience, "designed and led by inspiring locals" to boot. Airbnb Experiences, launched in 2016, uses the Airbnb platform to link guests with locals who can provide things like guided tours or cooking workshops. In June it added Airbnb Adventures, which arranges trips for up to 12 people in exotic places. People don't travel to sleep, Mr Chesky likes to say, but to have an experience.	爱彼迎有宏伟的计划，要从住宿扩展到覆盖出行全程：去哪里，做什么，怎么去，而不仅仅是住哪里。它打算与航空公司合作以"提升"航空旅行的体验。为此它在年初聘请了维珍美国航空（Virgin America）的第一任首席执行官弗雷德·里德（Fred Reid），但切斯基对细节守口如瓶。爱彼迎已开始为Luxe服务（可选择城堡和其他高档场所）的用户安排"行程规划师"，帮助他们安排交通、餐厅和其他额外服务。确实，爱彼迎的主要增长计划的核心是不仅仅为用户提供一张床，而是由"热心鼓舞的当地人设计和带领"的体验。爱彼迎"体验"（Experiences）于2016年推出，在平台访客与当地居民之间架起桥梁，由当地人提供导游或烹饪作坊等服务。今年6月，它又新增了爱彼迎"探险"（Adventures），为用户在异域安排冒险体验，每个团不超过12人。切斯基总喜欢说，人们去旅行不是为了睡懒觉的，而是为了获得体验。

原文	译文
So far, so Uber. The ride-hailing giant, too, has expanded into areas like food delivery and road freight. But here the similarities end, starting with money. Whereas Uber has yet to turn a profit (and, sceptics say, never will), Airbnb says it is already profitable (to be precise, EBITDA-positive) and has been since 2017, when it is thought to have earned $93m on revenues of $2.6bn. That is not the only distinction. For ride-hailing firms like Uber and Lyft, supply and demand must be matched in the same city; a driver in Manhattan is no use to a rider in Mumbai. Airbnb's listings, by contrast, are global. Any property anywhere can potentially appeal to any user; a Mumbaiker May want to stay in New York. A telltale sign of Airbnb's superior "network effects" is that whereas drivers for Uber often drive for Lyft, and vice versa, doing their utmost to play the platforms off against each other, most of Airbnb's listings do not appear on any other platform.	到这里，爱彼迎看起来很像优步。优步这个网约车巨头也已将服务拓展到送餐和公路货运等领域。但是，两者的相似点到此为止。差异首先在于钱。优步尚未实现盈利（持怀疑态度者认为它永远不会盈利），而爱彼迎自称已经盈利（确切地说是EBITDA为正），并且自2017年以来一直处于盈利状态，据估计它当年的收入为26亿美元，利润9300万美元。这不是唯一的区别。优步和Lyft这样的网约车公司只能在同一个城市里匹配供求——曼哈顿的司机没法去拉孟买的乘客。而爱彼迎的房源遍布全球，任何地方的任何房源都可能吸引到用户——比如说某个孟买的客户可能就想去纽约住几天。尤其能体现爱彼迎出众的"网络效应"的一点就是，它的大多数房源都不会出现在其他平台上，而优步和Lyft的司机经常通过对方的平台接单，使出浑身解数让两个平台相互竞争。
Unlike Uber drivers, few of whom were previously riders, Airbnb hosts typically start out as renters first. Since it is a middleman for property rather than labour, Airbnb has avoided the controversy about "gig economy" exploitation, and the vexed question of whether ride-hailing firms should treat drivers as employees.	优步司机以前只有少部分是司机，而爱彼迎屋主通常一开始就是租户[4]。由于爱彼迎是房产而非劳力的中间人，因此避开了有关"零工经济"压榨人的非议，以及网约车公司是否应将司机视为雇员的烦人问题。

难点1

原文：Chalk and Cheese

译文：优步与爱彼迎：风马牛不相及

分析："chalk and cheese"虽然字面意思为"粉笔和奶酪"，这两种事物在本质上没有任何相似之处，因此常常用来形容两个人或两件事迥然不同或完全不合拍，结合全文理解为优步和爱彼迎是完全不同的，为了更加贴合部分中文读者的阅读习惯，采用了增词和习语活用的标题翻译方法，译为"优步和爱彼迎：风马牛不相及"。

难点 2

原文：Founded in 2008 and 2009, respectively, Airbnb and Uber pioneered asset-light platforms to bring together providers and consumers of particular services — accommodation for the first, transport for second.

译文：爱彼迎和优步分别成立于2008年和2009年，它们率先推出了轻资产平台，将特定服务的供应商和消费者聚集在一起——爱彼迎是住宿，优步是出行。

分析：本句主干为"Airbnb and Uber pioneered asset light platforms"。"to bring together providers and consumers of particular services"中不定式"to do"作定语，修饰前面的名词"platforms"。而最后的"accommodation for the first, transport for second"则作为"services"的同位语。

难点 3

原文：Both firms became bywords for entire categories: startups now claim to be Airbnb for dogs or Uber for doctors.

译文：两家公司都成为了整个类别的代名词：创业公司如今都自称为宠物服务业的爱彼迎或医疗业的优步。

分析：首先要明白"bywords"的含义，意为"……的代名词"，比如："His name has become a byword for honesty in the community."因此"both firms became bywords for entire categories"可以理解为"两家公司都成了整个类别的代名词"，下文的"dogs"和"doctors"使用了押韵，可以理解为"宠物服务业"和"医疗业"。

难点 4

原文：Unlike Uber drivers, few of whom were previously riders, Airbnb hosts typically start out as renters first.

译文：优步司机以前只有少部分是司机，而爱彼迎屋主通常一开始就是租户。

分析：句子的前半部分如果按照原文句型结构译为"不像优步司机，他们中只有少数人之前是司机"，显得句型结构拖沓，可以合并成"优步司机以前只有少部分是司机"。

翻 译 练 习

一、词组翻译

市场份额
跳水
黄金地段

电子商务

贸易战

软着陆

泡沫经济

资本市场

摩根士丹利中国指数

投资热

外向型经济

牛市

deflation

brick and mortar

nasdaq industrial average

non-performing

repay

cross border money

IMF

in stock

the Dow Jones Industrial Average

二、句子翻译

(一) 汉译英

1. 中国连续五个月减持美国国债。

2. 据国家统计局网站消息,国家统计局今日公布的数据显示,2014 年 9 月中国非制造业商务活动指数为 54.0%,比上月回落 0.4 个百分点。

3. 消费对经济增长的贡献率达到 60%,消费升级也伴随着强劲增长。

4. 尽管增速有所放缓,中国经济正在朝着我们期待的方向,朝着更多立足内需和创新拉动的方向发展。

5. 中国每年新增城镇就业 1000 万人以上,居民可支配收入增长超过 GDP 增速。

(二) 英译汉

1. The agencies said that they will make sure borrowers have access to the information they need to responsibly repay their loans, to protections that will be treated fairly and to assurances that servicers will be held accountable for their behavior.

2. Wal-Mart said Tuesday that its operating income sank 8.8 percent in the most recent quarter as the big-box behemoth shoulders the cost of a wage increase for its workers and investments in boosting its e-commerce business.

3. Investors were calmed by positive signs in the U.S. economy; including a report that gross

domestic product grew more than initially expected in the second quarter.

4. The ADB in September forecast China's economy to grow 6.8 percent this year and 6.7 percent next year.

5. We are in a new macroeconomic epoch where the risk of deflation is higher than that of inflation, and we cannot rely on the self-restoring features of market economies.

三、语篇翻译

(一) 汉译英

经济特区

经济特区是中国最早对外开放的地区，是对外经济交流最活跃的地区，也是最能代表改革开放形象的地区。经济特区诞生于20世纪70年代末80年代初，是中共中央、国务院根据邓小平的倡导，为推进改革开放和社会主义现代化建设作出的重大决策。1979年4月，中共中央工作会议根据邓小平的提议，决定在深圳、珠海、汕头和厦门等划出一定地区，利用其毗邻港澳台、华侨众多的优势，在对外开放中"先走一步"，试办"出口特区"。1980年5月，中共中央、国务院将"出口特区"名称改为内涵更加丰富的"经济特区"。1980年8月，第五届全国人大常委会第15次会议决定，在广东省的深圳、珠海、汕头和福建省的厦门四市分别划出一定区域，设置经济特区，标志着中国经济特区的正式诞生。1988年4月，设立海南经济特区；2010年5月，批准新疆的霍尔果斯、喀什设立经济特区。经济特区实行特殊的经济政策和经济管理体制，坚持以外向型经济为发展目标，是中国利用境外资金、技术、人才和管理经验来发展本国和本地经济的重要手段，在中国改革开放中发挥了重要的窗口和示范作用。

(二) 英译汉

Rate Cuts Won't Fire Up Housing, Says JP Morgan

The Reverse Bank of Australia's expected interest rate cuts won't lift auction clearance rates above the 50 per cent mark nor stop housing prices from declining a further 5 per cent this year, JP Morgan says.

While weaker-than-expected economic growth figures last week prompted many economists to expect the central bank to cut, rather than raise, the benchmark lending rate this year, the effect of any further cuts would be less than the last rate-cutting cycle because there was less scope to cut rates, JP Morgan economist Tom Kennedy said.

The investment bank is now expecting a 50 basis-point cut this year, with two equal moves in July and August, but this would not fire up a housing market in which vendors had lowered their expectations to "more realistic" levels and were cutting expectations, Mr. Kennedy said.

Expected rate cuts will support the housing market, but not fire it up, economists say.

"It will support the housing market but I don't think that by the RBA recommencing an easing cycle, prices [will] do what they did between 2014 and 2016," Mr. Kennedy said. "The movement in the cash rate isn't large enough."

Australia's five-year housing boom was fuelled by a series of cuts that started when the central bank first reduced the cash rate from 4.75 per cent to 4.5 per cent in November 2011. But even over 2015 and 2016 the benchmark rate fell from 2.5 per cent to 1.5 per cent, marking a far greater reduction than the RBA was likely to make now, Mr. Kennedy said.

The JP Morgan comments are consistent with research by the central bank itself published on Monday, which said while interest rates were the primary driver in house price movements, the crucial factor was the degree of change in rates, rather than the level at which rates were at. In a research note titled "Australian Housing Auctions: Seasonally", Mr. Kennedy said the apparent stabilisation in auction clearance rates — which returned a preliminary 52 per cent last weekend — was unlikely to lead to a stabilisation in prices, as had been the case in the past, because vendor discounting was likely to subdue prices.

"At first pass the relationship indicates that the decline in house prices is overdone and poised to stabilise/turn higher in coming months," he said.

"We would caution against this interpretation given the wedge that has emerged between clearance rates and price growth is likely related to vendor discounting as sellers adjust expectations. With the dwelling construction pipeline still elevated and housing credit growth slowing, our expectation is for current dynamics to persist and for house price growth to remain under pressure in 2019."

◎ 参考文献

[1] 黄勤. 我国的新闻翻译研究：现状与展望[J]. 上海翻译, 2007(3): 23-27.

[2] 聂薇, 贾见. 英文期刊财经报道的语言特点分析：以《经济学人》为例[J]. 中国ESP研究, 2010(1): 52-63.

[3] 刘其中. 新闻翻译教程[M]. 北京：中国人民大学出版社, 2004.

[4] 王恩冕. 如何翻译英语报刊经济文章[M]. 北京：对外经济贸易大学出版社, 2005.

[5] 谢水璎. 英语报刊财经类新闻报道的语言风格[J]. 新闻战线, 2015(17): 147-148.

[6] 许明武. 新闻英语与翻译[M]. 北京：中国对外翻译出版公司, 2003.

第三章　经济研究与调查报告翻译

> ☞**思考题**
> 1. 什么是经济研究与调查报告？
> 2. 经济研究与调查报告遵循怎样的结构？
> 3. 该类文本有哪些翻译难点？

第一节　经济研究与调查报告文本分析

一、文本性质

经济研究报告是指运用科学的经济理论，以相关经济资料和调查材料为依据，对某一国家、地区或行业的经济活动，或某一项经济活动的情况进行系统客观的分析与总结的一种书面报告。而经济调查报告是反映某一经济活动调查结果的一种书面报告。调查主体在对特定对象进行深入考察的基础上，经过准确的归纳整理以及科学的分析研究，得出符合实际的结论，由此形成的汇报性应用文书即经济调查报告。

经济研究与调查报告具有以下几大特性：

1. 针对性：有比较明确的意向。
2. 写实性：实事求是地反映客观经济事物（真实客观性）。
3. 时效性：反映市场中经济活动的最新动向（市场是瞬息万变的，各种经济数据、经济指标也在发生变化）。
4. 逻辑性：在事实基础上进行严密论证，探明事物发展变化的原因，预测发展趋势，揭示本质和规律（不是简单的事实描述）。

二、文本特点

(一)英文文本特点

1. 词汇特点

(1)用词严谨正式

经济研究与调查报告作为书面的文字材料,用词严谨正式、简洁准确,语言表达忌口语化。

例1

However, keeping afloat firms that had taken on excessive risk **prior to** the pandemic could hamper economic recovery further down the line.

(International Business Settlement(IBS), *Annual Economic Report 2020*)

例2

Even **prior to** COVID-19, many OEMs were reducing their fleet mix, targeting profit improvement over sheer volume competition.

(J. P. Morgan, *Auto Sector: Post-COVID-19 World of Autos*)

在表达"在……之前"时,上述例句均使用的是更为正式的"prior to",而不是口语常用词汇"before"。

(2) 多专业术语与专业术语缩略语

经济研究与调查报告以具备一定专业知识的人群为目标受众,专业性较强,含有大量的专业术语与缩略语。

例3

That banks were in better shape than during the **GFC** was not the only silver lining in this crisis.

(IBS, *Annual Economic Report 2020*)

例4

Next, we turn to the main topic of the weekly: an update on **LIBOR** to **SOFR** transition.

(Morgan Stanley, *Global Macro Strategist: V for Vroom Vroom Vroom*)

在上述例句中,"GFC"的全称为"Great Financial Crisis",指的是2008年9月15日爆发并引发全球经济危机的金融危机。"LIBOR"的完整形式为"London Interbank Offered Rate",即伦敦银行同业拆借利率,指的是伦敦的第一流银行之间短期资金借贷的利率,是国际金融市场中大多数浮动利率的基础利率。"SOFR"的全称为"Secured Overnight Financing Rate",即担保隔夜融资利率。"SOFR"以美国国债作为抵押品,是一个用来计算隔夜借贷成本的广泛指标。

(3) 使用符号与缩略形式

经济研究与调查报告还会使用大量的符号以及各国名称、货币等的缩略形式,这样既可以在一定程度上缩减文章的篇幅,又凸显了专业性与规范性。

例 5

We expect the FOMC to leave rates unchanged, continue to offer soft forward guidance and a downbeat outlook, and announce an open-ended 'maintenance' QE program of **$80bn/month** in Treasuries and **$50bn/month** in net purchases of MBS.

(Morgan Stanley, *Global Macro Strategist: V for Vroom Vroom Vroom*)

例 6

Strong risk appetite and positive market sentiment around Europe have allowed **EUR/SEK** to weaken recently.

(Morgan Stanley, *Global Macro Strategist: V for Vroom Vroom Vroom*)

例 7

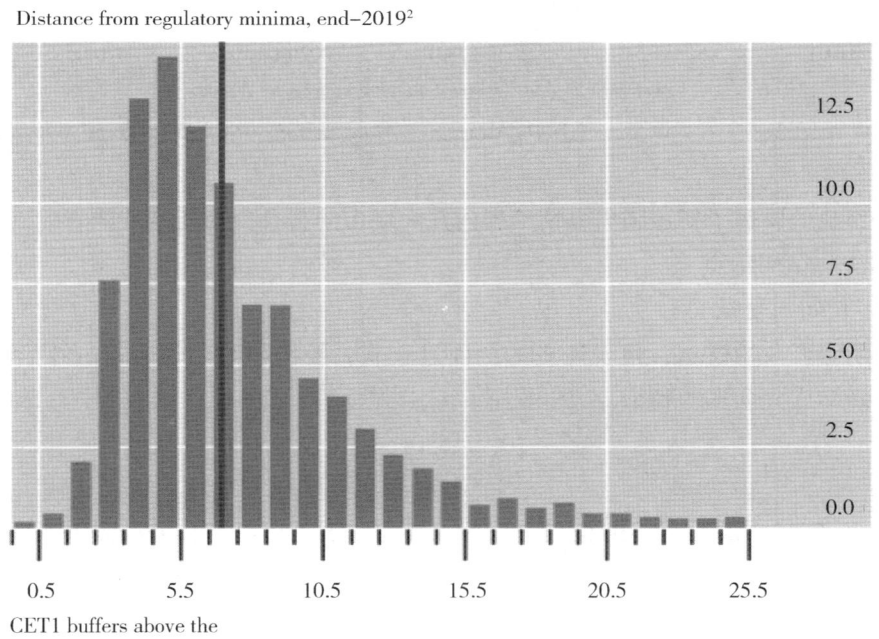

(IBS, *Annual Economic Report 2020*)

在例 5 中,符号"$"与"/"分别代表"美元(US dollar)"与"每,每一(per)","bn"为"十亿(billion)"的缩略形式。例 6 中的"EUR"与"SEK"分别为"欧元(euro)"与"瑞典克朗(Swedish Krona)"的缩略形式,这一例句中的"/"为除法符号,代表"一国货币兑换另一国货币的比率"。在例7中,"%"与"pts"的组合则代表着"百分点(percentage points)"。

(4)运用大量数据与图表

为了更直观准确地反映客观现实,经济研究与调查报告通常会引用大量的统计数据,并运用各类图表使得数据可视化,将抽象语言转变为更有表现力和说服力的具象可视图。

例8

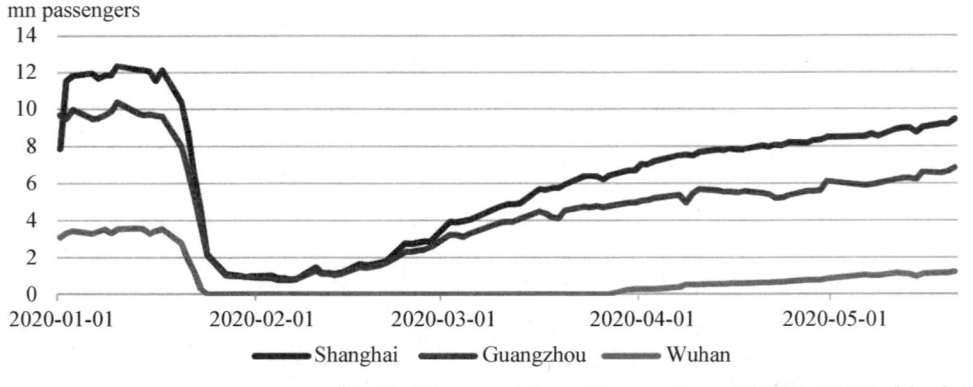

(J. P. Morgan, *Auto Sector*:*Post-COVID-19 World of Autos*)

例8直观地展示了新冠肺炎疫情给国内几大城市的公共交通所带来的影响。

2. 句法与结构特点

(1)多长句与复杂句

为了阐明复杂的概念,使表述更为全面且正式,经济研究与调查报告中含有大量结构复杂、修饰成分众多的句子。

例9

Back in 2012, the 10-year point had richened substantially on the 5s10s30s butterfly, **driven by a combination ever extending forward guidance and QE**①, **comparable to the levels** *where the fly is today*② (see blue shaded regions in Exhibit 10).

(Morgan Stanley, *Global Macro Strategist*:*V for Vroom Vroom Vroom*)

在该例句中,①和②均为非限制性的修饰成分,其中①为过去分词短语作后置定语,②为形容词短语作后置定语,且成分②中还包含了一个由"where"引导的定语从句。

(2)遵循类似的框架结构

英文经济研究与调查报告的撰写往往遵循大致相同的框架结构,如图3-1所示:

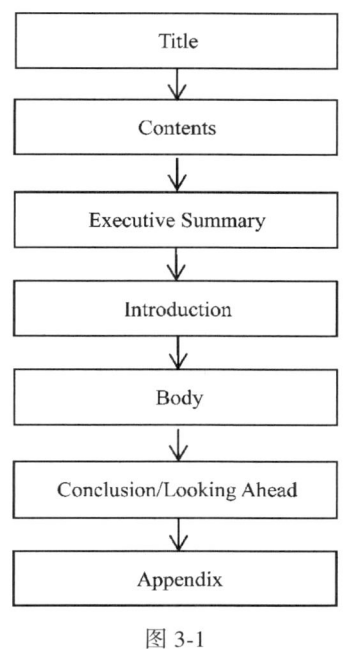

图 3-1

(二) 中文文本特点

1. 词汇特点

(1) 多专业术语

经济研究与调查报告通常是由权威机构发布的针对某一国家或地区的某一项经济活动的书面报告,涉及经济领域相关知识,常使用较多的专业术语。

例 10

尽管汇丰银行的整体**净息差**下降至 2.02%(较 2018 年下降 4 个基点),由于客户存款利差的改善以及再投资收益率的提高,汇丰银行香港业务的净息差增加了 1 个基点。

(毕马威中国,《2020 年香港银行业报告》)

该例句中的"净息差"指的是银行净利息收入和银行全部生息资产的比值。

(2) 使用数字缩略语

以《政府工作报告》为代表的一类经济研究与调查报告常使用含有数字的缩略语来表达固定的概念,这些缩略语借助数字将丰富的内容或好几层意思概括为寥寥几个字,言简意赅但内涵丰富,其构成分为"取字"和"取义"。所谓"取字",就是通过抽取原词语各组成部分中共有的字,再标以与项数相同的数字而构成的缩略形式。所谓"取义",是通过概括原词语中各组成部分所共有的"意义",并以一个确切的词语来表述概括出来的"意义",再在该词语前标以与项数相同的数字而构成。

第三章　经济研究与调查报告翻译

例 11

三大攻坚战

（2019 年《政府工作报告》）

例 12

"三去一降一补"

（2017 年《政府工作报告》）

（3）运用大量四字格

《政府工作报告》多处连用四字格，这样的结构词义丰富、蕴意深刻，读起来铿锵有力、朗朗上口，使得文章富有感染力和号召力。

例 13

攻坚克难，开拓进取

（2016 年《政府工作报告》）

例 14

稳中有变，变中有忧

（2019 年《政府工作报告》）

2. 句法与结构特点

（1）含大量无主句

无主句在中文的经济研究与调查报告中较为常见。这是因为中文重语义，是一种"意合"语言，句子内部的连接或句子间的连接采用语义手段，因此中文在构成上不太考虑语法，以达意为主，句中往往省略了一些语法成分，如主语、连接词等。

例 15

采取既利当前更惠长远的举措，着力推进供给侧结构性改革，适当扩大总需求，推动实现更高层次的供需动态平衡。

（2018 年《政府工作报告》）

（2）多用粘连句

如上所述，中文讲究"意合"，句子内部的结构较为松散，独立的分句往往只用逗号进行连接，被称为粘连句。经济研究与调查报告中也不可避免地存在这一类句子。

例 16

在以习近平同志为总书记的党中央坚强领导下，全国各族人民以坚定的信心和非凡的勇气，攻坚克难，开拓进取，／经济社会发展稳中有进、稳中有好，完成了全年主要目

50

标任务，改革开放和社会主义现代化建设取得新的重大成就。

（2016年《政府工作报告》）

原文包含了数个分句，但分句之间并没有任何的连接词。分析后发现，该句的前半部分为因，后半部分为果，译文应体现出这种逻辑关系。

(3) 框架结构

中文经济研究与调查报告的撰写也基本遵循下表的框架结构：

		标题
	简介	目录
		摘要
经济研究与调查报告		引言
	正文	主体部分
		结论
	附录	

第二节　翻译知识讲解

一、英译汉

(一) 词汇

1. 专业术语

例1

原文：If history is a guide and the law of gravity applies to China, China's economic growth is set to slow.

(*Emerging Markets Focus: Latin America*)

译文：如果正常的经济规律对中国适用，那么中国经济增长的速度将会放缓。

分析：意译是由于两种语言在表达方式上的差异性过大，在翻译过程中为了准确地转化源语的内容，而不得不打乱源语的语言形式，用符合译语表达习惯的句子结构进行转化的翻译方法。

"law of gravity"是物理中的专业词组，翻译为"万有引力定律"。根据上下文提到的人均GDP与国家经济发展之间关系的描述，"law of gravity"在这里指的就是这个规律。因此在翻译该句时，把"law of gravity"意译为"经济规律"才是文章想表达的意思。

例2

原文：Will demographics in general and labor supply in particular be a headwind or a tailwind to economic growth?

(*Emerging Markets Focus*：*Latin America*)

译文：总体人口，特别是劳动人口供给会成为经济增长的阻力还是动力？

分析："headwind"和"tailwind"的意思分别为"逆风"和"顺风"，均为地理气象里面的专业词汇，表示的是天气现象。通过文章的描述，这里研究的是人口变动对中国经济的影响。所以在这里为了把原文所要表达的真正含义表现出来，就可以把"headwind"和"tailwind"分别译为"阻力"和"动力"，以符合文本内在含义。

例3

原文：There are several mitigating factors at work.

(*Human Capital and Rural Economic Development*)

译文：当前仍有许多不利因素正在减缓这一进程。

分析："mitigating factors"是法律英语中的专业词汇，意为"减罪因素"。原文想要表达的意思是还不能确定减速的快慢程度，许多因素正在减缓工作进程。所以在这里把"mitigating factors"意译为"不利因素"，使得译文顺应原文本的意义。

2. 数量表达

在经济研究与调查报告中，对于某些经济现象的描述，比如其发展过程和走势等，往往需要运用大量的客观数据。而数据的准确性会对报告本身的可信度与权威性产生重大的影响。这就要求译者在翻译数量表达时，务必忠实于原文，做到精准翻译。

例4

原文：According to early IMF forecasts, the average primary fiscal deficits in AEs will **increase by** 8 percentage points of GDP between 2019 and 2020.

(IBS, *Annual Economic Report 2020*)

译文：根据国际货币基金组织的早期预测，2019年至2020年，阿拉伯联合酋长国的平均基本财政赤字将**增加**GDP的8个百分点。

例5

原文：When we published our AUD/USD framework in late March, we posited that AUD/USD would **rise to** 0.65 from roughly 0.60 once the USD shortage had abated.

(Morgan Stanley, *Global Macro Strategist*：*V for Vroom Vroom Vroom*)

译文：我们在3月底发布澳元兑美元的汇率分析框架时，曾假定一旦美元短缺的局面得到缓解，澳元兑美元的汇率将从0.60左右**上升至**0.65。

分析：经济研究与调查报告中用来表示"增长，上升"的高频词汇有"increase, rise, raise, jump, soar, surge"等，用来表示"减少，下跌"的高频词汇有"decrease, fall, down, drop, slump, plunge"等。译者在翻译时，应仔细判断原文表达的是"上升"还是"下跌"。此外，"from…to…"与"by…"是用来反映数据动态变化的两个高频表达，译者同样需要谨慎处理，分析清楚原文是"（上升或下跌）至"还是"（上升或下跌）了"。

3. 熟词僻义

例6

原文：In the same vein, we do not expect a move towards Yield Curve **Caps**（YCC）at the current meeting either.

译文：同样地，我们不认为对收益率曲线上限（YCC）的研究将在本次会议上取得进展。

（Morgan Stanley, *Global Macro Strategist*: *V for Vroom Vroom Vroom*）

分析：例句中的"cap"的本义为"（有帽舌的）帽子，便帽"，但这一含义显然不适用于原文的语境。其实，"cap"在此处已被引申为"an upper limit that is put on the amount of money that someone can earn, spend, or borrow"，中文可译为"上限，最高限额"，与"floor（下限，最低限额）"相对，如"pay caps"就是指"薪资上限"。据此，"Yield Curve Caps"可译为"收益率曲线上限"。

4. 隐喻意象

隐喻是人类的思维手段和认知方式，人类的认知根植于自身的身体经验和生活经验，在日常生活中往往参照他们熟知的、有形的、具体的概念来认识和对待无形的、难以定义的概念，形成了一个不同概念之间的相关关联的认知方式。许多科学的定义通过隐喻的方式便能清晰地表达出其内在含义。同样地，在许多经济类文本中，隐喻也常常被用来表现许多经济学现象和定义，使得经济类文本更为通俗易懂，更具吸引力。

例7

原文：In another words, the growth deceleration for the "flying geese" as a whole is much milder than that of the leading goose (i. e., Japan).

（*Flying Geese in Asia*）

译文：也就是说，东亚国家整体的减速幅度都比领头雁日本低。

分析：该句中的"flying goose"笔者直译为"领头雁"。查阅资料可知，"雁行模式"的提法起源于日本经济学家赤松要的"雁行产业发展形态论"。在这一理论模式中，赤松要认为，日本的产业发展实际上经历了进口、进口替代、出口、重新进口四个阶段，因为这四个阶段呈倒"V"形，在图表上酷似依次展飞的太雁，故得此名。所以，在此运用直译的方法便能够清晰表现出日本在其中的带头先锋作用，保留着原文的隐喻意象。

例 8

原文：As the world prepares to roll out 5G, a **healthy** and competitive market will help to ensure that the network infrastructure is installed as efficiently, quickly, and cheaply as possible.

(Oxford Economics, *An Economic Impact Study*: *Restricting Competition in 5G Network Equipment Throughout Europe*)

译文：随着 5G 在全球的推广，一个健康且竞争激烈的市场将有助于确保尽可能高效、快速且低价地安装网络基础设施。

例 9

原文：In some respects, the success of central banks in calming markets and shoring up confidence has even helped spark some market exuberance: at the time of writing, equity prices and corporate spreads in particular seem to have decoupled from the **weaker** real economy.

(IBS, *Annual Economic Report 2020*)

译文：在某些方面，央行在安抚市场和提振信心方面取得的成功甚至有助于市场繁荣：在撰写本报告之际，股票价格和企业利差似乎已经与愈发疲软的实体经济脱钩。

分析：人们常用身体或精神的健康状况来构建经济概念，经济的运行状况通过人的健康概念得到理解。经济实体常被概念化为需要关心照顾的病人；经济运行过程中存在的问题被理解为"疾病、顽症、慢性病"；经济运行良好是"健康、强劲"；经济运行状况不佳则是"疲软、虚弱"。

上述例句中的"a healthy market"与"a weak economy"经过多次重复映射，已形成了常规的隐喻表达，而且中文也有相对应的说法，因此，译者在译文中保留了此隐喻意象。

(二) 句法

1. 被动语态

经济研究与调查报告是一种典型的信息型文本，因为英语中的被动句对事物的表述比较客观和严谨，因此在经济研究与调查报告中通常会使用大量的被动语态来陈述一些客观事实和所获数据等信息。

(1) 译为无标志的汉语被动句

由于汉语自身的特点，有时无需特定的词等作为标志或者连接，也能表达一类意思。汉语中的被动句就属于这一类，尽管没有标志词，通过词语和句子的内部联系，也可以表示被动含义。

例 10

原文：This distinct disconnect between economic growth and employment growth in China **is further highlighted** by cross-country comparison.

(*China Economics*: *Labor Supply to Remain Abundant*)

译文：中国经济增长和就业增长之间的这一明显区别可以**通过**同别国进一步的比较**说明**。

分析：该句原文所要表达的意思是：中国经济增长和就业增长之间的这一明显区别被同别国进一步的比较来说明。

（2）译为汉语的无主句

在翻译英文中的被动句时，有的时候不需要或者根本就不知道动作的发出者，再或者是没有必要指出动作的发出者，这时除了上面提及的可以译成汉语的被动句以外，还可以将其译成汉语的无主句。

例 11

原文：While the decline in the average growth rate is significant, it should be stressed that growth decelerated from a high level.

(IBS, *Annual Economic Report 2020*)

译文：虽然平均增长率下降得相当明显，但**需要强调的是**减速是在经济增长到高位的基础上才会出现的。

分析：本句中的被动语态出现在后半句，由"it"作形式主语，如果把需要"强调"的这部分放在前面说，就会显得头重脚轻，因此原句使用被动语态进行表达。在很多情况下，英语中的被动句不需要或无法说出行为的主体，因此，翻译时往往译成汉语的无主句。此时，原句中的主语通常会被译成宾语。

（3）译为汉语的泛指主语句

在英语被动句的表达中会发现，之所以使用被动句是由于英语的表达习惯，有时没有必要指出动作的发出者，再有一种情况就是动作的发出者是普通大众，是泛指，因此不需要指出。

例 12

原文：Theoretically, the working-age population can be considered the sum of the "economically active" and "non-economically active" population, with the former further broken out into the "employed" and "unemployed".

(*China Economics: Labor Supply to Remain Abundant*)

译文：理论上说，我们可以把劳动人口作为"从事经济活动"人口与"不从事经济活动"人口之和，而前者又可以进一步分为"有工作"和"无工作"。

分析：如果译为"理论上说，劳动人口可以被认为是'从事经济活动'人口与'不从事经济活动'人口之和，而前者又可以进一步分为'有工作'和'无工作'"，看上去难免有些生硬，为了使译文通顺流畅，可以加上一个泛指的主语"我们"，并将其翻译成主动句。

二、汉译英

（一）词汇

1. 中国特色词汇的翻译

中文的经济研究与调查报告中包含了许多中国特色词汇，它们大多来自日常生活，并且被赋予了时代的烙印，如"择校""以旧换新""保障性安居工程"等。翻译时若仅仅依据其字面意义，会不得要领，相去甚远。这是因为这些词汇表达的是一种特定语境中词语概念意义之外的附加意义，代表着中国特定文化语境中的文化、社会、情景、历史以及政治意义等，与中国的国情和社会息息相关。因此，在翻译这类词汇时，只有在充分理解原文的基础上，注重特定语境中上下文词语的搭配关系，注重社会文化因素，才能用符合语境、符合规范、符合译文习惯的表达方式正确译出这类词汇的实际内涵。

（1）直译

例13

原文：习近平新时代中国特色社会主义思想

（2019年《政府工作报告》）

译文：Xi Jinping Thought on Socialism with Chinese Characteristics for a New Era

分析：近年来，"习近平新时代中国特色社会主义思想"这一我国特有的概念在《政府工作报告》中出现的频率很高。其中的"中国特色社会主义"已有了固定的英文表达，而且为外国读者所广泛接受。因此针对这一词汇的翻译，通过灵活地运用介词"on"与"for"（尤其是"for"，表达出了"统领、引领"之意），直译便能完整准确地传递其内涵。

（2）意译

例14

原文：深化国际产能合作，带动我国装备、技术、标准、服务走出去，实现优势互补。

（2017年《政府工作报告》）

译文：We will deepen international industrial-capacity cooperation, **promoting the export of** Chinese equipment, technologies, standards, and services, to see that China and other countries are able to draw on each other's strengths.

分析："走出去"也是一个具有中国特色的高频词。若依照其字面意思直译，外国读者自然是不知所云，因此需要结合原文的语境进行理解。此处的"走出去"指的是"走"到海外市场，即"出口"。翻译为"export"虽然不符合原文的形式，但却忠实准确地传递了原文的实质内容。

2. 数量表达

《政府工作报告》中出现的数字可以分为"具体数字"和"模糊数字"。

（1）"具体数字"——忠实，直译

例15

原文：根据 ISDA 报告，SOFR 挂钩期货的交易量从 **2019 年第一季度的 4.3 万亿美元增加到 2019 年第四季度的 11 万亿美元**，而 SOFR 挂钩掉期合约的交易量从 **2018 年的 60**

亿美元增加到 2019 年的 3930 亿美元(以名义价值计)。

(毕马威中国,《2020 年香港银行业报告》)

译文：According to an ISDA report, trading volume of SOFR futures **increased from US＄4.3 trillion in the first quarter of 2019 to US＄11 trillion in the fourth quarter of 2019**, while the trading of SOFR swaps also **increased from US＄6 billion in 2018 to US＄393 billion in 2019 in notional value.**

分析：在翻译此类具体数据时，可采用直译的方法。不仅要精准地译出数值大小，翻译时还要特别注意单位、变化方向、时间等，避免误译或漏译。

(2)"模糊数字"——意译

例 16

原文：是广大干部群众筚路蓝缕、千辛万苦干出来的

(2019 年《政府工作报告》)

译文：made by our people through perseverance and hard work

例 17

原文：让三百六十行人才荟萃、繁星璀璨

(2019 年《政府工作报告》)

译文：producing **a vast range** of talent ready to shine bright

分析：需要注意的是，此处的"三百六十行"并不是指具体的三百六十种职业，而是指代各行各业。在翻译此类模糊数字时，不必囿于原文的形式，可采用意译的方法，译出原文的实质内容即可。

3. 数字缩略语

指除"具体数字"之外的、常与汉字结合、意思高度浓缩的汉语含数字词语或短句，被称作"数字缩略词"或"数字略语"，主要包含以下几类：①**数字+名词**，如"一带一路""21 世纪海上丝绸之路"等，从内涵到缩略词均为名词；②**数字+动词**，如"两学一做""三去一降一补"等；③**数字+形容词或副词**，如"四个全面"；④**多词类混合**，如"双随机、一公开"(混合了数词、副词和动词)等。

(1)保留数字增译

保留数字，对汉字部分进行解释性翻译。

如"三大攻坚战"译为"the three critical battles against potential risk, poverty, and pollution"；"五位一体"译为"The 'Five-sphere Integrated Plan' is a plan to promote coordinated economic, political, cultural, social, and ecological advancement"。其中的"一体"指五个方面融为一体。

(2)数字减译

可以将数字全部或者部分去掉，甚至可以将其转换为其他的数字形式，以求表情

达意。

如"两不愁"译为"The basic living needs of rural poor populations are met";"三农"译为"agriculture, rural areas, and rural residents"。

(3) 灵活转译

遇到复杂的表达方式,可以综合考虑,摆脱汉语语言形式的束缚,灵活转译。

如"双随机、一公开"译为"the random selection of both inspectors and inspection targets and the prompt release of results"。

4. 连用四字格

四字格的使用使文章语言简洁凝练、气势磅礴、朗朗上口。四字格在《政府工作报告》中的运用主要包括并列、重复和递进。

(1) 并列关系

根据忠实原则,通常采用直译法。根据目的原则,一般采用意译的方法,这取决于文章的具体内容。

例 18

原文:为政以公,行胜于言

译文:Government works for the public; words can't compare with actions.

(2019 年《政府工作报告》)

分析:并列关系只有前后之分,没有主次之分。"为政以公"和"行胜于言"就是党一心为人民服务,为人民做实事,属于并列结构。根据目的论中的忠实原则,采用意译的方法,既保持了形式一致,又准确表达了中国共产党的执政思想,简洁明了。

例 19

原文:互联互通

译文:connectivity

(2019 年《政府工作报告》)

(2) 重复关系

一般根据语义,采用省译法。

例 20

原文:我们将**坚定不移**走和平发展道路,奉行互利共赢的开放战略,坚定维护多边主义和以联合国为核心的国际体系。

(2019 年《政府工作报告》)

译文:China will **remain** on the path of peaceful development, pursue mutually beneficial opening up, and resolutely uphold multilateralism and the international system built around the United Nations.

分析："坚定"和"不移"都意味着坚持不懈。因此，将它们作为一个整体来翻译，而不是分别转化为"坚定信念和坚持不变"。

例 21

原文：让三百六十行**人才荟萃、繁星璀璨**。

译文：producing a vast range of **talent ready to shine bright.**

（2019 年《政府工作报告》）

分析：人才荟萃"和"繁星璀璨"都是指以一技之长发光发热，实现价值。所以采用省译，用词简洁，也避免了重复。

（3）递进关系

例 22

原文：促进各民族和睦相处、和衷共济、和谐发展

译文：and enable the people of all our ethnic groups to live together happily, work together for a common cause, and develop in harmony

例 23

原文：深入推进政治建军、改革强军、科技兴军、依法治军。

译文：We will further efforts to ensure the political loyalty of the armed forces, strengthen them through reform, science and technology, and run them in accordance with law.

（2019 年《政府工作报告》）

分析：在词语内部也存在逻辑关系，"通过政治来建设军队""通过改革来强化军队""通过科学和技术来加强军队""通过法律来治理军队"。英语重"形合"，汉语重"意合"。翻译时用介词或者介词短语将内在的逻辑关系解释清楚。

5. 同词不同义

一个词在不同的语境下有不同的内涵，在翻译时需要区别对待。以"精神"一词为例：

表示会议精神、讲话精神时	the guiding principles
与物质相对应	cultural and ethical standards / progress
表示具有某种思想态度、精神内涵时	spirit
表示"……感"时	sense

（2019 年《政府工作报告》）

（二）句法

1. 无主句

（1）使用被动语态

例 24

原文：**提高**个人所得税起征点，**设立**6 项专项附加扣除。

（2019 年《政府工作报告》）

译文：The threshold for individual income tax **was raised** and six special additional deductions **were created**.

分析：这一例句含有两个动宾结构，译文通过使用被动语态，将原文的动宾结构调整为系表结构，由此原文的宾语便可以置于句首作主语。

（2）增补主语

例 25

原文：支持农民工在城镇购房，提高棚改货币化安置比例，房地产去库存取得积极成效。

（2017 年《政府工作报告》）

译文：**We** supported migrant workers in buying urban homes; and **we** increased the proportion of people affected by rebuilding in rundown urban areas receiving monetary compensation, making good progress in reducing real estate inventory.

分析：这一例句的译文通过增译代词"We"来给句子增补主语。

（3）使用形式主语"it"

例 26

原文：不能纸上谈兵、光说不练。

（2017 年《政府工作报告》）

译文：**It's** no good to just push paper and pay lip service.

分析：增补形式主语"it"也是在翻译汉语无主句时经常使用的一种方法。

（4）使用祈使句

例 27

原文：不忘初心，牢记使命。

（2017 年《十九大报告》）

译文：Remain true to our original aspiration and keep our mission firmly in mind.

2. 动宾短语

经济研究与调查报告，尤其是政府报告中，常见此类长句。翻译时，可重组句子，将同类信息整合在一起，还可适当使用被动语态、增补主语等，使句式富于变化。

例 28

原文:2018 年 11 月,中国国务院研究部署进一步扩大内需促进经济平稳较快增长的措施,确定了进一步扩大内需、促进经济增长的十项措施。具体包括:**加快**建设保障性安居工程;**加快**农村基础设施建设;**加快**铁路、公路和机场等重大基础设施建设;**加快**医疗卫生、文化教育事业发展;**加强**生态环境建设,**加快**自主创新和结构调整;**加快**地震灾区灾后重建各项工作;**提高**城乡居民收入;在全国所有地区、所有行业全面**实施**增值税转型改革,**鼓励**企业技术改造,**减轻**企业负担 1200 亿元;加大金融对经济增长的支持力度。

(《国务院常务会议部署扩大内需促进经济增长的措施》)

译文:For a stable and faster economic growth, in November, 2018, the State Council adopted ten measures to further expand the domestic demand. They are as follows: The construction of **national projects** should be accelerated, including indemnificatory housing project for low-income families, rural infrastructure, transport (e. g. railways, highways and airports). **More efficient efforts are needed in** developing health care, culture and education, enhancing ecological environment, innovation and economic restructuring, as well as rebuilding the earthquake-stricken areas. The urban and rural incomes **should be increased**. To stimulate the enterprises' initiatives for technical upgrading and innovation while reduce their business cost, the value-added tax reform **should be fully implemented** nationwide across all industries, which is expected to save 120 billion RMB for the enterprises. Financial supports **should be enhanced** for the economic growth in the future.

分析:此句为典型多动宾短语长句。首先可将同类信息整合在一起,"建设保障性安居工程""农村基础设施建设""重大基础设施建设"都属于"national projects",可以放在一起翻译。然后,为了避免句式单一,翻译余下的短语时,可变换句式,如,为动宾短语添加主语,使用被动语态,等等。

3. 独立短句

经济研究与调查报告中还有一种常见的长句,由多个独立短句构成。由于每个短句的主语不同而且相互之间没有明显的逻辑关系,如何避免译文冗长是一个难点。翻译时,可将独立短句译成短语,避免繁复。

例 29

原文:工业生产显著放缓,原材料价格和运输市场需求下降。部分企业经营更加困难,就业形势严峻。消费热点降温,房地产市场低迷,金融市场潜在风险不容忽视。

(《中国积极采取措施应对危机确保增长》)

译文:Meanwhile, China's industrial productivity was weakened which lowered the price of raw materials and the demand for transportation. **All these have led to more challenges for**

many businesses, **increased unemployment**, **cooled consumption** and **sluggish real estate**. The potential risks in the financial market could not be ignored any more.

分析：此句多独立短句，翻译时可将其译为短语。此外，还可添加连接词以衔接上下文。"all these"与前文构建桥梁，明确逻辑关系。

例30

原文：源于美国房地产价格泡沫的破灭，2007 年美国出现次贷危机，2008 年 9 月次贷危机急剧恶化，演变成为一场 20 世纪 30 年代大萧条以来最为严重的全球金融危机。

（《美国次贷危机的特殊根源及未来走向》）

译文：Triggered by the bursting of housing bubble, the U.S. subprime crisis broke out in out in 2007, **then** sharply deteriorated in September 2008, **and eventually** evolved into the worst global financial crisis since the Great Depression in the 1930s.

分析：汉语是隐性语言，注重"意合"；英语是显性语言，注重"形合"。经济研究与调查报告用语简洁，翻译时尤其要注意两种语言之间的差异，找出句子内部的逻辑关系，添加连接词，使译文各部分适当衔接。

原文以时间为顺序，意在说明金融危机发展的过程，译文中应体现出这一点。翻译时可添加表示时间的副词使译文前后衔接，理清金融危机发展的逻辑顺序。

经济研究与调查报告需遵循通顺性、忠实性和准确性的翻译原则。翻译时，需大量搜集平行文本，总结专业术语和专有名词，建立术语表；并通过阅读相关文献，了解话题背景知识；熟悉中英文表达习惯，掌握运用具体翻译技巧。

第三节　常用词汇与表达

原文	译文
balance of payments	国际收支差额
bond market	债券市场
consumer price index(CPI)	消费者物价指数
consumer surplus	消费者剩余
discount rate	贴现率
excess reserves	超额准备金
foreign direct investment(FDI)	外国直接投资
International Monetary Fund(IMF)	国际货币基金组织
marginal cost	边际成本

续表

原文	译文
Return on Assets(ROA)	资产收益率
第三产业	the tertiary industry
国民生产总值	gross national product(GNP)
国内需求	domestic demand
汇率	exchange rate
货币政策	monetary policy
经济特区	special economic zone(SEZ)
贸易顺差	trade surplus
实体经济	the real economy
收益率曲线	yield curve
资产负债表	balance sheet

第四节 译文赏析

一、汉译英

原文	译文
2015年以来，信用业务在证券市场中扮演了重要的角色，尤其以融资融券业务为代表：全年交易额达人民币35万亿元，较2014年增长了231%，占整个A股市场交易额比重达14%，已然成为中国证券市场的主要业务之一。截至2015年年末，全行业融资融券余额超过人民币1.1万亿元，股票质押式回购业务待回购初始交易金额人民币7087亿元，均较2014年年末有所增长。而受股票质押回购业务发展的影响，约定购回的待回购交易规模逐年降低，截至2015年年末约为人民币56亿元，与2014年年末相比，降幅为49%。	Since 2015, the credit business, primarily comprising margin financing and securities lending, is becoming one of the most important components of China's securities market. Its annual turnover reached RMB 35 trillion last year, an increase of 231 percent compared with 2014 and equivalent to 14 percent of the total turnover of the A-share market. As of the end of 2015, the balance of margin financing and securities lending exceeded RMB 1.1 trillion, while the balance of securities backed lending stood at RMB 708.7 billion[1], both increasing compared with the end of 2014. Following the growth of securities backed lending, the scale of stock repurchase business has been declining year-on-year, falling to approximately RMB 5.6 billion as of the end of 2015, a decrease of 49 percent compared with 2014[2].

原文	译文
2015年信用业务经历了曲折式发展，1月至6月融资融券业务持续高速增长，曾一度飙升至人民币2万亿元以上，而伴随着7月以来沪深指数的异常波动，避险情绪使得融资融券业务规模显著下降，余额又回落至1万亿元以下。与此同时，融资业务的信用风险和流动性风险也随之暴露，多只标的股票由于价格下跌导致部分投资者被强制平仓。此外，2015年7月以来市场下行也引发了股票质押式回购业务的强平危机，部分上市公司大股东通过资管计划在较高价位增持护盘，可能为日后埋下了杠杆危机。在当前资本市场形势下，如何通过合理有效的风险管理手段为信用业务保驾护航，是证券公司面临的巨大挑战之一。	The credit markets have undergone a difficult period in 2015. The turnover of margin financing and securities lending business exceeded RMB 2 trillion following rapid growth in the first six months of 2015. However, due to unusual volatility in the Shanghai and Shenzhen indices in July, the balance shrank to less than RMB 1 trillion[3]. This exposed credit and liquidity risks related to margin financing. Some investors were forced to liquidate their positions when the price of underlying stocks fell below a certain threshold. In addition, the fall in stock prices since July 2015 also triggered a liquidity crisis for the securities backed lending business. Although, some shareholders in listed companies are increasing their equity holdings through asset management plans with the intention of stabilising the market, this raises the possibility of a leverage crisis in the future. Under current market conditions, adopting prudent and effective risk management measures is one of the biggest challenges securities companies are faced with in relation to their credit business.
2015年7月1日，证监会发布了《证券公司融资融券业务管理办法》(以下简称"管理办法")，管理办法不仅建立了逆周期调节机制，对保证金比例、标的证券范围和业务集中度等进行动态调整和差异化控制；还将融资融券业务规模与证券公司净资本规模相匹配，要求业务规模不得超过证券公司净资本的4倍；同时优化了融资融券客户担保物违约处置标准和方式；完善了融资融券业务现有的风险监测监控机制，进一步强化了投资者权益保护。沪、深证券交易所根据修订后的法规，于2015年8月3日，将融券交易当日融券卖出后可还券改为次一交易日可还券；于2015年11月13日，将融资保证金比例从50%提高至100%，这些举措均有利于促进融资融券业务的健康发展，维护市场稳定。	On 1 July 2015, the CSRC issued the *Administrative Measures for Margin Financing and Securities Lending Business of Securities Companies* (the "Measures"). The purpose of the Measures is to establish a countercyclical adjustment mechanism by: i) adjusting and controlling the margin deposit ratio, the scope of underlying securities and the concentration of business; ii) matching the size of margin financing and securities lending with the securities companies' net capital, capping it at four times a brokerage's net capital[4]; iii) optimising the disposal criteria and collateral of margin clients in default and iv) refining existing risk monitoring and control mechanisms to further protect the interest of investors. Pursuant to the revised regulations, the SSE and the SZSE, beginning on 3 August 2015, require investors to return securities the following day after a short selling transaction instead of on the same day as they had done previously[5]. The margin deposit ratio was also raised from 50 percent to 100 percent beginning on 13 November 2015. These measures are designed to promote the sound development of margin financing and securities lending business and to contribute to market stability.

续表

原文	译文
2015年以来融资融券业务既实现了跨越式增长也出现了反转式下降,在市场行情波动较大的情况下,证券公司不仅需要积极应对监管机构出台的相关制度规则,还应当主动通过对信用业务风控体系、交易机制和投资者适当性等多方面科学合理的管理,减少资本市场"黑天鹅"事件的发生,保障信用业务健康平稳发展。	After achieving significant growth, margin financing and securities lending business started to decline since 2015. Following this volatility, securities companies should make sure not only to respond proactively to relevant rules and regulations issued by the authorities, but also to properly manage their credit risk control systems, trading mechanisms and the make-up of their investor base. This will help mitigate against the risk of "black swan" events[6] and ensure the stable and sound development of their credit business.

难点1

原文：**股票质押式回购业务**待回购初始交易金额人民币7087亿元

译文：the balance of **securities backed lending** stood at RMB 708.7 billion

分析："股票质押式回购业务"是指符合条件的资金融入方以所持有的股票或其他证券质押,向符合条件的资金融出方融入资金,并约定在未来返还资金、解除质押的交易。"back"在此处有"支持""担保"之意。

难点2

原文：而受股票质押回购业务发展的影响,约定购回的待回购交易规模**逐年**降低,截至2015年年末约为人民币56亿元,与2014年年末相比,降幅为49%。

译文：Following the growth of securities backed lending, the scale of stock repurchase business has been declining **year-on-year**, falling to approximately RMB 5.6 billion as of the end of 2015, a decrease of 49 percent compared with 2014.

分析：译文将"逐年"表达成了"year-on-year",而"year-on-year"的英文含义为"compared with the previous year",即"与去年相比",明显与原文的含义不符。根据"逐年"的具体含义"一年一年地,一年接一年",将其译为"year by year"更为恰当。

难点3

原文：2015年**信用业务**经历了曲折式发展,1月至6月**融资融券业务**持续高速增长,曾一度飙升至人民币2万亿元以上,而伴随着7月以来沪深指数的异常波动,避险情绪使得融资融券业务规模显著下降,**余额**又回落至1万亿元以下。

译文：The **credit markets** have undergone a difficult period in 2015. The turnover of **margin financing and securities lending business** exceeded RMB 2 trillion following rapid growth in the first six months of 2015. However, due to unusual volatility in the Shanghai and Shenzhen indices in July, **the balance** shrank to less than RMB 1 trillion.

分析：原文为典型的中文粘连句，句中包含多个独立的分句，分句之间仅用逗号进行连接。译文则依据意群进行分译，这样不仅使句子的逻辑关系更为显化，而且避免了译文过于冗长，增强了译文的可读性。

难点 4

原文：还将融资融券业务规模与证券公司净资本规模相匹配，**要求**业务规模**不得超过**证券公司净资本的 4 倍

译文：matching the size of margin financing and securities lending with the securities companies' net capital, **capping** it at four times a brokerage's net capital

分析：此处的"cap"意指"限制"，属熟词僻义。

难点 5

原文：沪、深证券交易所根据修订后的法规，于 2015 年 8 月 3 日，将融券交易当日融券**卖出**后可还券改为次一交易日可还券。

译文：Pursuant to the revised regulations, the SSE and the SZSE, beginning on 3 August 2015, require investors to return securities the following day after a **short selling** transaction instead of on the same day as they had done previously.

分析："short selling"是金融术语，意为"卖空"，指的是证券市场上的证券投机者利用证券价格飞涨的时机，先借入大批的证券在市场上高价售出，待将来证券价格下跌以后，再低价买回证券，归还所借证券，进而从中获利的一种证券投机交易。

难点 6

原文："黑天鹅"事件

译文："black swan" events

分析："黑天鹅"事件来自一个典故：欧洲人观察了上千年，见到的天鹅都是白色的，因此"所有的天鹅都是白色的"成了一个没有人怀疑的事实，直到人们在澳大利亚发现黑天鹅，推翻了上千年来千万次观察总结出来的结论。于是，"黑天鹅"事件被用来隐喻非常难以预测，且不寻常的事件，通常会引起市场连锁负面反应甚至颠覆。用"黑天鹅"作喻体本就起源于西方，而且至今已为读者广泛理解和接受。因此，译文选择保留隐喻，这对目标语读者而言，符合其文化思维，具有喻体共知性。

二、英译汉

原文	译文
CBO's Economic Forecasting Record: 2017 Update (Excerpt)	美国国会预算办公室经济预测记录:2017年更新(节选)
Summary	摘要
For four decades, the Congressional Budget Office has prepared economic forecasts to use in making its projections for the federal budget. Forecasts of output, inflation, interest rates, and wages and salaries, in particular, play a significant role in CBO's budget analysis. For example, to project receipts from individual income taxes, CBO uses its forecasts of wages and salaries.	四十年来,美国国会预算办公室编制了经济预测,用于为联邦预算制定项目。特别是对产量、通货膨胀、利率、工资和薪金的预测,在美国国会预算办公室的预算分析中发挥了重要作用。例如,为了预测个人所得税的收入,美国国会预算办公室使用其编制内容对工资和薪水进行预测。
CBO regularly evaluates the quality of its economic forecasts for several reasons. One is to determine if it needs to change its forecasting methods. For example, partly in response to past forecast errors, CBO has changed the way it forecasts productivity growth and interest rates in recent years. Another reason for evaluating past forecasts is to calculate the errors in those forecasts, which in turn can be used to approximate the range of errors or uncertainty in the agency's current forecasts. Finally, publishing such evaluations gives readers a tool to assess the usefulness of the agency's projections and is thus one way in which CBO demonstrates its commitment to transparency.	美国国会预算办公室出于以下几个原因定期评估其经济前景的质量。一是确定它是否需要更改其预测方法。例如,部分方法是为了应对过去的预测误差,美国国会预算办公室改变了近年来对生产力增长和利率的预测方式[6]。评估预测的另一个原因是计算这些预测中的误差,反过来可以用来估计目前预测中存在的误差或不确定性的范围。最后,发布评估以给读者提供一个评估机构预测是否有效的工具,由此,这也是美国国会预算办公室展示其提高透明度承诺的一种方式。
To evaluate its economic forecasts, CBO compares them with the economy's actual performance and with the Administration's forecasts, which are published in the Office of Management and Budget's annual budget documents, and the Blue Chip consensus—an average of about 50 private-sector forecasts published in Blue Chip Economic Indicators. Such comparisons can indicate the extent to which imperfect information and analysis may have caused CBO to miss patterns or turning points in the economy. They can also help the agency identify areas where it has tended to make larger errors than other analysts. This report evaluates CBO's economic forecasts over two-year and five-year periods. The span of years that CBO examined for this evaluation differs by variable and by forecast period on the basis of data availability.	为了评估其经济预测,美国国会预算办公室将它们与经济的实际绩效和政府的预测进行了比较,这些预测发表在行政管理和预算局的年度预算文件和蓝筹共识——约50个私营部门在蓝筹经济指标中公布的预测。这种比较表明信息和分析的不完善程度可能会导致美国国会预算办公室错过经济模式或转折点。这些数据还可以帮助该机构识别往往会比其他分析师发生更大误差的地方。该报告评估了美国国会预算办公室对两年期和五年期的经济预测。基于数据的可得性,美国国会预算办公室为这一评估所审查的年际因变量和预测时期的不同而不同。

续表

原文	译文
How Does CBO's Forecasting Record Compare with Those of the Administration and the Blue Consensus?	美国国会预算办公室的预测记录是如何与行政与蓝筹股共识进行对比的？
CBO's forecasting record is comparable in quality to those of the Administration and the Blue Chip consensus. When CBO's projections were inaccurate by large margins, the other two forecasters projections tended to have similar errors because all forecasters faced the same challenges. For example, all three sets of forecasts of inflation were relatively inaccurate during the late 1970s and early 1980s but generally became more accurate as inflation stabilized in more recent decades.	美国国会预算办公室的预测记录在质量上可与政府和蓝筹股共识相媲美。当美国国会预算办公室的预测存在很大偏差时，另外两个预测者的预测往往也会出现类似的错误，因为所有预测者都面临着同样的挑战。例如：在20世纪70年代末和20世纪80年代初，美国国会预算办公室、政府和蓝筹股共识三方均对通货膨胀预测相对不准确，但随着近几十年的通货膨胀稳定下来，一般都变得更加准确。
Do CBO's Forecasts Exhibit Statistical Bias?	美国国会预算办公室的预测是否存在统计偏差？
Statistical bias is the tendency of a forecaster's projections to be too low or too high over a period of time. A simple and widely used indicator of bias is the mean error. By that measure, CBO's forecasts of most economic indicators examined here have tended to be too high by small amounts but the agency's two-year forecasts of real (inflation-adjusted) output were slightly too low, on average. (CBO calculated averages of inflation in the consumer price index from calendar-year averages of monthly data published by the BLS.)	统计偏差是预测者在一段时间内过低或过高的预测趋势。简单而广泛使用的偏差指标是平均误差。根据这一措施，美国国会预算办公室对大多数经济部门的预测都略高，但该机构两年预测的实际（通货膨胀调整）产出的平均水平略低。（美国国会预算办公室根据美国劳工统计局公布的月度数据的历年平均值计算消费物价指数中的通货膨胀平均值[5]。）
After evaluating the mean errors of its forecasts, CBO reached two conclusions:	在评估了其预测的平均误差后，美国国会预算办公室得出了两个结论：
CBO's two-year forecasts of output growth and inflation have been less biased than its two-year forecasts of interest rates and the growth of wages and salaries, which exhibit a sizable upward bias—that is, they have tended to be higher than actual values by a larger amount.	美国国会预算办公室对产出增长和通货膨胀的两年预测低于其对利率及工资和薪金增长的两年预测，这显示出相当大的上升偏差——也就是说，它们往往比实际价值更高[1]。
For most economic indicators, the mean errors of CBO's five-year forecasts (which are discussed in the second half of the report) have been slightly larger than those of the agency's two-year forecasts. That pattern shows that CBO has a tendency to overestimate economic trends over the longer term.	对于大多数经济指标，美国国会预算办公室五年期预测的平均误差（在报告的后半部分中讨论）略大于该机构两年期预测的误差。这种模式表明，美国国会预算办公室倾向于高估长期经济趋势。

续表

原文	译文
How Accurate Are CBO's Forecasts?	美国国会预算办公室的预测准确率是多少？
Accuracy is the degree to which forecast values are dispersed around actual outcomes. One widely used measure of accuracy is the root mean square error (RMSE). By that measure, CBO's two-year forecasts are generally as accurate as those of the Blue Chip consensus and, for most economic indicators, slightly more accurate than the Administration's two-year forecasts. The accuracy of all three sets of five-year forecasts is comparable.	准确性是指预测值对实际结果的预测的程度。广泛使用的精确测量是均方根误差（RMSE）[2]。根据这一标准，美国国会预算办公室的两年预测通常与蓝筹共识的预测一样准确，对于大多数经济指标，比政府的两年预测精确率略高。三家机构五年期预测的准确性都是可比较的。
How Do Assumptions About Fiscal Policy Affect Forecast Errors?	关于财政政策的推测是如何影响预测误差的？
Fiscal policy refers to the federal government's policies on taxes and spending. Assumptions about fiscal policy are an important ingredient of an economic forecast because such policy affects output, inflation, interest rates, and wages and salaries. To provide lawmakers with a bench-mark against which they can assess potential changes in the law, CBO constructs its economic forecasts under the that federal fiscal policy will generally remain the same as under current law. By contrast, the Administration's forecasts reflect the assumption that the policies in the Presidents proposed budget will be adopted. Forecasters in the private sector (such as those who contribute to the Blue Chip consensus) form their own projections about the future of federal fiscal policy, so their forecasts reflect changes in law that they anticipate will be made.	财政政策是指联邦政府的税收和支出改策。关于财政政策的推测是经济预测的一个重要因素，因为这种政策影响产量、通货膨胀、利率、工资和薪金。为了向立法者提供一个基准点，他们可以评估法律的潜在变化，美国国会预算办公室根据联邦财政政策将大致保持与现行法律相同的假设，构建其经济预测。相比之下，政府的预测反映了将通过总统拟议预算的政策假定。私营部门的预测者（如对蓝筹共识作出贡献的人）形成了自己对联邦财政政策未来的预测，因此，他们的预测反映了他们预期将发生的法律变化。
CBO's Methods for Evaluating Forecasts	美国国会预算办公室的评估方法
CBO evaluates the quality of its forecasts by examining its past forecast errors and comparing them to the errors in the Administration's forecasts and the Blue Chip consensus. The Blue Chip consensus is particularly useful for comparisons because it incorporates a variety of forecasts and therefore reflects a broader blend of sources and methods than any single forecaster would use. Over time, composite forecasts like the Blue Chip consensus often provide better estimates than any projection made by a single forecaster or using a single method.	美国国会预算办公室通过审查过去的预测误差来评估其预测的质量，并将其与政府预测和蓝筹共识中的误差进行比较。与蓝筹共识的对比效果较为明显，因为它包含了各种预测，因此反映出它使用了比任何一家预测者都更广泛的来源及方法。随着时间的推移，像蓝筹共识这样的复合型预测者往往比单一型预测者或使用单一预测方法所做的预测能提供更准确的评估。

续表

原文	译文
This report evaluates CBO's economic forecasts over the first two years and over the first five years of CBO's 10-year baseline projection period. The forecasts are made at the beginning of a calendar year, and the errors are calculated by subtracting the average actual value over the forecast period from the average projected value. The two-year forecasts include the full period that is used to prepare the baseline budget for the upcoming fiscal year. The five-year forecasts are used to examine the accuracy of longer-term projections of several variables that are important for CBO's baseline budget projections.	该报告评估了美国国会预算办公室10年基线预测期在前两年和前五年的经济预测。预测是在历年开始时进行的,误差是通过从平均预测值减去预测期间的平均实际值来计算的。两年期预测包括用于编制下一个财政年度的基准预算的整个期间。用五年期预测来检验几个变量长期预测的准确性,这对美国国会预算办公室基线预算预测至关重要[3]。
Calculation of Forecast Errors	**预测误差的计算**
The method used to calculate the forecast errors for this report differs slightly from that used in CBO's evaluation of errors in revenue projections. In that evaluation, projection errors were calculated for a single fiscal year. For example, the error in CBO's two-year revenue projection for 2007 is the percentage difference between the actual amount of revenues received in fiscal year 2007 and the revenues projected for that year in January 2006.	本报告计算预测误差的方法与美国国会预算办公室在收入预测中的误差评估中使用的方法略有不同。在该评估中,计算了一个财政年度的预测误差[2]。例如,美国国会预算办公室对2007年两年期收入预测的误差是2007财政年度收到的实际收入与2006年1月预计的收入之间的百分比差额。
Limitations of the Forecast	**预测评价的局限性**
There are three reasons to be cautious when interpreting the results of this forecast evaluation: Forecasting methods change over times, different forecasters make different assumptions about future fiscal policy, and many of the actual values of the projected variables are periodically revised.	在解释这一预测评价的结果时,有三个理由需特别注意:预测方法随着时间的变化而变化;不同的预测者对未来的财政政策作出不同的假设,预计变量的许多实际价值将定期修订。
A third reason to be cautious when interpreting the results of this forecast evaluation is that the historical values of many of the data series that CBO and other analysts forecast are periodically revised by the agencies that compile those data. BEA and other agencies use various methods and statistical definitions to estimate gross domestic product (GDP) and other economic indicators on the basis of data that they and others collect.	在解释这一预测评估的结果时需要谨慎的第三个原因是,美国国会预算办公室和其他分析机构预测的系列数据的历史价值将由编译数据的机构定期修订[4]。美国经济分析局和其他机构以各自收集的数据为基础,通过各种方法和统计学定义来估算国内生产总值和其他经济指标[5]。

第四节 译文赏析

续表

原文	译文
Revisions to historical data can affect the calculations of forecast errors. For example, the RMSE of CBO's two-year forecasts of the growth of real output is 1.2 percentage points if calculated using the data that were available immediately after the two-year horizon of each forecast. But the RMSE is 1.3 percentage points if the most recently available data are used in the calculation.	对历史数据的修订可能影响预测误差的计算。例如，如果使用在每个预测的两年期后提供的数据计算，美国国会预算办公室两年预测实际产出增长的均方根误差为1.2个百分点。但如果使用最近提供的数据计算，则均方根误差为1.3个百分点。
Sources: Congressional Budget Office; Office of Management and Budget; Wolters Kluwer, *Blue Chip Economic Indicators*, Bureau of Economic Analysis; Bureau of Labor Statistics; Federal Reserve. Forecast errors are projected values minus actual values; thus, a positive error is an overestimate.	资料来源：美国国会预算办公室；管理和预算办公室；威科集团，《蓝筹股经济指标》，经济分析局；劳工统计局；联邦储备局。 预测误差是预测值减去实际值。因此，出现正误差是估算过高[6]。

难点1

在句法结构上，汉语以"意合"为主，强调篇章的整体结构和平衡，必须根据上下文和逻辑关系来判断意义。而英语重"形合"，注意句子结构是否严谨，语法关系是否清晰。一般意义可以从表层结构中得出。英语句子的主体是主谓结构，谓语只能由动词承担。然而，汉语除了动词之外，形容词、名词等词也可以用作谓语。

通过对英汉两种句法现象的比较，发现两种句法的主要区别在于句子结构、句子顺序和句子内容。因此，在翻译过程中，要注意句子的时间顺序和逻辑顺序的合理安排，并根据汉语表达的需要进行增删。

王佐良（1990）对英语长句的定义是："英语句子超过平均长度（17个单词）就可以称为长句。"就这个长度而言，材料中出现了大量结构复杂的长句。例如：

原文：CBO's two-year forecasts of output growth and inflation have been less biased than its two-year forecasts of interest rates and the growth of wages and salaries, which exhibit a sizable upward bias—that is, they have tended to be higher than actual values by a larger amount.

译文：美国国会预算办公室对产出增长和通货膨胀的两年预测低于其对利率及工资和薪金增长的两年预测，这显示出相当大的上升偏差——也就是说，它们往往比实际价值更高。

分析：此句采用了线性翻译。线性翻译方法保留了源语的内部句法关系，即按照源语的顺序进行翻译。当英语长句的内容与汉语的逻辑思维、顺序和结构一致时，通常会进行线性翻译，以达到源语和目的语的句法相似。句中的主语是"CBO's two-year forecasts…"，谓语是"have been less biased"，宾语是"its two-year forecasts…"，"which"引出一个非限制性定语从句，修饰第一句，在后面的句子中用破折号解释。虽然整个句子结构复杂，但逻辑清晰。在该句的翻译中，对原句法进行层层剖析，然后结合目的语的表达习惯，采用线性翻译的方法对该句进行翻译。在句子翻译中，分句就是按照一定的原则将一个长句、复杂句分成若干部分。经济类文章经常夹杂着长句和复合句。因此，在复杂结构的句子翻译过程中，应通过调整语序、结构或句子的划分和重组等方式来传达原始信息。这将使译文在译入语中更容易被接受，更符合译入语的习惯，从而实现了信息型文本和目的论的功能和意义。

难点 2

被动语态是英语中一种常见的语法现象。然而，在汉语中，由于缺乏被动词汇，以及被动语态被认为是"不幸的"的历史语境（刘宓庆，2005），很少使用被动语态。例如：

原文：One **widely used** measure of accuracy is the root mean square error（RMSE）.

译文：广泛使用的精确测量方法是均方根误差（RMSE）。

原文：In that evaluation, projection errors **were calculated** for a single fiscal year.

译文：在该评估中，计算了一个财政年度的预测误差。

分析：第一个句子用于解释计算误差的方法，是典型的信息性文本。信息的准确表达应该是翻译的首要任务。这种情况下采用的翻译方法是直译。句中"widely used"是被动语态，而作者在翻译时采用了"意义被动"，即不使用被动语态，而是表达被动语态的意思。因此，它被翻译为"广泛使用的方法"而不是"广泛被使用的方法"，更符合目的语的表达习惯。

连贯原则要求译文必须符合语内连贯的标准，即译文必须为接受者所理解，并且在译文所使用的目的语文化和交际环境中具有意义。翻译行为的目的决定了翻译行为的整个过程，即结果决定方法。（Vermeer，1989）英语和汉语是两种完全不同的语言系统。英语是分析性语言，汉语是综合性语言。在汉语中虽然可以使用"被"表达被动语态，但是在情感意义上，"被"这个词给人一种强迫的感觉，表达的情绪通常是不愿或不愉快。

因此，译者应在忠实于原文的基础上，力求符合汉语的写作风格和读者的阅读习惯。将被动语态转化为主动语态可以更好地向目标读者传达信息，符合目标文本读者的阅读习惯。

难点 3

材料中的经济术语是翻译的主要困难。对于这些专业术语，应通过阅读平行文本，参考背景资料和专业知识进行翻译。同时为了保证术语翻译的准确性和表现力，在理解了翻译术语的具体含义后，应采用直译和意译的翻译方法。在翻译过程中，译者应尊重原文作者，对译文读者承担责任，避免偏离原文。

可使用谷歌、维基百科等在线搜索渠道，结合《新编经济金融词典》（2015）、《英汉双解银行与金融词典》（2009）等工具，对这些经济术语进行理解和翻译。例如：

原文：The five-year forecasts are used to examine the accuracy of longer-term projections of several variables that are important for CBO's **baseline budget projections**.

译文：用五年期预测来检验几个变量的长期预测的准确性，这对美国国会预算办公室**基线预算预测**至关重要。

分析：译文采用直译法。维基百科上说"基线预算是美国联邦政府用来制定未来几年预算的一种会计方法"。所以，可以采用直译的方法，忠实于原文的形式和内容。此外，目的论认为翻译是以原文为基础的有目的的跨文化交际，译者可在段落末尾添加注释从而保证目的语读者更好地理解原文的意图和意义。以下是一些经济术语及其译文：

经济术语	译文
forecast errors	预测误差
statistical bias	统计偏差
proposed budget	拟议预算
disinflationary policy	控制通货膨胀政策
intermediate goods	中间产品
RMSE	均方根误差

难点4

原文：A third reason to be cautious when interpreting the results of this forecast evaluation is that the historical values of many of the data series that CBO and other analysts forecast are periodically revised by the agencies that compile those data.

译文：在解释这一预测评估的结果时需要谨慎的第三个原因是，美国国会预算办公室和其他分析机构预测的系列数据的历史价值将由编译数据的机构定期修订。

分析：目的论中的连贯性原则要求译文必须以符合接受者情境的方式被接受。连贯性不仅要考虑语言系统，确保表达的意思清晰，还要关注相关的背景信息等。在本句中，"analyst"是指分析事物的人。如果文本的主题是职业或工作，这里可以翻译成"分析师"。然而，原始文本的主题是三方的经济预测，所以把它翻译成"分析机构"。词汇翻译应当符合上下文及语篇规则。

难点5

专有名词是指特定的人、事物、地点、机构、团体、国家、节日等的名称。这份报告的一个明显特点是包含了大量政府部门和企业的名称。企业名称和政府部门名称的准确翻译是有效传递准确信息的关键。对于企业和政府部门名称的翻译，应根据不同情况采取不同的方法。其他必要的方法还有查阅工具书和利用网络资源，了解专有名词的背景知识，根据实际情况选择合适的译文。这样就避免了逐字直译造成的误解，从而达到准确、简洁、规范翻译的目的。在翻译材料中企业和政府部门名称的过程中，有必要确认是否存在中文官方名称。对于已有正式中文名称的实体，一般会遵循此正式翻译。对于缺乏官方翻译的，可采用直译法和意译法相结合的方法，提高读者的接受度。例如：

原文：**CBO** calculated averages of inflation in the consumer price index from calendar-year averages of monthly data published by the BLS.

译文：**美国国会预算办公室根据**美国劳工统计局公布的月度数据的历年平均值计算消费物价指数中的通货膨胀平均值。

原文：**BEA** and other agencies use various methods and statistical definitions to estimate gross domestic product（GDP）and other economic indicators on the basis of data that they and others collect.

译文：**美国经济分析局**和其他机构以各自收集的数据为基础，通过各种方法和统计学定义来估算国内生产总值和其他经济指标。

	原文	译文
publication name	*Blue Chip Economic Indicators* *Handbook off Economic Forecasting*	《蓝筹股经济指标》 《经济预测手册》
institution name	*Blue Chip* consensus BLS BCDC	蓝筹共识 美国劳工统计局 美国商业循环评定委员会
Other name	Wolters Kluwer	威科集团

难点 6

英语和汉语中都存在一词多义现象，因为有时一个词同时属于几个词类。在翻译过程中，有时一个词可能有多种意思，但在特定的语境中却有独特的意思，为了避免歧义，明确目的语，就必须保证多义词的准确性。例如：

原文：For example, partly in response to past forecast errors, CBO has changed the way it forecasts productivity growth and interest rates in recent years.

译文：例如，部分方法是为了应对过去的预测误差，美国国会预算委员会改变了近年来对**生产力**增长和利率的预测方式。

原文：Forecast errors are projected values minus actual values; thus, a **positive error** is an overestimate.

译文：预测误差是预测值减去实际值；因此，出现**正误差**是估算过高。

分析：许多经济文本没有区别"生产力"和"生产率"。然而，前者是一种关系，后者是一种生产积极性指标(《新编经济金融词典》,2015)。所以在翻译过程中,译者必须准确理解词的意思,同时根据词在句子中的词性及搭配并结合上下文和语境来选择和识别词义,从而实现信息文本的目的和功能。

翻 译 练 习

一、词组翻译

复工复产
援企稳岗
大众创业 万众创新
供给侧结构性改革
自贸试验区
综合保税区
减税降费
excess capacity
economies of scale
comparative advantage
alternative cost
non-performing loans
risk exposure
tariff concessions
financial repression

二、句子翻译

(一)汉译英

1. 国内消费、投资、出口下滑,就业压力显著加大,企业特别是中小微企业困难凸显,金融等领域风险有所积聚,基层财政收支矛盾加剧。

2. 受全球疫情冲击,世界经济严重衰退,产业链供应链循环受阻,国际贸易投资萎缩,大宗商品市场动荡。

3. 要用改革开放办法,稳就业、保民生、促消费,拉动市场、稳定增长,走出一条有效应对冲击、实现良性循环的新路子。

4. 加强监管,防止资金"空转"套利。金融机构与贷款企业共生共荣,鼓励银行合理让利。

5. 支持大中小企业融通发展。以公正监管维护公平竞争,持续打造市场化、法治化、国际化营商环境。

(二) 英译汉

1. At present, the treasury bond futures market is comprised of institutional investors including securities companies, securities investment funds, asset management products launched by futures companies and private equity funds.

2. Continuing the growth of previous years, total loans and advances of the surveyed banks increased by 6.4 percent, a significantly higher growth rate compared to 3.5 percent in 2018.

3. The top 10 surveyed banks showed a 4.7 percent increase in total operating income, offset by a 6.8 percent increase in total operating expenses. The weighted-average cost-to-income ratio of the top 10 banks slightly deteriorated from 40.4 percent in 2018 to 41.2 percent in 2019.

4. Given the expected emergence of a multi-layered securities market in China, this suggests there is ample room for development in a range of value-added services such as mergers & acquisitions, restructuring and financial advisory services.

5. With the rapid increase in share prices, investors piled into the A-share market and trading volumes increased rapidly, with the daily turnover repeatedly hitting new heights.

三、语篇翻译

The Impact of COVID-19 on Hong Kong's Banking Sector

The onset of COVID-19 has caused significant disruption and challenges to the banking sector in Hong Kong, and is expected to have a major impact on banks' financial results and business and operating models in 2020 and beyond.

Predicting financial results in these unprecedented times is not easy, but a big part of revenue for banks in Hong Kong comes from net interest income, and we expect banks to face a number of challenges that will impact their NIM. For example, interest rates are low in the US, which in turn will impact rates in Hong Kong and the ability of banks in Hong Kong to sustain the levels of income generated from asset yields and deposit spreads. Coupled with that, in 2020 we will see the eight new virtual banks launch in Hong Kong, which are expected to compete with traditional banks on price to attract customers and deposits and therefore push up the cost of funding. However, we expect deposits at virtual banks as a percent of total balances to be relatively minor, at around 2 to 3 percent of the total, at least in the short term, which will mitigate this particular pressure.

It is also important to remember that banks reflect underlying economic activity, and in an environment where the economy is forecasted to contract — and where the chance of businesses closing is real — there is likely to be less demand for loan financing from corporates in Hong Kong to expand and grow their businesses, which will have an impact on income.

The other aspect of revenue is non-interest income. This is where we believe the story might be slightly more optimistic. Anecdotally, we have seen that financial markets businesses —

whether for equity or fixed income products — have actually been quite strong in the first half of 2020, although we do not necessarily expect this to continue throughout the second half of the year. We have seen the stock market rally and a lot of the losses that were felt in March have been reversed. This volatility can help both investment management businesses and wealth managers. In our view, monetary policy measures implemented by central banks — such as increases in quantitative easing — and low interest rates on corporate bonds means that people are more likely to invest in the stock market in their search for better yield. This will likely continue for a while, but the big question is whether the recovery in the stock market is sustainable and underpinned by fundamentals.

In addition, we expect credit costs and loan impairment charges to increase, which will also have a significant impact on Hong Kong banks' performance in 2020. Hong Kong has, over the past 15 years or so, had quite low impairment ratios. More NPLs or impaired loans in the future will increase the impairment ratios and consequently drive higher loan impairment charges as loans move from provisions based on 12 months of expected credit losses to provisions based on lifetime expected credit losses. Furthermore, the underlying parameters for the calculations of expected credit losses, such as the probability of default and the loss given default, are expected to increase because of poorer performance, which would in turn drive higher impairment costs.

◎参考文献

[1] Halliday, M. A. K. & Hasen, R. *Coherence in English*[M]. London: Longman, 1976.

[2] Reiss, K. *Translation Criticism: The Potentials & Limitation*[M]. Shanghai: Shanghai Foreign Language Education Press, 2004.

[3] Vermeer, H. J. *Skopos and Translation Sauftrag Aufsatze*[M]. Heidelberg: Universitat, 1989.

[4] 刘法公. 谈汉英隐喻翻译中的喻体意象转换[J]. 中国翻译, 2007(6): 47-51, 96.

[5] 刘宓庆. 新编当代翻译理论[M]. 北京: 中国对外翻译出版公司, 2005.

[6] 陆谷孙. 英汉大词典(第二版)[M]. 上海: 上海译文出版社, 2007.

[7] 王佐良, 丁往道. 英语文体学引论[M]. 北京: 外语教学与研究出版社, 1990.

[8] 杨明基. 新编经济金融词典[M]. 北京: 中国金融出版社, 2015.

第四章　经济学论文翻译

> ☞**思考题**
> 1. 什么是经济学论文？经济学论文与其他文本相比，有什么特点？
> 2. 翻译经济学论文时有哪些注意事项？
> 3. 经济学论文翻译的难点在哪里？

第一节　经济学论文文本分析

一、经济学论文概述

(一) 概念

经济学是研究市场经济规律的学科，也是当前的热门学科之一。而经济学论文是对经济学领域的研究成果做出的结论性总结，主要内容是对社会生活中的经济现象、公司企业的典型案例等加以深入分析，继而得出理性的结论，并提出具有建设性的意见和解决方案，不断扩充经济领域的学术理论，扩大经济学研究范围和领域，可以学以致用，去解决社会经济发展中的实际问题。更重要的是，撰写经济学论文可以使作者开拓思路，提高认识水平，论文将体现出很高的学术价值和实际意义。

(二) 总体特点

1. 结构特点

经济学论文除了一般论文结构中包括的标题、摘要、关键词之外，其正文主要包括选题背景与意义、文献综述、理论模型、经验实证、研究结论、参考文献六大块，其中理论模型部分是在继承前人成果基础上所作的自己理论创新部分。这一部分是论文的主体，亦应是论文的精华所在；经验实证是应用材料对理论模型的论证和支撑，即通过古今中外的实证材料来证明自己理论模型的合理性。

2. 内容特点

(1) 鲜明的目的性

经济学论文是针对某一特定的经济问题，有目的地进行分析、研究、调查、论证并寻求解决问题的办法以指导下一阶段的实践,并要求达到预期的效果。

(2)理论的综合性

经济学论文必然渗透着许多学科的基本理论,包括社会科学、自然科学等方面;经济学论文在对某一经济活动进行分析、评价时,往往又采用多目标的各种指标体系,有技术指标、经济指标以及综合指标等。

(3)实践的应用性

经济学论文本身不仅论述经济社会实践中的问题、现象及其规律,而且其所使用的有关资料、信息等都来源于实践,来源于对客体的调查研究。

(4)科学的创见性

经济学论文应真实地反映客观的实际,要遵循客观规律;有新意,而不是对别人论断的重复。

3. 词汇特点

(1)专业术语丰富

经济学论文属科技类文本,多来源于国际经济期刊,内容关于当前经济发展的最新模式和经济理论的最新成果,其术语专业性较强,数量也较多。因此,在翻译经济学论文时,要求除了有较高的语言表达水平外,还必须掌握一定的专业知识或者专业主题方面的知识以及专业文本处理能力,从而能够准确捕捉并运用术语词汇。

(2)善用图表,数据庞杂

经济学论文涉及的经济知识具有较强的专业性,对于某些经济现象的发生原因、过程和走势需要通过大量的客观数据与图表来阐述经济现象,因此经济学论文中穿插着大量的数字变化与图表,而图表是经济文本中不可缺少的一部分,特别是在经济研究论文中,为了说明一些经济现象、显示调查信息或统计数据,包含了大量图表。大体可分为曲线图、柱形图和图表。图表的目的就是用最直观、最一目了然的方式把原文本的信息呈现给受众。

(3)抽象名词与缩略语的高频使用

经济学论文具有语言简洁明了、能高度概括文章内容的特点,而抽象名词具有言简意赅、高度概括的特点,所以经济学论文中抽象名词出现的频率较高,主要分为三类:由普通用词合成的抽象名词,固有抽象名词和由动词转化而来的抽象名词。而缩略语作为一种简洁明快的语言单位,以更简短的形式凝结起更丰富的信息,有效地增强了词汇的表现力,在经济学论文中使用频率也越来越高。

4. 句法特点

(1)句法规范,常用一般现在时

中英文在表达习惯上有所不同:中文体现东方的思维习惯,呈螺旋式发展;而英文在表达上直截了当,呈竹节式发展。汉语论文多为无主句,而英语需要有明显的主谓宾,论文研究的内容多为一般性的客观事实描述,因此以一般现在时为主。根据动态对等理论,翻译经济学论文时应遵循语义对等,以读者接受为导向,寻找语句间内在逻辑,保证一句一义。

例 1

原文：INFORMATION FRICTIONS IN TRADE

It is costly to learn about market conditions elsewhere, especially in developing countries. This paper examines how such information frictions affect trade. Using data on regional agricultural trade in the Philippines, I first document a number of information frictions. I then incorporate information frictions into a perfect competition trade model by embedding a process whereby heterogeneous producers engage in a costly sequential search process to determine where to sell their produce. I show that introducing information frictions reconciles the theory with the observe patterns in the data. Structural estimation of the model finds that information frictions are quantitatively important: roughly half the observed regional price dispersion is due to information frictions. Furthermore, incorporating information frictions improves the out-of-sample predictive power of the model.

分析：根据引用的国外经济学论文摘要可以看出，句子精简不冗余。所有句子都使用一般现在时，表明实验的一般适用性和有效性。同时，各句行文凝练，直击主题，符合句法规范。

（2）信息完整，文体结构与句型模式统一

自从采用计算机编辑和排印以来，经济学期刊中的论文摘要几乎已形成一套公式化的文体结构和句型模式，一般分为研究的目的、方法、结果以及结论四个部分。摘要是对论文要点的摘述，是不标注评论和补充解释，确切、简练地概括文献重要内容的短文。当它和论文一起刊出时，是论文的重要组成部分，当它以二次文献形式出现时，则具有独立性与自含性。

例 2

原文：Subjects in a laboratory experiment withdraw earnings from a cash reserve evolving according to an arithmetic Brownian motion in near-continuous time. Aggressive withdrawal policies expose subjects to risk of bankruptcy, but the policy that maximizes expected earnings need not maximize the odds of survival. When profit maximization is consistent with high rates of survival (HS parameters), subjects adjust decisively towards the optimum. When survival and profit maximization are sharply at odds (LS parameters), subjects persistently (and suboptimally) hoard excess cash in an evident effort to improve survival rates. The design endures that this hoarding is not due to standard risk aversion. Analysis of period-to-period adjustments in strategies suggests instead that hoarding is due to a widespread bias towards survival in the subject population. Robustness treatments varying feedback, parameters, and framing fail to eliminate the bias.

分析：首句"Subjects in a laboratory experiment…"介绍了研究背景，第二句是一个带有"but"的转折句，揭示了作者的写作目的，即增加预期收入的政策并不能增加经济存活的可能性，随之用两个"when"引导的时间状语从句介绍了研究的方法。"The design endures …subject population"指出了研究结果，最后一句则说明了研究结论。整篇摘要信息完整、扼要清晰，体现出了摘要的独立性与自含性。

二、经济学论文标题与摘要特点

本部分以经济学论文标题与摘要的翻译为切入点，通过发掘标题翻译和摘要翻译的普遍特点和规律，对其翻译策略和方法进行研究，以小见大，加深人们对经济学论文翻译中存在的具体问题的认识，从而进一步提高此类文本翻译的质量。

(一)经济学论文标题的特点

1. 经济学论文标题的功能

(1)信息功能

标题是论文基本思想的浓缩与概括，其作用在于表现文章的主要内容，同时也有利于读者检索、查阅及引用。当使用题名检索方式搜索文献时，如标题中的用词无法精准地反映论文的核心内容，将会产生检索遗漏，所以标题对于经济学论文的第一个作用就是发挥引导检索的信息功能。

(2)吸引功能

标题作为论文的"标签"或"门牌"，应当新颖、确切、鲜明、醒目，能扼要地从各个方面概括论文的基本思想，使读者能迅速准确地判明论文的基本内容，从而省去看摘要和正文的时间，来判断是否阅读全文。因此，如果题名取用不当，就会使其失去应有的吸引效用，使文章与读者擦肩而过。

2. 经济学论文标题的文体特点

(1)专业性

经济学论文标题常常包含经济学领域高度专业的词汇，这些专门术语语义精练、表意准确、概念专一，专业特点明显，这些用词不追求语言的艺术美，而追求逻辑的条理清晰和思维的准确严密。所以在翻译经济学论文标题时，要遵循这些特点，在措辞上应条理清楚、准确无误。

(2)正规性

从文体上看，经济学论文标题具有高度的正规性，其用词精练准确、规范严谨，原则上不带入任何私人的感情色彩和主观意愿，学术气味浓厚，正式化程度高，常用拉丁语派生词，以示高雅和正式。

(3)信息性

经济学论文的标题一般立意鲜明、短小精悍，包含的信息高度浓缩，对于文章的主题思想高度概括提炼。其通常由两部分组成：主题和题旨(即主题所在)，一般不宜过长，否则重点不突出。

3. 经济学论文标题的结构特点

英文论文常使用短语形式的名词性标题,其中名词短语被普遍使用,即标题的主体是一个或若干个名词,对于每个名词搭配一定数量的前置或后置定语,基本不包含谓语成分。标题多不用完整陈述语句,因为其判断语义太强,不符合标题主要发挥标示作用的宗旨。只有少数需要强调事实的情况下会使用陈述句式标题,或者使用疑问句作题名,以探讨性语气激发读者兴趣和往下探究的好奇心。

对于英文标题的标准结构,有两个需要强调的重点:第一,中心词的名词化。首先要确定标题的中心词,再对其进行修饰。中心词必须使用名词,如"Monetary Policy and Risk Avoidance of Commercial Banks",可以看到使用名词"Avoidance"而不是动词"Avoid"。第二,用词顺序问题。英文标题中词语的词序不当,可能会产生歧义。英语与汉语表达有所不同,英语中常用定语后置,这与汉语中定语置于中心词之前恰恰相反,其语言效用也更加强大,如"Analyses on the Effects of Labor & Capital on Income Distribution"。

(二)经济学论文摘要的特点

1. 经济学论文摘要的功能

论文摘要是位于正文前的一段提炼总结文章内容的概括性文字,是对论文内容简短扼要的陈述,不掺杂注释和评论,使读者不用阅读全文,就能获得必要的信息。摘要具有独立性和自明性,当摘要与论文一起搭配时,就成为论文的重要组成部分,而当其加上标题和关键词形成独立文体时,就变为二次文献。因此,摘要犹如论文的一份产品说明书,务求语言精简,语体规范专业,内容介绍全面、主次分明。

2. 经济学论文摘要的文体特点

摘要是一种规范性的文本,不可在撰写时添加公式、图标、引用文献编号等,其文体风格独特。首要特点是文体书面、正式,用语庄重规范、朴实自然;再者是用语简洁、凝练,无词语赘述且限制字数;最后是态度科学、客观,逻辑严谨且常以第三人称表述。

3. 经济学论文摘要的结构特点

论文摘要层次结构比较清晰,一般包括:目的,包括作者写论文的目的以及解决什么问题,或者论述的观点;方法,包括作者撰写论文的主要过程,甚至所采用的技术手段、试验方法等;结果,包括论文论证的结果、数据及关系式等规律性的内容;结论,包括文章要阐明的理论、现象或观点等。在摘要中上述层次关系按顺序展开,通过摘要读者能一目了然地了解文章的概貌。

按照层次关系表述摘要各部分内容时,常使用固定句型和语法,研究目的部分基本是以不定式开头的陈述句,如"In order to"。方法部分常用"study, consider, discuss, investigate, analysis, develop"等单词。结果部分直接使用简单句,并多用"present, report, illustrate"等表达结果的单词。结论部分通常简单明了地对文章发现的规律进行总结,常采用"summary, outline, rule"等词汇。

4. 经济学论文摘要的篇幅要求

虽然论文摘要有基本的规范和要求,但对于各个期刊社、检索目录,其要求各不相同。不同期刊有不同的摘要格式要求，以满足各大期刊社的版面设计要求。例如《当代外语研究》期刊对于摘要的要求是中文摘要约 250 字，英文摘要为 150~200 个单词。通常摘要的长度由文章的长度及其排版的位置决定。摘要的长度一般占文章长度的 3% 至 5%，但在排版时不应超过版面的 2/3。

第二节　翻译知识讲解

一、翻译原则

（一）准确性

1. 术语准确

在翻译经济学论文术语时，应注意术语翻译的准确性，做到同一术语译名一致。多个术语在同一文本中如具有同一含义，切不可为避免重复而另创新译，应根据语境进行变通翻译或编译，保证意思上的对等。术语表达是经济学期刊论文翻译的关键，正确的术语翻译能够保证译文的质量，促进跨领域交际的顺利进行。

2. 信息准确

在翻译经济学论文信息过程中，译者可以依据动态对等的基本要求，对原文的某些形式进行适当的增减，从而让译文信息能够准确、清晰地得到传达。当然这对译者本身的要求比较高，需要译者通读原文，在把握实质内容和意义的前提下进行翻译。这里的准确性不仅体现出翻译的基本原则要忠实和准确，更是突出翻译经济学论文时，译者可依据功能对等论翻译文本的实际意思，而非单纯的字面形式。

（二）规范性

经济学论文的翻译应该首先服务于目的语读者，在其形式和内容上应向目的语国家看齐。因此这里可以参考国外经济学论文写作的基本要求，让翻译首先在形式和规范性上满足功能对等的要求。但这里的规范性主要强调结构层面的规范，包括目的层面、方法层面、结果层面和结论层面四部分。

例 1

原文	译文
（研究什么？）中国宏观经济正面临前所未有的挑战，减税能否成为稳定中国经济增长的有效工具亟待研究。（怎么研究？）本文利用 2009 年增值税改革的政策冲击，基于微观数据考察增值税税率	（研究什么？）China's economy is facing unprecedentedly severe challenges, making it urgent to explore policy instruments to sustain economic growth. （怎么研究？）Using data from National Taxation Survey, this paper employs China's value-added tax reform in 2009 as an exogenous shock to identify how tax reduction

续表

原文	译文
变化对企业的影响,为理解减税对宏观经济的作用提供了微观基础。(得出什么?)研究发现,减税不仅可以提升短期总需求,还可以在长期内改善供给效率。具体而言,降低增值税有效税率短期内会刺激企业的固定资产投资,这一效果对于私营企业、中西部地区和非出口企业尤为明显;同时,减税可以提升供给效率,国有企业、东部地区和出口企业的资本和劳动产出效率明显增强。(什么意义?)本文对于制定稳定经济的减税政策乃至具体的减税方案都有一定的指导意义。	impacts firms' behavior and performance providing empirical evidence for the effect of tax reduction on China's economy. (得出什么?) It is found that tax cuts can not only boost aggregate demand in the short run, but also improve supply efficiening in the long run. To be specific, the decline in effective value-added tax rate encourages firms' investment in fixed assets, especially for private business, non-export firms, and those in central China; the productivity of capital and labor improves after value-added tax reform in almost all kinds of firms, implying that tax reduction will boost economic growth even in the long run. (什么意义?) This study can serve as guideline not only for general tax policy to stabilize the economy but for specific scheme of tax-cut as well.

分析:译文中,"China's economy…to sustain economic growth"说明了研究目的即减税对于提振中国经济的影响;"Using data from National Taxation Survey…China's economy"介绍了研究方法;"It is found that…in the long run"从两个角度说明研究结果;最后的"This study can serve as guideline…"即研究结论。行文中每一点都规范地按照摘要写作要求,在译文中加以呈现,保证了译文与原文在内容上和要点上的对等与规范。

(三)等效性

根据尤金·奈达的动态对等理论,原文与译文要求具有等效性,即原文与译文对读者产生的效果相同。经济学论文属于实用型文本,在其翻译过程中,再现其信息内容的重要性远超过保留其语言表达形式。之所以要翻译某一经济学论文,往往不是因为该文献在语言文学上有较高的价值,而完全是由于文献的实质内容可用于本国的生产或科研部门,具有可以借鉴的价值。

例2

原文	译文
近年来,中国债券市场的违约现象呈增加趋势,如何合理估计债券价格,有效度量政府隐性担保,保障投资者权益成为市场中的重要问题。(背景)本文在可违约债券 CIR 仿射定价模型基础上引入	In recent years, defaults in the Chinese bond market have been on the rise. How to reasonably estimate bond prices, effectively measure the implicit government guarantee, and protect investors' rights and interests has become an important issue in the market. Based on the CIR affine pricing model of defaultable bonds, this

续表

原文	译文
政府隐性担保作用,并运用卡尔曼滤波法对该隐性担保作用进行了实证考察。(方法)结果表明:(1)自2011年地方国有企业债、中央国有企业债和民营企业债开始频繁交易以来,政府隐性担保长期显著存在于我国债券市场中;(2)市场对于隐性担保预期理性,具体表现为不同信用评级、不同债券种类间隐性担保水平有明显区别:AA评级中央企业债和地方国有企业债的定价中,分别隐含着对应政府以39.9%和6.7%概率进行的隐性担保,而类似隐性担保在AA+评级中央企业债和国有企业债定价中分别为33.9%和1.2%(结果及结论)	paper introduces the implicit guarantee effect of government and makes an empirical study of the implicit guarantee effect by using Kalman filter. It is found that:(1) Since 2011, when local state-owned enterprise bonds, central state-owned enterprise bonds and private enterprise bonds began to be frequently traded, implicit government guarantee has existed significantly in China's bond market for a long time;(2) The market's expectation of implicit guarantee is rational, which is embodied in the obvious difference of implicit guarantee level between different type of bonds with different credit ratings: AA rated bonds issued by central and local government owned enterprises have predicted bailout possibility of 39.9% and 6.7% respectively, while those AA+ rated have 33.9% and 1.2%.

分析:由上例可知,最明显的对等内容即为重要的数据信息,保证内容上的真实性。同时,译者以"this paper"为关键词,把结构分为两部分,使得内容和结构均对等。在结构上,经济学论文摘要的目的、方法、结果、结论四部分并非平分秋色,而是以提供原文中的全部创新内容为前提。因此,目的、方法着墨较少,重点放在结果和结论上。在英译经济学论文摘要时,有的译者把握不住,就遇到了内容与形式、语义与文体、自然对应与形式对应之间的矛盾。根据尤金·奈达翻译过程的转换阶段学说,译者应竭尽所能保留原文内容,其次再考虑保留形式、保证对等。

二、经济学论文标题翻译策略

(一)字母大小写

英译时,常将题目中冠词(a, an, the)、介词(in, for, on)和连词(and, or)的首字母小写,而实词(名词、动词、形容词和副词等)的首字母一般大写。特别需要注意的是,如果冠词、介词等位于英文题目开头处时,首字母一般需要大写。

例3

原文:股市现状对国内经济影响的实证研究

译文:On Effect of Status of Stock Market on Chinese Economy

分析:上例中的介词"on"因为出现在英文题目的开头处,所以首字母应该大写,而题目中间出现的介词"of"和"on"首字母应该小写,其余实词首字母均大写。

(二) 短语型标题的翻译

动词短语、并列短语和偏正短语常被用作经济学论文的标题。

1. 动宾结构

动宾结构由动词及其宾语构成,可以翻译成英语的名词短语、分词短语或不定式短语。汉语标题中的动词"论""谈"等常译为介词"On"或"Towards"结构,放在句首强调主题。

例 4

原文:浅析领导者的权利基础

译文:On Right Base of Leaders

分析:为了使句子更为简洁,大多数情况下省译诸如"试论……""浅析……""……的研究"这样没有具体指代内容,不能反映研究方法、研究对象等的"虚词",以达到突出题目中最重要信息的目的。

例 5

原文:试论政策对经济发展的动态效应

译文:Dynamic Effects of Policy on Economic Development

分析:例 5 中的"试论"这样自谦的惯用表达可略去不译,从而使英文题目更言简意赅。

2. 并列结构

由并列结构构成的标题中,多数是以两个或三个名词短语为核心,采用直译方法,但也可将动词短语译为名词短语或使用冒号来突出主题。

例 6

原文:价格信息发布、消费者偏好差异与价格离中现象

译文:Price Information Advertisement, Diversity of Consumers' Preference and Price Dispersion

例 7

原文:工程失败原因分析及失败知识管理

译文:Analysis of Project Failure Reason and Failure Knowledge Management

例 8

原文:中美危机管理的基本概念、原则与变量

译文:Sino-U. S. Crisis Management: Concepts, Principles, and Variables

分析:例 6 和例 7 中标题的英译采用的是直译的方法,准确地传递了信息。例 8 中则

将原标题拆译，前半部分指明主题，后半部分解释其内容，更好地突出了主题。

3. 偏正结构

偏正结构是由修饰语和中心语组成，结构成分之间有修饰与被修饰关系，中文习惯上定语前置，而英文常用定语后置，因此英译时通常采用直译的方法，将中心词放在定语前面，常用的表明所使用的研究方法的中心词有这样一些名词："影响（effect/influence）、应用（application）、分析（analysis）、研究（research）、比较（comparison）"等，常用的介词有"of, for, on/upon, in, between, with"等。

例 9

原文：浙江民营企业实施多层次品牌战略的理性思考

译文：The Rational Consideration of Implementing Multilayer Brand Strategy in Zhejiang Private Enterprises

例 10

原文：企业在职培训的私人投资收益分析

译文：An Analysis of Employees' Return of On-the-Job Training Investment in Private Sector

分析：例 10 中"分析"与前面提及的动词结构中的虚词"分析"不同，其前有具体修饰语，就有了特定的含义，应该在英文题目的译写中体现出来。

(三) 分句型标题的翻译

分句型标题多为完整的一句话。句子式的题目诸如陈述句和疑问句在经济学论文题目中很普遍，英译时，通常将中文分句标题译为分词、不定式或介词短语，但表示号召性质的标题也会翻译成完整的英文句子。为了理解方便，建议遵循忠实原则，在翻译时保持形式和标点与原分句句型标题一致。同时，论文题目字数不宜太多，否则不能突出重点。在确保能够准确表达相应中文题目信息的前提下，字数越少越好，最好保持在 12 个单词以内，最多一般不要超过 16 个单词。

例 11

原文：用产权制度制约失信行为

译文：To Restrict the Conducts of Breaking Faith with the Aid of an Institution of Property Rights

例 12

原文：如何加快开发我国工程保险市场

译文：How to Accelerate the Development of Chinese Engineering Insurance Market

(四)带破折号或冒号的标题翻译

1. 带破折号的标题

破折号在中文里表示停顿或意思的转折,中文标题中常用破折号引出副标题,翻译时可采用直译、省译标题的一部分、合译前后两部分并省略破折号、用冒号代替破折号四种方法。直译是最常见的译法,将原标题中的每个短语都译为目的语中的相似结构。

例 13

原文:人力资本投资结构及其对经济增长的影响——基于扩展 MRW 模型的内生增长理论与实证研究

译文:Investment Structure in Human Capital and its Effect on Economic Growth Model

例 14

原文:上市公司审计委托关系的重构——加强审计独立性的路径

译文:Reconstructing the Audit Entrustment Matrix of Corporations and Strengthening Audit Independence

分析:例 13 原标题前半部分指明主题,后半部分解释其内容,在英译时省略后半部分以求在译文中突出最重要的信息。例 14 中的破折号省译同时增加并列连词"and",合译破折号前后两部分。

2. 带冒号的标题

标题中被冒号分开的两部分中的前半部分通常是文章主题,后半部分是补充说明部分,遵循目的原则和连贯原则,带冒号的标题可采用直译、省略标题的一部分、合译冒号前后部分并省略冒号、将冒号换为破折号等方法。

例 15

原文:政府投资工程造价审计分析:基于委托代理视角

译文:Analysis of Cost Auditing to Government Investment Projects Based on the Principal-agent Theory

例 16

原文:农民工的社会网络与职业阶层和收入:来自深圳调查的发现

译文:Social Network of Rural-urban Migrants and Their Occupation Stratum and Income —Findings from Survey in Shenzhen

尽管冒号和破折号在标题中的作用相似,但有人认为在英文标题中使用破折号不恰当,此外,英美报刊 *Time*, *Newsweek*, *Discover*, *Geographical*, *Studies in Higher Education* 的近几期均未出现一例标题使用破折号的情况,可见破折号不是英文标题常用的标点符号。

三、经济学论文摘要翻译策略

(一) 词汇层面

经济学论文摘要的显著特点是存在许多经济术语,其专业性表现在对专业术语翻译的准确度和精确性,是否达到这些要求决定了该文本是否具有参考价值。一般包括金融术语、股票术语、风投术语、银行术语等。

1. 准确判断词义

经济类术语有严格的科学界定,英汉互译的过程中必须准确规范,不得随意更改。如"国际游资"译为"hot money";"货币替代"译为"currency substitution";"政府采购"译为"government procurement"。

此外,注意不要局限于一种译法,灵活翻译使译文更符合译语习惯。例如"keen"在"keen competition""keen interest"和"keen price"三个经济类术语中应分别译成"激烈的竞争""强烈的兴趣"和"薄利的价格"。翻译中要多用常见词代替生僻词,狭义词代替广义词。

2. 缩写翻译

例 17

原文:电子商务背景下银行对**第三方物流**的激励模式
译文:Motivation Model of Bank on **TPL** Under E-Commerce

例 18

原文:基于**层次分析法**构建金融评价体系
译文:Construction of financial evaluation system based on **AHP**

分析:由于所有目标读者都是经济专业人士,因此当某些术语具有缩写表达并且在经济领域是已知的时,可以应用缩写翻译,且缩写版本比直译要简洁得多。

(二) 句法层面

1. 语态的翻译

英文论文摘要多使用被动语态,避免人称句,因为论文无须表现动作的执行者,重点在于客观事实和过程的描述,侧重推理,强调客观准确。英译时,为了使读者更有效地抓住重点、掌握主要信息,更清楚作者所要表达的研究内容、过程及结果,常将论文重点突出的问题、事实、概念等放在句首明显位置。

例 19

原文:本文叙述了林业的可持续发展,从林木遗传改良与无性系林业、森林集约栽培及管理、森林资源监控、木材加工利用等方面**验证了技术创新**是可持续发展的根本动力。

译文：**Technology innovation is proven to be** the driving force of forestry sustainable development, which is obvious in the forest tree genetic improvement and clonal forestry, forest-intensive cultivation and management, monitoring of forest resources, and timber processing, etc.

分析：本句将主动语态译成被动语态，更符合英语的句式特点，将技术创新置于醒目位置，其他次要信息用定语从句表示，也符合英语的行文习惯。

2. 拆译及合译

根据句子的长短和意义的关联程度，可将摘要原句进行拆译或合译。例如：

例 20

原文：实证结果表明住房公积金制度会显著促进房价上涨，当前如果取消住房公积金制度的话，将会使房价下降13.5%。

译文：The empirical results show that HPFS has positive effect on house price significantly. If HPFS were canceled, house price would decrease by 13.5%.

例 21

原文：本文叙述了林业的可持续发展，从林木遗传改良与无性系林业、森林集约栽培及管理、森林资源监控、木材加工利用等方面验证了技术创新是可持续发展的根本动力。

译文：Technology innovation is proven to be the driving force of forestry sustainable development, which is obvious in the forest tree genetic improvement and clonal forestry, forest-intensive cultivation and management, monitoring of forest resources, and timber processing, etc.

分析：上述两个例子中，分别采用了拆译和合译的翻译策略。摘要翻译中，对句子的处理是拆译还是合译，应根据具体句子来定，目的是更准确、更清楚明了地表达作者的意图。

3. 省译及增译

根据语句一些成分的意义，可将中文摘要内容冗余的部分删去不译，同时内容不全的地方则需要增译，为方便外国读者阅读，英文摘要的核心内容不妨详细一些。

例 22

原文：本文将不对称产出冲击的假设引入主权违约模型，**并以1993—2007年的阿根廷经济作为例子**，研究了该假设下的主权违约概率。

译文：This paper develops a sovereign default model with state-switching asymmetric output, which reflects the reality better.

例 23

原文：森林是由于具有强大的碳汇功能而在发展低碳经济中得到重视。

译文：People attach much importance to forest in developing low carbon economy because forest has large amount of carbon sink.

分析：例22的中文摘要和其英译摘要内容对等，但相较而言，英文更加言简意赅、行文紧凑，没有多余的内容，对无关紧要的阿根廷经济例子做了省略处理，直接阐述研究结果，是论文内容的高度凝练，保证了其实质性内容的等效表达。例23中，森林在发展低碳经济中得到重视，实则指的是得到人们的重视，这里应增译"People"。

四、经济学论文翻译中的译者素养

(一) 充分的译前准备

翻译实践工作需要将翻译知识和理论应用于实践，同时也能够学到其他专业的知识。准备翻译经济学论文前，需要先了解文本特点，了解经济类相关知识和其前沿科学动态，一个有效的途径是阅读相关论文，整理相关术语，总结常见的问题，以避免前人在翻译中出现的问题。通过阅读《经济学人》英文原版和由ECO论坛发表的中文版翻译，能够学习到许多经济类专业术语的地道表达。

(二) 扎实的双语基本功

对于译者而言，这是最基本的专业素养。译者首先要拥有扎实的双语功底、双语语言能力、文化能力，对于有着高度的逻辑性、准确性和严密性特点的经济文本，要在翻译时做到"忠实""准确""统一"。因此译者应该熟练驾驭源语和目的语，包括词汇、语法和惯用语等。如果对原文理解不准确，译文必然也会有问题，如果只是理解清晰，但表述不符合目的语的行文风格，同样难以完成翻译任务。

(三) 了解译入语论文撰写规范

经济学论文的翻译得到的产物本质上是一篇符合目的语论文规范的论文，而不同的国家，论文写作规范有所不同。因此在翻译过程中，要了解国际社会公认的论文撰写规范，以及译入语国家的论文撰写规范，在行文、格式等方面满足规范需求，以期达到更好的翻译效果，使读者阅读起来更为熟悉与自然。

(四) 利用资源、整合信息的能力

经济学论文翻译中，对于译者来说重要的是要学会如何解决遇到的各式各样的问题。译者要具备检索文献资源，熟练运用语料库、计算机辅助翻译技术、翻译工具和资源的能力，使用现代化信息技术，学习国际经济知识和百科知识，提高工作效率。同时还要注意在特定文化背景下所导致的差异，分类、整理和概括检索到的信息，利用资源更好地解决问题。

(五) 认真严谨的态度

论文的翻译与撰写一样要秉持认真严谨的态度。译者身上担负的不仅是语言转换的任务，更是充当着两个国家间相互沟通和交流的桥梁，翻译时应高度重视，保持谦逊和严谨的态度，不忽视任何细节。对于经济文本，需进行多方准备，不能急于求成。准备不充分而随意下笔必然会导致对原文信息的误传，甚至出现表达生硬拗口的地方，影响

经济学论文的学术性和说服力。

第三节　常用词汇与表达

一、专业术语

原文	译文
heterogeneous income	异质收入
search frictions	搜寻摩擦
idiosyncratic shock	特定冲击
supply-side shock	供给冲击
assortative matching	类聚效应
dynamic stochastic content	动态几率性内涵
economic divergence	经济差异
net gains	净利
partial equilibrium	局部均衡
general equilibrium	一般均衡
economy of scale	规模经济
game theory	博弈论
Gini coefficient	基尼系数
oligopoly	寡头垄断
Pareto improvement	帕累托改进
discrete-choice model	离散选择模型

二、缩略语

缩略语	原文	译文
NNP	Net National Product	国民生产净值
PMI	Purchase Management Index	采购经理指数
PPI	Producer Price Indexes	生产者物价指数

续表

缩略语	原文	译文
PI	Personal Income	个人收入
DPI	Disposable Personal Income	个人可支配收入
MC	Marginal Cost	边际成本
APC	Average Propensity to Consume	平均消费倾向
BD/BS	Budget Deficit/Budget Surplus	预算赤字/盈余
MPC	Marginal Propensity to Consume	边际消费倾向
MPS	Material Balance System	物质平衡体系
RBCT	Real Business Cycle Theory	真实经济周期理论
AFC	Average Fixed Cost	平均固定成本
AVC	Average Variable Cost	平均可变成本

第四节　译文赏析

一、汉译英

原文	译文
金融危机的新特征	**New Features of the Financial Crisis**
摘要：2007年爆发于美国的次贷危机，在2008年9月演变成为全球金融危机。美国长期的宽松货币政策和金融监管的失败，以及国际货币体系的不合理是引发美国次贷危机和引起世界金融危机的主要原因。与以往的经济危机相比，此次金融危机表现出一些新的特点。主要表现在各国应对危机的措施力度空前，各国政府联合共同刺激经济，发展中国家对世界的影响力增强，新能源、环保等产业备受关注，稳步推进国际金融体系改革达成基本共识等方面。	Abstract：The American subprime crisis broke out in 2007 evolved into a global financial crisis in September 2008. The failure of the U. S. long-term easy monetary policy and financial regulation as well as the irrational international monetary system jointly contributed to this U. S. subprime crisis which in turn caused a global financial crisis[1]. Compared with the previous economic crises, this financial crisis shows up some new features, mainly including the unprecedented measures taken by all countries to deal with the crisis, the jointing hands of all countries to stimulate economy, the growing influence of developing countries to the world, the increasing attention on new energy and environmental protection industries, and the consensus reached by all countries to steadily promote the reform of the international financial system.

续表

原文	译文
一、金融危机爆发和传导的过程	1. Outbreak and Spread of the Financial Crisis
源于美国房地产价格泡沫的破灭，2007 年美国出现次贷危机，2008 年 9 月次贷危机急剧恶化，演变成为一场自 20 世纪 30 年代大萧条以来最为严重的全球金融危机。美国在互联网泡沫破灭之后，美联储在很长时期内实施了过于宽松的货币政策。2004 年 6 月，美联储重新步入加息周期，房地产价格从 2006 年 6 月起开始下跌。美国房地产价格指数在 2000 年 1 月至 2006 年 5 月期间上涨了 1.24 倍。2007 年 8 月，美国第五大投资银行贝尔斯登宣布旗下对冲基金停止赎回，引发投资者撤资行为，从而触发了流动性危机。这被视为美国次贷危机全面爆发的标志。	Triggered by the bursting of housing bubble, the U.S. subprime crisis broke out in 2007, then sharply deteriorated in September 2008, and eventually evolved into the worst global financial crisis since the Great Depression in the 1930s[2]. After the Internet bubble collapsed, the U.S. Federal Reserve implemented the over-easy monetary policy for a long time. In June, 2004, the Federal Reserve started a new round of interest rate increase. As a result, the housing prices began to fall since June, 2006. Between January 2000 and May 2006, the U.S. real estate price index increased by 1.24 times. In August, 2007, Bear Stearns, the fifth largest U.S. investment bank, declared not to redeem its hedge funds, which caused investment withdrawal and finally triggered liquidity crisis. Thus, the U.S. subprime crisis completely broke out.
我们用标志性事件来看美国金融危机的过程，可划分为三个阶段：第一阶段为 2007 年 8 月至 2008 年 9 月中旬。危机表现为一场规模有限的次贷危机，危机集中反映在与次贷相关的结构性金融产品上。第二阶段为 2008 年 9 月中旬至 2008 年 10 月中旬。雷曼的破产引发了金融市场大面积信心危机，流动性紧缩从货币和信贷市场迅速传递到全球金融市场，使得规模有限的次贷危机上升成为全球性金融危机。第三阶段为 2008 年 10 月中旬至 2009 年 7 月，金融危机与经济衰退并行，世界经济形势甚至有恶化的趋势。面临此种形势，各国相继出台各种刺激经济的措施。经过各国的共同努力，从 2009 年第三季度开始，世界经济才有好转迹象。	According to the landmark events, the U.S. financial crisis can be divided into three phases[3]: the first phase is from August 2007 to mid-September 2008. The crisis manifests itself into a subprime crisis with limited size mainly reflecting on the structured finance products relating to the subprime. The second phase is from mid-September to mid-October 2008. Lehman's bankruptcy caused a severe confidence crisis in the financial market. A tight liquidity quickly expanded to the global financial market from currency and credit markets, upgrading the limited subprime crisis into a global financial crisis. The third phase is from mid October 2008 to July 2009. The financial crisis coexisted with the economic recession and the world economy even faced the trend of deterioration. Under this context, all countries set out various measures to spur economy in succession. With the concerted efforts of all nations, the world economy had a sign of recovery in the third quarter of 2009.

难点 1

原文：美国长期的宽松货币政策和金融监管的失败，以及国际货币体系的不合理是引发美国次贷危机和引起世界金融危机的主要原因。

译文：The failure of the U. S. long-term easy monetary policy and financial regulation as well as the irrational international monetary system jointly contributed to this U. S. subprime crisis which in turn caused a global financial crisis.

分析："宽松货币政策"和"次贷危机"都是专门的经济学术语，要找到对应的英文翻译，不能根据字面意思直译。

难点 2

原文：源于美国房地产价格泡沫的破灭，2007 年美国出现次贷危机，2008 年 9 月次贷危机急剧恶化，演变成为一场自 20 世纪 30 年代大萧条以来最为严重的全球金融危机。

译文：Triggered by the bursting of housing bubble, the U. S. subprime crisis broke out in 2007, then sharply deteriorated in September 2008, and eventually evolved into the worst global financial crisis since the Great Depression in the 1930s.

分析：原文清楚地表达了金融危机的发展，这在汉英翻译中应该是明确的。但是，仅仅翻译原文中的日期是远远不够的，通过增译时间副词"then""eventually"来阐明这次金融危机的逻辑发展，可以让译文更有条理、更生动。

难点 3

原文：我们用标志性事件来看美国金融危机的过程，可划分为三个阶段：

译文：According to the landmark events, the U. S. financial crisis can be divided into three phases：

分析：汉语重人称，常用主动式，英语重物称，常用被动式。非人称表达法是英语书面语中常见的表达方式，这种表达方式可以使叙述显得更加客观、公正，句子结构更加紧凑，语气更加缓和。在英译中，无法指明施事者时，一般选择采用被动句来表达。

二、英译汉

原文	译文
A Brief Refresher on Risk-Neutral Pricing	风险中性定价的简要回顾
Risk-neutral pricing is a technique widely used in mathematical finance to price contingent claims. In this section, we provide the reader with a brief review in order to motivate discussion on arbitrage-free pricing in Section 9 of this paper.	风险中性定价是一种广泛应用于数学金融学中的定价方法，用来进行未定权益定价。本节为读者提供了一个简要的回顾，以此引出本文第 9 节中关于无套利定价的讨论[1]。

续表

原文	译文
A market is considered to be complete if any contingent claim can be replicated by an admissible, self-financing trading strategy referred to as a replicating portfolio. The replicating portfolio is constructed from primary securities such as stocks and bonds, the market prices of which are unique. The price of the replicating portfolio is identical to all agents in the market, and is therefore independent of any assumptions of risk preferences, either averse or seeking. Regardless of their risk preferences, market participants will eliminate any discrepancy between the price of the replicating portfolio and the prices of its underlying primary securities by engaging in arbitrage trades.	当未定权益可以通过某种可采纳的、资金自筹的贸易策略(简称为复制投资组合)所复制时,市场则被视作完整市场。复制性投资组合由股票和债券等初级证券构成,其市场价格是唯一的。复制性投资组合的价格与市场中的所有代理相同,因此,不受来自于风险偏好的任何——无论是风险回避还是风险追求——假设的影响[2]。市场参与者不考虑他们的风险偏好,将通过参与套利交易的方式来消除复制性投资组合的价格与其标的初级证券的价格之间的任何差异。
Typically, the probabilities of events occurring are expressed in terms of the physical (i.e. "realworld") probability measure, which we denote as P in the probability space (Ω, $\mathcal{F}$, P). However, a problem arises because market participants discount the risk of a contract with varying interest rates according to their individual preferences for risk. Therefore, we apply Girsanov's theorem and use a probability measure, which we denote as Q, and is equivalent to P, under which market participants are insensitive to risk (i.e. risk-neutral). This is a powerful and tractable technique because it allows us to discount cash flows at the risk-free rate r when computing expectations under the probability measure Q.	通常,事件发生的概率以物理(即"现实世界")概率测度表示,我们在概率空间(Ω, $\mathcal{F}$, P)中将其表示为P。然而,问题的出现是由于市场参与者只考虑其个人风险偏好,却没有考虑到每个合约的利率各不相同,忽视了其中的风险。因此,在市场参与者对风险不敏感(即风险中性)的情况下,我们应用吉尔萨诺夫定理,使用概率测度,用Q表示,并等同于P。这是一个具有说服力且易于处理的方法,因为它允许我们在按照概率测度Q计算期望值时,以无风险利率r折现现金流。
A martingale is the mathematical formalization of a fair game (e.g. coin flip). The process X is said to be a martingale if $E[X_{t+i} \mid \mathcal{F}_t] = X_t$, for all i and t $\geqslant$ 0 (3.1)	鞅是公平游戏的数学形式化(例如,掷硬币)。若$E[X_{t+i} \mid \mathcal{F}_t] = X_t$,所有i和t$\geqslant$0 (3.1)那么,过程X就叫作鞅。
If we model the prices of financial contracts as martingales, then we can imply market participants are unable to consistently profit by trading these financial contracts.	如果我们将金融合约的价格建模为鞅,那么我们可以暗示市场参与者不能通过交易这些金融合约持续获利。

续表

原文	译文
A position in the derivative contract can be hedged with a position in Δ units of the underlying (Black & Scholes, 1973). In theory, this results in a riskless portfolio. However, the theory relies on a number of assumptions. One key assumption is that market participants are able to continuously and completely hedge away all of the risk. In practice, this is not possible because, inter alia, markets are incomplete. Therefore, according to the Second Fundamental Theorem of Asset Pricing, the preference for risk must be reintroduced into derivatives valuations, resulting in individual assessments of risk. The Law of One Price, an economic concept which states that two assets with identical cash flows and risk characteristics should have the same price in a market that is complete and arbitrage-free, no longer holds. Another assumption is the ability of market participants to borrow limitless amounts at the risk-free rate. This, too, is not possible in practice.	衍生品合约中的头寸可以与标的资产单位 Δ 中的头寸进行对冲(布莱克 & 斯科尔斯，1973)。理论上，这种做法产生了无风险的投资组合。然而，该理论依赖于许多假设。其中一个关键的假设是，市场参与者能够连续完全地对冲所有风险。而实际上，这根本无法实现，因为，除了个别情况以外，市场从来都不是完整的。因此，根据"资产定价的第二基本定理"，进行衍生品估值时，风险偏好必须被重新引入，对风险作出单独评估[3]。"一价定律"是一个经济概念，它指出两种具有相同现金流和风险特征的资产，在完整的市场中应具有相同的价格，因而，套利空间也就不复存在。另一个假设是市场参与者可以以无风险利率无限额地借入。但在实际操作中，这也不可能做到。
The reader is referred to Appendix A for a derivation of the pricing equation for a financial derivative contract.	读者可参考附录 A 来了解金融衍生品合约定价方程的推导过程。
As the interest rate swap market developed in the 1980s, LIBOR was perceived as the benchmark that most appropriately reflected the funding cost of interbank transactions, and was therefore used as the proxy for the "risk-free" rate. Collateralization had not yet been widely adopted. Best practices prescribed the use of a LIBOR zero-coupon curve to discount the cash flows of these non-collateralized derivatives contracts.	随着20世纪80年代利率互换市场的发展，伦敦同业拆利借率被当作一项基准，因其能够最恰当反映同业交易融资成本，因此被用作"无风险"利率的代理。抵押担保品还未被广泛采用。最佳实践做法规定，使用伦敦银行同业拆借利率零息票据收益曲线来对这些非抵押衍生品合约的现金流进行折现。
Prior to the financial crisis, LIBOR was considered to be the risk-free rate, as well as the rate at which banks could fund themselves. There was little distinction between the risk-free rate used for the purposes of discounting and a bank's cost of funding. The effects of credit risk, liquidity risk, collateral agreements and funding costs were largely ignored. The primary focus was to price the market risk of transactions. Collateralized and noncollateralized derivatives transactions had traditionally been priced using the LIBOR zero-coupon curve.	在金融危机之前，伦敦银行同业拆借利率被认为是无风险利率，同时银行可以对自己的利率进行调整。用于贴现的无风险利率和银行资金成本之间几乎毫无区别。信用风险、流动性风险、担保协议和融资成本的影响在很大程度上被忽略[4]。主要的焦点集中在交易的市场风险定价。抵押和非抵押衍生品交易习惯于使用伦敦同业拆借率的零息票据曲线来定价。

第四章　经济学论文翻译

难点 1

原文：In this section, we provide the reader with a brief review in order to motivate discussion on arbitrage-free pricing in Section 9 of this paper.

译文：本节为读者提供了一个简要的回顾，以此引出本文第 9 节中关于无套利定价的讨论。

分析：在源文本中，多次使用"we"作为人称主语，在翻译时，若将原文中的人称主语"we"直译出来，在中文的学术论文中出现"我们"等人称主语，则显得文章带有强烈的主观色彩，不够权威，不能体现出学术论文客观性的特点。为了避免这种情况的发生，用"本节"充当句子主语，其他内容则按照动宾结构逐一翻译，方能突出学术论文专业性、客观性的特点。

难点 2

原文：The price of the replicating portfolio is identical to all agents in the market, and is therefore independent of any assumptions of risk preferences, either averse or seeking.

译文：复制性投资组合的价格与市场中的所有代理相同，因此，不受来自于风险偏好的任何——无论是风险回避还是风险追求——假设的影响。

分析：学术论文具有专业化和规范化的文体特征。如果将"either averse or seeking"翻译为"无论回避还是追求"，虽然符合原意，但表达不够专业，较为口语化。经过句式分析，不难发现"either averse or seeking"是"risk preferences"的修饰成分。在《风险偏好类型与风险判断模式的实验分析》（李劲松、王重鸣，1998）一文中，作者将风险偏好划分为"风险回避、风险追求和风险中立"三种类型。故原句中的"averse"和"seeking"实为两个经济术语，应分别译为"风险回避"和"风险追求"。在句式上，为了符合学术论文严谨、规范的表达特点，将"either averse or seeking"作为插入语处理。

难点 3

原文：However, a problem arises because market participants discount the risk of a contract with varying interest rates according to their individual preferences for risk… Therefore, according to the Second Fundamental Theorem of Asset Pricing, the preference for risk must be reintroduced into derivatives valuations, resulting in individual assessments of risk.

译文：然而，问题的出现是由于市场参与者只考虑其个人风险偏好，却没有考虑到每个合约的利率各不相同，忽视了其中的风险……因此，根据"资产定价的第二基本定理"，进行衍生品估值时，风险偏好必须被重新引入，对风险作出单独评估。

分析：大多数的经济术语都采用"名词+名词"结构，在《银行词典》中可查到"risk preference"的汉译为"风险偏好"，但"preference for risk"却没有查到对应的汉译。转而回看原文，文中该部分的信息焦点为"风险偏好在衍生品定价过程中的重要性"，所以，可以推断"preference for risk"也应译为术语"风险偏好"。经过这样处理,使行文简洁,上下文内容统一、连贯,同时,也能减少中文读者对该句产生的歧义和困惑。

难点4

原文:The effects of credit risk, liquidity risk, collateral agreements and funding costs were largely ignored.

译文:信用风险、流动性风险、担保协议和融资成本的影响在很大程度上被忽略。

分析:英语中的词汇常常是一词多义,而在具体的语言背景下,结合上下文和不同的文本类型,一个词只有一个意义,这个词义需要通过上下文内容或文本类型进行判断。通过查找《柯林斯经济学词典》,"liquidity"一词作为经济学术语时既有"流动性"的意思,又有"偿还能力"的意思。此时,就需要根据上下文,结合具体的语境来判断词义。在此句中,"liquidity"与"risk"连用时,一般取"流动性"之意,译作"流动性风险"。

翻 译 练 习

一、词组翻译

difference-in-differences
quantitative equilibrium
global sourcing
expenditure switching
joint taxation
fundamental surplus
trade-off
supplemental security income
边际收益
异质性
最优配置
影子价格
空头支票
储备货币
逆向选择

二、句子翻译

(一)英译汉

1. The Margins of Global Sourcing: Theory and Evidence from US Firms

2. Are There Environmental Benefits from Driving Electric Vehicles? The Importance of Local Factors

3. As the interest rate swap market developed in the 1980s, LIBOR was perceived as the benchmark that most appropriately reflected the funding cost of interbank transactions, and was therefore used as the proxy for the "risk-free" rate.

4. An Overnight Index Swap (OIS) is a fixed-for-floating interest rate swap whose floating leg references an overnight index that resets each day during the specified term of the swap. Interest on the floating leg is computed through daily compounding of the overnight index. The floating rate index is typically the overnight secured lending rate between banks.

5. Market participants typically calibrated a single interest rate curve to liquid market products such as cash deposits, forward rate agreements, short-term interest rate futures (e. g. Eurodollar futures) and/or interest rate swaps.

(二) 汉译英

1. 信用风险、流动性风险、担保协议和融资成本的影响在很大程度上被忽略。

2. 复制性投资组合的价格与市场中的所有代理相同，因此，不受来自于风险偏好的任何假设的影响，无论是风险回避还是风险追求。

3. 对于过度诊疗与高水平诊疗的界定

4. 论 WTO 准入对中国加工企业业绩的影响

5. 在最终消费中可贸易部分的转变，主要是因为持续投资的有效性降低，因此贸易对于 GDP 贡献减少。

三、语篇翻译

本文介绍了主题的背景、意义、创新点和非正式制度与中国经济发展的概况，从分析非正式制度影响中国经济发展的理论研究入手，首先，通过分析选取了四个方面内容作为说明非正式制度与中国经济发展影响关系的传导媒介，并通过这四方面的传导媒介分析论证了非正式制度与中国经济发展之间的传导途径。从文化传统、意识形态、习俗习惯和伦理道德作为非正式制度的四个维度内容分别论证分析了与中国经济发展关系的内在机理和传导途径。建立了非正式制度与中国经济发展的理论基础。其次，在理论研究的基础上，分别从不同层面维度的测度标准、指标选取和指标趋势走向对非正式制度与中国经济发展分别进行了探讨。本文在论证分析过程中严格依照非正式制度性质、内容和中国经济的发展历程对每个维度进行测度定义，并按照国家经济发展标准、测度定义和鱼骨图问题追溯的思想选取符合非正式制度内容且具有经济特性的可测指标，实现构建非正式制度与中国经济发展的测度指标体系。并利用通过对数据的统一、筛选和优化过程最终确定非正式制度选取的 16 项测度指标和中国经济发展选取的 22 项测度指标，分别构成初始时序面板数据集，且依次绘制 16 项指标和 22 项指标的平滑曲线图和趋势走势图，借助数据的分布规律寻到异常临界点，并结合历史进程和中国经济发展特点给出较为基础的成因解释说明。再次，通过实证分析方法，建立非正式制度与中国经济发展的综合评价函数并进行关联，通过函数系数说明二者之间的关系。再根据中国经济发展选取的22项指标建立中国四个大区域的数据面板，分别建立非正式制度与中国四个区域经济发展的函数，论证非正式制度与区域经济发展存在的影响关系，进一步说明非正式制度对中国经济的影响。同时构建了非正式制度与中国经济发展之间传导媒介的测度指标体系，并分别建立了非正式制度与传导媒介、中国经济与传导媒介之间的函数关系，验证了非正式制度与中国经济发展之间的传导途径。最后，本文根据上文的理论分析，运用实证数据结果，分别从"正确引导意识形态高效变迁""加快市场经济文化建设""重视习俗习惯正向有效变迁""加速推广新时代社会主义道德观""加快有效正式制度改革，拉升非正式制度相融合发展""加大教育投入，提高人力资本文化价值"以及"坚持党和政府引领新理念，扩大有效供给增加消费需求"与非正式制度内容相关的七个方面提出推进中国向经济高质量发展的对策建议。

◎参考文献

[1]季蕊.动态对等理论指导下的经济类期刊论文摘要英译研究[D].河北科技大学，2017.

[2]金晶，杨占.医学科研论文与医学科普文章翻译探析[J].海外英语，2020(6)：30-31，40.

[3]李劲松，王重鸣.风险偏好类型与风险判断模式的实验分析[J].人类工效学，1998(3)：18-22，71.

[4]李益广.经济论文标题的文体特点及英译技巧[J].中国科技翻译，1997(4)：23-25.

[5]廖昌盛，钟平.经贸翻译的词义选择[J].赣南师范学院学报，2002(4)：93-94.

[6]凌民.学术论文标题的结构特点与英译[J].四川师范学院学报(哲学社会科学版)，2000(1)：92-95.

[7]王立丽.金融类学术期刊论文英汉翻译实践报告[D].黑龙江大学，2014.

[8]王中雨，刘雅芳.中医药论文题目英译的跨文化研究[J].文教资料，2020(5)：221-222.

[9]徐如秀.经济类论文标题翻译实践报告[D].电子科技大学，2016.

[10]袁予熙，赵玉闪.目的论指导下的经济论文标题英译[J].中国电力教育，2009(20)：210-211.

[11]云佼阳.*Crowdsourcing, Sharing Economy and Development* 英汉翻译实践报告[D].黑龙江大学，2019.

[12]张瑜.*CSA Discounting: Impacts on Pricing and Risk of Commodity Derivatives* 英汉翻译实践报告[D].黑龙江大学，2017.

第五章　经济学教材翻译

> ☞**思考题**
> 1. 什么是经济学教材？经济学教材有哪些特点？
> 2. 翻译经济学教材时有哪些注意事项？
> 3. 经济学教材翻译的难点在哪里？

第一节　经济学教材文本分析

一、经济学教材的总体介绍

经济学是研究人类社会在各个发展阶段上的各种经济活动和各种相应的经济关系及其运行、发展规律的学科。而经济学教材自然也就是系统反映学科内容的教学用书。作为课程的重要参与者和课程的具体化表现，教材的编写离不开课程和课程标准的制定。目前各大高校所教授的经济学大多以西方经济学课程为主，囊括微观经济学、宏观经济学等基础课，也包括金融学、财政学、计量经济学等其他相关或交叉学科。由于微观经济学和宏观经济学常作为基础课，其中又以微观经济学为基础中的基础，因此，本单元对经济学教材的翻译讨论主要以微观经济学为范本展开。

就西方而言，亚当·斯密的《国富论》标志着西方经济学的诞生，虽然以现在的角度来看《国富论》应当算作著作而非教材，但将其置于特定的历史时期，则显然已起到了启迪他人的作用。而狭义上，在大学中开设专业并聘任专职经济学教授的经济学，则始于19世纪初，如剑桥大学的马尔萨斯（Robert Malthus，1766—1834），他于1805年被东印度学院任命为政治经济学①教授，从而成为英国第一位职业经济学家，据说他当时就是以《国富论》为基础进行授课的，授课过程中甚至曾经进行过逐句解释的方法。另外，伦敦国王学院的理查德·琼斯也担任过政治经济学教授，他曾编写过《地租》，并将其概念化

---

① 在19世纪，经济学通用的名称为政治经济学（political economy），直到1890年马歇尔的《经济学原理》（*Principles of Economics*）出版后，"政治经济学"才逐渐被"经济学"所取代。

为一种剩余劳动的形式，从而赢得了马克思的辩护。在美国，哥伦比亚大学的麦克维尔（John McVickar，1787—1868）及利伯（Francis Lieber，1800—1872）、哈佛大学的鲍文（Francis Bowen，1811—1890）等，也都在这个时期开设了经济学课程。此后，正如《新帕尔格雷大经济学大辞典》所述，"在19世纪后半叶，随着剑桥作为经济学精英中心的崛起，1895年伦敦经济学院的创立，以及20世纪初美国哈佛大学、哥伦比亚大学、芝加哥大学的经济学教授的大量涌现，第一次有了集中的经济学教师、研究者和学生"。

我国的经济学课程则主要经历了中华人民共和国成立前、计划经济体制时期和市场经济体制时期三个阶段。最早将西方经济学著作较为完整地引入中国的，是京师同文馆的美国传教士丁韪良（W. A. P. Martin，1827—1916），他在同文馆中讲授了英国学者 H. Fawcett（1833—1884）的《政治经济学手册》，并与王凤藻一同将其翻译为中文。这本书也成为中国历史上第一部系统介绍西方古典主义政治经济学的译著。中华人民共和国成立后，受苏联影响，我国的经济以"计划经济学"为理论依据建立了一系列教育体系，如1950年成立的中国人民大学中便有"国民经济计划系"，课程以国民经济计划、统计学、经济地理、农业经济等为主。教材则有《资本论》《剩余价值学说史》，以及中国人民大学《国民经济计划》（六册）等。此书以苏联教授的讲稿为主。此外，《苏联国民经济工资计划》《苏联国民经济运输计划》等也经由翻译被引入了国内。然而，随着时间的推移，中国社会的发展，以及特定历史时期对经济生活的影响，苏联模式越来越难以跟上中国发展的脚步。在改革开放之后，西方经济学的相关原理得到了认可，在解放思想、实事求是思想的指导下，我国也引进了一大批西方经济学著作，如萨缪尔森的《经济学》、哈罗德的《动态经济学》等。本章所着重介绍的经济学教材——曼昆的《经济学原理：微观部分》，以及范里安的《微观经济学：现代观点》都可归于此类。

二、经济学教材的基本特征

西方经济学教材有着图文并茂、深入浅出、案例丰富，以及体系完备的特点。教材以学生为中心，重视学生自我学习能力和习惯的培养。

以《经济学原理：微观部分》为例，曼昆在前言中写到，他的目标是写一本学生爱看的经济学教材。以其第四章为例，除了文本内容外，还有非常丰富的补充材料，共有图表12幅，即问即答4条，关键词20个，新闻摘录和案例各1篇，章末内容提要9条。以图5-1为例，该图选自曼昆《经济学原理：微观部分》第二章，是该章首页，与普通教材相比，这一页选择了大面积色块铺底，同时页面二分之一的版面被女教师教授经济学知识的图片占据，从图中隐约可以看到 PPF（Production Possibility Frontier，生产可能性边界）以及 circular-flow diagram（循环流量图）等。从而可以得知，图中的教师正在教授经济学知识。同时该章节的标题"Thinking Like an Economist"的实词部分"thinking""like"以及"economist"也做了放大字号的处理。从以上方面可以看出，西方经济学教材非常重视对学生注意力的唤醒。（见图5-1）

第五章　经济学教材翻译

图 5-1　曼昆《经济学原理：微观部分》第二章章首页

除了使用图像等模态资源之外，西方经济学教材在结构上也乐于使用重复的方法，同样是"循环流量图"的概念，作者可能在文本中提到并以黑体字加粗，并在页侧空白处重复概念，最后在内容提要中再次重复其概念，这当中穿插图表和案例进行辅助说明。此外，部分教材还配有《学习指南》供学生练习使用。对于入门级别的经济学教材而言，学生需要掌握相当多的概念，而重复的使用使得学生可以更加方便快捷地找到重要信息，加深对重要概念的熟悉程度。（见图 5-2）

曼昆的《经济学原理：微观部分》属于经济学入门书籍，因此更注重可接受性。相较而言，为经济学专业设计的教材则更加注重逻辑顺序和推断。以范里安的《微观经济学：现代观点》为例，该书以市场和市场中的活动为线索，介绍供需理论和市场运作机制。图 5-3 选自该书前言部分，作者以一张图表简明扼要地介绍了《微观经济学：现代观点》所涵盖的内容，各章节以不同的颜色区分了重要程度，以虚实箭头等符号指明了各章节之间的关系，实线表示学习后章前需要仔细阅读学习前章，虚线则表示可以略微了解。相较于《经济学原理：微观部分》而言，这幅图的颜色并不丰富，画面内容也不够生动，但提供的信息量却非常大，读者不仅了解到了书籍内容，也对书籍中各部分的逻辑联系有了直观的感受。（见图 5-3）

第一节 经济学教材文本分析

Our First Model: The Circular-Flow Diagram

The economy consists of millions of people engaged in many activities—buying, selling, working, hiring, manufacturing, and so on. To understand how the economy works, we must find some way to simplify our thinking about all these activities. In other words, we need a model that explains, in general terms, how the economy is organized and how participants in the economy interact with one another.

Figure 1 presents a visual model of the economy called a *circular-flow diagram*. In this model, the economy is simplified to include only two types of decision makers—firms and households. Firms produce goods and services using inputs, such as labor, land, and capital (buildings and machines). These inputs are called the *factors of production*. Households own the factors of production and consume all the goods and services that the firms produce.

Households and firms interact in two types of markets. In the *markets for goods and services*, households are buyers, and firms are sellers. In particular, households buy the output of goods and services that firms produce. In the *markets for the factors of production*, households are sellers, and firms are buyers. In these markets, households provide the inputs that firms use to produce goods and services. The circular-flow diagram offers a simple way of organizing the economic transactions that occur between households and firms in the economy.

The two loops of the circular-flow diagram are distinct but related. The inner loop represents the flows of inputs and outputs. The households sell the use of

circular-flow diagram
a visual model of the economy that shows how dollars flow through markets among households and firms

空白处的定义

文本中加粗的概念

图 5-2 循环流量图

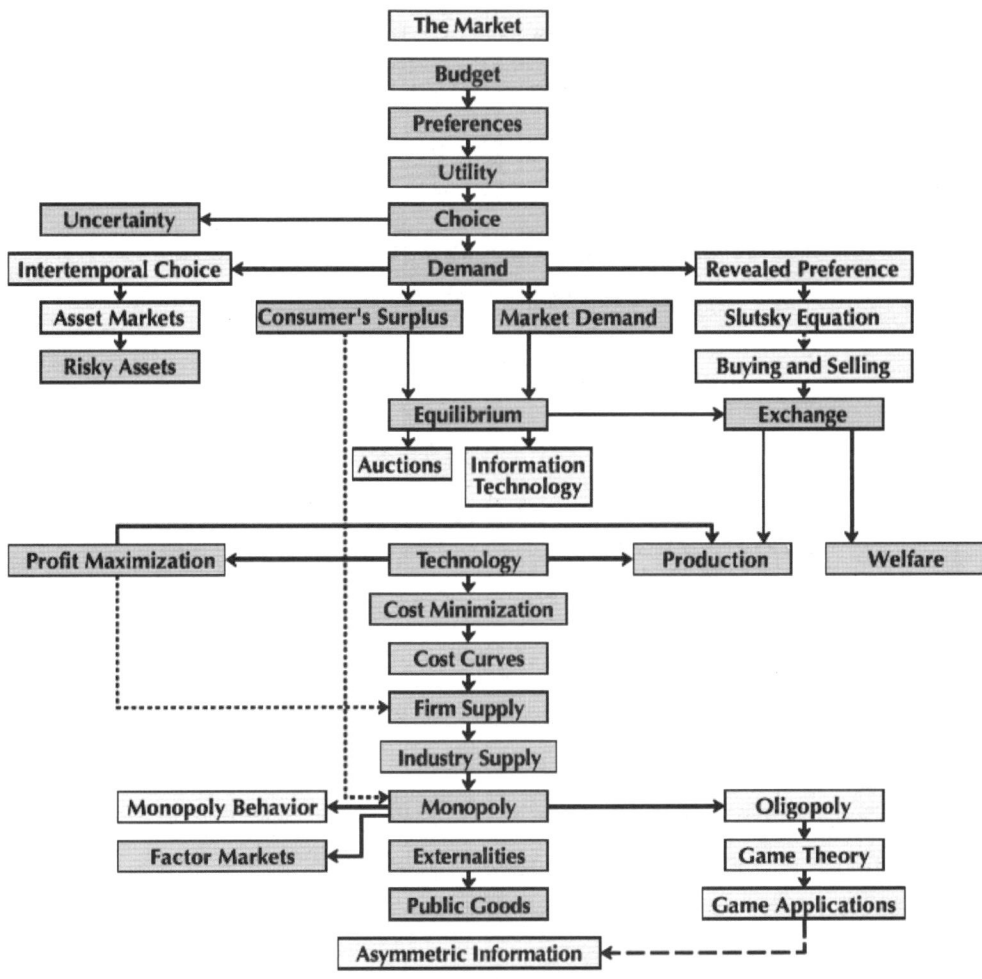

图 5-3 《微观经济学：现代观点》章节关系图

105

经济学教材在介绍和论证原理时，需要应用相当多的数学语言，因此可以发现教材中有相当多的算式和前后逻辑符号，如第五章介绍柯布-道格拉斯效用函数(Cobb-Douglas Utility Function)就用了多达 23 个算式，从而在理解上加大了译者的难度。(见图 5-4)

In Chapter 4 we introduced the **Cobb-Douglas utility function**

$$u(x_1, x_2) = x_1^c x_2^d.$$

Since utility functions are only defined up to a monotonic transformation, it is convenient to take logs of this expression and work with

$$\ln u(x_1, x_2) = c \ln x_1 + d \ln x_2.$$

Let's find the demand functions for x_1 and x_2 for the Cobb-Douglas utility function. The problem we want to solve is

$$\max_{x_1, x_2} c \ln x_1 + d \ln x_2$$

such that $p_1 x_1 + p_2 x_2 = m.$

There are at least three ways to solve this problem. One way is just to write down the MRS condition and the budget constraint. Using the expression for the MRS derived in Chapter 4, we have

$$\frac{cx_2}{dx_1} = \frac{p_1}{p_2}$$

$$p_1 x_1 + p_2 x_2 = m.$$

These are two equations in two unknowns that can be solved for the optimal choice of x_1 and x_2. One way to solve them is to substitute the second into the first to get

$$\frac{c(m/p_2 - x_1 p_1/p_2)}{dx_1} = \frac{p_1}{p_2}.$$

Cross multiplying gives

$$c(m - x_1 p_1) = dp_1 x_1.$$

Rearranging this equation gives

$$cm = (c + d)p_1 x_1$$

or

$$x_1 = \frac{c}{c+d} \frac{m}{p_1}.$$

This is the demand function for x_1. To find the demand function for x_2, substitute into the budget constraint to get

$$x_2 = \frac{m}{p_2} - \frac{p_1}{p_2} \frac{c}{c+d} \frac{m}{p_1}$$
$$= \frac{d}{c+d} \frac{m}{p_2}.$$

图 5-4 《微观经济学：现代观点》第五章柯布-道格拉斯函数

从上面几个例子可以看出，西方经济学教材种类多样，依据目标读者的不同，对内容进行了不同的区分。针对无基础的入门学生，作者采取了图文并茂、深入浅出的写作风格。而针对有一定经济学基础的学生，作者则采取了体系完备、逻辑严密的写作风格。

三、经济学教材的基本结构

一本经济学教材通常包含封面、版权页、序言、目录、正文、术语表、索引以及参考文献等部分。具体如表 5-1 所示：

表 5-1

结构	内容
封面	书名、作者、译者、出版社、版次等
版权页	除上述外，包括编辑、地址、出版日、开本、定价、标准书号等
序言	作者对作品、读者等要说的话，可以从中找到交际动机、发送者意图等
目录	对作品内容和结构的大致把握
正文	教材的主要部分、学科内容
术语表	正文部分出现的术语
索引及参考文献	作者参考的资料等（习题答案）

译者在进行翻译时，正文部分的内容固然应当重视，其他部分也不能有所缺憾。以一本教材而言，除正文外，序言也需要译者多加留心。序言通常用于表明作者著述或编写此书的意图，或是学者对该领域的问题的研究和看法。对于译者而言，序言的理解和翻译至关重要，因为译者在翻译过程中势必涉及文本分析，而通过对序言的阅读，可以了解到作者著述的体验、心理，以经济学教材而言，也可以大致推断作者属于什么样的学派，有着怎样的思想主张。以曼昆的《经济学原理：微观部分》为例，从序言部分作者列举的一系列问题（为什么有地租差异、为什么有工资差异、为什么国家经济发展水平存在差异）可以看出《经济学原理：微观部分》侧重的是对经济学原理的应用。因此译者在翻译时，原理的解释应当简单明了，意思准确；而在翻译案例时，则应该重视原文案例的语言风格和特征，如果案例语言诙谐幽默，则翻译为中文时也应该用诙谐幽默的语言，如果原文使用了庄重的语言，则译文也应当庄重。

此外，序言和目录也有可能帮助读者了解文本的外部环境。如以操纵学派的观点来看，翻译过程中的意识形态和赞助人等因素也会影响到译作。如在目录中发现其"市场是组织经济活动的一种好方法（Markets are usually a good way to organize economic activity）""相互依存性和贸易的好处（interdependence and the gains from trade）"以及"税收产生无谓损失（deadweight losses）"等观点，由此可以大致推断曼昆至少不是凯恩斯主义者，而是一位小政府、大市场的自由主义学者，这在一定程度上对正确把握正文内容提供了帮助。

四、经济学教材的语言特征

如上所述，西方经济学教材在编写过程中十分注意学生的接受性。因此，在结构上，教材的内容充斥大量图表、案例和新闻，这些除了补充教材信息外，很大程度上也是为了吸引学生的注意力。同时，在语言风格上，也是庄重与诙谐并重。可以参见如下两个例子：

例1

原文：Ogre to Slay? Outsource It to Chinese

A decade ago, no one would have asked which nation has a comparative advantage in slaying ogres.

译文：想打怪兽吗？外包给中国人吧

十年前，没人会对哪个国家在打怪兽游戏上有相对优势有疑问。

分析：这段话选自曼昆《经济学原理：微观部分》第三章的新闻摘录。主要目的是对分工和比较优势进行介绍。可以看到，首先标题使用了相当惹眼的词汇："Ogre to Slay?（打怪兽?）"，人们就能对这篇报道产生一种初始印象，即这篇报道讲的是电子游戏。从后一部分"Outsource it to Chinese（外包给中国人吧）"就能得知，这篇报道和中国有关，且可能是一种贸易，因为涉及外包活动。下一段话则重复了"打怪兽"，此外，这也是一个下位概念，其上位概念"打游戏"隐含其中。由于中文倾向于用概括性的表达，如果将其翻译为"十年前，没人会对哪国人更擅长打怪兽有疑问"，则读者可能认为"打怪兽"有点不知所云，因为现实生活中没有怪兽。因此可以翻译为："十年前，没人会对哪个国家在打怪兽游戏上有相对优势有疑问。"

例2

原文：An economist would describe the distinction between the prices of the two kinds of apartments in this model by saying that the price of the outer-ring apartment is an exogenous variable, while the price of the inner-ring apartments is an endogenous variable.

译文：在公寓模型中，对于两类公寓的价格的差别，经济学家会这么说，外环公寓的价格是一个外生变量，而内环公寓的价格是个内生变量。

分析：这个例句选自范里安《微观经济学：现代观点》的第一章。这段话介绍了两个概念：外生变量（exogenous variable）以及内生变量（endogenous variable）。在这段话之前，作者举了一个例子，该例子涉及租房边际成本问题。因此可以注意到，作者在这段话中介绍概念时，是结合上述例子进行说明的，外环住房（价格较低）的价格为外生变量，内环住房（价格较高）的价格为内生变量。虽然这段话比较平实，不难理解，也没有上一个例子那样诙谐幽默，但可以看出，经济学教材的语言风格是注重实感、非常具体的。

第二节　翻译知识讲解

因为经济学教材属于 ESP（English for Specific Purposes），翻译经济学教材时使用目的论和文本分析的理论最为合适。因为作者在编写教材的时候，最首要的考虑不是为了让语言多么地优美，多么地有赏析价值，而是借助语言传达相应的学科信息。换句话说，作者编写教材是带着目标的，具体到各个作者这个目标又不一样，如前文所述，曼昆的目的是"写一本学生喜欢的经济学教材"。而范里安在《微观经济学：现代观点》中针对的则是"welcome an analytical approach to microeconomiy at the undergraduate level"（对微观经济学采取分析方法的本科生），读者范围和《经济学原理：微观部分》有着很大差别。按照弗米尔的观点，在目的原则、连贯原则和忠实原则中，以目的原则为首要目的，译者应当根据译文的目的采取相应的翻译策略。

因此定下翻译原则后，可以根据翻译原则寻找相应的翻译方法，而不仅仅局限于归化、异化，直译、意译等。具体到经济学教材的翻译，可以根据不同的情况进行变通。例如在翻译吸引学生注意力的文段和表达的时候，可以适当采取归化的方法：

例1

原文：The gain from trade are most obvious if the rancher can produce only meat and the farmer can produce only potatoes. In one scenario, the rancher and the farmer could choose to have nothing to do with each other.

译文：如果牧场主只生产牛肉，而农场主只能生产土豆，那么，贸易的好处是显而易见的。在一种情况下，农场主和牧场主可能选择"老死不相往来"。

分析：这句话选自《经济学原理：微观部分》第三章，理解起来不会有任何问题，但最后一句却对译者的翻译水平有一定的考验。"have nothing to do with each other"一般直译为"和对方无关"。但这里作者在上文中，以农场主和牧场主举例，说明作者是想要以更加直观具体的方式呈现信息的。那么在翻译时应该采取更适合中国人的表达习惯，因此在译文中可以适用俗语，将其翻译为"老死不相往来"。

例2

原文：A subsidy is the opposite of a tax. In the case of a quantity subsidy, the government gives an amount to the consumer that depends on the amount of the good purchased. If, for example, the consumption of milk were subsidized, the government would pay some amount of money to each consumer of milk depending on the amount that consumer purchased. If the subsidy is s dollars per unit of consumption of good 1, then from the viewpoint of the consumer, the price of good 1 would be p1-s. This would therefore make the budget line flatter.

译文：补贴（subsidy）正好和税收相反。在从量补贴（quantity subsidy）的情形下，政府根据消费者购买某种商品的数量，给与他一定金额的补助。例如，假如政府补贴牛奶消费，则政府需要向消费牛奶的每个消费者支付补贴，补贴金额取决于消费者消费牛奶的数量。如果每消费一单位商品1可以获得s美元的补贴，则在消费者的眼里，商品1的价格变为 p1-s。这将会使预算线变得更平坦。

分析：这段话选自范里安的《微观经济学：现代观点》第二章。目标读者如上所述，是经济学专业的本科学生。此外，从这段话中也可以看出作者更倾向于用一个简单直接的态度来陈述补贴的概念，为了达到这个目的，作者甚至在概念中运用了数学符号。因此在进行翻译的时候就应该试图达到这种目的。直译显然能够达到这一点，但也要注意到，具体到句法层面，这里的"if, for example, the consumption of milk were subsidized"是被动语态，在翻译时，为了顺应中国人的表达习惯，还是适合将其转换为主动，译为"假如政府补贴牛奶消费"。（"政府"这一主语依据后文"the government would pay…"推断而来。）这样的表达也达到了作者进行简单清晰表达的目的。

例3

原文：…the choice that people plan to make in one state of nature should be independent from the choices that they plan to make in other states of nature. This assumption is known as the independence assumption.

译文：……人们在一种自然状态下作出的选择，应该和另外一种自然状态下作出的选择无关。这个假设称为独立性假设（independence assumption）。

分析：经济学教材还有一个明显的特点，可能也是其他英语材料共有的特点，那就是多用被动语态，叶斯伯森在《语法哲学》中就提到过，英语各类作品的被动句中有70%到94%是不会出现施动者的；但在汉语中，施动者常常是必须说出来的①。这种不一致也就加大了英汉转换的难度。被动语态具有客观性强的特点，隐去施动者更强调了内容的客观现实性，因为教材是人类对已发现的科学事实的客观陈述。此外，被动部分也起到了强调的作用，对于某些施动者众多的句子，被动语态也能够平衡句子的前后重量，使之连贯。在这个例子中，诸如"be known as"等被动语态，避免了"somebody"的出现，因为在作者所要表达的意思中，"谁"知道并不重要，重要的是这种现象的术语表达，因此这种静态化的描述不仅增强了客观性，也突出了重点信息。

例4

原文：Although both the competitive market and the discrimination monopolist generate Pareto efficient outcomes in the sense that there will be no further trades desire, they can result in quite different distributions of income.

译文：竞争的市场和歧视性垄断都能实现帕累托最优的结果，因为在这两种情况下，人们都不再有进一步交易的欲望。尽管如此，这两种情况会导致相当不同的收入分配。

例5

原文：The argument here rests on the fact that an arbitrary assignment of renters to apartments will generally involve someone living in the inner ring who is willing to pay less for an apartment than someone living in the outer-ring.

译文：这里的论点基于这样一个事实，即任意分配租房者到公寓通常会导致有的人

---

① 卢敏. 英语笔译实务[M]. 北京：外文出版社，2017.

住在内环公寓，有的人住在外环公寓，内环公寓租金更高，而分配到内环公寓的人比分配到外环公寓的人更加不愿意为住一套公寓支付更多的钱。

分析：由于经济学教材自身的学科属性，教材中常常出现较长的句子，在遇到这类句子的时候不应当害怕，句子结构就如同房屋，当中一定会有如同承重墙一般，起到主要支撑作用的成分，而这些成分通常就是句子的主语和谓语成分。找到之后，先判断句子是否存在并列句或者主从句，如果有，判断从句或并列句内部的主谓结构，最后去掉与主谓相关的限制短语或分句。逐步切割后，就可以捋顺句子各部分之间的联系，并将之消化，用中文反哺出来。上面两句话都有较多的从句，可以按照上述方法对这些句子做出切分，以助于理解。例4中，第一个句子的主语虽然长，但"although"所引导的部分全部是表让步的分句，真正的主语为逗号后的"they"，谓语则为"result in"，而在"although"这一分句中，也很容易能找到"competitive market"以及"discrimination monopolist"是主语，"generate"则为谓语。同样，例5也可以如法炮制，首先可以发现这个句子有一个"that"从句，也有一个"who"从句，粗略判断这里是需要切分的地方。接下来，可以发现"argument"是句子的主语，"rests on"为谓语。虽然这两句话都有一定长度，但在剖析完句子成分之后，理解起来是没有什么困难的。

在翻译经济学教材时最后一个要注意的地方在于学习经济学相关的知识，比如"escape clause""concessionary loan"等术语就不应译为"逃跑条款""特许贷款"。对合同等经济文件有了解的同学应当能够认识到它们指的是"免责条款"以及"优惠贷款"。类似的还有"engagement（委任）""non-disclosure（保密）"等。

第三节　常用词汇与表达

原文	译文
equilibrium	均衡
oligopoly	寡头
quasiconvex	凸函数
Nash equilibrium	纳什均衡
Slutsky equation	斯拉茨基方程
Strong axiom of revealed preference	强显现偏好公设
sunk cost	沉没成本
shoeleather cost	皮鞋成本
prisoner's dilemma	囚徒困境
deadweight losses	无谓损失

续表

原文	译文
tying	搭售
homo economics	理性经济人
externality	外部性
excludability	排他性
elasticity	弹性
complements	互补品
Giffen goods	吉芬物品
Game Theory	博弈论
asymmetric information	不对称信息
vertical intercept	纵截距
horizontal intercept	横截距
affine function	仿射函数
linear function	线性函数
residual claimant	剩余索取权
incentive compatibility constrain	激励相容约束

第四节 译 文 赏 析

一、英译汉

原文	译文
Because the market supply curve holds other things constant, the curve shifts when one of the factors changes. For example, suppose the price of sugar falls. Sugar is an input into producing ice cream, so the fall in the price of sugar makes selling ice cream more profitable. This raises the supply of ice cream: At any given price, sellers are now willing to produce a larger quantity. The supply curve for ice cream shifts to the right.	由于市场供给曲线假设其他条件不变,当这些因素中的一个因素变动时,该曲线将发生移动[1]。例如,假设糖的价格下降了。糖是生产冰淇淋的一种投入品,所以,糖的价格下降使销售冰淇淋更加有利可图。这就增加了冰淇淋的供给:在任何一种既定价格水平下,卖者现在愿意生产更多的冰淇淋。冰淇淋的供给曲线向右移动。

续表

原文	译文
Figure 7 illustrates shifts in supply. Any change that raises quantity supplied at every price, such as a fall in the price of sugar, shifts the supply curve to the right and is called an increase in supply. Similarly, any change that reduces the quantity supplied at every price shifts the supply curve to the left and is called a decrease in supply.	图 7 说明了供给曲线的移动。每一种价格水平下的供给量都增加的任何一种变动（例如糖的价格下降），都会使供给曲线向右移动，我们称之为供给增加[2]。同样，使每一种价格水平下的供给量都减少的任何一种变动，都会使供给曲线向左移动，我们称之为供给减少。
There are many variables that can shift the supply curve. Here are some of the most important.	有许多变量会使供给曲线移动，以下是一些最重要的变量。
Input Prices: To produce their output of ice cream, sellers use various inputs: cream, sugar, flavoring, ice-cream machines, the buildings in which the ice cream is made, and the labor of workers to mix the ingredients and operate the machines. When the price of one or more of these inputs rises, producing ice cream is less profitable, and firms supply less ice cream. If input prices rise substantially, a firm might shut down and supply no ice cream at all. Thus, the supply of a good is negatively related to the price of the inputs used to make the good.	投入品价格：为了生产冰淇淋，卖者使用各种投入品：奶油、糖、香料、冰淇淋机、生产冰淇淋的厂房，以及搅拌各种材料并操作机器的工人的劳动。当这些投入品中的一种或几种价格上升时，生产冰淇淋就变得不那么有利可图，企业供给的冰淇淋就会变少[3]。如果投入品价格大幅度上升，企业可能会停止营业，根本不再供给冰淇淋。因此，一种物品的供给量与生产这种物品所用的投入品价格负相关。
Technology: The technology for turning inputs into ice cream is another determinant of supply. The invention of the mechanized ice-cream machine, for example, reduced the amount of labor necessary to make ice cream. By reducing firms' costs, the advance in technology raised the supply of ice cream.	技术：把各种投入品变为冰淇淋的技术也是供给量的另一个决定因素。例如，机械化冰淇淋机的发明减少了生产冰淇淋所必需的劳动量。这一技术通过降低企业的生产成本而增加了冰淇淋的供给量。
Expectations: The amount of ice cream a firm supplies today may depend on its expectations about the future. For example, if a firm expects the price of ice cream to rise in the future, it will put some of its current production into storage and supply less to the market today.	预期：企业现在的冰淇淋供给量还取决于其对未来的预期。例如，如果预期未来冰淇淋的价格会上升，企业就会把现在生产的一些冰淇淋储存起来，而减少当前市场的供给。
Number of Sellers: In addition to the preceding factors, which influence the behavior of individual sellers, market supply depends on the number of these sellers. If Ben or Jerry were to retire from the ice-cream business, the supply in the market would fall.	卖者的数量：除了以上影响单个卖者行为的因素以外，市场供给还取决于这些卖者的数量。如果 Ben 或 Jerry 退出冰淇淋经营市场，市场供给将减少。

原文	译文
Summary: The supply curve shows what happens to the quantity supplied of a good when its price varies, holding constant all the other variables that influence sellers. When one of these other variables changes, the supply curve shifts. Table 2 lists the variables that influence how much producers choose to sell of a good.	总结：供给曲线表示在其他所有影响卖者的变量保持不变的情况下，一种物品的价格变动时，该物品的供给量会发生什么变动。当这些变量中的一个变动时，供给曲线就会发生移动[4]。表 2 列出了影响生产者出售物品数量的变量。

难点 1

原文：Because the market supply curve holds other things constant, the curve shifts when one of the factors changes.

译文一：由于市场供给曲线假设其他条件不变，当这些因素中的一个因素变动时，该曲线将发生移动。

译文二：由于市场供给曲线使得其他因素不变，当其中一个因素改变时，曲线随之移动。

分析：这一段话选自《经济学原理：微观部分》第二部分，主要介绍经济是如何运作的。第一句的重点在于"holds other things constant"。译文一将"holds constant"增译出了"假设"的含义，译文二则是直译。这里需要考察文本所要达到的目的，由于《经济学原理：微观部分》是一本设计给初学者的课本，用词应当更加口语化一些，因此这里译为"使得"比"假设"更合适。此外，根据汉语语料的查询结果来看，"假设"的主语一般为人称代词，如"你、我、他"，或某些作代词使用的名词，如"某某学者假设""某某记者假设"。用某一无生命的名词，如"市场供给曲线假设"则不符合中国人的表达习惯。

难点 2

原文：Any change that raises quantity supplied at every price, such as a fall in the price of sugar, shifts the supply curve to the right and is called an increase in supply.

译文：每一种价格水平下的供给量都增加的任何一种变动（例如糖的价格下降），都会使供给曲线向右移动，我们称之为供给增加。

分析：原句的结构中，"any change"是主语，"that"引导定语从句，"such as"作为插入成分举例说明何种变动，"shifts"是谓语，"supply curve"则为宾语，"to the right"为结果状语，"and"后是一个复合句。译文的处理方式为，将"such as"引导的插入成分用括号括起来，起到解释说明的作用。且在复合句中的"is called…"则使用的主被动转换的翻译技巧，增译了"我们"使之更加符合汉语表达习惯。

难点 3

原文：When the price of one or more of these inputs rises, producing ice cream is less profitable, and firms supply less ice cream.

译文：当这些投入品中的一种或几种价格上升时，生产冰淇淋就变得不那么有利可图，企业供给的冰淇淋就会变少。

分析：除了句法上的安排之外，还可以注意一下词汇上的英汉转换。这句话最关键的点在于"profitable"，意为"有益的，可得利的"。中文存在可以对应的四字格"有利可图"的时候，选用四字格更符合中文的表达习惯。

难点 4

原文：The supply curve shows what happens to the quantity supplied of a good when its price varies, holding constant all the other variables that influence sellers. When one of these other variables changes, the supply curve shifts.

译文：供给曲线表示在其他所有影响卖者的变量保持不变的情况下，一种物品的价格变动时，该物品的供给量会发生什么变动。当这些变量中的一个变动时，供给曲线就会发生移动。

分析：这段话体现了经济学教材注重逻辑的特点，该句使用了"when"引导的时间状语从句，并运用"holding"分词等方式来展现一个变量改变时，另一个变量的变化情况。特别要注意的是"holding"分词的翻译方法，由于英语的衔接是显性的，很容易发现这里是用分词作条件状语。由于状语在汉语中通常放在句子前面，因此在翻译时需要调整语序，译为"在其他所有影响卖者的变量保持不变的情况下……"。这样不仅更加符合汉语的表达习惯，也更加简洁明了。

二、汉译英

原文	译文
作为一种以巨大经济力量为支撑的建筑物，摩天大楼常常被民众和政客视为展示经济繁荣、社会进步的标志。有些经济学家则持完全相反的看法，认为摩天大楼的出现，特别是摩天大楼的纪录被刷新，往往预示着经济即将衰退。	For politicians and the general public at large, skyscrapers, gigantic buildings backed by huge economic strength, are a symbol of economic prosperity and social progress[1]. Contrary to this popular belief, some economists argue that the emergence of skyscrapers and those reaching new heights in particular, would more often than not precede economic downturns[2].

续表

原文	译文
就像日有昼夜、季有冬夏一样，经济也是存在景气周期的。任何商品的价格都会受到供需关系的影响。否极泰来，盛极而衰，低廉的利率、膨胀的需求、上涨的资本价格，以及大多数人盲目乐观的心态所集合产生的"黄金状态"构成了摩天大楼的需求，但这种状态是不可持续的。	Just as day follows night in a 24-hour period and seasonal variations occur in a year, the economy undergoes a boom-to-bust cycle, and all commodity prices respond to the forces of supply and demand[3]. As the Chinese saying goes, anything that reaches its climax returns cyclically to its opposite extreme. A market demand for the construction of skyscrapers emerges from what is called the "golden climate", which is created by a combination of factors: lower interest rates, greater demand, rising capital prices, and a general mood of excessive optimism among the vast majority of the general public. However, such a "golden climate" never lasts long[4].
所以，通常是在经济已经步入衰退的时候，摩天大楼才刚刚竣工；在它真正投入使用的时候，经济很可能已经深陷困境。这就导致了经济危机总是与摩天大楼的兴建如影随形，也常使全球第一建筑成为逝去繁荣的纪念碑。	It is therefore quite common that no sooner is a skyscraper completed than the economy enters a recession and then is thrown into deeper distress by the time the skyscraper is put to use. This best reveals the inseparable correlation between skyscrapers and economic downturns. Indeed, the world's tallest buildings often stand as monuments to prosperity[5].

难点 1

原文：作为一种**以巨大经济力量为支撑**的建筑物，摩天大楼常常**被民众和政客视为**展示经济繁荣、社会进步的标志。

译文：For politicians and the general public at large, skyscrapers, gigantic buildings **backed by** huge economic strength, are a symbol of economic prosperity and **social progress**.

分析：本句主要有两点需要注意，首先是中英文语言习惯的问题。英语有着"形合"的特征，其衔接手段通常是显性的，汉语则倾向于按照句子内部的顺序和内在关系来组织。因此在看到这句话的时候我们首先应该想到，这句话强调的是人们对摩天大楼的看法，即人们通常把摩天大楼和经济繁荣联系在一起，原因是建起一座摩天大楼，需要耗费相当大的人力物力，也就是说某一国家或者地区必须有着强劲的经济实力才行。而后文实际上对这种看法进行了批判，因此在翻译的时候，应当调整句子顺序，强调这是人们的看法。因此将"for politicians and general public"放在前面。第二点在于"支撑"这处含有隐喻意味的表达。这里作者想说的是，建造摩天大楼的背景是巨大的经济力量，因此可以翻译为"backed by"。

难点 2

原文：有些经济学家则持完全相反的看法，认为摩天大楼的出现，特别是摩天大楼的**纪录被刷新**，往往预示着经济即将衰退。

译文：Contrary to this popular belief, some economists argue that the emergence of skyscrapers and those **reaching new heights** in particular, would more often than not precede economic downturns.

分析：这一句的难点在于如何处理"摩天大楼的纪录被刷新"这一表达。译文巧妙地回避了汉语中"刷新纪录"这一主谓表达，而是以分词的形式表达了破纪录的摩天大楼的意思。而且在汉语中，人们更常用概括词、上位词或是抽象词，翻译为英文时应当注意将其具体化。在这里，我们就应当避免将"纪录"直译为record。摩天大楼所打破的纪录，显然应当是高度，因此应当将其翻译为"reaching new heights"。后文"预示经济即将衰退"译为了"precede economic downturns"，也是同样的道理。

难点 3

原文：就像**日有昼夜、季有冬夏**一样，经济也是存在景气周期的。

译文：Just as **day follows night in a 24-hour period and seasonal variations occur in a year**, the economy undergoes a boom-to-bust cycle, and all commodity prices respond to the forces of supply and demand.

分析：受文化传统影响，四字格因其朗朗上口的特点，一直以来都备受中国人的推崇，因此也就成为了译者不得不面对的翻译难点，译者需要仔细体会四字格所表达的含义才能将其翻译为恰当且通顺的英文句子。在这句话中，"日有昼夜，季有冬夏"强调的是经济活动有其自身规律。这种规律就像昼夜交替、春夏秋冬一样，是有着固定顺序且不为人的意志所转移的。如果译者将其简单翻译为"a day has day and night, a year has four seasons"，不仅不知所云，甚至不合逻辑。因此，译者可以将其意译为一天有24小时，一年有不同季节。

难点 4

原文：**否极泰来，盛极而衰**，低廉的利率、膨胀的需求、上涨的资本价格，以及大多数人盲目乐观的心态所集合产生的"黄金状态"构成了摩天大楼的需求，但这种状态是不可持续的。

译文：**As the Chinese saying goes, anything that reaches its climax returns cyclically to its opposite extreme**. A market demand for the construction of skyscrapers emerges from what is called the "golden climate", which is created by a combination of factors: lower interest rates, greater demand, rising capital prices, and a general mood of excessive optimism among the vast majority of the general public. However, such a "golden climate" never lasts long.

分析：与上一个例子类似，这句话使用了"否极泰来，盛极而衰"这样的中文特有成语，通常来说文化负载词很难在目标语中找到对应的词语，因此译者需要体会作者使用这一词汇的用意，并辅以一定的解释。"否极泰来"的重点分别是"否"和"泰"，在《周易》中，前者是不好的卦象，而后者则是吉兆。不好的东西到了极致，幸运就会降临。"盛极而衰"则是从另一个方面表达了类似的意思。而这种盛衰、吉凶之间的转化，在中国人看来有其自身的规律。因此，译者在这里用了阐释的方法，将这两个成语解释为"anything that reaches its climax returns cyclically to its opposite extreme"，不仅表达了两者之间的转化，也阐明这样的转化是周期性、循环性的。

难点 5

原文：这就导致了经济危机总是与摩天大楼的兴建**如影随形**，也常使全球第一建筑成为逝去繁荣的纪念碑。

译文：This best reveals the **inseparable correlation** between skyscrapers and economic downturns. Indeed, the world's tallest buildings often stand as monuments to prosperity.

分析："如影随形"这一成语不仅是文化负载词，也以形影之间的关系来暗喻两件事物之间的相关关系。译者在翻译时应当注意避免将其直译为"shadow and body"，而只需要强调两者之间关系紧密、不可分割就可以了。此外，也正是因为作者在这里强调两者之间密不可分的关系，这种关系也应该作为重点放在句子的主干部分。这里译者就以"inseparable correlation"为宾语放在了主干部分，同时由于前句强调关系，后句以纪念碑来形容全球第一建筑，两者之间关系并不紧密。译者便将其切分为两个句子，并以"stand"形象表达了这一比喻关系。

翻 译 练 习

一、词组翻译

exogenous variable
endogenous variable
the Optimization Principle
economic agents
reservation price
competitive market
comparative statics
monopoly

discriminating monopolist
excess demand
Pareto efficiency
consumption bundle
budget set
numeracies price
budget line
opportunity cost
strict preference
indifferent
value tax
quantity tax

二、句子翻译

(一)英译汉

1. At this price, each consumer who is willing to pay at least p* is able to find an apartment to rent, and each landlord will be able to rent apartment at the going market price.

2. A supply shock is an event that directly affects firms' costs of production and thus the prices they charge; it shifts the economy's aggregate-supply curve and, as a result, the Phillips curve.

3. Ogre to Slay? Outsource It to Chinese

4. The gain from trade are most obvious if the rancher can produce only meat and the farmer can produce only potatoes. In one scenario, the rancher and the farmer could choose to have nothing to do with each other.

5. A subsidy is the opposite of a tax. In the case of a quantity subsidy, the government gives an amount to the consumer that depends on the amount of the good purchased.

(二)汉译英

1. 图中所示的曲线称为需求曲线(demand curve):将需求量和价格关联起来的曲线。

2. 经济学家将一个人愿意支付的最高价格称为该人的保留价格(reservation price)。

3. 如果想租住公寓的人很多而且他们的保留价格相差很小,可以认为需求曲线是一条向下倾斜的平滑曲线,如图1.2所示。

4. 我们考虑的情形是这样的,即市场中有很多的房东,他们公开出租公寓,价格当然是越高越好,这种类型的市场称为竞争性市场。

5. 不管租金如何变化,公寓的数量都是既定的,也就是说当时所有的公寓都是现成的,拎包即可入住。

三、语篇翻译

(一)英译汉

All governments—from the federal government in Washington, D. C., to the local governments in small towns—use taxes to raise revenue for public projects, such as roads, schools, and national defense. Because taxes are such an important policy instrument, and because they affect our lives in many ways, we return to the study of taxes several times throughout this book. In this section, we begin our study of how taxes affect the economy.

To set the stage for our analysis, imagine that a local government decides to hold an annual ice-cream celebration—with a parade, fireworks, and speeches by town officials. To raise revenue to pay for the event, the town decides to place a \$0.50 tax on the sale of ice-cream cones. When the plan is announced, our two lobbying groups swing into action. The American Association of Ice-Cream Eaters claims that consumers of ice cream are having trouble making ends meet, and it argues that sellers of ice cream should pay the tax. The National Organization of Ice-Cream Makers claims that its members are struggling to survive in a competitive market, and it argues that buyers of ice cream should pay the tax. The town mayor, hoping to reach a compromise, suggests that half the tax be paid by the buyers and half be paid by the sellers.

To analyze these proposals, we need to address a simple but subtle question:

When the government levies a tax on a good, who actually bears the burden of the tax? The people buying the good? The people selling the good? Or if buyers and sellers share the tax burden, what determines how the burden is divided? Can the government simply legislate the division of the burden, as the mayor is suggesting, or is the division determined by more fundamental market forces? The term tax incidence refers to how the burden of a tax is distributed among the various people who make up the economy. As we will see, some surprising lessons about tax incidence can be learned by applying the tools of supply and demand.

How Taxes on Sellers Affect Market Outcomes

We begin by considering a tax levied on sellers of a good. Suppose the local government passes a law requiring sellers of ice-cream cones to send \$0.50 to the government for each cone they sell. How does this law affect the buyers and sellers of ice cream? To answer this question, we can follow the three steps in Chapter 4 for analyzing supply and demand: (1) We decide whether the law affects the supply curve or demand curve. (2) We decide which way the curve shifts. (3) We examine how the shift affects the equilibrium price and quantity.

Step One: The immediate impact of the tax is on the sellers of ice cream.

Because the tax is not levied on buyers, the quantity of ice cream demanded at any given price is the same; thus, the demand curve does not change. By contrast, the tax on sellers makes the ice-cream business less profitable at any given price, so it shifts the supply curve.

Step Two: Because the tax on sellers raises the cost of producing and selling ice cream, it reduces the quantity supplied at every price. The supply curve shifts to the left (or, equivalently, upward).

In addition to determining the direction in which the supply curve moves, we can also be precise about the size of the shift. For any market price of ice cream, the effective price to sellers—the amount they get to keep after paying the tax—is $0.50 lower. For example, if the market price of a cone happened to be $2.00, the effective price received by sellers would be $1.50. Whatever the market price, sellers will supply a quantity of ice cream as if the price were $0.50 lower than it is. Put differently, to induce sellers to supply any given quantity, the market price must now be $0.50 higher to compensate for the effect of the tax. Thus, as shown in Figure 6, the supply curve shifts upward from S1 to S2 by the exact size of the tax ($0.50).

Step Three: Having determined how the supply curve shifts, we can now compare the initial and the new equilibriums. The figure shows that the equilibrium price of ice cream rises from $3.00 to $3.30, and the equilibrium quantity falls from 100 to 90 cones. Because sellers sell less and buyers buy less in the new equilibrium, the tax reduces the size of the ice-cream market.

Implications: We can now return to the question of tax incidence: Who pays the tax? Although sellers send the entire tax to the government, buyers and sellers share the burden. Because the market price rises from $3.00 to $3.30 when the tax is introduced, buyers pay $0.30 more for each ice-cream cone than they did without the tax. Thus, the tax makes buyers worse off. Sellers get a higher price ($3.30) from buyers than they did previously, but the effective price after paying the tax falls from $3.00 before the tax to $2.80 with the tax ($3.30 - $0.50 = $2.80).

(二) 汉译英

帕累托效率

在比较不同经济制度的结果优劣时,可以选择一种称为帕累托效率(Pareto efficiency)或经济效率的概念作为评价标准。我们首先定义帕累托改进(Pareto improvement)这个概念:如果我们能找到一种方法,这种方法能使一些人的状况变好但同时又未使其他人的状况变差,则我们就得到了一个帕累托改进。如果某种配置存在帕累托改进,则将这种配置称为帕累托无效率(Pareto inefficient);如果某种配置不存在这样的帕累托改进,则称为帕累托有效率(Pareto efficient)。

帕累托无效率的配置是不受欢迎的,因为存在着利己但不损人的改进方法。这种配置方式也许有其他的优点,但帕累托无效率对它给予了致命一击:既然可以设法让一些人的状况变得更好的同时又不损害别人的利益,为什么不这么做?

帕累托效率思想是经济学中最重要的思想之一,在以后章节我们将详细研究。这个思想有很多微妙的细节,我们要慢慢分析,但是目前我们仍可以粗略地介绍一下它的思想。请看下面。

假设我们将内环公寓和外环公寓随机分配给租房者,但允许他们互相转租。有些想住在内环的人运气太差,最终被分配到外环。但是这些人可以从不想住在内环但又被分配在内环的人手里重新租得内环公寓。哪些人不想住在内环?认为内环公寓不值那么多租金的那些人。如果内外环公寓是随机分配的,必然有些人想转租公寓,只要他得到的补偿足够高。

例如,假设 A 分得了内环公寓但他认为它只值 200 美元租金,B 被分配到了外环,但他愿意以 300 美元的价格租入 A 的内环公寓。这种情形下存在着"交易收益(gain from trade)",因为如果 B 向 A 支付某些租金(200 美元到 300 美元之间),从而二人交换公寓后,两人的状况都变好了。具体的交易额并不重要。重要的是支付意愿最高的人得到了内环公寓——否则,只要有两人对内环公寓的评价不同,就可能存在着转租的可能。

假设所有的自愿交易都已进行完毕,因此交易的所有收益都被取尽,这种情形下的配置必然是帕累托有效率的。如若不然,就会存在某种交易,这种交易使得两人的状况变得更好但又不损害其他人的利益,可是如果是这样,就意味着交易的收益没有被取尽,与我们的假设矛盾。如果某种配置使得所有自愿交易已进行完毕,则这种配置必然是帕累托有效率的。

如果你注意到下列事实,你就能很快得到答案:对于内环公寓,内环的人的保留价格必然高于外环的人的保留价格;否则,他们就会交易从而使双方的状况都变好。因此,如果有 S 个内环公寓用于出租,则保留价格最高的前 S 名租房者最终得到了公寓。这种配置是帕累托有效率的,除此之外所有其他的配置都不是有效率的,因为其他任何配置方式都会存在交易,从而使至少两个人的状况变好,同时又没有损害其他人的利益。

◎ 参考文献

[1] Christiane Nord. 翻译的文本分析模式:理论、方法及教学应用[M].李明栋,译.厦门:厦门大学出版社,2013.

[2] Hal R. Varian. *Intermediate Microeconomics* [M]. New York:W. W. Norton & Company,2014.

[3] Hal R. Varian. *Microeconomics Analysis* [M]. New York:W. W. Norton & Company,1992.

[4] Hal R. Varian. 微观经济学:现代观点[M].费方域,朱保华等,译.上海:格致出版社,上海人民出版社,2014.

[5] N. Gregory Mankiw. 经济学原理[M].梁小民,梁砾,译.北京:北京大学出版社,2015.

[6] 卢敏.英语笔译实务[M].北京:外文出版社,2017.

第六章　经济学经典文献翻译

> ☞**思考题**
> 1. 如何定义经济学经典文献翻译？
> 2. 在翻译中应如何处理英文的隐喻？
> 3. 在翻译中应如何处理中文的文化负载词？

第一节　经济学经典文献文本分析

一、经济学经典文献定义

经济学经典文献是经济学领域的学者用艰苦创作凝结而成的，能够深刻反映人类文明，并经过一定时间考验的伟大成果。经典文献是文献总体中的少数，但它是优选的信息源，具有巨大的艺术及科学价值。阅读经典文献不是为了系统掌握某一学科的理论体系，而是从中感知原汁原味的经济学，领略经济学大师的迷人风采，体会经济学的深邃思想、严密逻辑和博大精深，经济学经典文献是攀登经济学巅峰的必由之路。

因此，经济学经典文献不是指书籍、论文等特定的形式，而是指著作本身带来的影响力。本章的经典文献翻译主要指西方经济学经典文献，因此讲述以英译汉为主。

二、西方经济学经典文献语言特点

(一) 文体风格为正式体

语言是人类最重要的交际工具，而语言活动都在相应的语境中进行，语境又反过来影响语言的使用。在漫长的人类社会语言交际过程中，人们在各种社会活动领域，针对不同对象、不同环境，有不同的特定的语言表达体式，这就是语体。美国语言学家马丁·裘斯(Martin Joos)在《五只时钟》(*The Five Clocks*)中将语言的使用分成5个级别：冷冻体(frozen style)、正式体(formal style)、询议体(consultative style)、随便体(casual style)和亲密体(intimate style)。其中，正式体不如冷冻体庄重严肃，但也适用于比较正式、重要的场合,因此,经济学经典文献的语言属于正式体,用词严谨,逻辑清晰有条理,思维准确严密。

(1)在表达"让步"概念时,正式文体常使用 yet,however,nevertheless,in spite of (despite),notwithstanding 等词语。

例 1

I shall venture, **nevertheless**, to put further stress upon two points, which may be among those which have a familiar ring, but which appear sometimes to be in danger of being forgotten.

(2)在构成"方式状语"时,正式文体则常借用由介词和与该同根的词构成的介词短语。例如:

例 2

Thus change becomes progressive and propagates itself **in a cumulative way**.

(3)在表达"原因""后果"等概念时,正式文体常用 on account of,accordingly,thus,hence,consequently,owing to (the fact that)等词或词组,且较常运用分词短语、独立主格结构等。例如:

例 3

... if **accordingly** we look too much at the individual firm or even, as I shall suggest presently, at the individual industry.

(4)由引导词 it 起始的句子(如 it is said that..)多见于正式文体;不用这一结构而表达同一意义的句子多见于非正式文体。例如:

例 4

It is encouraging to find that a fairly large number of commentators upon the volume of the American industrial product...

例 5

The successors of the early printers, **it has often been observed**, are not only the printers of today, with their own specialized establishments.

(二)频繁出现专业术语

经济学经典文献的专业性强,其在词汇上的表现主要为专业术语和表达的频繁使用。例如:

英文	中文	名词解释
property right	产权	是一个社会所强制实施的选择一种经济物品的使用的权利
externality	外部性	又称为溢出效应、外部影响、外差效应或外部效应、外部经济,指一个人或一群人的行动和决策使另一个人或一群人受损或受益的情况
cost	成本	生产某一产品所耗费的全部费用
communal ownership	共有制	一种由共同体的所有成员实施的权利,意味着共同体否定了国家或单个的市民干扰共同体内的任何人行使共有权利的权利
private ownership	私有制	意味着共同体承认所有者有权排除其他人行使所有者的私有权
state ownership	国有制	意味着只要国家是按照可接受的政治程序来决定谁不能使用国有资产,它就能排除任何人使用这一权利
economies of scale	规模经济	通过扩大生产规模而引起经济效益增加的现象
diseconomies of scale	规模不经济	因生产规模扩大而导致单位产品成本提高的现象

节选自 H. 登姆塞茨(Harold Demsetz)《关于产权的理论》(*Toward a Theory of Property Rights*)

(三)多用长句,句法关系复杂

经济活动复杂多样,该特点深刻影响着经济语言,因此也对经济学文献的翻译提出了更高的要求。经济学家必须使用科学语言来对经济活动和现象加以阐述和论证,这就要求有严谨的逻辑性。

例6

原文:But as I have used them, joined to the other half of my title, they are meant merely to dispel apprehensions, by suggesting that I do not propose to discuss any of those alluring but highly technical questions relating to the precise way in which some sort of equilibrium of supply and demand is achieved in the market for the products of industries which can increase their output without increasing their costs proportionately, or to the possible advantages of fostering the development of such industries while putting a handicap upon industries whose output can be increased only at the expense of a more than proportionate increase of costs.

(*Increasing Returns and Economic Progress*, written by Allyn A. Young)

译文:当我们把经济进步同报酬递增结合起来,就排除了这种理解。我不打算讨论那些富有诱惑力但却非常技术性的问题,即以某种精确的方式研究市场上供给和需求达到某种均衡,使某些产业能够在其成本没有按比例增长的情况下增加其产出,或者对那些只能靠成本按比例更快增长才能增加产出的产业加以限制,而使前述产业加快发展获得可能的收益。

分析:该长难句有一个宾语从句、三个定语从句和一个时间状语从句,共有108个词。乍一看不好理解，容易让人读了后面忘了前面，然而在经济学经典文献中，这种长难句比比皆是。

(四) 常用隐喻

由于经济学经典文献常常深入浅出地为读者介绍某一经济学观点，那么，为了避免语言枯燥乏味，作者常使用修辞手段来达到使语言生动的效果，吸引读者的阅读兴趣。最常见的修辞手法就是隐喻。隐喻，即利用一事物与另一事物的相似性，将指示该事物的词语从一种概念域投射(始源域)到另一个所想表达的物体的概念域(目标域)，这样就形成了认知语言学所说的认知投射或映射。简而言之，隐喻是利用具体、熟知的事物来描述、判断或推理抽象、陌生的事物，从而创造一种感染力，使表述新奇、生动和形象。隐喻有两个重要特征：(1)隐喻是奇特语言，不是一般语言。(2)隐喻是语言现象，不是思维现象。(叶子南，2013：176)麦克洛斯基(Deirdre Mc-Closkey)强调隐喻对经济学的重要作用，甚至认为"经济学就是漂浮在隐喻之上的"。隐喻有时直接把本体说成喻体，有时仅仅出现喻体，而没有出现本体，因此含义比较含蓄，需要读者根据上下文去领会，在没有深刻掌握经济学知识的情况下，读懂隐喻的寓意并非易事，而且作为译者，更重要的任务是要翻译出来。

关于经济学的隐喻现象不胜枚举。例如：

(1) "invisible hand(无形的手)"，比喻经济生活中支配资本分割的不可知的力量，后来人们又把"无形的手"引申为在经济现象背后操纵经济运行的规律。现如今，该比喻已为大部分人所接受，可以说它是经济思想史上最具代表性的隐喻之一。

(2) "gray rhino(灰犀牛)"，比喻那些显而易见却被忽略的，且影响巨大的高概率危机事件。最早出自于米歇尔·渥克的《灰犀牛：如何应对大概率危机》一书。

(3) "Black Swan Event(黑天鹅)"，比喻带来重大影响的不确定的小概率事件。出自于纳西姆·尼古拉斯·塔勒布的《黑天鹅——如何应对不可预知的未来》。

(4) "Placebo Test(安慰剂检验)"又名"Falsification Test"，取义自医学实验中的安慰剂(placebo)效应，指"病人虽然获得无效的治疗，却'预料'或'相信'治疗有效，而让病患症状得到舒缓的现象"。在微观实证计量中，我们常使用安慰剂检验做稳健性测试(robustness check)。检验核心的思想是定义一些不存在的"伪实验"，重新进行回归然后观察"伪实验"的系数是否显著，如果不显著的话，则符合我们的期望；如果显著，则意味着我们面临内生性问题的风险。

第二节　翻译知识讲解

一、英文文本翻译的难点与重点问题

(一) 词汇层面

在进行经济学文献翻译时，译者不能将原文本中令目的语读者感到陌生的概念原封不动地在译文中传递给他们，这样不仅不能将原文本作者意图准确传达给目的语读者，还会令目的语读者失去阅读的兴趣。因此，译者为了取得较好的翻译效果，可以充分考虑目的语读者的理解和接受水平，灵活运用翻译方法和技巧，保证源文本中的含义能够通过译文被有效地传递。在经济学文献中，原文作者经常借用一些属于其他领域的词汇，将它们运用在自己所要表达的经济学常识中，试图让作品中原有的复杂内容变得形象生动、浅显易懂。词汇翻译中的难点可以分为四类：对词义准确的判断和表达、专业术语、专有名词和词类转换。

1. 对词义准确的判断和表达

在翻译过程中，我们受原文表层语法结构的影响和字面意思的束缚，对约定俗成、固定搭配、成语等易产生望文生义的错误。由于经济学英语有其特殊性，因此要根据其主要词性、语法作用、词与词的搭配等来选择词义，用最恰当的词汇表达再现原文。如 bug：

We noticed tiny bugs that were all over the walls.

我们注意到墙上爬满了小虫。

a flu bug 流感

There's a stomach bug going round.

现在流行一种肠胃传染病。

There is a bug in the software.

软件有漏洞。

the travel bug 旅游狂热

I only did it to bug my parents.

我这么做只是为了让我父母心烦。

He heard that they were planning to bug his office.

他得知他们打算在他办公室安装窃听器。

可以看出，一个"bug"在不同的语境下有截然不同的意义，因此，在翻译的时候，要注意准确判断词义，并作相应的翻译。

请观察下列例句，仔细体会黑体词的翻译：

例 1

原文：Theories about what is causing the rally continue to **swirl** around the market.

（*The Price of EU Carbon Credits Soars to 14-year High*，written by Camilla Hodgson）

译文：对于导致此轮涨势的原因，各种理论继续在市场上流传。

分析："swirl"的基本意义是"盘旋、打旋"，"流传"为其衍生意义。

例 2

原文：With new facilities starting to export out of the US and China's commitment to make its economy greener, LNG could be perfect fit. There is a **wrinkle**, though.

(Coronavirus Gives China Get-out Clause for Buying US Energy, *Financial Times*)

译文：随着新设施开始从美国出口液化天然气，以及中国承诺让其经济更加环保，液化天然气可能是一个完美的选择。然而还是有一些小问题。

分析："wrinkle"一般指"皱纹、褶皱"等，但它有一个形象好用的衍生意义——"小问题"，相当于"a minor problem"。

例3

原文：The Chinese company's telecoms equipment business has faced severe political **headwinds**, while its consumer division has been affected by trade sanctions that stop its latest phones from using Google's suite of mobile phone software.

(Huawei Growth Slows After Sanctions and Political Pressure, *Financial Times*)

译文：这家中国公司的电信设备业务面临严重的政治阻力，而其消费者业务部门受到贸易制裁的影响。这些制裁禁止其新款手机使用谷歌的手机软件。

分析："headwind"是指"逆风、顶风"，例句中将其翻译为"阻力"，形象生动。

例4

原文：A widespread **propensity** to hoard money posed a problem for Say's vision.

(*The Economics*)

译文：人们普遍喜欢囤积货币，这对萨伊的观点构成了挑战。

分析："propensity"原本表示性格、行为方面的"倾向、习性"，比如受自然欲望驱使而来的习性。如今，更多的是用来表示某种"倾向、嗜好、癖好"，强调源于某种天生的或固有的无法控制的渴望。

2. 专业术语翻译

郑述谱认为："术语具备多重属性；学者从不同角度、不同学科出发，其属性也就各不相同。"首先我们对于术语进行大体的定义：它是指特定领域对一些特定事物的统一的称谓。那么，作为一种专业概念，其中涵盖了不止一种内在特征，译者不能只通过某个单一词义或者词组来传达作者想要表达的特定特征与意义。文本中的术语亦是如此，它在文本中具备的意义可能在其他文本中就截然不同。那么，如何有效处理这些术语？笔者首先考虑到的是其社会约定性。比如，"硬货币""牛市"或者"面值"，读者不能仅凭字面意义就能理解该类术语。所以在处理其意义的时候，我们就需要规定，"某信息指称的……而非它本身可能传达的……"，这样一来，就可以充分方便没有经济学基础的读者阅读经济学经典文献。

例5

原文：Unlike the standard **prisoners' dilemma**, in the iterated prisoners' dilemma the defection strategy is counter-intuitive and fails badly to predict the behavior of human players.

(*The Iterated Prisoners' Dilemma*, written by Graham Kendall, Xin Yao and Siang Yew Chong)

译文：与标准的囚徒困境(一种经济现象，博弈论中的代表性例子)不同，在重复性囚徒困境中，叛逃策略是反直觉的，不能很好地预测人类玩家的行为。

分析："囚徒困境"概念来自心理学，它是博弈论中非零和博弈最具代表性的例子，但只代表个人最佳抉择，而非整个团队。虽然它本质上是一种模型，但在实际生活中，这一博弈存在于价格竞争、环境保护等诸多方面。因此，作者在文章中使用这个概念属于术语借用，他是想论述某种经济现象，根据社会约定性，译者在翻译的时候，应通过加注的方法，将其与心理学中的概念区别开来。

例 6

原文：**Regional resilience** as a conceptual framework is useful in helping us to think about regions in a dynamic, holistic and systematic way.

(*The New Oxford Handbook of Economic Geography*, written by Gordon L. Clark, Maryann P. Feldman, and Meric S. Gertler)

译文：区域复原力作为一个概念框架，可帮助我们以一种动态、整体和系统的方式来思考区域。

分析："resilience"是一个使用范围极广、众多学科都热衷于研究的时髦术语，最早源自生态学，后来被许多社会科学领域的学科用作专业术语，如经济学、地理学、管理学、社会学以及区域经济学等。在不同的学科领域，"resilience"有不同的意思。如，在生态学中，"ecological resilience"是指生态系统通过抵抗破坏和迅速恢复来应对扰动或干扰的能力，译为"生态复原"；在组织学中，"organizational resilience"被定义为一个系统能够承受其环境变化并仍能发挥作用的能力，译为"组织弹性"；在心理学中，"psychological resilience"是指能够成功地应对危机并迅速恢复到危机前状态的能力，译为"心理韧性"。在翻译"resilience"时，首先应该坚决排除"弹性"这个译法，因为经济学中早就有了"弹性"这个专业术语，英文为"elasticity"，否则容易与经济学中的弹性概念混淆。"韧性"是较流行的译法，但是"韧性"基本上只是在物理学范围内使用，不能涵盖这一术语的全部内涵。在区域经济学领域，"regional resilience"研究一般偏重于讨论一个区域受到冲击后的反应过程、结果或反应能力以及相应的政策支持。从辞源角度分析，英文单词"resilience"来源于拉丁文词根"resilire"，意为受挫折后恢复原状(bounce back)。因此，根据规约性，将其译为"复原力"，直截了当、通俗易懂，也能让读者认定其意义。

例 7

原文：Recent literature on **regional branching** proposes that new industries emerge in regions where preexisting economic activities are technologically related to the emerging industry.

(*Regional Branching Reconsidered*:*Emergence of the Fuel Cell Industry in European Regions*,written by Anne Nygaard Tanner)

译文：最近，研究区域派生的文献提出，一些地区孕育了新产业，这些地区已有的经济活动在技术上与该产业相关。

分析："branching"一词在经济学、管理学等学科中早就存在，但是指设立分厂。"regional branching"不是指设立分厂，而是指区域内出现新的公司。中文对"regional branching"的译法大致有几种："区域（产业）分叉""区域分支""区域分化"和"区域衍生"。"区域（产业）分叉"的译法不可取，因为在新经济地理学中存在"分叉"一词，即"bifurcation"，这个英文术语也可译为"转折点"或"临界点"。该译法容易使人联想到"bifurcation"一词；"区域分支"这个译法没有揭示这个词的真正内涵，即通过技术关联性等产生新的企业；"区域分化"容易让人理解为区域之间的差别化或分异，因此此译法在内涵上不具有唯一性；"区域衍生"这个译法同样不可取，因为"衍生"在西方区域经济学中有一个专有词汇，即"spin-off"，一般指科技园孵化出的企业从园区内迁移至园区外。译成"区域衍生"会混淆"spin-off"与"branching"的区别。企业衍生是区域派生的直接来源之一。根据《汉语大词典》的解释，"派生"本指江河的源头产生出支流，引申为从一个主要事物的发展中分化出来。根据规约性，用中文"派生"一词的引申含义，读者可认定：区域派生是指一个区域由于现有企业与新出现的企业之间的技术关联性，或由于区域内企业与区域外应用新技术的市场之间的应用关联性而导致新企业的产生。

3. 专有名词翻译

专有名词指代人名、地名、官方机构名称，本章阐述的专有名词主要包含以下两类：一类是专家学者人名；另一类是官方机构名称。

根据中华人民共和国国家标准 GB/T19682-2019 翻译服务译文质量要求的规定，外国人名、地名、团体名、机构名、商标名的翻译原则如下：使用惯用译名（有特殊要求的按双方约定）；无惯用译名的，可自行翻译，必要时附注原文。

（1）专家学者人名

在翻译人名时可采用两大原则：约定俗成原则和按照英语人名本身的发音音译的规律。第一种规律是指按照被广泛和普遍使用的英语人名的翻译版本进行翻译，尽管有时这些版本不符合这些人名本身的发音。如，著名政治经济学家 Adam Smith 应翻译成"亚当·斯密"而非采用其直译——"亚当·史密斯"；第二种是音译，大多数情况下，译者都会采用。

（2）官方机构名称

官方机构和协议名称翻译的最核心原则就是准确性和社会合乎性，也就是说人们一听到这个名词的翻译就能产生联想意义，同时确信这一翻译的权威性。在这种情况下，通过查询相关官方资料便可确定其意义，译者切不可按照字面直接进行翻译。

4. 词类转换

汉语一个词类能充当的句子成分较多，一般无须改变词类；但英语一个词类能充当的句子成分较少，充当不同成分时常常要改变词类。因此，在翻译实践中，要做到既忠实于原文又符合译文的语言规范，就不能机械地按原文词类"对号入座"逐字硬译，而需要进行适当的词类转换。请看下表：

汉英词汇句法功能对照表

	汉语	英语
名词	主语；宾语；定语；状语；谓语	主语；宾语；表语；定语
形容词	定语；表语；主语；宾语；状语；谓语	宾补；表语；定语
动词	谓语；主语；宾语；定语；表语	谓语

翻译中的词类如何转译，要根据原文词义、译入语的表达习惯等而定，通常有四种情况：

（1）转译成动词

a. 名词转译成动词

b. 介词转译成动词

c. 形容词转译成动词

d. 副词转译成动词

（2）转译成名词

a. 名词派生的动词或由名词转用的动词转译成名词

b. 英语被动句式，可译成"受到/遭到……+名词"或"予以/加以……+名词结构"

（3）转译成形容词

（4）其他词类转译

a. 形容词与副词的互相转译

b. 英语动词译成汉语名词时，修饰该动词的副词往往转译成形容词。

c. 由于英汉两种语言表达方式不同，还有一些英语形容词可译为汉语副词。

以下仅举几则例子：

例 8

原文：Economic theory has suffered in the past from a failure to state clearly its assumption.

(*The Nature of Firm*, written by R. H. Coase)

译文：过去，经济理论一直因未能清楚地说明其假设而备受困扰。

分析："Failure"是名词，但是由于中英两种语言存在差异，中文多动词，因此需要改变词性，将名词转换为动词"未能"，此外，在英语写作上，用"fail to do"来表示否定含义，可让句型更为多样。

例9

原文：The words economic progress, taken by themselves, would suggest the pursuit of some philosophy of history, of some way of appraising the results of past and possible future changes in forms of economic organization and modes of economic activities.

(*Increasing Returns and Economic Progress*, written by Allyn A. Young)

译文：如果仅就经济进步这个词本身来看，它会被人们理解为研究某种历史哲学，评价经济组织形式和经济活动方式过去变迁的结果和未来可能的变迁。

分析：译者没有直译"the pursuit of"，而是同样转换了词性。对于"pursuit"的中译，译者根据不同的词组搭配，将它分别翻译为"研究"和"评价"，这种处理更符合目的语读者的阅读习惯，也在结构上更加严谨。在遇到"the+抽象名词+of"的结构时，有两种译法：(1)有动词词根常译为动词，如例句。(2)无动词词根的，增添动词。

例10

原文：The cedar logs are cut into small, pencil-length slats less than one-fourth of an inch in thickness.

(*I, Pencil*, written by Leonard E. Read)

译文：雪松圆木被切割成铅笔那么长的薄板条，只有1/4英寸厚。

分析："thickness"是名词，而翻译成中文时，如果直译为"……在厚度上是1/4英寸"，译文难免生硬，因此译者转换了词性，这样能充分保障译文的准确性和生动性。

(二) 句子层面

1. 句子形态重组

传统语法的一个核心部分就是词性，形容词修饰名词，副词修饰动词，连接词连接句子各成分。但作为译者，对语法过于毕恭毕敬，这样的翻译就如同"戴着镣铐跳舞"。事实上，是遵循源语言语法规则进行翻译，还是另辟蹊径，找到更适合目的语读者的翻译，要根据具体语境而定，不管怎么样，译者最忌讳的就是紧抱着原文的词性不放。

例11

原文：How often do we hear that modern life is so complex that government must impose its guiding hand to assure order in society?

(*I, Pencil* (preface), written by Leonard E. Read)

译文：我们是否经常听到这样的说法：现代生活极其复杂，所以，政府必须施加其指导之手以确保社会秩序？

例 12

原文：But still every person would prefer to see detection made more effective (if it were somehow possible to monitor costlessly) so that he, as part of the now more effectively producing team, could thereby realize a higher pecuniary pay and less leisure.

译文：但是，每个人仍然宁愿看到监督更为有效（如果以某种方式进行的监督是没有费用的），因此，他现在作为更为有效的生产队的一员，就可能被支付更高的现金报酬和较少的闲暇。

分析：在上面两个例句中，都出现了英语中常见的"so...that"结构来连接句子各成分，翻译为"如此……以至于"固然没有错，但是会出现翻译腔，不是最佳办法。译者要基于英语句子的意思，对原句的成分进行拆分，而后按照汉语句子结构的规律，重新组织汉语译句。

例 13

原文：But since this very broad specification gives results which are too general to be applicable to special problems...

(*Marxian Economics and Modern Economic Theory*, written by O. Lang)

译文：但由于这一非常宽泛的描述提供的结论太过笼统，因而无法应用于特殊问题……

分析："too...to"也是英语常见的词组，同样地，直译为"太……以至于……"过于生硬，该词组有一定程度上的因果关系，只要把这层关系翻译出来就可以了。

2. 句子语态重组

就句子的语态而言，英语和汉语也差别较大。英语中被动句的使用较汉语中被动句的使用要广。在翻译被动句时，既要考虑句子本身的特点和内容，又要照顾到与其他句子的衔接以及行文的需要。英语中的被动句一般可翻译为汉语的主动句、被动句以及无主句，有些还可以处理成固定短语。例如：

例 14

原文：A representative firm within the industry, maintaining its own identity and devoting itself to a given range of activities, is made to be the vehicle or medium through which the economies achieved by the industry as a whole are transmitted to the market and have their effect upon the price of the product.

(*Increasing Returns and Economic Progress*, written by Allyn A. Young)

译文：产业内的一个代表性企业，要保持自己的地位并投身于自己的经营范围，就要让自己成为纽带或中介。促使产业作为整体所达到的经济传输给市场,并对产品的价格发生影响。

分析:全句有三个被动语态:"is made to be the vehicle or medium..." "economies achieved by the industry..."和"...are transmitted to the market",如果完全按照被动语态的句式来翻译,译文的翻译腔会十分严重,所以译者采用被动转主动的方法,分别译为"让自己成为""所达到的经济"和"传输给市场"。

例 15

原文:It is generally agreed that Adam Smith, when he suggested that the division of labour leads to inventions because workmen engaged in specialized routine operations come to see better ways of accomplishing the same results, missed the main point.

(*Increasing Returns and Economic Progress*, written by Allyn A. Young)

译文:当亚当·斯密提出劳动分工导致发明的时候,人们普遍认为他没有抓住要点,因为从事某项专门操作的工人会找到更好的方法来完成同样的结果。

分析:这里的"It is generally agreed"经常被处理成固定短语,相类似的还有"It is suggested that"等,遇到类似的情况,译者可增加主语"人们"。

3. 句子语序重组

由于冠词、连词、介词等功能词的作用和非谓语动词及谓语动词等结构形式的存在,英语句子结构的一般特点是关系复杂但条理清晰。因此,要翻译好英语句子,首先要分清主次,例如简单句的主干部分、并列句的倾向性、复合句的关系性质;其次是要找出句子表述的顺序,如逻辑顺序、时间顺序以及空间顺序。然后,再根据具体的分析结构,结合汉语表达的需要综合考虑,选取翻译某一句子所需要的汉语句式、关键词语、翻译技巧、转换层次和表达顺序。此外,长句的翻译还需要适当的顺序变通,即是否要改变原文顺序以及怎样改变。就这一关系而言,可以归纳为三种基本方法(孙万彪,2010:178):

(1)顺叙法。即基本上按照原文顺序译出。

(2)逆序法。即基本上从原文结尾开始由后向前逆次译出。

(3)综合法。在尊重原文的基础上,通过重新地编码和解码,使翻译的句子符合目的语的表达习惯,达到功能对等的目的。

例 16

原文:It is generally agreed that Adam Smith, when he suggested that the division of labour leads to inventions because workmen engaged in specialized routine operations come to see better ways of accomplishing the same results, missed the main point.

(*Increasing Returns and Economic Progress*, written by Allyn A. Young)

译文：当亚当·斯密提出劳动分工导致发明的时候，人们普遍认为他没有抓住要点，因为从事某项专门操作的工人会找到更好的方法来实现同样的结果。

分析：首先，要分清主次：本句主干是"It is generally agreed that Adam Smith missed the main point"，其余的都是次要部分，然后找到句子的逻辑顺序，因此本句可采用综合法来翻译。

例17

原文：But as I have used them, joined to the other half of my title, they are meant merely to dispel apprehensions, by suggesting that I do not propose to discuss any of those alluring but highly technical questions relating to the precise way in which some sort of equilibrium of supply and demand is achieved in the market for the products of industries which can increase their output without increasing their costs proportionately, or to the possible advantages of fostering the development of such industries while putting a handicap upon industries whose output can be increased only at the expense of a more than proportionate increase of costs.

译文：但是，当我们把经济进步同报酬递增结合起来，就排除了这种理解，我不打算讨论那些富有诱惑力但却非常技术性的问题，即以某种精确的方式研究市场上供给和需求达到某种均衡，使某些产业能够在其成本没有按比例增长的情况下增加其产出或者对那些只能靠成本按比例更快增长才能增加产出的产业加以限制，而使前述产业加快发展获得可能的收益。

分析：本句属于长难句，主干是"they are meant merely to dispel apprehensions"，翻译长难句可以尝试切分句子：

①But as I have used them, joined to the other half of my title, they are meant merely to dispel apprehensions

②(apprehensions) by suggesting

③(suggesting) that I do not propose to discuss any of those alluring but highly technical questions relating to the precise way

④(the precise way) in which some sort of equilibrium of supply and demand is achieved in the market for the products of industries

⑤(industries) which can increase their output without increasing their costs proportionately, or to the possible advantages of fostering the development of such industries while putting a handicap upon industries

⑥(industries) whose output can be increased only at the expense of a more than proportionate increase of costs

在大致切分句子后，对该句的深层含义也有了一个清晰的把握，然后再根据上述步骤来翻译。

二、中文文本翻译的难点与重点问题

(一) 词汇层面

经济发展日新月异，同样地，新的经济现象和经济问题也不断涌现，因此经济类文本词汇也不断更新。词语的蕴涵意义是词语内涵的情感和联想意义，主要体现在词语的修辞色彩、问题特征、文化内涵等方面。中文词语的语言形式具有浓厚的修辞色彩，反映中华民族特有的思维模式和厚实的文化沉淀，中文经济词汇亦是如此。如"豆腐渣工程"被译为"jerry-built project"，"热钱"直译为"hot money"，如此生动、富有画面感的词汇极具中国特色，也便于人民群众的接受和理解。译者应在不影响指称意义传达的前提下，尽可能在译文中反映出原文独特的文化信息和审美价值。因此，翻译这些文化负载词给译者带来不小的挑战，再者，又该如何处理中文里常见的范畴词？

1. 文化负载词处理

语言是文化的载体，语言中的词汇是文化信息的积淀，反映出该民族的文化观和价值观。词汇意义往往带有独特的民族性，"不同文化用不同的语义范畴分解和描述世界。因此，一种文化里有的语义在另一种语言里可能就不存在"（陈宏薇，2018：76），这种现象被称为词义空缺。

例 18

原文：中行广东分行是中国首家为个人提供网上炒汇业务的银行。

（《外汇交易进阶》）

译文：The Bank of China's Guangdong Branch was the first bank in China to provide a program that allowed individuals to speculate in foreign currency online.

分析："炒汇"又称"汇价"，指一国货币以另一国货币表示的价格，或者说是两国货币间的比价。综合来说，炒汇是一个投资行为。"炒"有两个意思，一是把东西放在锅里搅拌着弄熟，这也是为多数人所熟知的意思；二是倒买倒卖。很显然，"炒汇"指的是第二个意思，所以要舍弃"炒"的语言形式和字面意义，着重传达其文化信息，译者可采用意译的策略来翻译该词语。

例 19

原文：由此可见，克强指数能够更加真实、更加灵敏地反映经济运行情况。

（《且说"克强指数"》）

译文：As a result, the Keqiang index provides a more realistic and sensitive picture of economic performance.

分析："克强指数（Keqiang index）"最早出现于英国著名杂志《经济学人》，全称为"李克强指数（Li Keqiang index）"。是该杂志在 2010 年推出的用于评估中国 GDP 增长量的指标，源于李克强总理2007年任职辽宁省委书记时，喜欢通过耗电量、铁路货运量和贷款发放量三个指标分析当时辽宁省经济状况。遇到以人物命名的理论、思想等，一般采用直译的策略。

例20

原文：2011年新年伊始，世行宣布将在香港市场发行5亿元人民币"点心债券"，表明中国可以而且正在尝试从这个方面堵塞权力流失，巩固乃至扩大自己对国际金融组织来之不易的话语权。

（《融资渠道也是影响力》）

译文：The Bank's announcement at the start of 2011 that it would issue a 500 million RMB "Dim Sum Bond" in the Hong Kong market shows that China can and is attempting to plug the power drain in this area and to consolidate and even expand its hard-won voice in international financial organizations.

分析："点心债券"是在香港发行的、以人民币计价的债券，又称"人民币计价债券"。人民币计价债券在香港发行量很小，就像点心一样味美但又吃不饱，因此被称为"点心债券"。"点心"是中国所特有的，其在英语文化中是完全缺失，因此可以采用音译法来将这些具有特殊文化内涵的词语"移植"到英语文化中去。

2. 范畴词处理

范畴词表示人或事物分类范畴的词语；常用在具体词的后面，对其进行分类总括，以便与其他词语搭配，具有概括意义。在汉语中，有些范畴词只是重复地概括已表达的意思，但它们在汉语语法上却是不可缺少的词，如"问题""环境""工作""状态""情况"等。这类词语表明事物的范畴或属性，大多没有实质内容。若把它们搬到英语中势必造成冗余，因此应该把它们省略不译。

对于汉语范畴词的英译，有两种方法：省译使表达抽象化和转译使表达具体化。

（1）省译使表达抽象化

将那些不必要的范畴词省去不译，再将其前面或后面的名词译成相应的英语抽象名词，化具体为抽象，贴近、自然地再现源语信息从而使译文符合英语的抽象表达习惯。

例21

原文：重工业的快速发展，不仅使大量资源被迅速消耗，而且环境污染问题也日益严重。

（《新中国成立初期工业化道路的选择及其影响》）

译文：The rapid development of heavy industry has not only led to the rapid depletion of large amounts of resources, but also to an increasingly serious problem of environmental pollution.

分析：范畴词前的名词"环境污染"译成抽象名词"environmental pollution"，范畴词"问题"略去不译，而原文意义丝毫未损。

（2）转译使表达具体化

英语多用抽象表达法，但这并不意味着英语就不用具体化表达手段。同样，汉语中有些范畴词的含义并不都是具体的，而是具有抽象意义。对于这种范畴词，译者可用英语具体化表达法来处理，这样使译文更自然流畅。

例22

原文：……欢欣之情溢于言表。

(《回顾与思考：共和国经济建设之路》)

译文：…his joy was palpable.

分析：范畴词"之情"连同它前面的名词"欢欣"一起构成一个抽象概念，译者运用具体化方法将其译成英语的具体名词"joy"，这样就使译文显得形象生动。

第三节 常用词汇与表达

原文	译文
实证科学	normative science
规范科学	regulative science
法定最低工资	legal minimum wage
实证分析	positive analysis
工资管制	wage control
关税	tariff
规模经济	scale economy
生产要素	production factor
定额税	quota tax
完全竞争	perfect competition
边际成本	marginal cost
需求曲线	demand curve
不完全竞争	imperfect competition
垄断竞争	monopolistic competition
新古典经济理论	new classical economics

第四节 译 文 赏 析

一、汉译英

原文	译文
本次三中全会公报中，59次提及"改革"，超过以往历届。这透露出了改革的艰难、迫切以及决心。从哪里改起？市场上众说纷纭。此次会议给出的"完善现代市场体系"等15个改革要点，给予了回应，也宣告了新的改革时代的启程。具体来讲，展望未来，中国市场经济体制的进一步升级值得期待。	In this Third Plenum Communique, the "reform" has been mentioned for 59 times, outnumbering the previous, which showed the reform hardship, urgency and resolution[1]. Where should we start the reform? People have different opinions about it. In response to this issue, this conference proposed the fifteen reform points including "improving modern market system", and also declared the beginning of new era of reform. Specifically, by looking into the future, the further upgrading of China market economic system is worthy to looking forward.
中国市场经济体制的确立，从1993年的十四届三中全会吹响号角。经过20年的发展，经济体制变革的红利，毋庸置疑地惠及了绝大多数中国人民，并且对世界经济格局产生了深远的影响。尽管过去20年中国市场化进程中积累了诸多的问题，尽管在改革的过程中，公众受益程度存在差别，但中国迈向市场经济的进程，相信已经是无人能改变的航向。这就迫切需要以更大的改革决心，化解改革中存在的问题，开启新的改革时代。	The Third Plenary Session of the Fourteenth Central Committee of the Party in 1993 blew the horn for the establishment of China market economy system[2]. Through the development of twenty years, the bonus of economic system reform definitely benefits a large number of people and exerts a deep influence on world economic pattern. Although there are still many problems in marketization over the past twenty years and differences in the degree of public benefit, the process of China proceeding to market economy is believed to be unchangeable. This forces us to solve the problems in the reform and open a new era of reform with more determined resolution.
如今回头看，可以说，过去20年的中国市场经济建设，是推动中国经济保持高速增长，成为世界第二大经济体的根本原因；但也不能否认，除了制度红利之外，还与加入WTO、积极融入世界经济体系的"全球化红利"密切相关。对于中国而言，世界已经逐渐变为"平的"，后发优势正在褪去。而今迈步从头越，升级尚不完善的市场经济体制，已经时不我待。要升级，就要勇于面对目前市场经济体制中存在的问题，并逐一克服。	Looking back, it can be said that China's market economy construction over the past twenty years is the fundamental reason why China has maintained rapid economic growth and become the world's second largest economy. We can't deny that except institutional dividend, our admission into WTO and active participation in global economic system has also greatly promoted our economic growth. China's late-mover advantage is fading as the world is developing to a relatively stable level[3]. However, now we speed up the process of upgrading incomplete market economic system, which is really urgent. If we want to upgrade the economic system, we need the courage to face the problems existing in current market economic system and overcome them.

续表

原文	译文
这些问题概括起来，就是从计划经济体制转型而来的中国市场经济体制，必然地保留了旧体制的影子，旧体制依然在牵绊着市场化改革的脚步。	Generally speaking, these problems can be concluded to one point, that is, China market economic system transferring from planned economic system must maintain the old system, which still hinders market reform.
比如，我们看到，经济运行中，"计划"穿上"审批"的马甲，依然大量存在。审批以一个美好的目的继续存在，但并没有真正实现美好的目标，反而可能成为寻租的工具。比如，每一个钢厂的建设都必须经过层层审批，但最终我们建成了一个产能严重过剩的市场。	We can see that there is still the phenomenon that plan is closely related to examination and approval in the market operation[4]. Examination and approval exist for its good purpose but it doesn't guarantee the achievement of great goals while becomes the tool for rent-seeking. For an example, the construction of every steel mill must go through layers of approval, but eventually, we established a market of severe overcapacity.
比如，从中央到地方，我们对每一个产业都有明确的规划，但却一次次面临着产业结构必须调整的现实。而在那些管制较少的产业，却极少出现过这样的麻烦。出现这些问题的原因，首先是市场在资源配置中的作用在一定程度上受到制约，市场与政府的关系依然没有处理好；其次是国内市场依然存在割裂、不统一的情况。	For another example, from the central government to local levels, we have clear planning of every industry but have to adjust the industry structure again and again. However, there are little such troubles among those less regulated industries. There are two reasons for these problems. First, to some degree, the function of market in resources distribution is restricted and the relationship between market and government is not dealt well. Second, there are still separation and disunity in domestic market[5].
十八届三中全会明确指出，经济体制改革是全面深化改革的重点，核心问题是处理好政府和市场的关系，使市场在资源配置中起决定性作用，建设统一开放、竞争有序的市场体系。这是对20年来中国市场经济体制病灶的一个总的回应，那就是，要充分尊重市场，放权给市场，使市场在法治之下透明运行。这预示着中国经济体制升级在望。	The Third Plenary Session of the 18th CPC Central Committee clearly pointed out that economic structural reform is the focus of comprehensively deepening reform, the core issue is to properly handle the relationship between the government and the market, let the market play a decisive role in the allocation of resources, and build a unified, open, competitive and orderly market system[6]. This is a general response to the disadvantage of Chinese market economic system over the past 20 years[7], that is, respect the market completely and deliver the right to the market, making the market operate under the law. This indicates that Chinese economic system upgrading is in sight.

原文	译文
按照经济学家吴敬琏的说法,之前中国的市场经济是 1.0 版本,而在十八届三中全会之后,升级的市场经济体制将成为 2.0 版本。在 2.0 版本的市场经济体制之下,产权应该得到充分保护;价格应该充分放开;政府管理市场的边界应该清晰;垄断与地区保护应该破除;民营资本与国有资本应该平等……这些均寄希望于十八届三中全会所指出的,要"处理好政府和市场的关系",而处理好政府和市场的关系,有赖于政府向市场放权。	According to economics Wu Jinglian's opinion, before the Third Plenary Session of the Eighteenth Central Committee of the Party, the market economy is 1.0 Version, and after that the upgrading market economy will be 2.0 Version. Under the 2.0 version market economy, property should be protected fully, the price should be open, the range of government management market should be clear, monopoly and local protection should be eradicate, and private capital and government capital should be equalized and so on. The accomplishment of all these goals lies on the balance of the government and the market, while the good relationship between the government and the market depends on the government decentralizing power to the market.
此外,三中全会宣示,毫不动摇地巩固和发展公有制经济、毫不动摇地鼓励支持引导非公有制经济,真正将国有资本和民间资本放到一视同仁的地位,也是市场经济体制升级的必然步骤。	In addition, the Third Plenary Session declares that we must unswervingly consolidate and develop the public sector of the economy and unswervingly encourage, support and guide non-public economy so as to treat government capital and private capital equally without discrimination, which is the necessary steps for upgrading market economy.
此次三中全会,被看作中国全面深化改革再出发的蓝图。就经济改革而言,所谓蓝图还只是一场新征程的开端。	This Third Plenary Session is regarded as the blueprint of fully deepening reform. As for economic reform, the blueprint is only can be called the beginning of a new journey.

(节选自《改革新蓝图》,五洲传播出版社,2013)

难点 1

原文:本次三中全会公报中,59 次提及"改革",超过以往历届。这透露出了改革的艰难、迫切以及决心。

译文:In this Third Plenum Communique, the "reform" has been mentioned for 59 times, outnumbering the previous, which showed the reform hardship, urgency and resolution.

分析:中文多用短句,而英文多长句,因此先要整理原文中的内在逻辑关系,再整合成英文长句。

难点 2

原文：中国市场经济体制的确立，从 1993 年的十四届三中全会吹响号角。

译文：The Third Plenary Session of the Fourteenth Central Committee of the Party in 1993 blew the horn for the establishment of China market economy system.

分析：中文是主题突出型语言，而英文是主语突出型语言。"中国市场经济体制的确立"便是原文的主题，翻译成英文时，译者没有采用直译，而是将"十四届三中全会"作为主语，根据时间顺序来表达语义。

难点 3

原文：对于中国而言，世界已经逐渐变为"平的"，后发优势正在褪去。

译文：China's late-mover advantage is fading as the world is developing to a relatively stable level.

分析：首先，原文中的"平的"是指世界发展速度变缓，即发展稳定。其次，"世界已经逐渐……"和"后发优势……"存在一定的因果关系，在翻译中，为了让目的语读者更清晰，有必要将逻辑关系点明。

难点 4

原文：比如，我们看到，经济运行中，"计划"穿上"审批"的马甲，依然大量存在。

译文：We can see that there are still the phenomenon that plan is closely related to examination and approval in the market operation.

分析："'计划'穿上'审批'的马甲"的表达较为口语化，意思是"计划"和"审批"关系十分紧密。在翻译中，译者需要将原作者的隐藏意义表达出来，否则会大大损害译文的可接受性。

难点 5

原文：出现这些问题的原因，首先是市场在资源配置中的作用在一定程度上受到制约，市场与政府的关系依然没有处理好；其次是国内市场依然存在割裂、不统一的情况。

译文：There are two reasons for these problems. First, to some degree, the function of market in resources distribution is restricted and the relationship between market and government is not dealt well. Second, there are still separation and disunity in domestic market.

分析：译者增译的"There are two reasons for these problems"可以使本句逻辑更为清晰，符合英语行文特点。

难点 6

原文：十八届三中全会明确指出，经济体制改革是全面深化改革的重点，核心问题是处理好政府和市场的关系,使市场在资源配置中起决定性作用,建设统一开放、竞争有序的市场体系。

译文:The Third Plenary Session of the 18th CPC Central Committee Clearly pointed out that economic structural reform is the focus of comprehensively deepening reform, the core issue is to properly handle the relationship between the government and the market, let the market play a decisive role in the allocation of resources, and build a unified, open, competitive and orderly market system.

分析:对于中文流水句的处理,首先要梳理句子之间的逻辑关系。在本句中,主语是"十八届三中全会",谓语是"指出",宾语是后面的整个句子。在宾语中有两层含义,分别是"全面深化改革的重点"和"核心问题"。句中还对"处理好政府和市场的关系"这一"核心问题"的目标做了补充说明,具体就是"使市场在资源配置中起决定性作用,建设统一开放、竞争有序的市场体系"。

难点7

原文:这是对20年来中国市场经济体制病灶的一个总的回应……

译文:This is a general response to the disadvantage of Chinese market economic system over the past 20 years…

分析:"病灶"原是临床解剖学和病理学的概念,指肉体发生病变的关键部位。在经济学上,它特指问题的关键原因。根据《牛津高阶词典》,"disadvantage"指的是"something that causes problems and tends to stop sb. /sth. from succeeding or making progress",符合作者的表达意图。

二、英译汉

原文	译文
Economic theory has suffered in the past from a failure to state clearly its assumption.	过去,经济理论一直因未能清楚地说明其假设而备受困扰。
Economists in building up a theory have often omitted to examine the foundations on which it was erected.	在建立一种理论时,经济学家常常忽略对其赖以成立的基础的考察。
This examination is, however, essential not only to prevent the misunderstanding and needles controversy which arise from a lack of knowledge of the assumptions on which a theory is based, but also because of the extreme importance for economics of good judgment in choosing between rival sets of assumptions.	然而,由于有人对相关理论赖以成立的假设缺乏了解而产生误解,并引起不必要的争论,为了防止该情况出现,这种考察不仅不可或缺,而且,对于经济学在一系列不同假设的选择中作出正确的判断,考察也是极为重要的[1]。

续表

原文	译文
For instance, it is suggested that the use of the word "firm" in economics may be different from the use of the term by the "plain man".	例如，值得一提的是，"企业"这个词在经济学中的使用方式与"一般人"的使用方式就有所不同。
Since there is apparently a trend in economic theory towards starting analysis with the individual firm and not with the industry, it is all the more necessary not only that a clear definition of the word "firm" should be given but that its difference from a firm in the "real world", if it exists, should be made clear.	由于经济理论中存在一种从私人企业而不是从产业开始分析的倾向性，因此就更加[2]有必要不仅对"企业"这个词给出明确的定义，而且要弄清它与"现实世界"中的企业的不同之处——假如存在的话，就应该搞清楚。
Mrs. Robinson has said that "the two questions to be asked of a set of assumptions in economics are: Are they tractable? and: Do they correspond with the real world?"	罗宾逊夫人曾说过："对于经济学中的一系列假设，需要提出的两个问题是：它们易于处理吗？它们与现实世界相吻合吗？"
Though, as Mrs. Robinson points out, "More often one set will be manageable and the other realistic," yet there may well be branches of theory where assumptions may be both manageable and realistic.	尽管正如罗宾逊夫人所指出的，"较通常的是，一种假设是可处理的，而另一种假设则是现实的"，可能还有这样的理论分支，其中的假设既是可处理的，又是现实的[3]。
It is hoped to show in the following paper that a definition of a firm may be obtained which is not only realistic in that it corresponds to what is meant by a firm in the real world, but is tractable by two of the most powerful instruments of economic analysis developed by Marshall, the idea of the margin and that of substitution, together giving the idea of substitution at the margin. Our definition must, of course, "relate to formal relations which are capable of being conceived exactly".	下文将表明，一种不仅是现实的（即能与现实世界中的企业含义相吻合），而且是易于处理的（即能用马歇尔所发展起来的两种最强有力的经济分析工具来处理），企业的定义是可以获得的。这两种分析工具就是边际概念和替代概念，两者合在一起就是边际替代概念[4]。当然，我们的定义必须"与能被准确表达的正规叙述相联系"。
I	I
It is convenient if, in searching for a definition of a firm, we first consider the economic system as it is normally treated by the economist.	在探索企业的定义时，像经济学家通常所做的那样，首先考察经济体制或许是比较合适的。
"The normal economic system works itself. For its current operation it is under no central control, it needs no central survey. Over the whole range of human activity and human need, supply is adjusted to demand, and production to consumption, by a process that is automatic, elastic and responsive."	"正常的经济体制自行运行。它的日常运行不在集中控制之下，它不需要中央的监查。就人类活动和人类需要的整个领域而言，供给根据需求而调整，生产根据消费而调整[5]，这个过程是自动的、有弹性的和反应灵敏的。"

续表

原文	译文
An economist thinks of the economic system as being coordinated by the price mechanism and society becomes not an organization but an organism.	经济学家认为，经济体制是由价格机制来协调的，而社会是一个有机体而不是一个组织[6]。
The economic system "works itself". This does not mean that there is no planning by individuals.	经济体制"自行运行"，这并不意味着没有私人计划。
These exercise foresight and choose between alternatives.	人们都在不同方案之间进行着预测和选择。
This is necessarily so if there is to be order in the system.	假如要使经济体制有秩序的话，这就是不可或缺的。
But this theory assumes that the direction of resources is dependent directly on the price mechanism.	但这种理论假定资源的流动方向直接依赖于价格机制。
Indeed, it is often considered to be an objection to economic planning that it merely tries to do what is already done by the price mechanism.	确实，人们常常认为，仅仅试图去做已由价格机制做完的事是反对经济计划工作的一个理由[7]。
Sir Arthur Salter's description, however, gives a very incomplete picture of our economic system.	然而，阿瑟·索尔特爵士的描述却给出了一个有关我们经济体制的非常不完整的画面。
Within a firm, the description does not fit at all.	在企业中，这种描述根本不适用。
For instance, in economic theory we find that the allocation of factors of production between different uses is determined by the price mechanism.	例如，我们发现在经济理论中生产要素在各种不同的用途之间的配置是由价格机制决定的。
The price of factor A becomes higher in X than in Y. As a result, A moves from Y to X until the difference between the prices in X and Y, except if so far as it compensates for other differential advantages, disappears.	如果要素 A 的价格在 X 比在 Y 高，则 A 就会从 Y 流向 X，直到 X 和 Y 之间的价格差消失为止，除非存在着某种程度上的其他方面的利益补偿。
Yet in the real world, we find that there are many areas where this does not apply.	然而，在现实世界中，我们发现这种说法在许多地方并不适用。
If a workman moves from department Y to department X, he does not go because of a change in relative prices, but because he is ordered to do so.	如果一个工人从部门 Y 流向部门 X，他这样做并不是因为相对价格的变化，而是因为他被命令这样做。

续表

原文	译文
Those who object to economic planning on the grounds that the problem is solved by price movements can be answered by pointing out that there is planning within our economic system which is quite different from the individual planning mentioned above and which is akin to what is normally called economic planning.	那些反对经济计划工作的人的理由是，问题已被价格机制解决了。对于这种观点，应该指出，我们的经济体制中存在的计划完全不同于上面所提到的私人计划，而类似于通常所说的经济计划。
The example given above is typical of a large sphere in our modern economic system. Of course, this fact has not been ignored by economists.	上面这个例子在我们的现代经济体制中具有大范围的典型意义。当然，经济学家们并没有忽视这一事实。
Marshall introduces organization as a fourth factor of production; J. B. Clark gives the coordinating function to the entrepreneur; Professor Knight introduces managers who coordinate.	马歇尔把组织作为第四种生产要素引入经济学理论；J. B. 克拉克赋予企业家以统筹职能；奈特教授强调了经理的协调作用。
As D. H Robertson points out, we find "islands of conscious power in this ocean of unconscious cooperation like lumps of butter coagulating in a pail of buttermilk".	正如 D. H. 罗伯逊所指出的，我们发现了"在这无意识合作的海洋中，自觉力量的岛屿就像凝结在一桶牛乳中的黄油块一样"。
But in view of the fact that it is usually argued that coordination will be done by the price mechanism, why is such organization necessary?	但既然人们通常认为统筹协调能通过价格机制来实现，那么，为什么这样的组织是必需的呢[8]？
Why are there these "islands of conscious power"?	为什么会存在"自觉力量的岛屿"呢？
Outside the firm, price movements direct production, which is coordinated through a series of exchange transactions on the market.	在企业之外，价格变动决定生产，这是通过一系列市场交易来协调的。
Within a firm, these markets transactions are eliminated and in place of the complicated market structure with exchange transactions is substituted the entrepreneur coordinator, who directs production. It is clear that these are alternative methods of coordinating production.	在企业之内，市场交易遭到取消，伴随着交易的复杂的市场结构为企业家所替代，企业家指挥生产。显然，存在着协调生产的替代方法。
Yet, having regard to the fact that if production is regulated by price movements, production could be carried on without any organization at all, well might we ask, why is there any organization?	然而，假如生产是由价格机制调节的，生产就能在根本不存在任何组织的情况下进行，面对这一事实，我们要问：组织为什么存在？

（节选自《企业的性质》*The Nature of Firm*）

难点 1

原文：This examination is, however, essential not only to prevent the misunderstanding and needles controversy which arise from a lack of knowledge of the assumptions on which a theory is based, but also because of the extreme importance for economics of good judgment in choosing between rival sets of assumptions.

译文：然而，由于有人对相关理论赖以成立的假设缺乏了解而产生误解，并引起不必要的争论，为了防止该情况出现，这种考察不仅不可或缺，而且，对于经济学在一系列不同假设的选择中作出正确的判断，考察也是极为重要的。

分析：该句为长难句，句子主干为"This examination is essential"，"not only…but also…"为关联词组，将"prevent the misunderstanding and needles controversy"和"because of the extreme importance for economics"并列起来，其中，限制性定语从句"which arise from a lack of knowledge…"的先行词是"misunderstanding and needles controversy"；而第二个定语从句"on which a theory is based"所指代的对象就是第一个定语从句中的"assumptions"，这种从句套从句现象在长难句中十分常见。"because of"后接的是名词性短语，由于中文喜动，因此在翻译成中文时，可适当更改词性，将名词翻译成动词。

难点 2

原文：all the more

译文：更加

分析："all the more"与"more""even more"最大的区别是："all the more"前后文说出来原因或隐含不明言原因，如文中的"it is all the more necessary not only that a clear definition of the word 'firm' should be given"与前文是存在因果关系的。

难点 3

原文：…"the two questions to be asked of a set of assumptions in economics are: Are they tractable? and: Do they correspond with the real world?"… "More often one set will be manageable and the other realistic"…

译文：……"对于经济学中的一系列假设，需要提出的两个问题是：它们易于处理吗？它们与现实世界相吻合吗？"……"较通常的是，一种假设是可处理的，而另一种假设则是现实的"……

分析：由于英语重句法结构、多用长句等特点，因此上文提到的往往在下文就会省略，并列结构中尤其如此，如文中的"one…the other"。而汉语重语义，多短句，多重复和补充。因此在翻译中，译者将省略的词语都补充上了。

难点 4

原文：It is hoped to show in the following paper that a definition of a firm may be obtained which is not only realistic in that it corresponds to what is meant by a firm in the real world, but is tractable by two of the most powerful instruments of economic analysis developed by Marshall, the idea of the margin and that of substitution, together giving the idea of substitution at the margin.

译文：下文将表明，一种不仅是现实的（即能与现实世界中的企业含义相吻合），而且是易于处理的（即能用马歇尔所发展起来的两种最强有力的经济分析工具来处理），企业的定义是可以获得的。这两种分析工具就是边际概念和替代概念，两者合在一起就是边际替代概念。

分析：本句主干是"It is hoped to show in the following paper…"，宾语从句有两个，而定语从句、状语从句、主语从句和同位语从句各有一个。遇到类似的长难句，可采用综合法来翻译，即综合运用顺序法、逆序法和分译法。用分译法翻译状语从句，用逆序法翻译同位语从句。

难点 5

原文：… supply is adjusted to demand, and production to consumption…

译文：……供给根据需求而调整，生产根据消费而调整……

分析：在并列句中，如果后一分句与前一分句中的谓语动词重复，常省略谓语动词或谓语的一部分，但介词不能省略，避免引起歧义。

难点 6

原文：An economist thinks of the economic system as being coordinated by the price mechanism and society becomes not an organization but an organism.

译文：经济学家认为，经济体制是由价格机制来协调的，而社会是一个有机体而不是一个组织。

分析：此句中的"an economist"并非特指某一位具体的经济学家，而是泛指经济学家这一类人，意在表达经济学家作为专业人士的观点和看法，所以不用翻译为"一位经济学家"。此外，此句意群较多，根据中文的表达特点，翻译时将其拆分为几部分，更符合中文读者的阅读习惯。

难点 7

原文：…it is often considered to be an objection to economic planning that it merely tries to do what is already done by the price mechanism.

译文：……人们常常认为，仅仅试图去做已由价格机制完成的事是反对经济计划工作的一个理由。

分析：本句由"it"作形式主语，真正的主语是从句"it merely tries to do what is already done by the price mechanism"，在翻译时，应该增加主语"人们"。

难点 8

原文：But in view of the fact that it is usually argued that coordination will be done by the price mechanism, why is such organization necessary?

译文：但既然人们通常认为统筹协调能通过价格机制来实现，那么，为什么这样的组织是必需的呢？

分析：按英语习惯，介词后面通常不能直接跟一个 that 从句作宾语，因此，可以在 that 从句前使用"the fact"。这样一来，就变成了"the fact"用作介词的宾语，而其后的 that 从句则成了"the fact"的同位语从句。在英语写作中，可采用此策略，为译文增色。

翻 译 练 习

一、词组翻译

二次探底
恩格尔系数
反垄断调查
点心债券
次级债务
不完全信息
"使用财产就要付费"体制
"let-him-buy-his-way out" system
personal income tax
Purchasing Managers Index of non-manufacturing sector
employment discrimination
scarcity of resource
equilibrium price
Indifference Curve
Ability-to-pay Principle

二、句子翻译

(一) 英译汉

1. The capital of the landlord, on the contrary, which is fixed in the improvement of his

land, seems to be as well secured as the nature of human affairs can admit of.

2. The economy is still paying the price for this in terms of continued high levels and duration of unemployment.

3. If human institutions had never thwarted those natural inclinations, the towns could not where have increased beyond what the improvement and cultivation of the territory in which they were situated could support; till such time, at least, as the whole of that territory was completely cultivated and improved.

4. If in the same neighborhood, there was any employment evidently either more or less advantageous than the rest, so many people would crowd into it in the one case, and so many would desert it in the other, that its advantages would soon return to the level of other employments.

5. Factors which may be relevant in this respect include, inter alia, the volume and prices of imports not sold at dumping prices, contraction in demand or changes in the patterns of consumption, trade restrictive practices of and competition between the foreign and domestic producers, developments in technology and the export performance and productivity of the domestic industry.

(二)汉译英

1. 如果他能更好地享受生活的乐趣,他很快就会把劳动的任何进一步增加的负效用看作一种罪恶,而且这种罪恶不再被预期的劳动带来的间接满足感的进一步增加所抵消。

2. 只有当雇主们能够垄断每种生产过程中不可或缺的生产要素并且以垄断的方式限制该要素的使用时,雇主们才能采用统一行动来拉低工人们的工资。

3. 一千个在亚洲落后地区的小工匠商店里使用传统老式工具的人,即使每周工作超过四十小时的情况下,也只能生产出少于 m 双的鞋子。

4. 从这个意义上讲,第一次转型的制度安排的重要特征是"摸着石头过河"。

5. 应当看到,在行业利益的诱惑下,实现政企分开、政资分开,实现国有资产的公益性还有很长的路要走。

三、语篇翻译

(一)英译汉

I. The Problem to Be Examined

This paper is concerned with those actions of business firms which have harmful effects on others. The standard example is that of a factory the smoke from which has harmful effects on those occupying neighbouring properties. The economic analysis of such a situation has usually proceeded in terms of a divergence between the private and social product of the factory, in which economists have largely followed the treatment of Pigou in *The Economics of Welfare*. The conclusions to which this kind of analysis seems to have led most economists is that it would be desirable to make the owner of the factory liable for the damage caused to those injured by the smoke, or alternatively, to place a tax on the factory owner varying with the amount of smoke produced and equivalent in money terms to the damage it would cause, or finally, to exclude the factory from residential districts (and presumably from other areas in which the emission of smoke would have harmful effects on others). It is my contention that the suggested courses of action are inappropriate, in that they lead to results which are not necessarily, or even usually, desirable.

II. The Reciprocal Nature of the Problem

The traditional approach has tended to obscure the nature of the choice that has to be made. The question is commonly thought of as one in which A inflicts harm on B and what has to be decided is: how should we restrain A? But this is wrong. We are dealing with a problem of a reciprocal nature. To avoid the harm to B would inflict harm on A. The real question that has to be decided is: should A be allowed to harm B or should B be allowed to harm A? The problem is to avoid the more serious harm. I instanced in my previous article 2 the case of a confectioner the noise and vibrations from whose machinery disturbed a doctor in his work. To avoid harming the doctor would inflict harm on the confectioner. The problem posed by this case was essentially whether it was worthwhile, as a result of restricting the methods of production which could be used by the confectioner, to secure more doctoring at the cost of a reduced supply of confectionery products. Another example is afforded by the problem of straying cattle which destroy crops on neighbouring land. If it is inevitable that some cattle ill stray, an increase in the supply of meat can only be obtained at the expense of a decrease in the supply of crops. The nature of the choice is clear: meat or crops. What answer should be given is, of course, not clear unless we know the value of what is obtained as well as the value of what is sacrificed to obtain it. To give another example, Professor George J. Stigler instances the contamination of a stream. If we assume that the harmful effect of the pollution is that it kills the fish, the question to be decided is: is the value of the fish lost greater or less than the value of the product which the contamination of the stream makes possible. It goes almost without saying that this problem has to be looked at in total and at the margin.

(二)汉译英

未来农村经济增长点在特色小镇。目前，全国有建制镇约1.8万个，成规模的乡镇约2万个，二次城市化要解决近4万个乡镇的经济发展问题。按照规划，到2020年，我国将建设1000个特色小镇。每个镇行政区划一般几十到几百平方公里，具有城市形态的核心镇域约2~3平方公里，基本实现需要3年投资50亿元人民币，仅1000个特色小镇的投资总额就将达到5万亿元人民币。而未来二三十年，4万个镇都将发生类似的重大变化，对GDP的支撑力度不可估量。二次城市化中，特色小镇将成为城乡经济勾兑的枢纽。被树为典型的特色镇，没有一个是与城市经济毫无关联的，相反，越是成功的小镇，越是充分利用了城乡经济相融合的梯度红利与创新红利。同时，老经济在上一轮城市化、工业化登峰造极的过程中已全面走向过剩,新经济需要新空间,新空间也乐于接纳环境友好的新经济,特色小镇自然成为新经济的制高点。此外,特色小镇集产业、旅游、体闲、消费等诸多体验经济元素于一身,恰好是商业投资新的切入口。

◎参考文献

[1]Joan Pinkham. 中式英语之鉴[M]. 北京:外语教学与研究出版社,2000.

[2]陈宏薇,李亚丹. 新编汉英翻译教程(第2版)[M]. 上海:上海外语教育出版社,2013.

[3]陈宏薇,李亚丹. 汉英翻译教程[M]. 上海:上海外语教育出版社,2018.

[4]陈加旭. 金融报道中的隐喻认知及其翻译研究[J]. 上海翻译,2016(6):22-27.

[5]李长栓. 非文学翻译理论与实践[M]. 北京:中国对外翻译出版公司,2004.

[6]卢敏. 英语笔译实务(2级)[M]. 北京:外文出版社,2010.

[7]孙万彪. 英汉法律翻译教程[M]. 上海:上海外语教育出版社,2010.

[8]叶子南. 高级英汉翻译理论与实践(第三版)[M]. 北京:清华大学出版社,2013.

[9]张可云,李晨. 区域派生理论与经验研究进展[M]. 经济学动态,2019(12):123-128.

[10]中国日报网. 最新汉英特色词汇词典(第7版)[M]. 北京:清华大学出版社,2010.

第七章 经济会议演讲发言翻译

> ☞**思考题**
> 1. 经济会议演讲发言有哪些语言特点？
> 2. 经济会议演讲发言的主要功能是什么？
> 3. 该类文本翻译的难点是什么？

第一节 经济会议演讲文本分析

一、文本概述

经济会议的召开是通过对话的形式，加强与各国人民之间的经济贸易往来和经济合作，研究和探讨世界经济领域存在的问题，促进国际经济合作与交流。经济会议演讲发言翻译作为一种口语和书面形式结合的文体形式，其语体正式，篇章逻辑清晰、结构紧凑，话题集中，涉及部分专业知识，因此区别于日常对话。但是由于其能够获得听众的及时反馈且依赖声音的传播，又区别于纯粹的书面文体。演讲发言中的修辞手法、话题的政治性，以及演讲者自身的语言特点，这些方面都是其区别于其他文体的重要内容。如何传递信息，实现跨文化交际，实现有效的经济活动，取得预期效果都是译者面临的困难。

经济会议又可以划分为国际经济会议和国内经济会议。国际经济会议是通过经济对话，加强与各国人民之间的经济贸易往来和经济合作，研究和探讨世界经济领域存在的问题，促进国际经济合作与交流。国内经济会议是总结目前的经济工作成绩，分析研判当前经济情况形势，制定经济发展规划，解决具体出现的经济问题。本书中主要研究的是语际翻译，所以主要讨论的是国际经济会议。

经济会议演讲发言整体结构主要分为以下五个部分：

（1）打招呼。演讲者与听众打招呼，建立友好融洽的关系，这是演讲中必不可少的环节。

（2）介绍主题。演讲者一般采用引用名人名言、讲故事、陈述客观事实或数据、提问等方式吸引观众的注意，就相关话题进行本次讨论。

（3）旁征博引。这是演讲的主题部分，演讲者通过举例子、给数据、分享经验等方式达到使听众信服的目的，涉及相关政治经济术语和知识。

(4) 总结演讲主题。主要通过引用名句、给出建议和提出开放性的问题，对本次演讲进行总结。

(5) 表示感谢。对听众表示感谢，演讲自然结束，给人留下良好的印象。

二、文本特点

经济会议演讲发言也属于外宣文本，其语言特征主要是准确性、专业性和正式性。准确性是指语言层次清晰，逻辑性强，表达不含糊。专业性是指经济会议演讲中有一些专业术语、专有名词、相关经济背景知识。正式性是指语言风格相对正式，无浓烈的感情色彩，以规范的陈述句为主。这就决定了在翻译时要保留源语文本的特点，遵循原文风格，全面理解原文的意思，注意遣词造句，忠实地传达原文的语义。下文将从词汇、句法和修辞层面进行分析，从而得出英中两类经济会议演讲发言的具体语言特点，帮助英语学习者进一步了解此类文体。

(一) 英文文本特点

1. 词汇层面

经济会议演讲发言在词汇方面的第一个特点主要表现在多专业术语，包括政治和经济专业知识以及部分缩略语。例如："Phillips curve（菲利普斯曲线）""nominal rates（名义利率）""inflation（通货膨胀）""FOMC（美联储联邦公开市场委员会）"。

第二个特点主要表现在人称代词的使用上，尤其是第一人称复数的频繁使用。在经济会议中，演讲者发言时多使用代词"we""our""us"等。通过这些人称代词的使用，演讲者可以更加鲜明地表明自己的主张和立场，以及观点和态度，从而得到听众的认可和赞同。同时还能拉近演讲者和听众之间的距离，建立相互信任和密切的关系。

2. 句法层面

句法层面的第一个特点就是多使用陈述句。根据功能划分，英文句子可分为陈述句、疑问句、祈使句和感叹句。在经济会议演讲中演讲者多使用陈述句来体现文本的严肃、专业的特性，但是在演讲的结尾演讲者往往喜欢使用祈使句，可以达到煽动听众的目的。

第二个特点就是多长难句。由于参与经济会议的一般是专业学者或各政府首脑，他们的文化素养和专业水平较高，长难句可包含更多的信息，使得语言更加正式。例如："Policymakers also had deeper concerns about the legitimacy and effectiveness of attempting to bind some future FOMC to take actions that could be objectionable from a short-term perspective when the time came to deliver."

3. 修辞层面

为了吸引听众的注意力，演讲者会使用恰当的修饰手法达到这一目的，让演讲更加生动活泼。通常使用的修饰手法有隐喻、反复和排比。修饰手法的使用可以使抽象的概念简单化，语言也更加生动形象。例如："Particularly striking in comparing the UK and US experience is the different trends in working age inactivity—historically an **Achilles Heel** for the UK after previous recessions."

(二) 中文文本特点

1. 词汇层面

中文经济会议演讲发言的词汇特点主要是使用具有中国特色的专业术语，包括新词语、成语、诗句等。新词语的使用代表着新时代新的经济政策方针，例如"双创""命运共同体""互联网+""一带一路"等。演讲者还常使用一些成语或者诗句来增加语言的生动性和形象性，具有一定的文学色彩，例如："同舟共济、立己达人""横看成岭侧成峰，远近高低各不同"，等等。

2. 句法层面

首先从句类来看，主要使用陈述句和祈使句，陈述句可以客观准确地陈述事实、表达观点。祈使句直接明了，提出建议和措施。从句型来看，语句灵活多变，既兼顾书面语的严谨，又具有口语的简单明了，以流水句、单句使用为主，复杂句较少，多无主句。流水句是汉语的一大特色，句子的信息容量不受语法形式的限制，弹性较大，这与英文重"形合"的特点相反。

3. 修辞层面

演讲对语言进行加工，体现了说话的艺术。演讲者通常会使用一种或多种修辞手段传递信息，感染受众，达到交际的目的。语言上多使用比喻、重复、引用、反复等修辞手段，将中国的经济政治政策以亲和有力的方式进行传播，增强演讲的感染力和信服力。

第二节　翻译知识讲解

目的论是德国功能翻译派的核心理论之一，也是德国功能翻译派的重要组成部分。创立者弗米尔在其所著文章《普通翻译理论框架》中首次提出目的论这一概念，其后，弗米尔和赖斯合著的《翻译的理论基础》具体介绍了目的论的相关原则。功能目的论的中心思想是，一切行为都有一定的目的，行为者要达到预期目的就要根据实际环境选择最佳的行为方式。翻译是一种社会行为，任何翻译都有其预期目的，译者也需要以翻译目的为导向，综合考虑各种因素选择最恰当的翻译策略和翻译方法。经济会议演讲发言无非有三个目的：一是向受众传递经济信息。二是增进各方面合作，吸引投资，促进经济发展。三是拉近与受众之间的距离，树立良好的形象。功能目的论的三大原则是：目的原则，连贯原则，忠实原则。

目的原则认为，翻译目的决定着翻译策略及翻译手段。因此译者应在给定的翻译语境中明确其特定目的，并根据这一目的来决定应该采用何种翻译策略、方法和技巧。翻译策略是翻译活动中，为实现特定的翻译目的所依据的原则和所采纳的方案集合，包括归化和异化两种翻译策略，归化策略下包括意译、仿译、改译、创译等翻译方法；异化策略下包括零翻译、音译、逐词翻译、直译等翻译方法。翻译中又有增译、减译、分译、合译、转换等翻译策略。翻译时应该根据翻译目的选择不同的翻译方法和技巧,以下选取了一些翻译案例。

一、增译

指通过对文化负载词的注解,弥补文化间的差异,以有效传达源语信息的方法。

例1

原文:坚持创新驱动发展,把"双创"引向纵深,推动大中小企业、科研机构和社会创客融通创新。

译文:We will keep to innovation-driven development, seek greater progress in mass entrepreneurship and innovation, and push forward integrated innovation among large companies, SMEs, research institutions and makers.

分析:"双创"一词,源语读者一听便知,意为"大众创业,万众创新"。如何将"双创"二字译出与源语相同的效果,需要译者对其进行相应增译。

例2

原文:The alternative plan still being presented is a return to higher borrowing, more debt, more instability, lost jobs, rising interest rates and higher taxes.

译文:替代方案会造成的结果是:回归更高借贷水平,更多贷款,更多不稳定性,更高失业率,更高利率和税款。

分析:英文中"lost jobs"没有说"更高",但在翻译成中文时,为了和前后句式结构一致,增加了"更高",以增强表现力和表达效果。

二、省译

指为避免译文累赘,删减原文中重复、无实义的表达,使译文简洁的翻译策略。

例3

原文:中国经济继续保持稳重向好发展态势,发展新动能在持续成长,基本面是健康的。

译文:On the whole, the Chinese economy has stayed on the track of steady progress, with growing new drivers and sound fundamentals.

分析:"稳中向好"指发展态势,"发展新动能"有成长之意,将其省译为"steady progress""growing new drivers",可避免译文冗长烦琐。

三、直译

强调保持文本的形式与语言风格,以展现源语语言特色。

例 4

原文：着力推动大众创业、万众创新，进一步推进"互联网+"行动，广泛运用物联网、大数据、云计算等新一代信息技术。

译文：We will also advocate mass entrepreneurship and innovation, further promote the "Internet+" strategy, extensively apply the new generation of information technologies such as the Internet of Things, big data and cloud computing.

分析：本句的关键点在于"互联网+""物联网""大数据""云计算"等特色词汇。政治经济文本注重新政策、新观念宣传，将其分别直译为"Internet +""Internet of Things""big data""cloud computing"，既保留了源语文本的特色，也有利于译语读者了解新的发展形势与成果，易于被读者接受。

四、意译

指在翻译过程中打破形式，以表意为出发点的翻译方法。意译法不注重形式对等，更重视传情达意。

例 5

原文：中国无论发展到什么阶段，都需要与世界各国取长补短、互学互鉴，对外开放的大门会越开越大。

译文：No matter how developed China will become, it will always need mutual-learning with the rest of the world, and it will open still wider to the outside.

分析：句中"取长补短"不是"长"与"短"的关系；"对外开放的大门"并不是"门"的意思。基于连贯性原则要求译文要为译语读者所接受，采用意译法，用"mutual-learning"表达"取长补短、互学互鉴"之意，"open to the outside"展现"对外开放"之意，既简洁精练，又意义明确。

五、转换

指在翻译中的词性转换。

例 6

原文：But I also warned of the dangers of market instability and said that forward guidance under our new MPC remit could be a useful tool to manage expectations as the economy recovered.

译文：但我也警告过会有市场不稳定的危险，而在经济复苏时，新货币政策委员会能进行前瞻性指导，有效引导预期。

分析：中文是动态语言，多用动词；英文是静态语言，多用名词。英文中的名词"useful tool"在译为中文时转换为动词"有效引导"，符合中文表达习惯。

第三节 常用词汇与表达

原文	译文
IMS (International Monetary System)	国际货币基金体系
EEC (European Economic Community)	欧洲经济共同体
IPO (initial public offering)	首次公开招募；上市
bubble economy	泡沫经济
labor intensive industry	劳动密集型产业
extensive/intensive operation	粗放式/集约式经营
ceiling price	最高限价
zero-sum game	零和博弈
outward-looking economy	外向型经济
emerging economies	新兴经济
贵宾	distinguished guests
与会人员	attendees
致开幕词	give/make/deliver an opening address
战略对话	strategic dialogue
试点	pilot program
全方位外交	all-round diplomacy
走出怪圈	break loose from the old pattern
巧实力	smart power
软实力	soft power
预祝……圆满成功	wish…a complete success

第四节 译文赏析

一、英译汉

原文	译文
Good morning. I am very pleased to welcome you here today. This conference is part of a first-ever public review by the Federal Open Market Committee of our monetary policy strategy, tools, and communications. We have a distinguished group of experts from academics and other walks of life here to share perspectives on how monetary policy can best serve the public.	早上好。欢迎诸位的到来。本次会议是美联储联邦公开市场委员会（FOMC）首次就我们的货币政策策略、工具和沟通举行公开评审的一个环节。会议聚集了来自学界和其他各行各业的顶尖专家，与诸位分享货币政策如何最好地为公众服务的观点。

第四节 译文赏析

续表

原文	译文
I'd like first to say a word about recent developments involving trade negotiations and other matters. We do not know how or when these issues will be resolved. We are closely monitoring the implications of these developments for the U. S. economic outlook and, as always, we will act as appropriate to sustain the expansion, with a strong labor market and inflation near our symmetric 2 percent objective. My comments today, like this conference, will focus on longer-run issues that will remain even as the issues of the moment evolve.	首先，我想谈谈涉及贸易谈判和其他事态的最新进展。我们并不知道这些问题会在何时以怎样的方式得到解决。我们正在密切关注这些进展对美国经济前景的影响；面对强劲的劳动力市场和接近2%的对称性通胀目标，我们也将一如既往地采取适当的行动来维系经济扩张[1]。我的评论和本次会议，都将集中讨论那些哪怕现状出现变化也仍会继续困扰我们的长期问题。
While central banks face a challenging environment today, those challenges are not entirely new. In fact, in 1999 the Federal Reserve System hosted a conference titled "Monetary Policy in a Low Inflation Environment". Conference participants discussed new challenges that were emerging after the then-recent victory over the Great Inflation. They focused on many questions posed by low inflation and, in particular, on what unconventional tools a central bank might use to support the economy if interest rates fell to what we now call the effective lower bound (ELB). Even though the Bank of Japan was grappling with the ELB as the conference met, the issue seemed remote for the United States. The conference received little coverage in the financial press, but a Reuters wire service story titled "Fed Conference Timing on Inflation Odd, but Useful" emphasized the remoteness of the risk. Participants at the conference could not have anticipated that only 10 years later, the world would be engulfed in a deep financial crisis, with unemployment soaring and central banks around the world making extensive use of new strategies, tools, and ways to communicate.	虽然中央银行目前面临一个充满挑战的环境，但这些挑战对我们并非完全陌生。事实上，在1999年美联储主办了一次题为"低通胀环境下的货币政策"的会议。与会者讨论了当时刚刚战胜大通胀后出现的新挑战。他们关注的是低通胀带来的许多问题，特别是如果利率下降到我们现在称之为有效下限（ELB）的水平，中央银行可能会用什么非常规工具来支持经济[2]。尽管日本央行在会议召开期间正努力解决ELB带来的问题，但这个问题对当时的美国而言似乎遥不可及。该次会议在财经媒体上几乎没有得到报道，路透社的报道题为"美联储会议对通货膨胀关注的时机奇怪，但确有用"，报道中强调我们距离风险还远。当时的与会者无法预料到，在仅仅10年后，世界将陷入严重金融危机中，失业率飙升，世界各地的中央银行广泛使用新的策略、工具和沟通方式。
The next time policy rates hit the ELB — and there will be a next time — it will not be a surprise. We are now well aware of the challenges the ELB presents, and we have the painful experience of the Global Financial Crisis and its aftermath to guide us. Our obligation to the public we serve is to take those measures now that will put us in the best position deal with our next encounter with the ELB. And with the economy growing, unemployment low, and inflation low and stable, this is the right time to engage the public broadly on these topics.	下一次政策利率触及ELB时，一定会有下一次，这不会令人感到意外。我们现在很清楚ELB所带来的挑战，同时我们还拥有全球金融危机的惨痛教训，其后果也将继续指引我们。我们对公众的义务是在当下采取措施，当利率再次跌到有效下限时，能够做好万全准备[3]。随着经济增长，失业率走低，通货膨胀稳定保持在低位，现在正是让公众广泛参与这些话题的最佳时机[4]。

159

续表

原文	译文
The review has several parts, all of which are intended to open our monetary policy to critical examination. We are holding a series of Fed Listens events around the country to help us understand the perspectives of people from diverse backgrounds and with varied interests. This conference and many other engagements will help us bring to bear the best thinking from policymakers and experts. Beginning later this year, the FOMC will devote time at a series of our regular meetings to assess lessons from these events, supported by staff analysis performed throughout the Federal Reserve System. We will publicly report the outcome of our discussions. In the meantime, anyone who is interested in participating or learning more can find information on the Federal Reserve Board's website.	评审分为几个环节,所有环节都是为货币政策公开征求批判性评论。我们正在全国范围内举办一系列"美联储在聆听"(Fed Listens)活动,以帮助我们了解来自各种背景、有着不同利益诉求的人们的观点。这次会议和其他活动将帮助我们充分运用政策制定者和专家们的独到见解。今年晚些时候,联邦公开市场委员会将在一系列定期会议上评估这些活动带来的经验成果,联储系统的全体员工都将参与到对成果的分析当中。我们将公开报告讨论结果。与此同时,任何有兴趣参与或了解更多的人都可以在美联储的官方网站上找到相关信息。
Before turning to the specifics of the review, I want to focus a little more closely on the challenges we face today. For a reference point, at the time of the 1999 conference, the United States was eight years into an expansion; core inflation was 1.4 percent, and the unemployment rate was 4.1 percent — not so different from today. Macroeconomists were puzzling over the flatness of the Phillips curve, the level of the natural rate of unemployment, and a possible acceleration in productivity growth—questions that are also with us today.	谈及评审的具体细节之前,我想首先讨论一下当前所面临的挑战。作为参考比较,在1999年的会议召开时,美国经济扩张已经持续了八年之久;核心通胀率为1.4%,失业率为4.1%,与当下的情况没有太大的差异。宏观经济学家们对菲利普斯曲线的平坦形态、自然失业率的水平以及生产率增长可能加速感到困惑,这些同样是我们今天所面临的问题。
The big difference between then and now is that the federal funds rate was 5.2 percent — which, to underscore the point, put the rate 20 quarter-point rate cuts away from the ELB. Since then, standard estimates of the longer-run normal or neutral rate of interest have declined between 2 and 3 percentage points, and some argue that the effective decline is even larger. The combination of lower real interest rates and low inflation translates into lower nominal rates and a much higher likelihood that rates will fall to the ELB in a downturn.	当时与目前的状况最大的区别在于,当时的联邦基金利率为5.2%,重点来说,这意味着在利率水平触及ELB之前,可以进行20次每次25bp的降息操作。自那时以来,长期正常或中性利率的标准估计值下降了2到3个百分点,有人认为实际下降的幅度更大。更低实际利率和更低通货膨胀的结合转化为更低的名义利率,并且在经济低迷时利率下滑触及ELB的可能性要高得多。

续表

原文	译文
As the experience of the past decade showed, extended ELB episodes can be associated with painfully high unemployment and slow growth or recession. Economic weakness puts downward pressure on inflation, which can raise real interest rates and reinforce the challenge of supporting needed job growth. In addition, over time, inflation has become much less sensitive to tightness in resource utilization. This insensitivity can be a blessing in avoiding deflation when unemployment is high, but it means that much greater labor market tightness may ultimately be required to bring inflation back to target in a recovery. Using monetary policy to push sufficiently hard on labor markets to lift inflation could pose risks of destabilizing excesses in financial markets or elsewhere.	正如过去十年的经验所表明的那样，利率长期处在ELB水平，可能伴随着痛苦的高失业率和增速放缓或经济衰退。经济疲软给通胀带来下行压力，这可能会提高实际利率并加剧支持所需就业增长的挑战。此外，随着时间的推移，通货膨胀对资源利用的紧俏程度变得不那么敏感了[5]。当失业率居高不下时，这种不敏感性可以成为避免通货紧缩的福音，但这意味着最终可能需要劳动力市场更加紧俏，才能使通货膨胀回归复苏目标。利用货币政策充分推动劳动力市场以提振通胀，可能会造成金融市场或其他部门过剩的不稳定风险。
In short, the proximity of interest rates to the ELB has become the preeminent monetary policy challenge of our time, tainting all manner of issues with ELB risk and imbuing many old challenges with greater significance. For example, the behavior of inflation now draws much sharper focus. When nominal interest rates were around 4 or 5 percent, a low-side surprise of a few tenths on inflation did not raise the specter of the ELB. But the world has changed. Core inflation is currently running a bit below 2 percent on a trailing 12-month basis. In this setting, a similar low-side surprise, if it were to persist, would bring us uncomfortably closer to the ELB. My FOMC colleagues and I must — and do — take seriously the risk that inflation shortfalls that persist even in a robust economy could precipitate a difficult-to-arrest downward drift in inflation expectations. At the heart of the review is the evaluation of potential changes to our strategy designed to strengthen the credibility of our symmetric 2 percent inflation objective.	简而言之，利率水平逼近有效下限已经成为我们这个时代不可忽视的货币政策挑战，这种风险衍生出各种问题，许多旧挑战也变得更加严重[6]。例如，通胀表现如今需要更多关注。当名义利率为4%或5%时，通货膨胀几个分位的意外下行并不会加剧触及ELB的风险。但世界已经发生变化。在过去12个月中，核心通胀略低于2%。在这种情况下，类似的意外下行如果持续发生，会过于接近ELB。我和我的同事们必须，并且确实在认真对待此类风险，即在强劲经济中持续存在的通货膨胀疲软，可能导致通货膨胀预期难以遏制地向下偏离。本次评审的核心在于评估我们策略的潜在变动，旨在加强2%对称通胀目标的可信度。

原文	译文
Let me conclude by saying that I look forward to our discussions here and to the ongoing work of the review that lies ahead. We need the best tools and strategies possible for dealing with the challenges we now face, and we must communicate them in a clear and credible way. My colleagues and I welcome your best thinking on these issues.	最后，我想说的是，我非常期待本次会议上的讨论以及未来持续的评审工作。我们需要最好的工具和策略来应对现在面临的挑战，我们必须以清晰可信的方式进行沟通。我和我的同事们欢迎大家就这些问题提出独到的见解[7]。

（节选自 Jerome H. Powell, Opening Remarks at the "Conference on Monetary Policy Strategy, Tools, and Communications Practices", Federal Reserve Board-Speeches, June. 4th, 2019）

难点 1

原文：We are closely monitoring the implications of these developments for the U.S. economic outlook and, as always, we will act as appropriate to sustain the expansion, with a strong labor market and inflation near our symmetric 2 percent objective.

译文：我们正在密切关注这些进展对美国经济前景的影响；面对强劲的劳动力市场和接近2%的对称性通胀目标，我们也将一如既往地采取适当的行动来维系经济扩张。

分析："as always"是一个插入语，介词"with"引导的状语，如果将这两个句子成分放在原位置进行翻译，译文的可读性不高，所以将插入语处理为副词"一如既往地"，"with"引导的状语放在主句前面翻译，调整句式，在不改变原文意义的前提下，使译文信息传递更加明确。

难点 2

原文：They focused on many questions posed by low inflation and, in particular, on what unconventional tools a central bank might use to support the economy if interest rates fell to what we now call the effective lower bound (ELB).

译文：他们关注的是低通胀带来的许多问题，特别是如果利率下降到我们现在称之为有效下限（ELB）的水平，中央银行可能会用什么非常规工具来支持经济。

分析：这句话的主干是"They focused on …"，句子较长，成分较多，从句中还有定语、插入语和条件状语，翻译时可以进行切分，对句子顺序进行调整。

难点 3

原文：Our obligation to the public we serve is to take those measures now that will put us in the best position deal with our next encounter with the ELB.

译文：我们对公众的义务是在当下采取措施，当利率再次跌到有效下限时，能够做好万全准备。

分析："put us in the best position"如果直译意思是"处于比较好的位置"，但是此处为了让译文符合目的语表达习惯，改变语序，将其放到最后译，处理为"做好万全准备"，在不改变原文意思的前提下，利用转译法照顾到译语结构。"encounter with"意思是"遇见、碰到"，ELB(effective lower bound)是一个专业术语，指"名义利率的有效下限"，直译这部分意思是"碰到有效下限"，虽然保留了原来形象化的表达，但是不符合汉语表达习惯，所以此处去掉形象化表达，转译为"跌到有效下限"，提高了译文的可读性。

难点 4

原文：And with the economy growing, unemployment low, and inflation low and stable, this is the right time to engage the public broadly on these topics.

译文：随着经济增长，失业率走低，通货膨胀稳定保持在低位，现在正是让公众广泛参与这些话题的最佳时机。

分析："economy growing, unemployment low, and inflation low and stable"都是名词短语，翻译时将其处理为动宾结构和短句，更加符合中文的动态表达习惯。

难点 5

原文：In addition, over time, inflation has become much less sensitive to tightness in resource utilization.

译文：此外，随着时间的推移，通货膨胀对资源利用的紧俏程度变得不那么敏感了。

分析：原文中"tightness"是一个抽象名词，意思是"紧张"，如果仅仅将译文处理为"紧张"一词，意思并不明确，具体的内涵意义无法表达出来，译者将其处理为"紧俏程度"，增加了一个范畴词"程度"，表达为通货膨胀对资源的紧俏程度更敏感，意思更加完整，整体表达更加清晰明了。

难点 6

原文：In short, the proximity of interest rates to the ELB has become the preeminent monetary policy challenge of our time, tainting all manner of issues with ELB risk and imbuing many old challenges with greater significance.

译文：简而言之，利率水平逼近有效下限已经成为我们这个时代不可忽视的货币政策挑战，这种风险衍生出各种问题，许多旧挑战也变得更加严重。

分析："tainting"意思是"污染，玷污"，"imbuing"意思是"充满，灌输"；这两个词在整句话中是一个形象化的表达，首先我们要理解原文的意思，主要表达了三个层面的意思：一是利率逼近有效下限是一个挑战，二是挑战带来新的问题，三是挑战使得旧问题更加严重。译者将"tainting"和"imbuing"两个具有形象化表达的词语利用转译法处理为去

163

形象化，保留主旨意思。

难点7

原文：My colleagues and I welcome your best thinking on these issues.

译文：我和我的同事们欢迎大家就这些问题提出独到的见解。

分析：英文多名词，中文多动词，此处将"thinking"翻译为名词"见解"，并且在前面增加了一个动词，处理为"提出见解"，可以使得语言更加正式，语气更礼貌。

二、汉译英

原文	译文
克里国务卿， 雅各布·卢财长， 各位来宾， 女士们，先生们，朋友们：	Secretary of State John Kerry, Secretary of the Treasury Jacob Lew, Distinguished Guests, Ladies and Gentlemen, Friends,
今天，第八轮中美战略与经济对话和第七轮中美人文交流高层磋商在北京举行。首先，我对对话和磋商的开幕，表示衷心的祝贺！对远道而来的美国朋友，表示热烈的欢迎！	Today, the eighth round of the China-US Strategic and Economic Dialogue (S&ED) and the seventh round of the China-US High-level Consultation on People-to-People Exchange (CPE) are held here in Beijing. Let me begin by extending hearty congratulations on the opening of the S&ED and the CPE and a big welcome to American friends who have traveled all the way to China[1].
3年前的这个时节，我同奥巴马总统在安纳伯格庄园举行会晤，双方同意加强战略沟通，拓展务实合作，妥善管控分歧，努力构建中美新型大国关系。	Almost around this time three years ago, President Obama and I met at the Annenberg Estate where agreement was reached for the two sides to step up strategic communication, expand practical cooperation[2], properly manage differences and work vigorously to build a new model of major-country relationship between China and the United States.
一分耕耘，一分收获。3年耕耘，我们有了不少收获。在双方努力下，中美两国在双边、地区、全球层面众多领域开展合作，推动两国关系发展取得新成果。两国贸易额和双向投资达到历史新高，人文和地方交流更加密切，网络、执法等领域合作和两军交往取得新进展。	Hard work pays off, and our efforts over the past three years have come to fruition. Thanks to our concerted efforts, our two countries have cooperated at the bilateral, regional and global levels in a wide range of areas, registering new progress in our relations. We witnessed record highs in trade and two-way investment, enjoyed closer people-to-people and sub-national exchanges, and made new headway in cooperation in cyberspace, law enforcement and military-to-military exchanges.

原文	译文
3年的成果来之不易，也给了我们很多启示，最根本的一条就是双方要坚持不冲突不对抗、相互尊重、合作共赢的原则，坚定不移推进中美新型大国关系建设。这个选择符合中美两国人民根本利益，也是各国人民普遍愿望。无论国际风云如何变幻，我们都应该坚持这个大方向，毫不动摇为之努力。	What we achieved over the past three years has not come by easily, and could well serve as guide for the growth of China-US relations in the time to come. Most important, I believe, is that the two sides need to stay committed to the principles of non-confrontation, non-conflict, mutual respect and win-win cooperation, and work steadily toward this new model of major-country relations, for this is a choice that meets the fundamental interests of both the Chinese and American people as well as the wish of all people in the world. Whatever changes in the international landscape, we need to stay on track and work unswervingly toward this overarching goal[3].
现在，我们正处在一个快速发展变化的世界里。世界多极化、经济全球化、社会信息化深入推进，各种挑战层出不穷，各国利益紧密相连。零和博弈、冲突对抗早已不合时宜，同舟共济、合作共赢成为时代要求。作为世界上最大的发展中国家、最大的发达国家和前两大经济体，中美两国更应该从两国人民和各国人民根本利益出发，勇于担当，朝着构建中美新型大国关系的方向奋力前行。	We now live in a world of rapid development and changes. The move toward multi-polarity, the increasing trend of globalization, and the quick application of information technologies have all been accompanied by growing challenges of various sorts, and have brought countries even closer than ever before. It is a time when ideas of zero-sum game and conflicts and confrontation must give way to common development and win-win cooperation. It thus falls upon China and the US, the largest developing and developed country respectively, and the two largest economies in the world, to act in the fundamental interests of our people and people of the world, and move steadily forward along the path of building this new model of major-country relationship.
我们要增强两国互信。中国人历来讲究"信"。2000多年前，孔子就说："人而无信，不知其可也。"信任是人与人关系的基础、国与国交往的前提。我们要防止浮云遮眼，避免战略误判，就要通过经常性沟通，积累战略互信。这个问题解决好了，中美合作基础就会更加坚实，动力就会更加强劲。	China and the US need to increase mutual trust. For the Chinese, trust is always something to be cherished. In the word of Confucius, who lived over 2,000 years ago, a man without trust can hardly accomplish anything. Trust stands as the basis of relationship among people, and provides a prerequisite for state-to-state exchanges. For China and the US, we need to maintain frequent communication and build up strategic mutual trust in order to avoid strategic misjudgment and prevent temporary problems from affecting our overall relations[4]. With sufficient mutual trust, China-US cooperation will stand on a more solid basis and enjoy even more robust growth.

续表

原文	译文
女士们、先生们、朋友们！今年是中国实施"十三五"规划开局之年。中国将贯彻全面建成小康社会、全面深化改革、全面依法治国、全面从严治党的战略布局，落实创新、协调、绿色、开放、共享的发展理念，着力推进供给侧结构性改革，推动转方式调结构，继续完善对外开放布局。我们对实现中国经济社会发展既定目标充满信心。中国将会为世界提供更多发展机遇，将会同包括美国在内的世界各国开展更密切的合作。	Ladies and Gentlemen, Friends, This year marks the beginning of China's 13th Five-Year Plan[5]. China will follow its strategic plan to build a society of moderate prosperity in all respects, and will comprehensively deepen reform, strengthen the rule of law, and enhance Party discipline[6]. China's development will be guided by the principle of innovative, coordinated, green, open and shared development. China will redouble efforts to promote supply-side structural reforms, shift growth model through restructuring, and achieve better opening-up. We are confident that the goals set for economic and social development will be met as planned. China's development will mean more opportunities for the world and China will have even closer cooperation with the US and other countries.
中国宋代诗人辛弃疾有一句名句，叫作"青山遮不住，毕竟东流去"。意思是天下的大江大河千回百转，历经多少曲折，最终都会奔流到海。只要我们坚定方向、锲而不舍，就一定能推动中美新型大国关系建设得到更大发展，更好造福两国人民和各国人民。最后，祝本轮中美战略与经济对话和人文交流高层磋商取得圆满成功！ 　　谢谢大家。	Xin Qiji, a poet in China's Song Dynasty[7], once wrote, "Thick mountains could not stop the river from flowing into the sea[8]." In fact, all rivers have to travel a meandering course before reaching their destination. For China and the US, as long as we stay focused on our goal and persevere in our efforts, we will be able to make even greater progress in building the new model of major-country relationship and deliver greater benefits not just to the people of our two countries but to people of all countries in the world. To conclude, I wish this round of the China-US S&ED and CPE a complete success. 　　Thank you.

（节选自习近平主席在第八轮中美战略与经济对话和第七轮中美人文交流高层磋商联合开幕式上的讲话，http://www.china.org.cn/chinese/cat/node_7225250.htm）

难点 1

原文：首先，我对对话和磋商的开幕，表示衷心的祝贺！对远道而来的美国朋友，表示热烈的欢迎！

译文：Let me begin by extending hearty congratulations on the opening of the S&ED and the CPE and a big welcome to American friends who have traveled all the way to China.

分析："对……表示衷心的感谢，对……表示热烈的欢迎"是经济会议演讲中演讲者常用的套话，我们要识记它们的固定表达才能在翻译时运用自如。比如英文常用"extend hearty congratulations on sth. and a big welcome to sb."来表达对某人某事的感谢和欢迎。

难点 2

原文：3年前的这个时节，我同奥巴马总统在安纳伯格庄园举行会晤，双方同意加强战略沟通，拓展务实合作。

译文：Almost around this time three years ago, President Obama and I met at the Annenberg Estate where agreement was reached for the two sides to step up strategic communication, expand practical cooperation.

分析：中文多用主动语态，一般用人作主语；英文多用被动语态，用物作主语，多用"无灵主语+有灵动词"的搭配。中文中的"同意"是主动语态，但在英文中变成了被动语态，采用"无灵主语+有灵动词"的搭配，符合英文的表达习惯。

难点 3

原文：无论国际风云如何变幻，我们都应该坚持这个大方向，毫不动摇为之努力。

译文：Whatever changes in the international landscape, we need to stay on track and work unswervingly toward this overarching goal.

分析：中文是动态语言，多用动词；英文是静态语言，多用名词。中文中用的动词"变换"，英文改变词性，使用的是名词词性的"changes"，将"国际风云"译为地点状语"in the international landscape"。在英文中要注意多用名词，中文中要多用动词。

难点 4

原文：防止浮云遮眼

译文：prevent temporary problems from affecting our overall relations

分析：中文中，尤其是在演讲中，发言者喜欢用中国成语使演讲更加生动形象，增强感染力，这也给译者的翻译带来了一定挑战。译者在翻译时一般采取意译中的释译法。比如本文中的"我们要防止浮云遮眼，避免战略误判，就要通过经常性沟通，积累战略互信"，"浮云遮眼"是中国特有的成语，译者采取了意译，译为"prevent temporary problems from affecting our overall relations"。

难点 5

原文：今年是中国实施"十三五"规划开局之年。

译文：This year marks the beginning of China's 13th Five-Year Plan.

分析："是"译为"mark"更地道。英文中有一些特殊动词可以用于这些句型，比如"witness""see"等。"这三年经济迅速发展"可以译为"The three years witness the fast development of economy"。

难点 6

原文：中国将贯彻全面建成小康社会、全面深化改革、全面依法治国、全面从严治党的战略布局……

译文：China will follow its strategic plan to build a society of moderate prosperity in all respects, and will comprehensively deepen reform, strengthen the rule of law, and enhance Party discipline…

分析：中文的经济会议演讲往往包含很多政治性词汇以及政策方针，比如"全面建成小康社会、全面深化改革、全面依法治国、全面从严治党的战略布局""创新、协调、绿色、开放、共享的发展理念"等，译者一般采用其约定俗成的已有的译法，平时要注重多积累这些固定表达。

难点 7

原文：中国宋代诗人辛弃疾

译文：Xin Qiji, a poet in China's Song Dynasty

分析：中文在介绍某个人时，一般先说职位再说人名，但英文在介绍某个人时，一般先说人名再说职位，翻译时要注意中英差异。

难点 8

原文：青山遮不住，毕竟东流去

译文：Thick mountains could not stop the river from flowing into the sea

分析：中文演讲者在发言时会经常用到诗句，译者一般采用意译法，译出主要信息即可，从而使得目的语读者能产生与原文读者相同的反应。比如"青山遮不住，毕竟东流去"没有将"青山"直译出来，也没有翻译"东"，而是意译为"Thick mountains could not stop the river from flowing into the sea"，外文读者能够明了其意思。

翻 译 练 习

一、词组翻译

global financial architecture
stagnant trade
financial system
energy economy

International monetary fund

industrial subsidies

bilateral trade agreements

transfer payment from the exchequer

关税壁垒

国内投资

反倾销

休会

第三产业

高层会谈

自由贸易区

二、句子翻译

(一) 英译汉

1. History shows that prosperity is greatest when government allow not just the free exchange of goods but the free exchange of ideas, that innovation, which thrives in open economies and societies, thrives in open economies and societies.

2. We are facing all changes with new solutions and we are seizing new opportunities with brimming confidence and boundless resolve.

3. But I also warned of the dangers of market instability and said that forward guidance under our new MPC remit could be a useful tool to manage expectations as the economy recovered.

4. A number of them remarked on the fact that it pointed to lessons that they could take away in revitalizing manufacturing towns in their home countries.

5. It's worth recalling the situation we faced six months ago — a contracting economy, skyrocketing unemployment, stagnant trade, and a financial system that was nearly frozen.

(二) 汉译英

1. 作为世界主要经济体领导人，我们有责任在关键时刻为世界经济和全球治理把准航向，为市场增强信心，给人民带来希望。

2. 中国有信心走好自己的路、办好自己的事，同世界各国和平共处、合作共赢，共建人类命运共同体，为创造世界经济更加美好的明天不懈努力。

3. 很高兴同大家在这里相聚，共商架设合作之桥、促进共同繁荣大计。

4. 我们要坚持走开放发展、互利共赢之路，共同做大世界经济的蛋糕。

5. 让我们携手合作，推动联动增长，促进共同繁荣，不断向着构建人类命运共同体的目标迈进！

三、语篇翻译

登高望远,牢牢把握世界经济正确方向
——在二十国集团领导人峰会第一阶段会议上的发言

尊敬的马克里总统,

各位同事:

今年是国际金融危机发生10周年,也是二十国集团领导人峰会10周年。尽管世界经济整体保持增长,但危机的深层次影响仍未消除,经济增长新旧动能转换尚未完成,各类风险加快积聚。新一轮科技革命和产业变革引发深刻变化,贫富差距和社会矛盾压力不断增加。世界经济再一次面临历史性的选择。

"以史为鉴,可以知兴替。"二十国集团要从历史大势中把握规律,引领方向。人类发展进步大潮滚滚向前,世界经济时有波折起伏,但各国走向开放、走向融合的大趋势没有改变。产业链、价值链、供应链不断延伸和拓展,带动了生产要素全球流动,助力数十亿人口脱贫致富。各国相互协作、优势互补是生产力发展的客观要求,也代表着生产关系演变的前进方向。在这一进程中,各国逐渐形成利益共同体、责任共同体、命运共同体。无论前途是晴是雨,携手合作、互利共赢是唯一正确选择。这既是经济规律使然,也符合人类社会发展的历史逻辑。面对重重挑战,我们既要增强紧迫感,也要保持理性,登高望远,以负责任态度把握世界经济大方向。

保持世界经济稳定发展的共同需要催生了二十国集团。10年来,我们同舟共济、勠力同心,推动世界经济走出衰退深渊,走上了复苏增长的轨道。10年后,我们应该再次拿出勇气,展示战略视野,引领世界经济沿着正确轨道向前发展。

第一,坚持开放合作,维护多边贸易体制。5年前,我第一次出席二十国集团领导人峰会,呼吁共同维护和建设开放型世界经济。现在看,这一任务更加迫切。二十国集团成员间月均新增贸易限制措施比半年前翻了一番,2018年全球货物贸易量增速可能下滑0.3%。我们应该坚定维护自由贸易和基于规则的多边贸易体制。中方赞成对世界贸易组织进行必要改革,关键是要维护开放、包容、非歧视等世界贸易组织核心价值和基本原则,保障发展中国家发展利益和政策空间。要坚持各方广泛协商,循序推进,不搞"一言堂"。

第二,坚持伙伴精神,加强宏观政策协调。伙伴精神是二十国集团最宝贵的财富。无论遇到什么困难,二十国集团成员都应该团结一致,共克时艰。各方应该坚持财政、货币、结构性改革"三位一体"的政策工具,努力推动世界经济强劲、平衡、可持续、包容增长。加强政策协调既是世界经济增长的客观需要,也是主要经济体理应担负的责任。发达经济体在采取货币和财政政策时,应该更加关注并努力减少对新兴市场国家和发展中国家的冲击。国际货币基金组织第十五轮份额总检查应该按期完成,国际货币体系应该继续朝着多元化方向迈进,要构筑更加牢固的全球金融安全网。

第三,坚持创新引领,挖掘经济增长动力。世界经济数字化转型是大势所趋,新的工业革命将深刻重塑人类社会。我们既要鼓励创新,促进数字经济和实体经济深度融合,也要关注新技术应用带来的风险挑战,加强制度和法律体系建设,重视教育和就业培训。我们既要立足自身发展,充分发掘创新潜力,也要敞开大门,鼓励新技术、新知识传播,让创新造福更多国家和人民。为更好引领和适应技术创新,建议二十国集团将"新技术应用及其影响"作为一项重点工作深入研究,认真探索合作思路和举措。

(节选自习近平主席在二十国集团领导人峰会第一阶段会议上的发言)

◎参考文献

[1] Nord, C. *Translating as a Purposeful Activity: Functionalist Approaches Explained*. Shanghai: Shanghai Foreign Language Education Press, 2002.

[2] 陈小慰. 对德国翻译功能目的论的修辞反思[J]. 外语研究, 2012(1): 91-95.

[3] 胡维佳. 功能翻译理论指导下的专有名词翻译[J]. 上海翻译, 2006(4): 34-36.

[4] 黄友义. 坚持"外宣三贴近"原则,处理好外宣翻译中的难点问题[J]. 中国翻译, 2004(6): 27-28.

[5] 李长栓. 非文学翻译理论与实践[M]. 北京: 中国对外翻译出版公司, 2004.

[6] 梁勇. 演讲辞文本翻译失误与策略探讨[J]. 淮南师范学院学报, 2018(4): 76-79.

[7] 廖七一. 当代西方翻译理论探索[M]. 南京: 译林出版社, 2000.

[8] 王军平. 演讲翻译的尺度[J]. 中国科技翻译, 2009(4): 33-37.

[9] 余樟亚. 英语政治演讲的翻译策略[J]. 中国科技翻译, 2019(4): 52-54.

第八章 经济会议联合公报翻译

> ☞**思考题**
> 1. 你知道哪些经济会议？它们开会的内容一般是什么？
> 2. 对于经济会议联合公报的格式内容你了解多少？
> 3. 作为译者，在翻译此类文本时你会注意些什么？

第一节 经济会议联合公报文本分析

在介绍经济会议联合公报之前，我们先要了解什么是公报，什么是联合公报，它们有什么区别和联系。作为经济会议联合公报，它和政治会议联合公报是否会有不一样的地方？下面请一起详细了解。

一、名词解释

公报：公报一般指国家、政府、政党、团体或其领导人所发表的关于重大事件或会议经过和决议等的正式文件。也有以会议的名义发表的公报。关于会议会谈进展、经过，或就某些问题达成协议的正式文件，称"公报""联合公报"或"新闻公报"。有时其中包含有关于这些国家间相互权利和义务的协议，具有条约的性质。由一国政府编印的专门登载法律、法令、决议、命令、条约、协定或其他官方文件的刊物，有时也称"公报"。例如联合国贸易和发展会议公报、中国共产党第十八届中央委员会第四次全体会议公报、政府公报、税务公报等。

联合公报：联合公报是指两个或两个以上的国家、政府、政党就有关重大国际问题、事件的会谈进展、经过、达成的协议等所发表的正式文件，是用以表明双方或多方对同一问题的共同看法的报道，或是经过谈判达成的具有承担权利和义务的协议文书。例如中美联合公报、中俄总理第二十四次定期会晤联合公报、中日韩三国会计准则制定机构会议联合公报、"一带一路"国际合作高峰论坛圆桌峰会联合公报、中德关于全面推进战略伙伴关系的联合公报等。

政治会议联合公报：简单而言，本章的政治会议联合公报即两个或两个以上的国家、政府、政党或经济组织就有关重大国际政治问题、事件的会谈进展、经过、达成的协议等所发表的正式文件,是用以表明双方或多方对同一问题的共同看法的报道,或是经过谈判达成的具有承担权利和义务的协议文书。

经济会议联合公报:顾名思义,本章所指的经济会议联合公报即为两个或两个以上的国家、政府、政党或经济组织就有关重大国际经济问题、事件的会谈进展、经过、达成的协议等所发表的正式文件,是用以表明双方或多方对同一问题的共同看法的报道,或是经过谈判达成的具有承担权利和义务的协议文书。

国际经济会议联合公报主要来源:G20各国财政部长及央行行长会议;"一带一路"国际合作高峰论坛,APEC(亚太经合组织),WB(世界银行),IMF(国际货币基金组织),等等。

既然公报有这么多种类,本章主要侧重经济会议联合公报的翻译。通过更加专业的学习,让我们翻译此类文本时更加得心应手。

例如《G20各国财政部长及央行行长会议联合公报》(*G20 Finance Ministers and Central Bank Governors Meeting Communiqué* | STBZ),里面就是各国财政部长及央行行长会议讨论后达成一致的协议文书。我们可以翻译以下内容进一步理解经济会议联合公报的特点:

Scope of creditors · All official bilateral creditors will participate in the initiative. · Private creditors will be called upon publicly to participate in the initiative on comparable terms. · Multilateral development banks will be asked to further explore the options for the suspension of debt service payments over the suspension period, while maintaining their current rating and low cost of funding. —*G20 Finance Ministers and Central Bank Governors Meeting Communiqué*/ Annex Ⅱ: Debt Service Suspension Initiative for Poorest Countries—Term Sheet

二、经济会议联合公报的基本特征

联合公报是融入新闻语体与政论语体的外交公文。联合公报一般在报纸、电台、电视台、网络等媒体上公开发布,具有报道重大事件的功能,拥有新闻语体的风格。联合公报需要正面阐述国家间的政治主张,又具有政论语体的风格。联合公报作为外交领域的公文,还具备外交公文的语体特点。

三、经济会议联合公报基本结构(标题(大标题和小标题)、正文、尾部)

以 *G20 Finance Ministers and Central Bank Governors Meeting Communiqué* 为例,其行文

结构如下：

1. 文件头（标题）

2. 正文
3. 附录

4. 附录小标题

Annex II: Debt Service Suspension Initiative for Poorest Countries — Term Sheet
Scope of beneficiary countries
- All IDA-countries, that are current on any debt service to the IMF and the World Bank.
- All least developed countries as defined by the United Nations, that are current on any debt service to the IMF and the World Bank.

Setting the right incentives

5. 尾部

有些联合公报没有尾部，有些联合公报以双方或多方签署作为尾部。

四、联合公报的语言特点

（一）语音

联合公报的语音，双音节组合占绝对优势。例如《第二届"一带一路"国际合作高峰论坛圆桌峰会联合公报》的第一部分。这一部分除了专有名词之外，其他词语以"二字格"为主，例如"主席""总统""酋长""总理""聚首""出席""共建""开创""欢迎""与会""峰会""主持"都是"二字格"。联合公报的内容经常通过电台、电视台播出，这就要求联合公报的语言具有明显的节奏感，便于播音员播发。双音节组合，播音员朗读起来，朗朗上口，铿锵有力，契合联合公报庄重严肃的总体风格。

英文中则不具备此特点。因此，在英译汉时，要注意词语的庄重严肃风格，如果有播报需要的话，更要注意语音的节奏感。

(二) 词汇

联合公报的词汇除了上面提到的双音节词占优势之外，还有以下特点：

1. 用词准确规范，书面语词多，口语词、方言词少

联合公报是一种正式文体，发布的均是国家间的重大事项，关系到国家间的利益。联合公报的用词力求正式规范、准确无误，不能含糊不清，不能有歧义。所以，联合公报多用标准的书面语词，很少使用口语词、方言词。

2. 用词典雅，使用一些具有文言色彩的词或短语

联合公报有时使用一些具有文言色彩的词，例如"之""于""至""此""及"等，使得联合公报的语言庄重典雅。因此在英译汉时，要突出中国特色。

3. 词汇时效性高，新词新语多

联合公报关注的是发文当时国家间最重大、最现实的事项，所用词语一般是反映各国新事物、新发展、新动态的新词新语。例如《第二届"一带一路"国际合作高峰论坛圆桌峰会联合公报》中出现的"杭州峰会""一带一路""古丝绸之路精神""共商共建共享"等近年才有的新词新语。

4. 词义宏大，关乎国家、民族，政治词汇多

联合公报发布的均是有关国家、政府、政党间的重大事项，攸关国家或政党利益。联合公报的性质决定联合公报必然使用很多政治领域的词汇。

(三) 语法

1. 句子结构完整

(1) 主谓句多，非主谓句少

联合公报要明确各方的权利与义务，行为主体、行为过程、行为客体都必须明确，所以多用结构完整的主谓句，一般不使用所指不明确的非主谓句。

(2) 多用长定语、长状语、长宾语

外交公文的语言要求准确严密，经常需要用定语、状语、补语等补充相关信息。例如：

我们相聚于世界经济机遇和挑战并存、世界正发生快速而深刻变化的(定语)时刻。我们重申加强多边主义对应对全球挑战至关重要。我们相信，构建开放、包容、联动、可持续和以人民为中心的(定语)世界经济，有利于促进共同繁荣。

We met at a time when(状语从句) the world economy is facing both expanding opportunities and rising challenges, complicated by profound and rapid changes in the world. We reaffirm that (宾语从句) strengthening multilateralism remains essential in addressing global challenges. We also believe that (宾语从句) an open, inclusive, interconnected, sustainable and people-centered world economy can contribute to prosperity for all. (《第二届"一带一路"国际合作高峰论坛圆桌峰会联合公报》)

2. 谓词性宾语的广泛应用

联合公报的语言逻辑严密，句子的语义层次清晰，为突出其动感作、操作性、程序性，多用谓词性宾语。例如《第二届"一带一路"国际合作高峰论坛圆桌峰会联合公报》中出现的"加强税收合作""鼓励达成更多避免双重征税协定""促进增长友好型的税收政策"等结构中的宾语都是谓词性的。这些谓词性宾语如"合作""协定""税收政策"等具有"双方性",体现了联合公报的双边功能。

3. 句式固定

联合公报中有很多固定句式,比如"我们相聚在……的时刻""我们坚信/决心、相信/承诺……""我们将……以……""我们重申……以……""……我们支持……""根据……""为……我们……""……特别是……""我们感谢……期待……再会"等。

4. 多陈述句,少祈使句、疑问句、感叹句

从语气角度来看,联合公报的句式基本上是陈述句,一般没有祈使句、疑问句或感叹句。

5. 修辞

联合公报主要是排比修辞格。例如《二十国集团领导人杭州峰会联合公报》中的"发挥引领作用、秉持伙伴关系、保持开放精神、体现包容风格、践行创意理念、发挥协同效应、展现灵活态度"用了排比修辞格。

6. 篇章

(1)层次清晰

联合公报的主要功能是要公开宣示发布方在哪些方面、项目、条款上达成了共识,需要在语言形式上凸显每一项共识,为此,联合公报经常采用以下方式:

①分段列举

让每一段呈现一项共识,所以联合公报的段落特别多。为进一步凸显是"双方"的共识,联合公报的段落经常有明显的段首标记,经常每一段都以"我们"起始。

②破折号列举

为进一步凸显双方每一条款的共识,甚至一句话的宾语中的每一条内容,都可以分段列举,每一段以破折号起始。

(2)直截了当,正面阐述

联合公报是双方或多方主张和共识的正式发布,语篇推进模式以正面陈述为主,少批驳,不迂回,不曲折,肯定句多,否定句少。

第二节　翻译知识讲解

一、翻译方法与技巧

(一)专有名词翻译

例1

原文:We welcome the IMF's rapid and enhanced deployment of access to emergency financing, including a temporary doubling of the annual access limit under the Rapid Credit Facility (RCF) and the Rapid Financing Instrument (RFI).

译文：我们欢迎国际货币基金组织加快紧急融资部署，包括快速信贷工具(Rapid Credit Facility，RCF)和快速融资工具(Rapid Financing Instrument，RFI)下的年度准入限额暂时翻一番。

分析：在原文中，有许多专有名词，如"国际货币基金组织""年度准入限额""快速信贷工具(RCF)"和"快速融资工具(RFI)"。在这种情况下，根据纽马克的语义翻译，译者应该使目标文本更加准确、忠实和具有可读性，以传递正确的信息。

(二) 长句翻译

1. 遵循原句法顺序

例2

原文：We are determined to spare no effort, both individually and collectively, to protect lives, bring the pandemic under control, safeguard people's jobs and incomes, support the global economy during and after this phase and ensure the resilience of the financial system.

译文：我们决心始终不遗余力，一道保护生命，控制疫情，保障人民就业和收入，维持全球经济，确保金融体系韧性。

分析：根据纽马克的文本类型理论，联合公报具有严肃性、权威性和准确性，属于表达性文本，翻译应与原文本具有相同的风格。因此，应采用语义翻译的翻译策略。为了保持原文的风格、体现原文的句式特点，译文不仅逐字逐句再现原文的内容，也保留了原文的格式。

2. 句式重组

例3

原文：As mandated by the extraordinary G20 Leaders' Summit, we endorse the G20 Action Plan in response to the COVID-19 pandemic, which sets out the key principles guiding our response, and our commitments to specific actions to drive forward international economic cooperation as we navigate this crisis and look ahead to a robust, sustained and inclusive global economic recovery.

译文：根据二十国集团领导人特别峰会的授权，我们核准了《G20行动计划——支持全球经济渡过新冠肺炎危机》，提出了G20政策行动的关键指导原则和应对危机，促进全球经济强劲、可持续和包容性复苏，推动国际经济合作的具体承诺。

分析：此处使用了句子结构重组的方法。在原文本中，只有一个谓语"endorse"，后面跟随着一个从句，以"sets"作从句谓语。为了使读者更好地理解，译文打破了单谓语结构，使用了两个平行的谓词，即"核准了"和"提出了"，这更符合中国读者的表达习惯，实现了翻译的交际意义。

(三) 篇章翻译

联合公报主要是传达国家间的共同政治主张，但有时也能容纳国家间的不同政治主张，这就要在共同表述的大框架内，容许不同国家的各自表述。例如，《G20各国财政部长及央行行长会议联合公报》中"we"共出现156次，"we"一词正唤起世界共同应对COVID-19的主人翁意识。另一方面，汉译英时，目的语经常带有中国特色的话语。因此，翻译的时候应注重对外话语体系的建设，树立中国形象，从而增强交际意义。

(四) 中国特色社会俗语翻译

政治话语体系是对外话语体系的核心，它集中体现了党和政府的执政理念和治国经验。准确全面地翻译领袖著作和重大会议文件，打造融通中外的新概念、新范畴、新表述，帮助国际社会正确理解中国在政治、经济、外交、文化等方面的路线、方针、政策，增强外界对中国发展的理解，提升中国特色社会主义道路的国际认同，提高国家文化软实力，都将是对外翻译的重点。中文的经济会议联合公报不仅能使世界了解中国的经济政策，还可以展示中文政治经济话语的独特魅力。在中国领导人的重要讲话中，给大家印象最为深刻的便是一些中国人民耳熟能详的俗语的运用。用俗语来表达一些较为深奥的政治术语，通俗易懂，因而，在对外翻译中，对这些俗语的翻译应该体现出这种亲民、求实、干练的风格，既能忠实地翻译出原文的含义，又能展示出独特的语言魅力，给目的语读者深刻的印象。为达到这一目的，翻译中可以遵循以下三个原则：

1. 端正文风

文如其人，文风体现作风，译者应充分了解原作者的思想轨迹及其行事作风，从而在翻译中既体现原作者的亲民实干，又体现语言的生动性和文章的可读性。

例 4

原文：打铁还需自身硬。

译文：The iron must be of good quality to be hammered/struck into a tool.

分析：这句俗语是习近平主席在会见中外记者时所说的一句话，"打铁还需自身硬"是一句中国传统俗语，人们常挂嘴边。在翻译时，译者没有直接翻译出"自身硬"这个相对抽象的概念，也没有解释说明性的文字，只是用简单的"quality"表达出品质的含义，使人易懂并影响深刻。

2. 转译文化

在中文的政治经济话语体系中有不少地方语言风格呈现出明显的形象比喻性，很多表述是典型的中国式表述，是中国传统文化的产物，简练精干，传情达意。在翻译中应谨慎对待这些特点，体现文化翻译精神，而不是生拉硬拽，弄巧反拙。

例 5

原文：要给权力涂上防腐剂，套上紧箍咒。

译文 1：Power should be covered with antiseptic and be kept in a straitjacket.

译文2:Power should be insulated from corruption.
译文3:Power should be bridled.

分析:原文中"防腐剂"是很常见的生活用品,而"紧箍咒"又出自家喻户晓的名著《西游记》,在西方并没有对应的文化词,因此不宜直译,在译文1中,译者将"防腐剂"译为"antiseptic",而不是更为常见的"preservative",对于"紧箍咒",译者将之转译为西方读者更为接受的"straitjacket",意为紧身衣。在译文2和译文3中,译者采取了意译的方法,用解释性的文字使读者更容易理解和接受。

3. 专业表达

专业表达原则是指在翻译外交新词时,译文的表达和措辞要专业、经济、简洁,符合外交语言的习惯用法,译文既不能俗气,也不能太长。

例6

原文:把权力关进制度的笼子。

译文1:Keep power in the cage of systemic checks/oversight.

译文2:Power should be placed under close oversight/checks.

分析:在中国人的传统思维里,把东西关进笼子有困住、管住的意思,这种俗语的表达便于大众的理解。译文1采用了直译的翻译方法,直观易懂,译文2采用意译的方法,保留了原文的简练、直接。治国理政论述翻译是一项综合事业,译者应该具备综合素质,与作者及其所代表的多元主体融为一体,置身其中,掌握其思想轨迹,了解其行为方式,进而才能成就理想的译文。在翻译治国理政论述中的俗语时更是如此,既要保留原文中的文化特色、发言人的亲民实干作风,又要使译文产生最大的共鸣,更好地向世界说明中国,让世界理解中国。

(五)隐喻

1. 直译法

隐喻立足文化、语言及思维之中,其作用是增强语言表达效果。而翻译是跨文化的语言交流过程,其隐喻翻译便是对文化系统的整体性移植,是利用第二语言重新构筑母语文化的形式,是将语言文化所呈现的认知思维通过第二语言传播到其他文化的流程。由于不同文化的国家拥有相同的知识体系,诸民族间又具备类似的认知机理,因此不同语言间可能存在着认知模式的相同,可以认为意象在目的语与母语的使用文本与频率相当,因而在政治文件隐喻翻译中可利用直译法进行翻译。例如"增强反腐斗争(隐喻)和党内廉政构建"可直译为"Strengthen the fight against corruption and build a clean government within the party"。又如,"将节能产业发展为我国的重要支柱"(隐喻)可直译为"The energy conservation industry will be developed as an important pillar of our country"。此种方法将政治文件中的隐喻表现直接置于英语语境中,使原文意境得以保留。读者可充分理解原政治文件的表达特点和思维方式,更有助于母语体系向目的语体系的渗透,进而在政治文件中联通译文与原文的文化气韵。

2. 替译法

隐喻翻译并非对词汇的直接对应，这是由于中文与英文的思维结构与认知方式不同所形成的。汉语蕴涵着汉族智慧与哲学；英语则反映着西方的价值观、历史文化、宗教思想及生活方式等。因而中西方在表现相同概念或意义时，会应用不尽相同的喻体，即运用不同的喻体表现相同的本体。因而，政治文件翻译的目的不应是文字符号的表现模式，而是读者对内容的反应。并且应将这"反应"与原文的"反应"进行对比，因此在政治文件翻译中，应依托英文的运用习惯，分析比喻概念和不同民族的人文环境，将原文的隐喻转变为目的语国家所能理解的隐喻，使其适应目的语国家的语言表达习惯，准确认知原文内容。例如"幸福之基是健康"替译后为"The root for happiness is health"。在译文中，将喻体"基"转变为植物的"根"，由于在英语用语习惯中"benchmark"与"root"相当，所以能有效传递政治文件含义。

(六) 四字格翻译

四字格是汉语词汇的一大特点。有些是自由词组，可以随意拆散，重新组合，例如"技术精湛""质量优良"等，而有些固定词组是一个整体，不能拆开、随意更换，其中包括一些成语，例如"寅吃卯粮""奇货可居"。汉语四字格的突出特点是：内容言简意赅，形式整齐划一，语音顺口悦耳，表达效果形象生动。汉语四字格的英语翻译方法各式各样：可以将其译成单词、词组或套用习语，也可以采用综合法进行翻译。具体采用哪种译法，应该根据不同的情况灵活处理。总的翻译原则是，使译文和原文在意义上形成对应关系，而不仅仅拘泥于形式上的简单对等。

二、翻译理论

语义翻译和交际翻译是纽马克翻译理论中最重要、最有特色的组成部分。语义翻译法具有绝对意义，交际翻译法具有相对意义。语义翻译法集逐字翻译、直译和忠实翻译的优势，交际翻译法集归化、意译和地道翻译的优势。在纽马克的翻译理论中，强调把语义翻译与交际翻译看成一个整体，翻译中不可能孤立地使用某种方法，也不能说语义翻译与交际翻译哪一个更好。二者在翻译中常常交替使用，只是侧重点不同而已，有时两种方法还会合二为一。在翻译本章文本时，可以采用该翻译理论。

三、翻译原则

联合公报是融入新闻语体与政论语体的外交公文。联合公报一般在报纸、电台、电视台、网络等媒体上公开发布，具有报道重大事件的功能，拥有新闻语体的风格。联合公报需要正面阐述国家间的政治主张，又具有政论语体的风格。联合公报作为外交领域的公文，还具备外交公文的语体特点。因此，翻译时应注意以下几个原则：

(一) 忠实为本原则

忠实、求信乃翻译之首要任务，只不过政论翻译要求更为严格。至于不同文体、文本翻译中，信于何或忠实于什么？内涵不尽相同，各有侧重。文学翻译信于艺术之美；

科技翻译信于指涉之意(referential meaning);而政论翻译则信于相关政治思想与见解主张。一般而言,政论翻译由于较为严肃,害怕出错,较少"不忠的美人",但译者大多拘泥于字当句对的被动硬译,看似字面忠实,往往不够准确或令人难以理解,所以政论翻译中的忠实为本所强调的是,译者应在兼顾语义与交际翻译的基础上,能动阐释,力求文字与思想的统一。

(二)话语逻辑原则

政论翻译表述不能只满足于语言通顺与否,还应注重话语逻辑规范。政论语言的思辨和说理性主要得益于其严密逻辑性:时空逻辑、指代逻辑、数的逻辑、施受逻辑、虚实逻辑、序数逻辑。由于英汉逻辑思维上存在着"形合"与"意合"本质上的不同,政论译文表达时要注意逻辑衔接和语义重心的处理,尤其要注意这种逻辑思维差异所引发的语言性、数、格、时态、语态等细节方面的不同,这样就能做到钱锺书所说的"依义旨以传,如风格以出",更有利于原文思想内容的传达。

(三)政治敏感原则

程镇球先生曾有专文论及:"政治文章的翻译要讲政治。"政论不仅是作者阶级立场、政治主张的"广而告之",有时甚至带有强烈的意识形态主体本位性和功利性。译者必须具备政治修养和敏感意识,才能从政治语境中对那些政策性较强的词汇、概念加以准确地理解和表达。特别是,在思想情感表述上,语气态度刚柔相济,虚实隐显,弦外留音,言外存意,如果没有较强的政治敏感性,就无法做到把握分寸、适度而译。

(四)社会属性原则

社会宣传与实践导向是政论固有的交际职能和功用价值。文章乃为事而作,亦为时而作,政论翻译尤其应注重其社会属性,即将文本目的、译者目的和读者目的有机地统一起来。这一方面要求译者吃透原文的交际目的和特色,笔者认为,大致可划分为立场声明、国策宣告、精神鼓舞、感悟抒怀、思想评述、号召响应、批判谬误、揶揄讽刺、问责诘难、针砭时弊等几类;另一方面还要求译者充分考虑到目标读者群的接受习惯和期待视野。

(五)文化处理原则

"翻译的最初对象是话语,最终对象是文化信息。"[1]政论翻译本质上是一种文化活动,而文化处理策略不外乎归化与异化两大价值取向。具体而言,对政论中那些文化差异较大但并未承载丰富政治内涵的谚语、习语或修辞手段,可最大限度地发挥译语优势,采取借译、替代、套用等归化手法处理;而对于那些政治色彩浓厚、思想深刻,涉及相关政治主张、立场态度的关键性词汇表达,即使在译语文化中存在着空缺或不相适应的情况,也不得随意归化,更不能省略或删减,必须异化出之,保持原汁原味,同时译文可采取一些直译加注或直译加意义诠释等手法,以利于读者理解和接受。

---

[1] 黄忠廉. 翻译本质论[M]. 武汉:华中师范大学出版社,2000.

四、译者素养

(一) 保持正确的政治立场

保持正确的政治立场是周恩来总理当年对外交翻译提出的要求，也是任何一个国家对它的外交官和外交翻译的要求。要真正做到这一点，翻译工作者就必须了解、理解、拥护党和国家的各项方针政策，特别是外交政策。例如，我国对香港恢复行使主权不能译为"to reclaim sovereignty over Hongkong"，而应该是"to resume the exercise of sovereignty over Hongkong"，因为我国从未放弃过对香港的主权。

(二) 准确理解政策，提高政策水平

翻译只有在知道、理解形势的复杂性、问题的症结所在、矛盾分歧的根源与表现、斗争的焦点、问题的敏感处，才能准确把握领导人的讲话意图，准确翻译他们的讲话。例如朱镕基总理1999年4月在美国麻省理工学院讲演时指出中美贸易顺差的性质时说："美国对华贸易虽存在逆差，但这种逆差不是竞争性的，并不形成对美国国内产业和就业的冲击。"要翻译这句话，就必须研究它的实质含义。"不是竞争性"是指中国出口的是劳动密集型产品，不存在与美国企业竞争的问题，相反有助于美国产业结构升级和竞争力的提高，有利于美国集中精力发展高科技产业，所以说这种逆差不是竞争性的。弄清实质含义后，就不应该译为："Although there is a deficit on the US side, the deficit is not a competitive one and has no impact on the US domestic industries and employment."似可译为："Although the US side has got a deficit in its trade with China, the deficit is not caused by a competitive Sino-US trade structure and has no impact on the US domestic industries and employment."总之，对外交翻译来说，要译得好，译得到位，译出深度，译得准确，最重要的是了解背景，掌握政策，提高政策敏感性。

(三) 工作认真严谨，具有钻研精神

作为外交翻译，要能够把握词的细微差别，要研究讲话的深层含义。如我国曾表示希望我国与某国外交部的对话磋商机制规范化。一开始译为"to standardize the dialogue and consultation mechanism"。向有关地区司了解后发现，"规范化"意指我国与该国外交部口头上已达成要进行对话与磋商的谅解，尚未用书面形式确定下来。显然这样翻译就不准确了。后改为："We hope to have a mechanism put in place for regular dialogue and consultation."又如"要用法律来规范市场行为"，不能译为："We need laws to standardize the market behaviour.""规范市场行为"不是要统一行为，而是要对市场行为规定一些行为准则，或者说游戏规则。所以译为"We need laws to regulate market behavior"更好一些。从事外交翻译，绝不能想当然，绝不能望词生意。在今天这么一个知识经济、信息爆炸的时代，国际、国内形势瞬息万变。我们如果不密切跟踪形势的发展，势必做不好外交翻译。北约轰炸南联盟后，江泽民主席立即作出反应，谴责以美国为首的北约绕过联合国、肆意践踏《联合国宪章》，把一个纯属一国内政的问题变为对一个主权国家动武的事件。随团翻译如果对情况一点都不了解，翻译时就会感到没有把握，心里就会没底。因此，

对口译员来说，除了要看事先准备的各种材料和宣传口径以外，还要密切了解最新动向和消息，包括用词。再者，任何一个国家都会有自己独特含义的用语。这是由各国的政治制度、发展模式、意识形态、价值观念、生活方式等不同而造成的。这类词汇的翻译是我们外交翻译的又一难点。要翻译好这类词汇，必须认真研究它们的内涵。例如"精神文明""建设有中国特色的社会主义政治（political life under socialism with Chinese characteristics，不能译为 the socialist politics with Chinese characteristics）"等。

(四) 严守国家机密，严守外事纪律

由于工作的需要，外交翻译需要参加一些重要的会见、会谈、国际会议等双边、多边外事活动，有时还需要参加一些内部讨论，直接听到领导人对一些问题的看法，知道一些政府决策的"内幕"，看到一些内部文件。但翻译决不允许以任何方式传播机密内容，连对自己的家人、亲朋好友都不能"吹风"。由于语言相通，翻译接触外宾的机会比较多，外宾也愿找翻译谈，但翻译没有直接回答问题和处理问题的"任务"。

(五) 具备良好的翻译职业道德

各行各业都有一定的职业道德和行为规范需要遵循。作为外交翻译，应做到不篡改原话原意，不随心所欲瞎译。翻译仅仅起桥梁和沟通作用。为此，译员对原话原作不能随个人好恶而有所改变或取舍，不能偷工减料，不能嫌讲话者啰唆而随意删改。

第三节　常用词汇与表达

原文	译文
the International Financial Institutions (IFIs)	国际金融机构
the annual access limit	年度准入限额
the Rapid Credit Facility (RCF)	快速信贷工具
the Rapid Financing Instrument (RFI)	快速融资工具
Short-Term Liquidity Line	短期流动资金额度
the Financial Stability Board's (FSB)	金融稳定委员会
the *International Health Regulations* (IHR 2005)	《国际卫生条例》(2005年)
Organization for Economic Co-operation and Development (OECD)	经济合作与发展组织
regional financing arrangements (RFAs)	区域性融资安排
the Poverty Reduction and Growth Trust (PRGT)	减贫和增长信托基金 (PRGT)
the Catastrophe Containment and Relief Trust (CCRT)	灾难遏制和救济信托基金
We are determined to	我们决心

续表

原文	译文
We commit to	我们承诺
We welcome	我们欢迎
We support	我们支持
We agreed on	我们商定
We call on	我们呼吁
We ask	我们请求
We reiterate our commitment	我们重申，我们承诺
We have taken... measures to	我们已采取……的措施
we recognize	我们认识到
互联互通	connectivity
重振……精神	restoring and rejuvenating such spirit
经济走廊	economic corridors
政策沟通、设施联通、贸易畅通、资金融通和民心相通	promoting development of policy synergy, infrastructure development, unimpeded trade, financial cooperation and people-to-people bond
共商共建共享	extensive consultation, joint contribution and shared benefits

第四节 译文赏析

一、汉译英

原文	译文
我们支持在遵守各国法律法规的基础上开展国际反腐败合作，对腐败问题采取零容忍态度。我们呼吁各国根据自身在《联合国反腐败公约》等国际公约和相关双边条约下的义务，加强相关国际合作。我们期待在交流有益经验和开展务实合作方面加强合作。	We support international anti-corruption cooperation and work towards zero tolerance in anti-corruption, consistent with national laws and regulations[1]. We call for more international cooperation in line with our applicable respective obligations under international conventions, such as UN Convention Against Corruption (UNCAC), and relevant bilateral treaties. We look forward to strengthening international cooperation and exchanges of good practices and practical cooperation.

第四节 译文赏析

续表

原文	译文
加强务实合作	Strengthening Practical Cooperation
为实现共同繁荣，我们应加强务实合作。有关合作应坚持以人民为中心，坚持结果导向和增长导向，遵守市场规则及各国法律，必要时政府可提供相应支持。我们鼓励包括中小微企业在内的各国企业参与合作。我们强调在遵守各国法律法规的基础上，采取开放、透明和非歧视的公共采购程序的重要性，并欢迎交流有益经验。	To achieve and sustain shared prosperity, practical cooperation should be strengthened. Such cooperation needs to be people-centered, result-based and growth-oriented[2], in accordance with market rules and our respective legal frameworks supported by the government when necessary. We encourage the participation by enterprises from all countries in the cooperation, including micro, small and medium enterprises. We highlight the importance of open, transparent and non-discriminatory public procurement procedures in accordance with national laws and regulations and welcome the exchanges of good practices.
我们支持各国在已有进展的基础上，继续建设经济走廊、经贸合作区（见附件）和同"一带一路"相关的合作项目，加强价值链、产业链、供应链合作。	We support continued efforts to build on the progress already made in developing economic corridors and economic and trade cooperation zones (as annexed) as well as other cooperation projects across all areas related to the "Belt and Road" Initiatives[3], and further cooperation on value chains, industry chains and supply chains.
我们将在遵守国际法和各国法律的前提下，继续加强多式联运，包括运用内陆国的内河水道、公路和铁路网络、陆海空港口及管道。我们鼓励借鉴国际良好实践，加强包括跨境高速光缆在内的数字基础设施，发展电子商务和智慧城市，缩小数字鸿沟。	We will continue our efforts towards strengthening multi-modal transportation including inland waterways in landlocked countries, roads, railway networks, air, land and sea ports and pipelines in line with international law and respective domestic laws. We encourage digital infrastructure including transnational fiber-optic highways, promoting e-commerce and smart cities, and helping narrow the digital divide while drawing on international good practices.
我们鼓励开展第三方市场合作、三方合作及政府和社会资本合作，欢迎企业和有关国际组织在符合各国法律法规的前提下就此做出更多努力。我们欢迎开展法务合作，包括为工商界提供争端解决服务和法律援助。	We encourage third-market, tripartite cooperation and Public Private Partnership (PPP)[4] cooperation and welcome more efforts by enterprises and relevant international organizations consistent with national laws and regulations. We welcome legal cooperation, including the availability of dispute resolution services and legal assistance for the business sector.

185

原文	译文
我们支持各国金融机构和国际金融机构开展合作，为有关项目提供多元化和可持续的融资支持。在尊重各国国内优先事项、法律法规、国际承诺以及联合国大会在债务可持续性方面通过的有关原则的同时，我们鼓励本币融资和互设金融机构，更好地发挥开发性金融的作用。我们鼓励多边开发银行和其他国际金融机构以财政可持续的方式加大对互联互通项目的支持，并根据当地需求动员民间资本投资相关项目。	We support collaboration among national and international financial institutions to provide diversified and sustainable financial supports for projects. We encourage local currency financing, mutual establishment of financial institutions, and a greater role of development in finance in line with respective national priorities, laws, regulations and international commitments, and the agreed principles by the UNGA on debt sustainability[5]. We encourage multilateral development banks and other international financial institutions to reinforce their support to connectivity projects in fiscally sustainable ways as well as the mobilization of private capital into projects in line with local needs.
为保障粮食安全和支持可持续发展，我们强调发展节水技术和开展农业创新的重要性。我们重视通过加强动植物卫生检疫合作，促进农产品贸易和投资。	We stress the importance of the development of water-saving technologies and agricultural innovations as an important component providing food security and supporting sustainable development. We stress the importance of cooperation on veterinary-sanitary and phytosanitary matters[6] for agricultural products in order to facilitate trade and investment.
我们注意到附件中列出的各专业领域"一带一路"合作平台。	We take note of the thematic sectoral platforms as seen in the annex.
加强人文交流	Advancing People-to-People Exchanges
互联互通让不同国家、人民和社会之间的联系更加紧密。我们相信"一带一路"合作有利于促进各国人民以及不同文化和文明间的对话交流、互学互鉴。我们欢迎扩大人文交流的努力，包括加强青年间的交往。	Considering connectivity as a means of bringing countries, peoples and societies closer together, we believe the "Belt and Road" cooperation promotes exchanges, mutual learning and dialogue among different peoples, cultures and civilizations[7]. We welcome efforts to expand people-to-people exchanges including those between the youth.

(选自《第二届"一带一路"国际合作高峰论坛圆桌峰会联合公报》)

难点1

原文：我们支持在遵守各国法律法规的基础上开展国际反腐败合作，对腐败问题采取零容忍态度。

译文：We support international anti-corruption cooperation and work towards zero tolerance in anti-corruption, consistent with national laws and regulations.

分析：汉语多用动词表达，而英文更倾向于其他词性，翻译时不必保留汉语的词性。例如本句中"遵守"对应翻译使用了形容词短语"consistent with"；"开展""采取"则没有用动词翻译。

难点 2

原文：结果导向和增长导向

译文：result-based and growth-oriented

分析：中文有时会使用相同的表达，例如这里的"导向"，而英文会避免使用相同的表达，因此这里的两个"导向"分别用"-based""-oriented"进行翻译。

难点 3

原文："一带一路"

译文：the "Belt and Road" Initiatives

分析："一带一路"曾经使用过"One Belt One Road"进行翻译，但是 2015 年国家发改委、外交部、商务部和外文局正式确认了"一带一路"的英文官方翻译是"the 'Belt and Road' Initiatives"。我们需要及时了解官方表达的变化，并作出相应调整。

难点 4

原文：政府和社会资本合作

译文：Public Private Partnership (PPP)

分析：有些专有名词除了翻译以外，还需要给出缩写。又如，"《联合国反腐败公约》"翻译为"*UN Convention Against Corruption* (UNCAC)"。有时则只用缩写，如"UNGA"（联合国大会）。

难点 5

原文：在尊重各国国内优先事项、法律法规、国际承诺以及联合国大会在债务可持续性方面通过的有关原则的同时，我们鼓励本币融资和互设金融机构，更好地发挥开发性金融的作用。

译文：We encourage local currency financing, mutual establishment of financial institutions, and a greater role of development in finance in line with respective national priorities, laws, regulations and international commitments, and the agreed principles by the UNGA on debt sustainability.

分析：中文更多状语在前，主句在后，而英文更习惯先表达主句的内容，翻译时应该调整顺序，这样更符合英文的表达习惯。

第八章 经济会议联合公报翻译

难点 6

原文：动植物卫生检疫

译文：veterinary-sanitary and phytosanitary matters

分析："植物卫生检疫"有对应的英文表达"phytosanitary"，"动物"在这里应该选择"veterinary（兽医的）"进行处理。平时应加强相关词汇的积累。

难点 7

原文：互联互通让不同国家、人民和社会之间的联系更加紧密。我们相信"一带一路"合作有利于促进各国人民以及不同文化和文明间的对话交流、互学互鉴。

译文：Considering connectivity as a means of bringing countries, peoples and societies closer together, we believe the "Belt and Road" cooperation promotes exchanges, mutual learning and dialogue among different peoples, cultures and civilizations.

分析：中文的第一个句子实际上可以理解为第二个句子的状语，此处增加"considering"把第一句转换成分词状语更符合英文表达习惯。翻译时我们应该考虑句子之间的关联性，不要逐句翻译。

二、英译汉

原文	译文
Annex I: G20 Action Plan—Supporting the Global Economy Through the COVID-19 Pandemic **Introduction** 　　COVID-19 is first and foremost a global health emergency. The restrictions and containment measures put in place are vital to reduce the spread of the pandemic. But we also recognize that the measures are having a profound impact on our economies. We, the G20 members, must therefore work collectively and decisively to protect and support our citizens and businesses, prevent long-term damage and lift restrictions as soon as our health conditions allow. G20 Leaders have asked Finance Ministers and Central Bank Governors to develop an Action Plan in response to COVID-19. Our collective goal, set by G20 Leaders, is to protect lives; safeguard people's jobs and incomes; restore confidence, preserve financial stability, revive growth and recover stronger; minimize disruptions to global supply chains; provide help to all countries in need of assistance; and coordinate on public health and financial measures.	**附件一：G20 行动计划——支持全球经济度过新冠肺炎危机**[1] **简介** 　　新冠肺炎疫情首先是全球卫生紧急事件。遏制措施的实施对于减少疫情蔓延至关重要[2]。但我们也认识到，这些措施正在对我们的经济产生深远影响。我们，二十国集团成员，为此，必须采取集体和果断的行动，保护和支持我们的公民和企业，防止长期受损，一旦我们的健康状况允许，立即解除限制[3]。二十国集团领导人已要求财政部长和中央银行行长[4]制订一项应对新冠肺炎的行动计划。我们二十国集团领导人将致力于保护生命，保障人民的就业和收入，重振信心，保持金融稳定与恢复增长，最大限度减少对全球供应链的干扰，帮助全部有需要的国家，以及协调公共卫生和财务措施[5]。

188

续表

原文	译文
This *Action Plan* is a living document and the first step in our collective response. It sets out the key principles guiding our response, and our commitments to specific actions to drive forward international economic co-operation as we navigate this crisis and look ahead to a robust and sustained global economic recovery, while making sure the design of our response and its implementation remain consistent with achieving strong, sustainable, balanced and inclusive growth.	《行动计划》是一份现存文件，也是我们共同应对的第一步。它阐述了我们共同行动的关键指导原则和应对危机，促进全球经济强劲、可持续和包容性复苏，推动国际经济合作的具体承诺，同时确保我们的应对措施的计划与执行同强劲、可持续、平衡和包容性增长保持一致[6]。
Health Response—Saving Lives	**卫生措施——拯救生命**
Finance Ministers have a clear role to play in ensuring that all elements of the health-care response are fully funded, to ensure we save lives through reducing the spread of infection and preventing waves of reinfection. Enhanced collaboration and increased funding are urgently needed to support accelerated research and development for diagnostics, therapeutics and vaccines. We will work in close collaboration with G20 Health Ministers and with Trade and Investment Ministers to support the availability of essential medical supplies and pharmaceuticals.	财政部长应确保所有医疗措施有足够资金，确保新增病例减少和防止二次感染。我们迫切需要加强合作和增加资金，以加快诊断学、治疗学和疫苗的研究和开发。我们将与二十国集团卫生部长以及贸易和投资部长密切合作，提供基本医疗用品和药品支持。
As G20 members, we will undertake the following actions and make the following commitments to support the health response:	作为二十国集团成员，我们将采取以下行动，并作出以下承诺，以支持卫生措施：
· We commit to full compliance with the International Health Regulations (IHR 2005) and the continued sharing of timely, transparent and standardised data and information between countries including on health measures and the effectiveness of non-pharmaceutical interventions.	· 我们承诺全面遵守《国际卫生条例》（2005年），并继续在各国间及时分享透明和标准的数据和信息，包括卫生措施和非药物干预措施的有效性。
· We will take forward the G20 Leaders' commitment to provide immediate resources to key entities in global health, on a voluntary basis. We will quickly work together and with stakeholders to close the financing gap in global health.	· 我们将推动二十国集团领导人自愿承诺为全球卫生关键领域提供即时资源。我们将迅速与利益攸关方合作，缩小全球卫生领域的资金缺口。

续表

原文	译文
·We encourage voluntary contributions to all relevant initiatives, organisations and financing platforms that contribute towards the development, manufacturing and distribution of COVID-19 diagnostics, therapeutics and vaccines.	·我们鼓励向所有致力于开发、制造和分销新冠肺炎诊断、治疗和疫苗的相关倡议、组织和融资平台提供自愿捐款。
·We call on the relevant International Organisations and expert bodies and alliances to produce an evidence-based report, under the leadership of the WHO, highlighting the actions necessary and the financing gaps for COVID-19 that need to be filled.	·我们呼吁有关国际组织、专家机构和联盟在世卫组织的领导下编写一份循证报告，强调需要填补的新冠肺炎的必要行动和资金缺口。
·We agree that emergency trade measures designed to tackle COVID-19, if deemed necessary, must be targeted, proportionate, transparent and temporary, and that they do not create unnecessary barriers to trade or disruption to global supply chains, and are consistent with WTO rules. We are actively working to ensure the continued flow of vital medical supplies and equipment.	·我们同意，旨在应对新冠肺炎的紧急贸易措施，如果认为必要的话，必须具有针对性、适度化、透明化、临时性[7]，且不会对贸易造成不必要的障碍或破坏全球供应链，并符合世贸组织的规则。我们正致力于保证重要医疗用品和设备的持续流动。
·We commit to work with Health Ministers to address and mitigate the impacts of the COVID-19 pandemic and look forward to a joint meeting of Finance and Health Ministers in the coming months. ——G20 Finance Ministers and Central Bank Governors Meeting	·我们承诺与卫生部长合作，解决或缓解新冠肺炎疫情的影响，期待在未来几个月举行财政部长和卫生部长联席会议。

难点 1

原文：COVID-19 Pandemic

译文：新冠肺炎危机

分析："pandemic"本义为"全国性的流行病；全世界性的流行病"，也经常翻译为"疫情"，而在此处翻译为"危机"更符合上下文的语义。

难点 2

原文：COVID-19 is first and foremost a global health emergency. The restrictions and containment measures put in place are vital to reduce the spread of the pandemic.

译文：新冠肺炎疫情首先是全球卫生紧急事件。遏制措施的实施对于减少疫情蔓延至关重要。

分析：原文两句中的"COVID-19"和"the pandemic"表达的意思一致，因此都用"疫情"进行翻译更加合理。

难点 3

原文：lift restrictions

译文：解除限制

分析：此处"lift"本义为"举起，升高"，容易误解为"提高"，根据上下文的语义应该翻译为"解除"。

难点 4

原文：Central Bank Governors

译文：中央银行行长

分析："governor"通常翻译为"统治者；总督；省长；美国州长；管辖者；支配者"。此处翻译为"行长"更符合中文习惯。

难点 5

原文：Our collective goal, set by G20 Leaders, is to protect lives; safeguard people's jobs and incomes; restore confidence, preserve financial stability, revive growth and recover stronger; minimize disruptions to global supply chains; provide help to all countries in need of assistance; and coordinate on public health and financial measures.

译文：我们二十国集团领导人将致力于保护生命，保障人民的就业和收入，重振信心，保持金融稳定与恢复增长，最大限度减少对全球供应链的干扰，帮助全部有需要的国家，以及协调公共卫生和财务措施。

分析：英文的主语"goal"在此处处理成动词"致力于"更符合汉语的习惯，也更便于后文大量动词短语的表达。

难点 6

原文：It sets out the key principles guiding our response, and our commitments to specific actions to drive forward international economic co-operation as we navigate this crisis and look ahead to a robust and sustained global economic recovery, while making sure the design of our response and its implementation remain consistent with achieving strong, sustainable, balanced and inclusive growth.

译文：它阐述了我们共同行动的关键指导原则和应对危机，促进全球经济强劲、可持续和包容性复苏,推动国际经济合作的具体承诺,同时确保我们的应对措施的计划与执行同强劲、可持续、平衡和包容性增长保持一致。

分析:这句话的主干是"It sets out the key principles…and our commitments …",句子较长,成分较多,翻译时可以根据汉语的表达习惯进行切分,对句子顺序进行调整。

难点7

原文:We agree that emergency trade measures designed to tackle COVID-19, if deemed necessary, must be targeted, proportionate, transparent and temporary…

译文:我们同意,旨在应对新冠肺炎的紧急贸易措施,如果认为必要的话,必须具有针对性、适度化、透明化、临时性……

分析:此句中选择用"……性""……化"对原文进行翻译,避免了直译,更加符合中文表达的特点,值得在今后的翻译中借鉴。

翻 译 练 习

一、词组翻译

制度
治理
完善
健全
优势
联动增长
基础设施互联互通
精简
lending capacity
regional financing arrangements
swift disbursements
the Flexible Credit Line(FCL)
the Precautionary and Liquidity Line(PLL)
Debt Limit Policy(DLP)
non-concessional borrowing

二、句子翻译

(一)汉译英

1. 我们决心构建创新、活力、联动、包容的世界经济,并结合《2030年可持续发展议程》《亚的斯亚贝巴行动议程》和《巴黎协定》,开创全球经济增长和可持续发展的新时代。

(《二十国集团领导人杭州峰会公报》)

2. 实现有活力的增长并创造更多就业,必须挖掘增长新动力。我们重申提振全球需求以支持短期增长的重要性,同时认为必须消除供给侧制约,以持续提升劳动生产率,拓展生产的边界,释放中长期增长潜力。

(《二十国集团领导人杭州峰会公报》)

3. 展望未来,我们将高质量共建"一带一路",通过促进政策沟通、设施联通、贸易畅通、资金融通和民心相通,加强各方互联互通,深化务实合作,增进各国人民福祉。在此方面,我们期待合作伙伴做出更多努力。

(《第二届"一带一路"国际合作高峰论坛圆桌峰会联合公报》)

4. 我们将努力建设高质量、可靠、抗风险、可持续的基础设施。我们强调,高质量基础设施应确保在全周期内切实可行、价格合理、包容可及、广泛受益,有助于参与国可持续发展和发展中国家工业化。

(《第二届"一带一路"国际合作高峰论坛圆桌峰会联合公报》)

5. 我们呼吁在世界范围内快速、有效和普遍落实金融行动特别工作组标准和联合国安理会2253号决议条款。

(《二十国集团领导人杭州峰会公报》)

(二) 英译汉

1. We reiterate our commitment to ensure a stronger global financial safety net with a strong, quota-based, and adequately resourced IMF at its center, and will keep demands on the IMF resources under close review.

(G20 Finance Ministers and Central Bank Governors Meeting)

2. Our collective goal, set by G20 Leaders, is to protect lives; safeguard people's jobs and incomes; restore confidence, preserve financial stability, revive growth and recover stronger; minimize disruptions to global supply chains; provide help to all countries in need of assistance; and coordinate on public health and financial measures.

(G20 Finance Ministers and Central Bank Governors Meeting)

3. We agree that emergency trade measures designed to tackle COVID-19, if deemed necessary, must be targeted, proportionate, transparent and temporary, and that they do not create unnecessary barriers to trade or disruption to global supply chains, and are consistent with WTO rules.

(G20 Finance Ministers and Central Bank Governors Meeting)

4. As agreed by Trade and Investment Ministers, we will continue to work together to deliver a free, fair, non-discriminatory, transparent, predictable and stable trade and investment environment, and to keep our markets open.

(G20 Finance Ministers and Central Bank Governors Meeting)

5. We will share the latest information and country experiences on COVID-19 containment measures, their implementation and subsequent removal to minimize negative spillover and second wave effects, including the risk of secondary waves of infections.

(G20 Finance Ministers and Central Bank Governors Meeting)

三、语篇翻译

Attachment I to the *Action Plan*—COVID-19 International Support to Countries in Need

Global action is required to combat the COVID-19 outbreak and its health and economic impacts.

We welcome the important steps already taken by the IMF, World Bank, Regional Development Banks, and central banks, including through the deployment and expansion of bilateral swap lines.

This financial response should include: delivering a comprehensive IMF support package and using available tools from regional financing arrangements (RFAs); implementing swiftly the support proposed by the World Bank and Regional Development Banks; providing debt service suspension for the poorest countries; and ensuring efficiency and operational coordination to optimize the use of resources. We welcome the actions taken by central banks to support financial stability.

1. Delivering a comprehensive IMF support package and using available tools from regional financing arrangements (RFAs)

We welcome the temporary doubling of annual access limits to IMF emergency facilities (Rapid Financing Instrument / Rapid Credit Facility), which will provide financing to countries with urgent balance-of-payments needs. We support the full use of existing instruments and lending capacities, including precautionary instruments such as the Flexible Credit Line (FCL) and the Precautionary and Liquidity Line (PLL), as well as the IMF's readiness to mobilize its US $1 trillion lending capacity to meet members' needs through augmenting existing programs or new programs. We also support streamlining and accelerating internal procedures allowing for swift disbursements.

Furthermore, we support the adoption of a Short-Term Liquidity Line, including a review in 2022, that will help countries with very strong fundamentals and policies through predictable and renewable access to IMF resources. We also call on the IMF to explore additional tools that could serve its members' needs as the crisis evolves, drawing on relevant experiences from previous crises.

We reiterate our commitment to a strong, quota-based and adequately resourced IMF at the center of the Global Financial Safety Net (GFSN). We welcome the steps already taken by countries to implement the necessary domestic measures that are needed to maintain the IMF's current resource envelope and urge others to act swiftly. We remain committed to revisiting the adequacy of quotas and continuing the process of IMF governance reform under the 16th General Review of Quotas, including a new quota formula as a guide, by December 15, 2023.

We welcome the tools provided by regional financing arrangements (RFAs) and call for further progress to deepen the cooperation between IMF and RFAs.

2. Implementing swiftly the support proposed by the World Bank and Regional Development Banks

We welcome the timely decisions taken by the Multilateral Development Banks (MDBs) through their Boards to define and adopt comprehensive emergency response packages, based on their respective mandates and geographical scopes. The financial support presented by MDBs amounts to a total of more than US $ 200 billion of financing for emerging and low-income countries. This includes (i) targeted investment programs in the health sector in coordination with specialized institutions such as the WHO, (ii) support to the poorest through safety nets and cash transfer programs, (iii) emergency fiscal support to affected countries, notably through general and sectorial budget supports consistent with IMF programs, (iv) support to private sector, including companies and financial institutions, notably through trade finance, liquidity and working capital programs. MDBs will continue to increase their commitments, maximizing their lending capacity and mobilizing all resources. We look forward to swift implementation of this funding.

We encourage MDBs to work closely together and with development partners at the country level to ensure consistency, optimize the use of resources, ensure debt remains sustainable and maximize the development impact. We look forward to an update by MDBs on further implementation of country-owned platforms.

We look forward to further discussion on the role of MDBs after the pandemic crisis, as they will have a key role to play to facilitate the recovery from the crisis and restore strong, sustainable, balanced and inclusive growth for the developing countries.

3. Providing debt service suspension for the poorest countries

We welcome the contributions already announced and call for more contributions to replenish the Poverty Reduction and Growth Trust (PRGT) and the Catastrophe Containment and Relief Trust (CCRT) that will help the poorest countries reduce their debt obligations to the IMF.

We support a time-bound suspension of debt service payments for the poorest countries that request forbearance. We agreed on a coordinated approach with a common term sheet providing the key features for this debt service suspension initiative, which is also agreed by the Paris Club. All bilateral official creditors will participate in this initiative, consistent with their national laws and internal procedures. We call on private creditors, working through the Institute of

International Finance, to participate in the initiative on comparable terms. We ask Multilateral Development Banks to further explore the options for the suspension of debt service payments over the suspension period, while maintaining their current rating and low cost of funding. We call on creditors to continue to closely coordinate in the implementation phase of this initiative.

◎参考文献

[1]黄兵.联合公报的语言风格[J].新闻知识,2017(8):27-30.

[2]黄友义,黄长奇,丁洁.重视党政文献对外翻译,加强对外话语体系建设[J].中国翻译,2014,35(3):5-7.

[3]李特夫.翻译中的"政治":政论翻译研究[J].江西师范大学学报(哲学社会科学版),2007(2):130-133.

[4]刘军平.西方翻译理论通史[M].武汉:武汉大学出版社,2009.

[5]原虹.论语义翻译和交际翻译[J].中国科技翻译,2003(2):1-2.

第九章　经济发展计划翻译

> **思考题**
> 1. 什么是经济发展计划？
> 2. 有哪些较为典型的经济发展计划？
> 3. 翻译经济发展计划的难点有哪些？

第一节　经济发展计划文本分析

该部分主要对经济发展计划文本进行分析，主要介绍了经济发展计划的内容、文本类型以及文本特点。

一、文本介绍

经济社会发展计划主要是政府或者组织为推动社会经济发展而制订的计划，主要包括经济发展状况、发展目标、发展理念、经济发展政策以及要采取的措施等，旨在促进经济持续稳定发展。其中较为典型的中国经济发展计划是国民经济和社会发展计划。国民经济和社会发展计划是指国家对一定时期内国民经济的主要活动、科学技术、教育事业和社会发展所作的规划和安排。国民经济和社会发展计划是指导经济和社会发展的纲领性文件。分为长期计划（十年至二十年）、中期计划（一般为五年）、年度计划，较为典型的为《国民经济和社会发展第十三个五年规划纲要》，简称"十三五"规划，于2016年至2020年执行。国外的经济发展计划有马歇尔计划、欧盟新《循环经济行动计划》以及《"一个纽约"计划概要》等。马歇尔计划（The Marshall Plan），官方名称为欧洲复兴计划（European Recovery Program），是第二次世界大战结束后，美国对被战争破坏的西欧各国进行经济援助、协助重建的计划，于1947年7月启动。新《循环经济行动计划》由欧盟委员会于2020年3月11日发布，拟在未来3年推出35项立法建议，推动欧洲经济适应绿色未来，激励环境保护与竞争力齐头并进，赋予消费者更多权益。《"一个纽约"计划概要》由纽约市政府发行，主要介绍了纽约城市发展的目标愿景、规划以及发展策略。

二、文本类型

纽马克在《翻译问题探讨》(Approaches to Translation)一书中将文本功能分为以下几种类型：表情功能、信息功能、呼唤功能、审美功能、寒暄功能以及元语言功能。其中信息功能强调外在语境、话题的事实以及语言之外的因素等，旨在传递文本信息。经济发展计划旨在传递经济发展的目标、计划以及促进经济发展的相关举措等信息，具有信息传递功能，属于信息型文本。

三、文本特点

经济发展计划作为经济类文本，具有权威性，以及实用性强、真实性强、时效性强的特点，且格式固定、内容规范、用词专业、语言严谨，下面将针对中文经济发展计划和英文经济发展计划的特点分别进行介绍。

(一) 中文文本特点

中国的经济发展计划有其独特的特点，如具有政治色彩以及中国特色，下面将从词汇层面和句子层面进行分析。

1. 词汇层面

(1) 政治专有词汇多

中国的经济计划文件中具有较多政治专有词汇，用词规范，具有较强的政治色彩。如"三农""一带一路""精准扶贫"等，这些政治性词汇一般与国家的政策密切相关，政治性较强，翻译时一定要充分了解相关的政策、背景知识，切忌出现政治性错误。

(2) 中国特色词汇多

中国经济计划中有较多的中国特色词汇，极具中国特色，体现了中国文化内涵，展现了中国文化的独特魅力。如"标兵""抓手""普惠性"等。这些词蕴涵着中国文化精神，具有独特的意义，彰显了中国文化特色。

(3) 四字格多

四字格是中文中常用的表达，具有音律上的节奏美、形式上的整齐美以及内容上的意象美，中国经济计划中四字格的使用也较为频繁。如"创新发展、绿色发展""勇于实践、善于创新""坚定信心、迎难而上"等。四字词语读起来朗朗上口，通顺流畅，具有节奏美，使得文本更为生动形象，可读性强。

(4) 重复性动词多

经济计划中有较多的动词，体现了政策的实施，且这些动词频繁出现，强调了对执行相关政策及方针的重视。如"坚持""构建""形成""推进"等。文中出现大量动词，是贯彻国家政策的体现，且这些动词反复出现，出现频率较高，具有一定的强调作用。

(5) 范畴词多

范畴词指汉语中倾向于加范畴的词语，在经济计划中也较为常见，使得句子更加流畅。如"活动""关系""问题""行动"等。这些范畴词没有实际含义，其目的是为了使得句子结构平衡，避免出现头重脚轻或头轻脚重的情况，在翻译的时候可以省去不译。

2. 句子层面

(1) 长句多

中文经济计划中有较多的长句，一个长句一般由多个分句组成，且这些分句之间没有连接词，一般用逗号隔开。如："商业类国有企业以增强国有经济活力、放大国有资本功能、实现国有资产保值增值为主要目标，依法独立自主开展生产经营活动，实现优胜劣汰、有序进退。"(选自"十三五"规划)此类长句中分句较多，用逗号隔开，没有逻辑词连接，符合中文表达习惯。

(2) 对偶句和排比句多

中文经济计划中对偶句和排比句较多，对偶句读起来朗朗上口、生动形象，排比句可以增强语式，使得句子结构更加完整。如："健全社会监管机制，畅通投诉举报渠道。"(选自"十三五"规划)这一句便是一个对仗工整的对偶句，能高度概括所要表达的内容，语句凝练，且具有节奏感，可读性强。

(3) 省略主语的陈述句和祈使句多

中文经济计划中一般陈述句和祈使句较多，且这些陈述句和祈使句通常没有主语。如："转变监管理念，加强事中事后监管。"(选自"十三五"规划)陈述句和祈使句在原文中出现较为频繁，且一般没有主语，多为动宾结构，符合中文表达习惯，译成英文时可适当添加主语。

(4) 主动句多

中文经济计划原文中的句子大多以主动语态出现，这符合中文行文习惯。如："在全国范围内建立了困难残疾人生活补贴和重度残疾人护理补贴制度。"(选自《2017年国民经济和社会发展计划报告》)这个句子为主动句，且没有主语，但英语必须有主语，所以译成英文可将其转化为被动语态，这样可以使句子更加通顺。

(二) 英文文本特点

英文经济发展计划在词汇和句子层面都有其相应的特点，下面将从这两个方面分别讨论文本特点。

1. 词汇层面

(1) 专业术语多

专业术语词形固定，词义单一，不容易混淆。英文经济计划有较多的专业术语，这些术语一般与经济学相关，体现了一定的专业性。如"circular economy(循环经济)""workforce(劳动力)""asset(资产)"，这些专业术语的使用使得文章更具有专业性和权威性。

(2) 缩略词多

由于缩略词书写方便、简洁，容易识别和记忆，因此英文经济计划中会使用一些缩略词，这样使文章更加简洁明了。如《纽约 2050 总规》中的 NYC（纽约城市）和 GHG（温室气体）以及欧洲《循环经济行动计划》中的 SME（中小企业）和 GDP（国内生产总值），这些缩略词一般由大家较为熟知的词语或短语缩写而成，简洁明了，可读性强。

（3）经济数据多

英文经济计划中会经常列出一些经济数据，用以表明经济发展状况以及呈现的经济特征，这样可以清晰反映经济发展状况。如："A recent study estimates that applying circular economy principles across the EU economy has the potential to increase EU GDP by an additional 0.5% by 2030 creating around 700,000 new jobs."（选自欧洲《循环经济行动计划》）这里用了"0.5%""700,000"这样的数字表明 GDP 的增幅以及工作岗位的情况，客观清晰，极具说服力。

2. 句子层面

（1）复合句多

汉语多短句，英语多长句，英文经济计划中有大量的长句和复杂句，一般表现为复合句，这种复合句通常有连接词连接，体现了句子之间的逻辑关系，展现了经济发展计划文本的逻辑性和连贯性。如："The sustainability challenge posed by key value chains requires urgent, comprehensive and coordinated actions, which will form an integral part of the sustainable product policy framework outlined in section 2."（选自欧盟《循环经济行动计划》）这个长句由两个句子构成，主句为"which"前面的句子，后面是"which"引导的非限制性定语从句，修饰"actions"，翻译的时候需要考虑句子间的关系，将长句拆分成短句，化繁为简，让中文读者更加理解句子的含义。

（2）被动句多

汉语多主动，英语多被动。英文经济计划中被动句使用频繁，这符合英文表达习惯。如："A world in which every woman and girl enjoys full gender equality and all legal, social and economic barriers to their empowerment have been removed."（选自联合国《2030 年可持续发展议程》）这个句子的主语为"a world"，"which"引导一个定语从句修饰"a world"，谓语为"have been removed"，这是一个被动句，隐含了施动者，译成中文可考虑化被动为主动，使其更符合中文表达习惯。

（3）小标题多

英文经济计划中一般会有较多的小标题，总领下文，且小标题一般为动宾结构，或者为名词短语形式，这些小标题简单明了，概括出后面的内容。如"Designing Sustainable Products""Empowering Consumers and Public Buyers"及"Circularity in Production Processes"（选自欧洲《循环经济行动计划》）。这些小标题或为动宾结构，或为名词短语，清晰明了，使文章层次分明、条理清晰。

中英文经济发展计划的特点总结如下表：

经济发展计划的特点	中文特点	英文特点
词汇层面	政治专有词汇多，具有较强的中国政治特色	专业术语多，体现了文本的专业性
	中国特色词汇较多，蕴涵着独特的中国文化	缩略词多，简洁明了
	四字格使用频繁	经济数据多，客观真实地反映经济特征
	重复性动词多，体现了政策的执行	
	范畴词多，维持句子结构平衡	
句子层面	长句较多，句子结构松散	长句和复杂句多，多为从句，有逻辑词连接
	对偶句和排比句多，增强语式，使句子更有节奏感	
	省略主语的陈述句和祈使句较多，符合中文表达习惯	小标题多，清晰明了，具有概括性
	主动句较多	被动句多

总之，经济发展计划正式且规范，语言严谨，表达专业，客观真实，具有较强的时效性和实用性。

第二节 翻译知识讲解

一、译文的可接受性简述

功能派翻译理论认为翻译是一种跨文化的交际活动，其过程是通过传递译文的文本信息来达到与目的语读者交际的目的，换言之，其最终目的是服务于译文读者的——这与传统语言学翻译理论强调以源语文本为准，为源语文本服务的思想相反。

有翻译学家认为，译文的文本必须遵循语际连贯法则，即译文的接受者应能够理解译文；其次，译文文本在目的语的交际场合中与目的语所在文化是相合的——若译文对于目的语接受者不存在意义，那么该译文文本也就没有意义。因此目的语读者对于译文文本的接受情况是能够作为评判翻译好坏的标准之一的。

译文的可接受性指的是译文的语言符合目的语的规范、思维习惯、表达习惯等，并能为目的语读者理解、接受、认同。因此，翻译理论中的异化、归化、意译、直译和各种翻译技巧、策略的讨论，其实都是围绕译文的可接受性展开的。译文的可接受性是一种以目的语读者为导向的翻译评价标准，是该译文文本在目的语读者中产生的一种直接交际效果。而以往翻译理论把忠实性作为判断译作可接受性的唯一标准是行不通的，因为照此标准，许多忠实程度看似与原文相差甚远，实则达到了很好的宣传、交际等功能的译作会被判断成谬误。

词无定义，译无定法。但不同的译文质量有高低之分，有理解是否到位和表达是否准确之别，译文可接受性也存在差异。判断译文质量有多种方法，从言内因素（如语法性、习惯性、语用性、修辞性、逻辑性、语篇性等）分析译文是一种方法，而评价读者反应是另一种方法。本书以读者的可接受性为指导思想，就经济发展计划文本中译本的可接受度进行研究和分析，旨在为时政话语规范翻译提供参考依据。

(一) 词汇的处理

1. 特色名词或名词短语

在政府文件中，最为常见的一种情况就是具有中国特色、地方特点的名词和名词短语，其翻译策略是尽量直译，亦步亦趋贴着原文走。

例 1

原文："十二五"期间，要高举中国特色社会主义伟大旗帜，以邓小平理论和"三个代表"重要思想为指导，深入贯彻落实科学发展观。（《上海市国民经济与社会发展第十二个五年规划纲要》）

译文：During the Twelfth "Five-year" Plan period, Shanghai Municipality shall uphold the great banner of socialism with Chinese characteristics, take Deng Xiaoping Theory and the important thought of the "Three Represents" Theory as its guideline, and further implement the Scientific Concept of Development.

例 2

原文：中国改革已进入深水区。（《习近平谈治国理政》）

译文：China's reform has entered a deep-water zone.

分析：我们不难发现，例 1 句子中的"十二五""中国特色社会主义""邓小平理论""'三个代表'重要思想""科学发展观"以及例 2 中的"深水区"都是当前有关中国改革开放的理论基础和指导思想，已有固定的英语翻译。译者在翻译这类句子时，应当对这类时政词汇保持敏锐度，及时调用最官方、最合理的译本。例如，译者可以通过浏览中华人民共和国外交部发言人讲话稿英文稿或历年来双语版的《政府工作报告》，积累表达，查证翻译的准确性。

然而，正如波兰学者沙夫说："一个表达式的意义是随着它所在的那个领域而不同的。这是由于：语言的表达式是含混的，它容许人们做出各种不同的解释。"语言特点是运用有限的符号来表达无限的对象和意念，这就导致了语言材料的多义性、模糊性和随意性。

语言意义的不确定性导致翻译的不确定性，一语多译不可避免。另一方面，不同译者有不同的理解，译文自然不同。在无法进行直译的情况下，未必一定要一板一眼地采用与原文相同短语或句式进行翻译处理，而是应该根据实际情况采用比较灵活的翻译处理方法。如意译或者对其进行解释。

例3

原文：坚持"拆、改、留、修"并举，全面实施旧区改造新机制和政策，继续推进旧区改造和旧住房综合改造。(《上海市国民经济与社会发展第十二个五年规划纲要》)

译文：Shanghai shall adopt and implement new policies to further advance the reconstruction of old areas and houses through tearing down, transforming, preserving and repairing.

例4

原文："十三五"时期是脱贫攻坚**啃硬骨头**、攻城拔寨的时期。(《习近平总书记参加青海代表团审议时发言》)

译文1：chew tough bones

译文2：solve difficult problems

译文3：crack the hard nuts

分析：显然，例3中"坚持'拆、改、留、修'并举"一句，如果不结合上下文进行理解翻译，只是用词语拼凑是无法让人信服的，这里译者采用了解释性的翻译方法，在理顺整句话的逻辑后，将这些举措放在句子末尾，用动名词的形式表现出来。例4中对"啃硬骨头"这一短语给出了三种不同的表达，第一种为直译，第二种和第三种为解释性翻译。中文的"啃硬骨头"是一种比喻，指将艰难的任务一点一点完成，体现其坚韧不拔的精神。考虑到读者的可接受性，将"啃硬骨头"生硬地译为"chew tough bone"容易让外国读者感到迷惑，不易产生联想，而第三种译文则套用了英文中"a hard nut to crack"的表达，形容事情很棘手，恰好表明了原文中所要表现的意思。

2. 重复词

在中国的政府文件中，常常会使用大量的重复性词汇或句子，在英语中常常称为parallelism，使句子看上去整齐划一。对于这样的句子或结构，翻译处理一般采用两种方式，一是结构跟着中文原文"依瓢画葫芦"；二是根据英语的习惯，在翻译时对原文的结构做适当的调整。

例5

原文：建设服务全国的贸易促进和服务平台，打造集多种媒体、多领域、多语种于一体的财经信息综合服务平台。(《上海市国民经济与社会发展第十二个五年规划纲要》)

译文：The city shall strive to construct the trade promotion and service platform serving the whole nation, and forge a multi-media, multi-field, and multi-language comprehensive business information service platform.

分析：这句话中连续用了 3 个"多"字作为前置修饰语，英语译文中也用 3 个"multi-"来作前置修饰语。一般来说，翻译处理时也采用原文的平行结构，能够比较好地向英语读者传达原文的语言特色，而英语读者也会欣然接受这样的译文，因为平行结构也是英语的一种修辞手段。

例 6

原文：社会主义经济建设、政治建设、文化建设、社会建设、生态文明建设取得重大进展，谱写了中国特色社会主义事业新篇章。(《中华人民共和国国民经济和社会发展第十三个五年规划纲要》)

译文：We made significant socialist economic, political, cultural, social, and ecological progress, and wrote a new chapter in building socialism with Chinese characteristics.

分析：在政治文献中，一个词语重复出现是很常见的情况。汉语喜欢用排比结构，但英语表达并非如此，英语中常避免重复的情况出现。原文中连着出现了五个"建设"，如果直译，在英文中连着出现五个"construction"则会显得冗余，不符合译入语的表达习惯。所以在处理的时候要进行适当的省略，将五个"建设"省略为一个既符合译文读者的表达习惯，又能很好地体现原意的表达。

3. 数字词

中国正式文件中专有名词中还有一个比较独特的现象，即常常含有数字。这种译文处理相对比较复杂。数字翻译常常有如下五种方法：保留数字直译、变动数字改译、舍弃数字意译、解释性翻译和创造性背叛。本书将以部分句子为例对其进行解释分析。

例 7

原文：探索完善居民区党组织、居委会、业委会和物业服务企业"四位一体"的协调机制，加快完善住房产权和物业管理。(《上海市国民经济与社会发展第十二个五年规划纲要》)

译文：Besides, the city shall try to enhance the "quaternary" negotiation mechanism between residential Party organizations, neighborhood committees, owners committees and property management companies, so as to improve housing property right and property management.

例 8

原文：实施"百姓健身设施工程"，公共运动场实现社区全覆盖。新建健身步道 300 公里。建设"一村一场""一镇一池""一街一中心"。(《上海市国民经济与社会发展第十二

个五年规划纲要》)

译文：The city shall carry out its Citizens Fitness Facilities Development Plan, and one of its aims is that every community shall have access to public sports grounds. According to the Plan, a total of 300 kilometers of fitness trails shall be built, and "every village shall have a sports ground, a town shall have a swimming pool, and every street shall have a fitness center".

分析：对于例7中的"四位一体"的翻译，通过具体分析，我们可以简单用一个英语单词"quaternary"来表示其含义，基本意思为由四要素构成的；由于文化背景的差异，为了避免误解和错译，必要时需加注或者解释，对于例8中"一村一场""一镇一池""一街一中心"的翻译，如果简单用数字进行翻译，必然会使得译文读者产生误解，因此这里采取了"挖掘隐含意义，使之显豁"的策略，即解释性翻译，译为"every village shall have a sports ground, a town shall have a swimming pool, and every street shall have a fitness center"。

4. 文化负载词

在政府文件里，我们常常会见到一些习语，我们在这里将其称为文化负载词。在汉语里，习语也称为"熟语"，包括短语、成语、俗语、谚语、格言、箴言、名言、警句、隽语、俚语、粗话、行话、歇后语等。在外宣翻译中，习语是常见的一类特色词汇，常常引用习语来使外宣材料的表达更生动、更体现中华文化。习语是语言的精华，同样也是文化的结晶。有的汉语习语可以在英语中找到对等的翻译，而由于文化空缺，有的习语在英语中无法找到完全对等的语言。汉英习语由于地理环境、宗教信仰、文化背景等不同，有着不同的表达方式。

例9

原文：小人有眼不识泰山。(《习语节选》)

译文：to entertain an angel unawares

分析：原文中"泰山"一词是中国特有的地理名胜，如果不加解释，外国人可能不知道"mountain Tai"指的是什么。译文"to entertain an angel unawares"是《圣经·新约》中的一句话，同"有眼不识泰山"的深层含义一样，都是"有眼无珠"的意思，这样翻译这句习语，则可以让译文读者在自己的文化背景下更深入、生动地理解原文意义。一门语言的发展是受多方面影响的，地理环境是很重要的一个因素，中国人自古以来面朝黄土背朝天，所以很多习语都与土地有关，如"土生土长""挥金如土"，而英国靠海，所以其习语多与水有关，所以在翻译的时候要多考虑译文读者的地理环境影响，如将"挥金如土"译为"spend money like water"，从译者的角度出发，这样能起到更好的效果。

例10

原文：回头是岸(《习语节选》)

译文：It is never too late to mend.

分析："回头是岸"是佛家语，指"有罪的人只要回心转意、痛改前非就可以登上"彼岸"，获得超度。后用来比喻做坏事的人只要悔改就不晚。该词出自佛家，而英语国家多信仰基督教、天主教，所以在翻译此词的时候就要尽量避免有宗教的色彩，只要译出其深层意义即可，如"it is never too late to mend"。同英文习语很多来自《圣经》一样，汉语中有很多谚语、成语都来自佛家经典、道家经典，如"借花献佛""五体投地"等，我们在翻译时要尽量避免宗教信仰，这样可以避免同译文读者的信仰冲突。

(二) 句式的处理

1. 并列句

平行结构是英语的一种修辞手段。一般来说，中文的时政文本中会出现相当多的并列句，在翻译处理时，译者也常常采用原文的平行结构，这样能够比较好地向英语读者传达原文的语言特色，而英语读者也会欣然接受这样的译文。

例 11

原文：面对新机遇、新挑战，我们必须：增强机遇意识、忧患意识、使命意识和创新意识。(《中华人民共和国国民经济和社会发展第十三个五年规划纲要》)

译文：In the situation where new opportunities and new challenges co-exist, we shall heighten its awareness of opportunities, of unexpected crisis, of mission, and of innovation.

例 12

原文：我国发展中长期积累的矛盾还没有根本解决，不平衡、不协调、不可持续问题依然突出，上海发展环境的不稳定、不确定因素明显增多。(《上海市国民经济与社会发展第十二个五年规划纲要》)

译文：The contradiction long accumulated in China's development remains fundamentally unsettled; the problems such as disproportion, incongruence, and unsustainability in development are unquestionably acute. So there are still many unstable elements in the environments and increasing uncertainties, which might constitute obstacles to the city's development.

分析：以上两句话中都包含了平行结构，但是在翻译时的处理却大不相同。例 11 中有 4 个作为名词的"意识"，但是英语译文却用一个"awareness"，后面再跟 4 个介词"of"来统领 4 个不同的名词或名词短语。例 12 中有 5 个表示否定意义的"不"字，但在英语译文中却分别连续用了 3 个名词："disproportion, incongruence, and unsustainability"，接着又用一个形容词"unstable"和一个名词"uncertainties"。这样的翻译处理隐没了原文的平行结构，而是靠英语词汇来转达原文中隐含在平行结构中的意义，是一种翻译处理手段，但不是翻译平行结构原文的一个最有效的手段。

2. 句式重组

英语是注重"形合"的语言，而汉语则是注重"意合"的语言。汉语的句式是比较散的，如果直接译为英文，可能会造成译文读者的意义混淆，所以在翻译时要特别注意英语的结构，汉语中一个以句号为单位的句子可能要拆成英语中的几句话，或者几句汉语要组合成一句英语。

例 13

原文：无论传统产业还是新兴产业、劳动密集型产业还是资金密集型产业，都有发展的空间，重要的是优化资源配置和产业布局，解决产能过剩、核心技术缺乏、产品附加值低的问题，解决低水平重复建设和地区产业结构趋同的问题。(《2013年政府工作报告》)

译文：Industries, whether traditional or emerging, labor-intensive or capital-intensive, all have room for development. The important task is to optimize resources allocation and industrial distribution, and solve the following problems: excess production capacity, the lack of core technology, products with low value-added, low-level and redundant industrial projects, and different regions having similar industrial structures.

例 14

原文：Improving the lives of our residents and future generations by cutting greenhouse gas emissions, reducing waste, protecting air and water quality and conditions, cleaning brown fields, and enhancing public open spaces. (《"一个纽约"计划概要》)

译文：通过减少温室气体排放、废弃物，保护水和空气的质量，清理棕地，增加公共开放空间等提高居民和未来子孙的生活。

例 15

原文：We cannot achieve health equity without guaranteeing the right to quality health care, and enrolling as many New Yorkers as possible in health insurance. New York City has steadily reduced the number of uninsured residents since the *Affordable Care Act* was launched in 2013. (《"一个纽约"计划概要》)

译文：我们只有保证市民享有高质量医保的权利，让更多人加入医保项目，才能促进公平的健康服务。自2013年推行《平价医疗法案》(*Affordable Care Act*)以来，纽约市享有医保的市民数量持续上升。

分析：例14和例15是典型的结果加条件句，从英文翻译成中文时，要采取贴近译文读者的策略，将顺序重新组合，采用符合中文读者表达习惯的句式。因此，可以先译出条件句，后翻译结果句，即先表达通过一系列的努力，然后再表达实现了一定的目标。

例 16

原文：社会建设与人民幸福安康息息相关。必须在经济发展的基础上，更加注重社会建设，着力保障和改善民生，推进社会体制改革，扩大公共服务，完善社会管理，促进社会公平正义，努力使全体人民学有所教、劳有所得、病有所医、老有所养、住有所居，推动建设和谐社会。（《中国共产党十七大报告》）

译文：Social development is closely related to the people's well-being. More importance must therefore be attached to social development on the basis of economic growth to ensure and improve people's livelihood, carry out social restructuring, expand public services, improve social management and promote social equity and justice. We must do our best to ensure that all our people enjoy their rights to education, employment, medical and old-age care, and housing, so as to build a harmonious society.

分析：在汉语中，经常会出现格式一样、没有明显逻辑的四字词组的罗列，在英语中则不会出现，在翻译时要根据意思将这些四字词组重组成有逻辑关系的一句话。例子中的"学有所教""劳有所得""病有所医"等四字动宾短语处理为名词，并用"so as to"来表明句子的逻辑关系，这样处理符合贴近读者的原则，不但能够很好地体现出原文的逻辑关系，也是从读者的角度出发，让读者充分地理解原意。

经济发展计划的翻译技巧总结如下表：

经济发展计划的翻译技巧

直译法	在译文中既保持原文内容，又保持原文形式
意译法	根据原文的大意来进行翻译，不作逐字逐句的翻译
省译法	提取并传达主要信息，省略不必要的冗余信息
结构整合与重组	在翻译过程中重新排列句子结构和顺序，这种翻译方法考虑到中英文表达习惯的差异性，重新布局整个句子

第三节　常用词汇与表达

原文	译文
第一动力	primary engine
新常态	new normal
协同创新	collaborative innovation
大众创新	crowd innovation
城乡发展一体化	urban-rural integration
知识产权强国	IPR powerhouse

续表

原文	译文
小康社会	moderately prosperous society
循环经济	circular economy
中小企业	SMEs
可持续发展	sustainable development
先行者	front runner
贸易保护主义	trade protectionism
带动消费结构升级	help improve the consumption mix
纵向横向经济轴带	formation of north-south and east-west intersecting economic belts
激发创新创业活力	invigorate innovation and entrepreneurship
发展一批中心城市	develop principal cities
鼓励发展众创、众包、众扶、众筹空间	encourage the development of crowd innovation, crowd support, crowdsourcing, and crowdfunding
走农业现代化道路	enable China to embark on a path to modern agriculture
优化劳动力、资本、土地、技术、管理等要素配置	ensure better allocation of factors of production such as labor, capital, land, technology, and management
发挥消费对增长的基础作用	ensure consumption plays the fundamental role in stimulating growth
城镇居民基本医疗保险	the basic medical insurance for non-working urban residents
国内国际经济联动效应	the interconnectedness of domestic and international economies
中高速增长	a medium-high rate of growth
新业态	new forms of business
开放型经济新体制	new systems for an open economy
人均 GDP	GDP per capita
推进供给侧结构性改革	advancing supply-side structural reform
统筹推进稳增长、促改革、调结构、惠民生、防风险各项工作	coordinate all work to maintain stable growth, promote reform, make structural adjustments, improve living standards, and guard against risk
就业比较充分	operate near full employment

第四节 译 文 赏 析

一、汉译英

原文	译文
展望新世纪初的国内外形势，未来五到十年，是我国经济和社会发展极为重要的时期。世界新科技革命迅猛发展，经济全球化趋势增强，许多国家积极推进产业结构调整，周边国家正在加快发展。国际环境既对我们提出了严峻挑战，也为我们提供了迎头赶上、实现跨越式发展的历史性机遇。从国内看，我们正处在经济结构调整的关键时期，改革处于攻坚阶段，加入世贸组织又会带来一些新的问题。各方面任务十分繁重，许多深层次矛盾需要解决，形势要求我们必须抓住机遇，加快发展。同时，我们也具备许多有利条件，能够在一个较长时期实现国民经济较快发展。	Looking ahead at the situation at home and abroad at the beginning of the 21st century, it can be said that the next five to ten years will be an extremely important period for China's economic and social development. The worldwide new scientific and technological revolution is progressing rapidly with great momentum[1]. The economic globalization trend is gaining strength. Many countries are actively restructuring their industries, and our neighboring countries are accelerating their development. All this serves as a severe challenge and a historic opportunity for us to strive to catch up and achieve development by leaps and bounds[2]. At home, we are at a crucial juncture in economic restructuring, and reform is in a very difficult period. Our entry into the World Trade Organization will bring us a number of new problems. We are facing many arduous tasks. Many deep-seated problems need to be solved. All this requires us to seize the opportunity and accelerate development. At the same time, there are many favorable conditions for our national economy to achieve rather rapid development over a fairly long period.
根据"十五"期间的形势和任务，《纲要》提出今后五年经济和社会发展的主要目标是：国民经济保持较快发展速度，经济结构战略性调整取得明显成效，经济增长质量和效益显著提高，为到 2010 年国内生产总值比 2000 年翻一番奠定坚实基础；国有企业建立现代企业制度取得重大进展，社会保障制度比较健全，社会主义市场经济体制逐步完善，对外开放和国际合作进一步开展；就业渠道拓宽，城乡居民收入持续增加，物质文化生活有较大改善，生态建设和环境保护得到加强；科技、教育加快发展，国民素质进一步提高，精神文明建设和民主法制建设取得明显进展。	In light of the situation and tasks facing us during the Tenth Five-Year Plan period[3], the *Outline* sets forth the main targets for economic and social development in the next five years as follows: maintain a fairly rapid growth rate in the national economy, achieve noticeable success in the strategic restructuring of the economy, and make marked improvement in the quality and benefits of economic growth to lay a solid foundation for doubling the 2000 GDP by 2010[4]; make significant progress in establishing a modern corporate structure in state-owned enterprises, increase the soundness of the social security system, improve the socialist market economy, and open wider to the outside world and strengthen cooperation with other countries; expand avenues of employment, increase the income of urban and rural residents steadily, improve people's material and cultural standards of living, and improve ecological conservation and environmental protection; accelerate the development of science, technology and education, further improve the quality of the Chinese people, socialist spiritual civilization, democracy and the legal system.

续表

原文	译文
"十五"计划《纲要》体现了以下重要指导方针。 坚持把发展作为主题。强调速度与效益相统一，在提高效益的前提下实现较快的发展。有市场、有效益的速度，才是真正的发展，才是硬道理。综合考虑各方面因素，"十五"期间年均经济增长速度预期目标为7%左右。这个速度虽然比"九五"实际达到的速度低一点，但仍然是一个较高的速度。要在提高效益的基础上实现这个目标，必须付出艰巨努力。同时，由于国际国内都存在一些不确定因素，计划的预期目标要留有余地。这样，有利于引导各方面把主要精力放在调整结构和提高效益上，也有利于防止经济过热和重复建设。	The *Outline of the Tenth Five-Year Plan* embodies the following major guiding principles. Making development the central theme. We stress a balance between high growth rate and good economic returns and attaining fairly rapid growth by improving economic returns. Sound economic growth must be based on strong market demand and good economic returns. This is a fundamental principle. Based on an overall analysis of conditions in all sectors of the economy, we have set the target for the average annual economic growth rate in the Tenth Five-Year Plan period at around 7%. Though slightly lower than the actual growth rate of the Ninth Five-Year Plan period, it is still fairly high. Arduous efforts have to be made to attain this target through better economic performance[5]. However, as there exist some uncertainties both at home and abroad, we have to leave some leeway when defining our target[6]. This will help people focus on restructuring and improving economic returns, and also help prevent overheating of the economy and poor quality or redundant development.
坚持把结构调整作为主线。我国经济已经到了不调整就不能发展的时候。按原有结构和粗放增长方式发展经济，不仅产品没有市场，资源、环境也难以承受。必须在发展中调整结构，在结构调整中保持较快发展。今后五年要着力调整产业结构、地区结构和城乡结构，特别要把产业结构调整作为关键。要巩固和加强农业基础地位，加快工业改组改造和结构优化升级，大力发展服务业，加快国民经济和社会信息化，继续加强基础设施建设。	Concentrating on economic restructuring. We have already reached the point where we cannot further develop the economy without making structural adjustments. Under the old economic structure and its crude manner of growth, products will not be marketable, and it will be impossible to sustain resources and preserve the environment. We must adjust the economic structure in developing the economy and maintain a relatively rapid growth in structural adjustments. In the next five years, efforts should be intensified to adjust the patterns of economic development between different industries, between different regions, and between urban and rural areas, with emphasis on the industrial structure. We should stabilize and strengthen agriculture as the foundation of the economy, accelerate industrial reform, reorganization, upgrading and optimization, vigorously develop the service industry, accelerate efforts to base the national economy and society on information, and continue to reinforce the infrastructure.

续表

原文	译文
坚持把改革开放和科技进步作为动力。经济发展和结构调整都要靠体制创新和科技创新来推动。今后五年要坚定不移地推进改革，扩大开放，突破影响生产力发展的体制性障碍，为经济社会发展提供强大动力。要把发展科技、教育放在突出位置，进一步实施科教兴国战略，振兴科技，培养人才，促进科技、教育与经济紧密结合。	Making reform and opening up and technological progress the driving force. The success of both economic development and structural adjustment depends on institutional, scientific and technological innovation. In the next five years, we must unswervingly pursue reform, open China wider to the outside world, and break down the institutional obstacles to the development of productive forces[7]. This will provide a strong impetus for economic and social development. In addition, we have to give priority to the development of science, technology and education, further implement the strategy of developing China through science and education, invigorate science and technology, train more skilled personnel, and better integrate science, technology and education with the economy.
坚持把提高人民生活水平作为根本出发点，不断改善城乡人民生活，既是我们发展经济的根本目的，也是扩大内需、促进经济持续增长的迫切需要。要坚持把提高人民生活水平摆在重要位置，扩大就业门路，增加居民收入，合理调节收入分配关系，健全社会保障体系，保证人民群众向更加宽裕的小康生活迈进。	Making improvement of the people's living standards as the basic starting point. Raising the people's living standards in both urban and rural areas is the basic goal of our economic development and a crucial factor for expanding domestic demand and stimulating sustained economic growth. We must give priority to raising the people's living standards. To accomplish this we must create more jobs, increase personal income, distribute income more equitably, improve the social security system, and ensure a more comfortable life for the people.
坚持把经济发展和社会发展结合起来。大力加强社会主义精神文明和民主法制建设，处理好改革、发展、稳定的关系，促进各项社会事业发展，确保社会稳定。高度重视和认真解决人口、资源和生态环境问题，进一步实施可持续发展战略，推动经济、社会、生态环境协调发展。	Coordinating economic development with social development. We should make great efforts to improve socialist spiritual civilization, democracy and the legal system, balance reform, development and stability, accelerate development of various social undertakings and ensure social stability. We need to pay close attention to and solve issues of population, resources and the ecological environment, take further steps to implement the strategy of sustainable development, and stimulate coordinated economic and social development.

续表

原文	译文
"十五"计划《纲要》突出了战略性、宏观性、政策性，减少实物指标，增加反映结构变化的预期指标；围绕要解决的主要问题和重点发展领域，提出努力方向和相应的政策措施。强调计划的实施要充分发挥市场机制的作用，政府宏观调控要更多地运用经济杠杆、经济政策和法律手段。在计划制订方法上，力求提高社会参与度，使计划制订过程成为发扬民主、集思广益的过程，成为各有关方面达成共识的过程。	The *Outline of the Tenth Five-Year Plan* emphasizes its strategic, macroeconomic and policy characteristics. It contains fewer specific targets and sets more tentative ones adjustable to structural changes[8]. The *Outline* focuses on key development areas and the settlement of major problems, orients our efforts, and presents corresponding policies and measures. It stresses that the role of market mechanisms should be fully exercised in the implementation of the Plan, and that economic levers, economic policy and legislation be further employed in the government's macro-control. In the process of formulating the Plan, we need to encourage more participation by all elements of society, thus making it a process of giving full scope to democracy, absorbing all useful ideas, and reaching agreement among all sides.

（节选自《"十五"期间的奋斗目标和指导方针——关于国民经济和社会发展第十个五年计划纲要的报告》）

难点 1

原文：世界新科技革命迅猛发展……

译文：The worldwide new scientific and technological revolution is progressing rapidly with great momentum.

分析："迅猛发展"强调了两个点，既要翻译出快速发展，也要译出发展势头强劲之意，而"momentum"有"动力、势头"的意思，因此译为"progressing rapidly with great momentum"。

难点 2

原文：国际环境既对我们提出了严峻挑战，也为我们提供了迎头赶上、实现跨越式发展的历史性机遇。

译文：All this serves as a severe challenge and a historic opportunity for us to strive to catch up and achieve development by leaps and bounds.

分析：我们常常使用"strive to"表示付出巨大努力去做某事，"迎头赶上"就是努力追赶、实现目标的意思。"leaps and bounds"为固定短语搭配，用来形容巨大或者快速的进展，在文章中即"跨越式发展"。

难点 3

原文：根据"十五"期间的形势和任务

译文：In light of the situation and tasks facing us during the Tenth Five-Year Plan period

分析："根据"有多种译法，文章中使用了"in light of"，其他同样能表达"根据"意思的短语还有"in line with, according to, on the basis of, on the grounds of"等。

难点 4

原文：为到 2010 年国内生产总值比 2000 年翻一番奠定坚实基础

译文：to lay a solid foundation for doubling the 2000 GDP by 2010

分析：在政经类文本中，由于涉及数字，经常会出现"翻一番，翻了一倍"之类的说法。我们常见的"翻一番"就是原来的两倍的意思，因此用"double"表示即可，同样地，我们用"triple"表示三倍，"quadruple"表示四倍。

难点 5

原文：要在提高效益的基础上实现这个目标，必须付出艰巨努力。

译文：Arduous efforts have to be made to attain this target through better economic performance.

分析："arduous"表示"艰巨的，费力的"，同样用来形容任务艰巨的短语有"formidable task, onerous task"等。

难点 6

原文：同时，由于国际国内都存在一些不确定因素，计划的预期目标要留有余地。

译文：However, as there exist some uncertainties both at home and abroad, we have to leave some leeway when defining our target.

分析："留有余地"比喻不把话说死或者不把事办绝，留下进退回旋的地步，"leave some leeway"的英文解释就是"allow for some unforeseen circumstances"，常见的用法为"留有足够余地(leave adequate leeway)"。

难点 7

原文：今后五年要坚定不移地推进改革，扩大开放，突破影响生产力发展的体制性障碍，为经济社会发展提供强大动力。

译文：In the next five years, we must unswervingly pursue reform, open China wider to the outside world, and break down the institutional obstacles to the development of productive forces.

分析："坚定不移地推进改革，扩大开放"是政论文中常见的与改革开放相关的表达，"unswervingly pursue reform, open China wider to the outside world"应该作为知识储备，记住固定译法。

难点 8

原文：减少实物指标，增加反映结构变化的预期指标

译文：It contains fewer specific targets and sets more tentative ones adjustable to structural changes.

分析："减少实物指标"在译文中换了一种表达，转译为"涵盖更少的实物指标（contains fewer specific targets）"，这样更加符合英文读者的阅读习惯。

二、英译汉

原文	译文
2. A SUSTAINABLE PRODUCT POLICY FRAMEWORK 2.1 Designing sustainable products 　　While up to 80% of products' environmental impacts are determined at the design phase, the linear pattern of "take-make-use-dispose" does not provide producers with sufficient incentives to make their products more circular. Many products break down too quickly, cannot be easily reused, repaired or recycled, and many are made for single use only. At the same time, the single market provides a critical mass enabling the EU to set global standards in product sustainability and to influence product design and value chain management worldwide.	2. 可持续产品政策框架 2.1　设计可持续产品 　　尽管产品的环境影响中有高达80%在设计阶段就已经确定了，但"取—造—用—弃"的线性模式无法充分激励制造商提高其产品的循环性[1]。许多产品太易损坏，无法重复使用、维修或回收再生，或其制造初衷即为一次性用品。同时，单一市场会产生集群效应[2]，赋能欧盟设定产品可持续性的全球标准，影响全世界的产品设计和价值链管理。
EU initiatives and legislation already address to a certain extent sustainability aspects of products, either on a mandatory or voluntary basis. Notably, the Ecodesign Directive successfully regulates energy efficiency and some circularity features of energy-related products. At the same time, instruments such as the EU Ecolabel or the EU green public procurement (GPP) criteria are broader in scope but have reduced impact due to the limitations of voluntary approaches. In fact, there is no comprehensive set of requirements to ensure that all products placed on the EU market become increasingly sustainable and stand the test of circularity.	欧盟已经有一些倡议和立法，在一定程度上对产品的可持续性施加或强制或自愿的监管。尤其是生态设计指令[3]，对能源相关产品的能效和某些循环性特征进行了有效的监管。同时，欧盟生态标签（EU Ecolabel）或者欧盟绿色公共采购（GPP）标准等工具的适用范围更广，但受其本身自愿性所限，其影响力较低。事实上，欧洲并没有任何综合性要求，来保障在欧盟市场上市的所有产品会具有越来越高的可持续性，能够通过循环性测试。

215

续表

原文	译文
In order to make products fit for a climate-neutral, resource-efficient and circular economy, reduce waste and ensure that the performance of front-runners in sustainability progressively becomes the norm, the Commission will propose a sustainable product policy legislative initiative. The core of this legislative initiative will be to widen the Ecodesign Directive beyond energy-related products so as to make the Ecodesign framework applicable to the broadest possible range of products and make it deliver on circularity.	为了使产品适合气候中和、资源节约的循环经济，减少废弃物，并确保领军国家[4]在可持续性方面的表现逐步成为规范，欧洲委员会将提出关于可持续产品政策的立法建议。此立法建议的核心是在能源相关产品之外，拓宽生态设计指令的应用范围，以使生态设计框架适用于尽可能多的产品类别，实现可持续性。
As part of this legislative initiative, and, where appropriate, through complementary legislative proposals, the Commission will consider establishing sustainability principles and other appropriate ways to regulate the following aspects: · improving product durability, reusability, upgradability and reparability, addressing the presence of hazardous chemicals in products, and increasing their energy and resource efficiency; · increasing recycled content in products, while ensuring their performance and safety; · enabling remanufacturing and high-quality recycling; · reducing carbon and environmental footprints; · restricting single-use and countering premature obsolescence; · introducing a ban on the destruction of unsold durable goods; · incentivising product-as-a-service or other models where producers keep the ownership of the product or the responsibility for its performance throughout its lifecycle; · mobilising the potential of digitalisation of product information, including solutions such as digital passports, tagging and watermarks; · rewarding products based on their different sustainability performance, including by linking high performance levels to incentives.	作为此立法建议的一部分，在适当的情况下，欧洲委员会将通过补充性立法建议，考虑设定可持续性原则及其他适当的方式，以对以下方面进行监管： · 提高产品耐久性、可重用性、可升级性和可修复性，处理产品中存在的危险化学物质，提高产品的能源和资源效率； · 在确保产品性能和安全性的同时，提高产品中可回收物质的含量； · 促成再制造和高质量回收利用； · 减少碳足迹[5]和环境足迹； · 限制一次性用品，防止过早淘汰； · 出台禁止销毁未经售出的耐用品的禁令； · 以激励措施推广"产品即服务"模型，或者由生产者保留产品所有权或者在整个寿命期内为产品性能负责的其他模型； · 发挥产品信息数字化的潜力，包括数字护照、标签和水印等解决方案； · 基于不同的可持续性表现为产品提供奖励，包括将高可持续性与激励措施挂钩[6]。

续表

原文	译文
Priority will be given to addressing product groups identified in the context of the value chains featuring in this Action Plan, such as electronics, ICT and textiles but also furniture and high impact intermediary products such as steel, cement and chemicals. Further product groups will be identified based on their environmental impact and circularity potential.	此行动计划的特色在于价值链，应优先处理在此种价值链背景下确认的产品类别[7]，例如电子产品、信息通信技术（ICT）[8]、纺织品、家具以及钢材、水泥、化学制品等高影响力的中间产品。进一步的产品类别将基于其环境影响和循环性潜力确定。
This legislative initiative and any other complementary regulatory or voluntary approaches will be developed in a way to improve the coherence with existing instruments regulating products along various phases of their life cycle. It is the intention of the Commission that the product sustainability principles will guide broader policy and legislative developments in the future. The Commission will also increase the effectiveness of the current Ecodesign framework for energy-related products, including by swiftly adopting and implementing a new *Ecodesign and Energy Labeling Working Plan 2020-2024* for individual product groups.	此立法建议以及任何其他补充性监管或自愿方法还将进一步发展，以提高其与现有的产品寿命期各阶段监管工具的一致性。欧洲委员会的意图是未来以产品可持续性原则为引导，制定更广泛的政策和立法[9]。欧洲委员会还将提高现行能源相关产品生态设计框架的效力，包括快速通过及实施针对各产品类别的新《2020—2024年生态设计和能源标签工作计划》。

（节选自欧盟《循环经济行动计划》）

难点1

原文：While up to 80% of products' environmental impacts are determined at the design phase, the linear pattern of "take-make-use-dispose" does not provide producers with sufficient incentives to **make their products more circular.**

译文：尽管产品的环境影响中有高达80%在设计阶段就已经确定了，但"取—造—用—弃"的线性模式无法充分激励制造商提高其产品的循环性。

分析：这里的"provide producers with sufficient incentives"没有直接翻译成"提供给制造商充分的激励"，而是将"provide"省去不译，将"incentives"转化为动词，译为"充分激励制造商"，这样表达更为流畅、通顺。"make their products more circular"没有译成"使……更……"，而是译为"提高其产品的循环性"，这样更符合中文表达习惯，使中文读者更易接受。当遇到"提高……性/度"这样的中文表达时，也可直接将其译为"make...more+形容词"的形式。

第九章　经济发展计划翻译

难点 2

原文：critical mass

译文：集群效应

分析："critical mass"指"集群效应"，这是一个社会动力学的名词，用来描述在一个社会系统里，某件事情的存在已达至一个足够的动量，使它能够自我维持，并为往后的成长提供动力。

难点 3

原文：Ecodesign Directive

译文：生态设计指令

分析："Ecodesign Directive"指"生态设计指令"，是欧盟制定的用以改善产品能效和环保性能的经济政策。

难点 4

原文：front-runners

译文：领军国家

分析："front-runners"本义为"先行者、领跑者"，这里根据上下文的语境将其译为"领军国家"，指经济发展处于领先状态的国家。

难点 5

原文：carbon footprint

译文：碳足迹

分析："carbon footprint"一般译为"碳足迹"，是指企业机构、活动、产品或个人通过交通运输、食品生产和消费以及各类生产过程等引起的温室气体排放的集合。

难点 6

原文：…rewarding products based on their different sustainability performance, including by linking high performance levels to incentives.

译文：基于不同的可持续性表现为产品提供奖励，包括将高可持续性与激励措施挂钩。

分析："link"的本义为"联系、连接"，此处译成"与……挂钩"，更符合中文表达习惯，更加地道。

难点 7

原文：Priority will be given to addressing product groups identified in the context of the value chains featuring in this Action Plan...

译文：此行动计划的特色在于价值链，应优先处理在此种价值链背景下确认的产品类别……

分析：原文为以"priority"为主语的被动句，而中文更习惯于使用主动句，此处化被动为主动，译为"应优先处理"，更符合中文行文习惯。

难点 8

原文：ICT

译文：信息通信技术

分析：ICT 的全称为 Information and Communication Technology，译为"信息通信技术"。

难点 9

原文：It is the intention of the Commission that the product sustainability principles will guide broader policy and legislative developments in the future.

译文：欧洲委员会的意图是未来以产品可持续性原则为引导，制定更广泛的政策和立法。

分析：原文为"that"引导的同位语从句，主语为"it"，译文直接将"欧洲委员会的意图"作为主语，并将原句进行拆分，添加动词"制定"，这样使译文更通俗易懂。

翻 译 练 习

一、词组翻译

精准扶贫
高质量发展
共有产权住房
新型城镇化
党的领导、人民当家作主、依法治国
党的基本理论、基本路线、基本纲领、基本经验
纠正"四风"（形式主义、官僚主义、享乐主义、奢靡之风）
西电东输、西气东送
shared development
macro regulation
commodity
ecological conservation redline
negative list

overcapacity

spirit of craftsmanship

二、句子翻译

(一) 汉译英

1. 全党同志要充分认识这场变革的重大现实意义和深远历史意义，统一思想，协调行动，深化改革，开拓前进，推动我国发展迈上新台阶。

2. 必须把创新摆在国家发展全局的核心位置，不断推进理论创新、制度创新、科技创新、文化创新等各方面创新。

3. 保护合法收入，规范隐性收入，遏制以权力、行政垄断等非市场因素获取收入，取缔非法收入。

4. 城市和农村居民家庭人均可支配收入年均增长率分别达到 11.3% 和 10.5%。

5. 实施更加积极的就业政策，创造更多就业岗位，着力解决结构性就业矛盾，鼓励以创业带就业，实现比较充分和高质量就业。

(二) 英译汉

1. For business, working together on creating the framework for sustainable products will provide new opportunities in the EU and beyond.

2. Innovative models based on a closer relationship with customers, mass customisation, the sharing and collaborative economy, and powered by digital technologies, such as the Internet of things, big data, block chain and artificial intelligence, will not only accelerate circularity but also the dematerialisation of our economy and make Europe less dependent on primary materials.

3. It foresees the further development of a sound monitoring framework contributing to measuring well-being beyond GDP.

4. The long-term growth of Japan's real GDP has been low, handicapped by an aging and declining population, making negative growth more likely.

5. During this time, the United States agreed to delay increasing its tariffs on $200 billion worth of Chinese imports from 10 to 25 percent, as had been scheduled to occur on January 1, 2019, until March 1, 2019.

三、语篇翻译

(一) 汉译英

坚持把扩大就业放在经济社会发展的优先位置，将促进产业发展和扩大就业相结合，创造平等就业机会，努力实现充分就业。

实施更加积极的就业政策。大力发展服务业、劳动密集型产业，采取信贷、税收优惠政策扶持小型企业发展，多形式、多渠道开发就业岗位。建立健全重大项目建设带动就业机制。完善税费减免、岗位补贴、培训补贴、社会保险补贴、技能鉴定补贴等政策，鼓励企业吸纳更多劳动者就业。深入推进全民创业，完善和落实小额担保贷款、财政贴息、场地安排等鼓励自主创业政策，健全创业服务体系，力争五年开展创业培训 50 万人次。鼓励外出务工人员返乡创业。

做好重点群体就业工作。加强高校毕业生就业服务和政策扶持，畅通大学生到城乡基层、中小企业和自主创业的就业渠道。在大力发展劳务输出的同时，加快产业集聚区、专业园区建设，发展农村二、三产业，推动农副产品加工业向产区集中布局，促进农村劳动力就地就近就业，力争五年累计转移农业劳动力 500 万人。做好城镇就业困难人员、退役军人就业工作，强化就业服务和援助，实施公益性岗位安置计划，力争每年开发 10 万个左右公益性岗位。

大力开展劳动技能培训。健全面向全体劳动者的职业培训制度，紧密围绕我省产业结构调整和承接产业转移需要，以培养高素质产业技能人才为重点，大规模开展职业技能培训，全面提升劳动者就业、创业能力。对下岗失业人员、农民工等开展免费实用技能培训，对未能升学的应届初高中毕业生等新成长劳动力普遍实行劳动预备制培训。实施全民技能振兴工程，到 2013 年，全省完成农村劳动力转移就业技能培训 1000 万人次、企业在岗职工技能提升培训 200 万人次、失业人员转岗职业技能培训 150 万人次，新培养技师、高级技师 10 万人。

加强公共就业服务。健全统一、规范、灵活的人力资源市场，加强县、乡基层就业服务设施建设，建成覆盖城乡的公共就业服务体系。完善劳动就业监测体系，健全失业监测预警制度。全面推行劳动合同制度，加强劳动定额标准管理，加强劳动争议调解仲裁，加强劳动保障监察执法，切实维护劳动者权益。发挥政府、工会和企业的作用，努力形成企业和职工利益共享机制，构建和谐劳动关系。

（二）英译汉

Empowering consumers and providing them with cost-saving opportunities is a key building block of the sustainable product policy framework. To enhance the participation of consumers in the circular economy, the Commission will propose a revision of EU consumer law to ensure that consumers receive trustworthy and relevant information on products at the point of sale, including on their lifespan and on the availability of repair services, spare parts and repair manuals. The Commission will also consider further strengthening consumer protection against green washing and premature obsolescence, setting minimum requirements for sustainability labels/logos and for information tools.

In addition, the Commission will work towards establishing a new "right to repair" and consider new horizontal material rights for consumers for instance as regards availability of spare parts or access to repair and, in the case of ICT and electronics, to upgrading services. Regarding the role that guarantees can play in providing more circular products, the Commission will explore possible changes also in the context of the review of Directive 2019/771.

The Commission will also propose that companies substantiate their environmental claims using Product and Organisation Environmental Footprint methods. The Commission will test the integration of these methods in the EU Ecolabel and include more systematically durability, recyclability and recycled content in the EU Ecolabel criteria. Public authorities' purchasing power represents 14% of EU GDP and can serve as a powerful driver of the demand for sustainable products. To tap into this potential, the Commission will propose minimum mandatory green public procurement (GPP) criteria and targets in sectoral legislation and phase in compulsory reporting to monitor the uptake of Green Public Procurement (GPP) without creating unjustified administrative burden for public buyers. Furthermore, the Commission will continue to support capacity building with guidance, training and dissemination of good practices and encouraging public buyers to take part in a "Public Buyers for Climate and Environment" initiative, which will facilitate exchanges among buyers committed to GPP implementation.

Circularity is an essential part of a wider transformation of industry towards climate-neutrality and long term competitiveness. It can deliver substantial material savings throughout value chains and production processes, generate extra value and unlock economic opportunities. In synergy with the objectives laid out in the Industrial Strategy, the Commission will enable greater circularity in industry by:

• assessing options for further promoting circularity in industrial processes in the context of the review of the Industrial Emissions Directive17, including the integration of circular economy practices in upcoming Best Available Techniques reference documents;

• facilitating industrial symbiosis by developing an industry-led reporting and certification system, and enabling the implementation of industrial symbiosis;

• supporting the sustainable and circular bio-based sector through the implementation of the Bioeconomy Action Plan;

• promoting the use of digital technologies for tracking, tracing and mapping of resources;

• promoting the uptake of green technologies through a system of solid verification by registering the EU Environmental Technology Verification scheme as an EU certification mark.

The new SME Strategy will foster circular industrial collaboration among SMEs building on training, advice under the Enterprise Europe Network on cluster collaboration, and on knowledge transfer via the European Resource Efficiency Knowledge Centre.

◎ 参考文献

[1] 蔡立坚. 政府公文英译浅析[J]. 中国翻译, 2015, 36(6): 81-87.

[2] 邓中敏, 曾剑平. 政治话语同词句异译可接受性研究[J]. 中国科技翻译, 2020, 33(2): 35, 51-54.

［3］胡芳毅. 操纵理论视角下的外宣翻译——政治文本翻译的改写［J］. 中国科技翻译, 2014, 27(2): 40-42, 39.

［4］韦孟芬. 英语科技术语的词汇特征及翻译［J］. 中国科技翻译, 2014, 27(1): 5-7, 23.

［5］张丽红, 刘祥清. 生态翻译论对外宣翻译的启示［J］. 中国科技翻译, 2014, 27(2): 43-46.

第十章 经济合同相关法律法规翻译

> **☞思考题**
> 1. 什么是经济合同？什么是商务合同？二者有什么区别？
> 2. 经济合同相关法律法规有哪些基本特征？
> 3. 有哪些翻译原则、方法和技巧适用于经济合同相关法律法规的翻译？

第一节 经济合同相关法律法规分析

一、经济合同的定义

合同伴随着人类从野蛮状态进入文明社会，由交易的法律形式进化为任何领域、任何主体自愿相互接受约束的法律形式，是一种最古老又最现代的法律关系和社会关系。根据1999年10月1日起施行的《中华人民共和国合同法》（以下简称《合同法》）第二条，合同是平等主体的自然人、法人、其他组织之间设立、变更、终止民事权利义务关系意思表示一致的协议。本章指的经济合同是指合同一方是政府或者由政府或法律授权的机构，或者一方或两方以上就合同的订立、合同的条件内容及合同内容的实现对政府负有义务，直接体现以政府意志表达出来的公共政策要求或其他公共利益要求，具有经济目的或经济内容的合同。

需要注意的是，经济合同和商务合同是有所区别的。商务合同是指有关各方之间在进行某种商务合作时，为了确定各自的权利和义务，而正式依法订立的，并且经过公证的、必须共同遵守的协议条文。商务合同中需要注明的要素有商品品名、质量、数量、价格、包装、交货、付款方式、保险、检验、索赔、违约、仲裁、不可抗力、专利、保密、培训、适用法律和其他等。

根据以上关于合同和经济合同的定义可以得知经济合同的性质。经济合同是直接体现政府意志的具有经济内容的合同，其本质是国家或政府在经济活动或经济管理中，将其意志体现到原本是私人自治的契约关系中。此外，经济合同是公与私融合，行政和"商事"、经济的交织，要直接服从市场和经济的规律，而不是单纯的行政运作手段，所以属于经济法而非行政法范畴。

由此，经济合同的范围也可以有所界定。第一，经济合同与不直接体现国家或政府意志的其他具有经济目的的合同有所区别，一般的民商事合同和行政管理性合同都不属于经济合同。第二，经济合同不包括含有政府意志但并不表达或无须表达的公共政策要求，如国家机关基于自身消费需要，并不或不需要纳入政府采购程序的民事合同。

二、经济合同的基本内容

经济合同的订立、效力、履行、变更、终止、违约责任等，要适用作为合同普通法的《合同法》的一般原则和规则。同时，《中华人民共和国招标投标法》《中华人民共和国政府采购法》《中华人民共和国城镇国有土地使用权出让和转让暂行条例》《中华人民共和国农村土地承包法》和《中华人民共和国农村土地承包经营纠纷调解仲裁法》等法律法规有特殊规定的，须优先适用相应特别法中涉及合同的规定。

在经济合同订立的要约和承诺阶段直接体现出政府或国家的意志。首先，一些经济合同超越当事人的意志，是依法或依政策、集体决定等必须订立的，如农村土地承包合同等，当事人的意思只能在一定范围内协商确定合同条款或变通、落实法定合同条件。其次，经济合同的订立原则上应当公开透明，贯彻公开、公平、公正的"三公"原则。而民商事合同原则上不必公开，出于商业和个人的原因可以秘密订立，也不存在对政府等公共管理主体的公正要求。公开、公正表现为法律要求通过招标、拍卖等竞争性方式，在监督和救济等程序之下订立合同。既然政府希望将其意志表达为合同的订立及条款，则负有秉公行事的义务，并就其行为接受当事人和公众的问责，承担相应的法律责任。

经济合同成立后具有法律效力，当事人必须全面适当地履行合同义务，而政府对于合同订立和内容的主导性，导致了在合同变更、解除和违约责任认定上的复杂性。直接体现政府或国家意志的合同条款，往往同时就是法律的规定、政府的政策、决定或措施，政府一方的违约与其基于公共管理权力的合同变更、解除难以分辨，可能掩盖其违约、违法行为或逃避其责任。在这种情况下，应当区分政府的行为是基于法律的一般规定、政策或抽象行政行为还是出于其单方具体行政行为。如为后者，政府作为合同一方原则上应当承担违约责任；如为前者，则政府原则上不必承担违约责任，但基于财产权保护的要求和合同的法律效力，政府对因此受到损害的合同当事人应给予适当补偿，或通过政策调整加以一定的弥补。

三、经济合同的种类

经济合同在不同的历史时期有不同的表现形式和作用。经济合同最早产生于20世纪30年代的苏联，其目的和作用是使计划指标具体化、明确化。当时苏联颁布了许多有关物资供应和建设承包合同的法规和决议，具有代表性的有1931年《关于国家联合企业、托拉斯和其他经济组织的流转手段》的决议、《关于订立1933年度合同》和《关于订立1934年度合同》的决议等。我国在计划经济时期没有制定合同法，改革开放后不久，《中华人民共和国经济合同法》(以下简称《经济合同法》)于 1981 年颁行。当时我国正处于计划经济体制转轨、变革时期,该法的宗旨是将计划与商品货币关系相结合,当时的法人组织主要还是受到计划管理的公有制企业。随着市场化改革的不断深入,市场逐步在资源配置中发挥决定性作用,指令性计划缩减殆尽,国有及公有制主体也在意思自治的基础上从事流转和协作活动。随着改革实践的推进,《经济合同法》的作用不再如昔,立法机关遂以一部统一的民事合同法即《中华人民共和国合同法》取代"三足鼎立"的《中华人民共和国经济合同法》《中华人民共和国技术合同法》和《中华人民共和国涉外经济合同法》。市场对资源起决定性的配置作用和放弃行政性的流通、协作,并不意味着在"横向"的流通和协作领域里不再有直接体现政府意志或政府主导的经济合同关系。这是我国合同制度的一个合乎逻辑的、正常的发展。

本章主要讲市场经济条件下的经济合同关系,主要表现为以下两种类型:

第一,国家通过政府机构或设立企业、委托代理人直接参与经济活动或进入经济关系,或者当事人直接受制于国家政策或政府意志订立合同而形成的合同关系。这类关系的一方或双方当事人是国家机关或必须执行国家政策的主体,合同内容需要体现国家的政策或政府意志。

第二,平等的国家机关或财政主体之间的经济协作关系。作为在行政或财政上互相没有隶属关系的所谓平等国家机关或财政主体,它们在利益或政策驱动下,在平等互利的经济协作中为明确相互权利义务并保证协作事项的实现而订立的协议,也属于经济合同和经济法调整的范围。

我国经济合同不完全列举如下:

(1) 国有土地使用权出让合同。这种合同将国家法律和政策确定的条件和政府土地管理的要求与合同条款有机紧密地结合,并由政府作为合同一方当事人,是一种十分典型的经济合同。

(2) 政府采购合同。这是作为采购人的国家机关和其他主体采购纳入政府采购管理的货物、工程和服务,适用《中华人民共和国政府采购法》,而与供应商订立的合同。不在此范围的"政府采购"则属于民商事合同的范畴。

(3) 中央银行和政策性银行与其他主体订立的借贷合同等。这种合同与落实和实现国家政策和政府管理目的相联系,主要是借贷合同,也包括中央银行在公开市场操作中买卖货币而订立的合同等。

(4) 国有企业或公司承包、租赁合同。这是落实国家(中央或地方)与国有企业、公司之间责、权、利关系的一种法律形式。其形式多种多样,从所有者代表一方看,既可以是作为具体股东的出资者,也可能是行使所有者职能的财政部门,甚至是企业的董事会;从企业一方看,则既可以是企业或公司本身,也可能是特定的经营者如总经理或董事长等或管理层整体与代表所有者的一方订立合同;从合同内容看,既可以全面涵盖各种经营指标,也可能仅包括某方面内容或某种指标,如经营者报酬与经营如何挂钩、扭亏为盈或审计责任等。

(5)政府和社会资本合作(Public-Private Partnership，简称"PPP")和政府特许经营合同。在政府与社会合作从事基础设施和市政等建设和公用事业引入竞争和民营化，以及在自然垄断和法定垄断领域，这种合同的运用越来越普遍。通过这种法律形式，把对企业的公共性要求，由政府作为合同一方当事人表达出来，落实为合同内容，既强化了企业一方的权利和义务，也对政府的公共管理提出了更高的要求。因为政府受到了合同的具体细致条款的约束，不能再凭行政权力单方面行事，稍有疏忽懈怠就可能被告上法庭，以致承担高额的赔偿或补偿责任。在政府对国有企业或公司特许经营的情况下，所订合同也可归为承包范畴，为广义的承包合同。

(6)政府担保合同。政府为特定债务提供担保，如《中华人民共和国担保法》中提及的为使用外国政府或者国际经济组织贷款进行转贷所提供的担保等，在公共财政用于经济目的和公共性投资、贷款越来越普遍的情况下，这是十分必要的。没有政府信用和财政的支持保证，这些活动就难以正常进行。由于担保的后果最终需由财政来承担，所以对其须依法加以一定的管理和控制，建立相应的程序和监督制度。

(7)指令性合同。随着社会主义市场经济体制的建立，我国的指令性计划趋于消亡，国家对经济的管理已从行政性的计划手段转为主要运用间接的经济手段，但在一定条件下，如救灾或发生紧急状态时，或者对于涉及国家重要经济利益和国家安全或为实现国家某种目标的特定产品和项目，仍可能予以行政性安排、调拨、指令性生产和国家订货等，从而形成指令性合同。这种合同与计划经济时期的指令性计划合同并无本质区别，是行政性很强的经济合同。

(8)农村土地承包合同。这种合同与村民自治和集体所有紧密相关，事关基层和社会稳定，加之农民处于弱势且分散状态，所以通过法律、党和国家的政策、政府的指导和管理等，对合同的订立和主要合同条件作具体的规定和要求，使之获得了经济合同的性质。

(9)互无隶属关系的国家机关或财政主体间的经济协作合同。如省、直辖市和自治区之间、中央部委与地方之间等双方或多方的协议或合同，内容包括投资建设道路、机场、水坝和林场，电力建设和电力供应，省际或市际对口协作和支援等。这类经济合同中不存在居于主导的一方，当事人之间是平等的，但其订立、履行都直接体现国家意志，是政府参与和调控经济的手段，具有较强的政策性，因而也属于经济合同，对于区域经济平衡协调发展等具有重要意义。

四、经济合同相关法律法规的基本特征

关于经济合同相关法律法规的基本特征，本章将从法律层面和语言层面分别展开。

从法律层面上讲，经济合同相关法律法规具有以下主要特征：

第一，经济合同相关法律法规的基本条件或主要条件由政府规定或确定。这种规定或确定，既可以是一般规定，如某种产品买卖合同执行具体收购政策或国家定价，农村土地承包经营合同适用政策法规的有关具体规定；也可以由作为合同一方的政府或其授

权机构，根据既定的目标、政策或项目的要求而拟订，如政府采购、国有土地使用权出让合同等。

第二，主体一方通常是政府或经授权执行公共政策的机构，如政府采购合同或土地使用权出让合同，主导的一方是代表政府的部门或机关。政府也可以通过其授权或法律直接授权的机构来订立经济合同，如通过法定机构或政策性企业的活动及合同来实现一定的公共政策或公共利益目标，就是国际上常见的情形，如中央银行或政策性银行作为合同一方当事人，国有粮食企业向农民收购粮食等。政府往往还通过代理人订立合同，如需要采购的政府部门通过集中采购机关进行采购活动。同时，有些主体都不是政府或特殊企业等，之所以认为其属于经济合同相关法律法规，是因为合同的一方或双方就合同的订立、合同的条件及其实现对政府负有义务。其典型情况是供销合作社根据政府的政策向农民收购棉花和其他规定的农副产品、村集体与村民订立土地承包经营合同等。

第三，经济合同相关法律法规具有经济性或商事性，也即经济目的（或商事目的）和经济内容。因具有直接政府意志性而较易于与民商事合同相区别，其经济性或商事性表明经济合同的媒介是物质利益关系，而非政府行政关系，其本质是市场交易。尽管政府在合同中起主导作用，经济性或商事性也要求其遵循市场规律和合同的平等要求，如对价和承诺、违约救济和赔偿等。

第四，经济合同相关法律法规中存在着事实上或合同上的政府主导性。一是政府在合同订立中运用促进竞争等构造买方市场的手段，来取得事实上的优势或主导地位，这常见于政府采购合同；二是政府基于公共政策或公共利益，要求在合同中加入保证政府主导性的权力，使权力和权利不再清晰可辨，比如监督管理权、撤销或终止合同的权力，在公共工程建设、委托或授权经营公共设施、土地使用权出让等合同中都有表现；三是在政府不作为合同当事人的情况下，通过政策和法律的规定和指导监督，取得对合同的主导。

第五，经济合同相关法律法规与政府及其运作机制有着密切联系。经济合同的公私法交融决定了它在遵守市场规律和规则的同时，必须遵循政府活动和运作的基本要求，这些要求包括：执行国家政策，厉行节约，政府一方公开操作，在缔约和履约中发挥民主机制，在条件许可的情况下由企业或其他主体以公平竞争方式与政府缔约，国有资产保值增值，严格监管和反腐败等。这些相关的制度或机制要求与经济合同制度不可截然分割。

从语言层面上讲，本章主要是从词汇、句法和篇章三个角度分析经济合同相关法律法规的基本特征。

（一）从词汇出发，经济合同相关法律法规的词汇特征

（1）对于经济合同相关法律法规中部分重复的内容，中文多使用重复的词汇以明确规定权利和义务和保证法律语言的规范性、准确性和严谨性；英文较少使用代词以尽可能防止出现因指代不清而产生歧义的情况，如有出现代词的情况，代词所指的内容则清晰明了，别无他意。

例1

原文：第一百零九条　当事人一方未支付价款或者报酬的，对方可以要求其支付价款或者报酬。

(《中华人民共和国合同法》)

译文：Article 109　If a party fails to pay the price or remuneration, the other party may request it to make the payment.

例2

原文：In the absence of contractual intention, an agreement, even if supported by consideration, cannot be enforced. Whether the parties to an agreement intended to create legally binding relations between **them** is a question determined by an objective assessment of the relevant facts.

(《新加坡合同法》*The Law of Contract* 8.4.1)

译文：如缺乏合同意旨，即使有对价支持，协议也不能执行。应该通过对相关事实的客观评估来确定各当事方是否愿意在彼此之间建立有法律约束力的关系。

分析：在上述例句中，例1中的"(支付)价款或者报酬"重复出现是对"对方可以要求其支付"的具体内容补充，避免因为省略部分宾语而引起歧义。例2中出现了代词"them"，根据前后文可以很明显地得知代词所指代的是"the parties"，可以避免引起不同的解读。

(2)经济合同明确当事人权利和义务时，中文多出现"不得""应当""必须"或"可以"等，英文多出现相对应的情态动词"no…may…""shall""must"或"may"等。

例3

原文：第十二条　招标人有权自行选择招标代理机构，委托其办理招标事宜。任何单位和个人不得以任何方式为招标人指定招标代理机构。招标人具有编制招标文件和组织评标能力的，可以自行办理招标事宜。任何单位和个人不得强制其委托招标代理机构办理招标事宜。依法必须进行招标的项目，招标人自行办理招标事宜的，应当向有关行政监督部门备案。

(《中华人民共和国招标投标法》)

译文：Article 12　A tenderer shall have the right to choose, on his own, a procuratorial agency and authorize it to carry out the tender. **No** unit or person **may** designate a procuratorial agency for the tenderer in any form. A tenderer who has the capability of preparing his tender documents and organizing bid assessments **may** carry out the tender by himself. **No** unit or person **may** compel the tenderer to authorize a procuratorial agency to carry out the tender. If a tenderer carries out the tender by himself for a project subject to tender according to law, the matter shall be reported to the relevant department for administrative supervision for the record.

例 4

原文：(1)The price in a contract of sale **may** be fixed by the contract, or **may** be left to be fixed in a manner agreed by the contract, or **may** be determined by the course of dealing between the parties.

(2)Where the price is not determined as mentioned in sub-section (1)above the buyer **must** pay a reasonable price.

(《英国货物买卖法》Sale of Goods Act 1979 [England] 8.)

译文：(1)买卖合同中的价格可由合同确定，也可留给合同所认同的其他方式确定，或者还可以由双方当事人在交易过程中来确定。

(2)如果价格并未依上述第(1)款得到确定，则买方必须支付合理的价格。

分析：在上述例句中，例3和例4中的原文和译文体现了规定权利和义务时用词的选择。在表示强制性的法律法规中，中文多用"不得""应当"或"必须"的字眼，英文多用"no…may…""shall"或"must"来表达。如果是表示选择性的或者非强制性的法律法规，中文多用"可"或"可以"的字眼，英文根据语态选择"may"或"may be"来表达。

英文经济合同相关法律法规中会出现古体词，中文中则没有古体词。古体词即英文单词"there""here"或"where"与介词"after""from""by""in""of""to"或"under"分别相结合以代指文中部分内容或者表明文中内容逻辑关系。

例 5

原文：§2-616. Procedure on Notice Claiming Excuse

(1)Where the buyer receives notification of a material or indefinite delay or an allocation justified under the preceding section he may by written notification to the seller as to any delivery concerned, and where the prospective deficiency substantially impairs the value of the whole contract under the provisions of this Article relating to breach of installment contracts (Section 2-612), then also as to the whole,

(a)terminate and thereby discharge any unexecuted portion of the contract; or

(b)modify the contract by agreeing to take his available quota in substitution.

(《美国统一商法典》U. C. C. -ARTICLE 2-SALES (2002) § 2-616.)

译文：第 2-616 条　收到主张免责之通知后的程序

(1)买方在收到通知，了解到根据上述合理理由，交货将要长期或无限延迟，或交货将只限于某一数额时，可以书面通知卖方，就任何有关部分货物，或如果依本篇关于违反分批交货合同的规定确认交货之不足部分已致整个合同的价值严重降低(第2-612条)，则就全部货物：

(a)终止合同，从而解除合同中任何未履行部分；或

(b)同意按替代办法收取他可以得到的数额,从而修改合同。

分析:在例5中出现了古体词"thereby",根据《柯林斯英汉双解大词典》可以得知该古体词的英文释义为"You use thereby to introduce an important result or consequence of the event or action you have just mentioned",即该古体词表因果关系,可以译为"从而"以起到承接上文原因和启示下文结果的作用。

(3)英文经济合同相关法律法规中会出现缩写词,中文则没有缩写词。

例6

原文:The term **C. I. F.** means that the price includes in a lump sum the cost of the goods and the insurance and freight to the named destination. The term **C. & F.** or **C. F.** means that the price so includes cost and freight to the named destination.

(《美国统一商法典》U. C. C. -ARTICLE 2-SALES (2002) § 2-320.)

译文:成本加运保费条件指价格中总括地包含了货物价格和将货物运达指定目的地的保险费和运费。成本加运费条件指价格中包含了货物价格和将货物运达指定目的地的运费。

分析:在上述例句中,C. I. F.、C. & F.或C. F.都是国际贸易中常见的贸易术语,这些术语的缩写形式已经为大众所接受,出现在英文经济合同相关法律法规中显得相对简洁。

(二)从句法出发,经济合同相关法律法规的句法特征

(1)中英文经济合同相关法律法规都有完整的句子结构,二者都有明确的主语和谓语,句子相对较长。句子结构清晰,表达明确,尽可能避免因内容省略或成分缺失造成理解偏差或者产生歧义。

(2)中英文经济合同相关法律法规都多用陈述句,较少用或者不用疑问句、祈使句和感叹句。本章所引用的六份参考经济合同文本中均没有出现疑问句、祈使句和感叹句。

(3)中英文经济合同相关法律法规都会使用条件句来考虑可能发生的情况。

例7

原文:第二十三条　汇票上记载付款日期、付款地、出票地等事项的,应当清楚、明确。

汇票上未记载付款日期的,为见票即付。

汇票上未记载付款地的,付款人的营业场所、住所或者经常居住地为付款地。

汇票上未记载出票地的,出票人的营业场所、住所或者经常居住地为出票地。

(《中华人民共和国票据法》)

译文:Article 23　The date of payment, place of payment and place of draft recorded on the draft shall be clear and definite.

If a draft does not bear the date of payment, it is a draft payable at sight.

If a draft does not bear the place of payment, the place of payment shall be the business site or the residence of the payer or the place where the payer often lives.

If a draft does not bear the place of draft, the place of draft shall be taken as the business site or residence of the drawer or the place where the drawer often lives.

例8

原文：Rule 4

When goods are delivered to the buyer on approval or on sale or return or other similar terms the property in the goods passes to the buyer：

(a) when he signifies his approval or acceptance to the seller or does any other act adopting the transaction；

(b) if he does not signify his approval or acceptance to the seller but retains the goods without giving notice of rejection, then, if a time has been fixed for the return of the goods on the expiration of that time, and if no time has been fixed, on the expiration of a reasonable time.

(《英国货物买卖法》Sale of Goods Act 1979 [England] 18.)

译文：规则4

当货物以试验买卖、余货退回或其他类似条款将货物交付买方时，货物所有权转移至买方：

(a) 买方向卖方表明认可或接受交易，或以其他方式确认这项交易时，货物有权转移给买方；

(b) 如果买方没有向卖方表示认可或接受该项货物，但他保留了货物并没有发出退货通知，如果合同规定有固定的退货期限，且期限届满，或者，合同没有规定退货期限，但经过了一段合理时间。

分析：通过以上两个例句可知，经济合同相关法律法规中，中文多分别罗列可能出现的情况，英文则多出现"when"或"if"引导的条件状语从句来表现可能出现的情况，并针对不同情况提出对应的处理方式或者明确对应的结果。

经济合同相关法律法规中出现明确权利和义务的内容时，中文英译版本或英文相关法律法规一般会根据相对应的情况使用主动语态以降低理解难度，也会使用被动语态和名词化结构来强调事实的客观性和真实性。

例9

原文：第三百四十四条　专利实施许可合同只在该专利权的存续期间内有效。专利权有效期限届满或者专利权被宣布无效的，专利权人不得就该专利与他人订立专利实施许可合同。

(《中华人民共和国合同法》)

译文：Article 344　A patent licensing contract is only valid during the term of the patent.

Where the term of the patent expires or the patent is invalidated, the patentee may not enter into a patent licensing contract with any other person in respect thereof.

例 10

原文：Subject to this and any other Act, a contract of sale may be made in writing (either with or without seal), or by word of mouth, or partly in writing and partly by word of mouth, or may be implied from the conduct of the parties.

(《英国货物买卖法》*Sale of Goods Act* 1979 [*England*] 4.)

译文：依据本法及其他任何法律，买卖合同的形式可依书面形式（需不需要签章均可），也可依口头形式，或部分书面形式部分口头形式，也可从当事人的行为中推断。

分析：在上述两个例句中，例9中的"专利实施许可合同"是事物，它需要在人为因素的干涉下才能生效，但是译文中直接使用主动语态以降低理解难度和增强译文的可读性。例10中，事物"a contract of sale"（买卖合同）作主语，原文中说明买卖合同的具体形式时使用被动语态以强调其客观性和真实性。

（三）从篇章出发，经济合同相关法律法规语篇规整，条目罗列清晰有序，逻辑严谨，明确当事人的权利和义务

例 11

原文：第十三条　招标代理机构是依法设立、从事招标代理业务并提供相关服务的社会中介组织。招标代理机构应当具备下列条件：

（一）有从事招标代理业务的营业场所和相应资金；

（二）有能够编制招标文件和组织评标的相应专业力量；

（三）有符合本法第三十七条第三款规定条件，可以作为评标委员会成员人选的技术、经济等方面的专家库。

(《中华人民共和国招标投标法》)

译文：Article 13 A procuratorial agency is a social intermediary organization which is established according to law to engage in the procuratorial tender business and to provide related services. A procuratorial agency shall satisfy the following conditions:

1. Having a business site and necessary amount of capital for carrying out the procuratorial tender business;

2. Having a qualified technical and academic force capable of preparing the tender documents and organizing bid assessments; and

3. Having a bank of experts in such fields as technology and economics who satisfy the conditions laid down in Paragraph 3 of Article 37 of this Law and can serve as candidates of members of the bid assessment committees.

例 12

原文: 30. Delivery of wrong quantity

(1) Where the seller delivers to the buyer a quantity of goods less than he contracted to sell, the buyer may reject them, but if the buyer accepts the goods so delivered he must pay for them at the contract rate.

(2) Where the seller delivers to the buyer a quantity of goods larger than he contracted to sell, the buyer may accept the goods included in the contract and reject the rest, or he may reject the whole.

(3) Where the seller delivers to the buyer a quantity of goods larger than he contracted to sell and the buyer accepts the whole of the goods so delivered he must pay for them at the contract rate.

(4) Where the seller delivers to the buyer the goods he contracted to sell mixed with goods of a different description not included in the contract, the buyer may accept the goods which are in accordance with the contract and reject the rest, or he may reject the whole.

(5) This section is subject to any usage of trade, special agreement, or of course of dealing between the parties.

(《英国货物买卖法》 *Sale of Goods Act* 1979 [*England*] 30.)

译文: 第三十条 错误数量的交付

(1) 当卖方所交货物少于合同订立的数量时,买方可以拒收货物,但是一旦买方接受了这样交付的货物,就必须按合同价格支付货物价款。

(2) 如果卖方交付至买方的货物多于合同订货数量时,买方可以接受合同数量而拒收多余数量,或拒收全部。

(3) 如买方接受了卖方交付的超过合同订货的数量,就必须按合同价格支付全部货物价款。

(4) 如果卖方交付至买方的货物为多种规格货物的混合,买方可以接受合同订货的货物,而拒收其他规格货物,或拒收全部货物。

(5) 本款适用于所有的贸易、特定协议或交易。

分析: 在上述两个例子中,例 11 中罗列出招标代理机构应当符合的三个条件,分别是从事招标业务的经营场所和资金、专业力量和专家库;例 12 罗列出了在进行货物买卖时可能出现交付错误数量货物的情况,交付错误数量货物分为交付数量多于合同规定的数量和交付数量少于合同规定的数量两种情况,而面对这两种情况,买方可以选择接受或者拒绝这批数量与合同规定不一致的货物,针对买方不同的选择也会有相对应的规定。经济合同相关法律法规条目清晰全面,考虑到可能发生的不同情况,有利于明确当事人的权利和义务。

第二节　翻译知识讲解

本节关于经济合同相关法律法规的翻译探索是在翻译功能对等理论的指导下进行的。在翻译功能对等理论的指导下，本节对经济合同相关法律法规的翻译原则、方法和技巧进行了相对详细的阐述。

一、翻译功能对等理论

翻译功能对等理论由美国语言学家尤金·A. 奈达(Eugene A. Nida)提出。奈达认为翻译是用最恰当、自然和对等的语言从语义到文体再现源语的信息。所谓"功能对等"，就是说翻译时不求文字表面的死板对应，而要在两种语言间达成功能上的对等。

根据《翻译的科学探索》(*Toward a Science of Translating*)(Eugene A. Nida，1964)可知，功能对等主要体现在四个方面：①词汇对等；②句法对等；③语篇对等；④文体对等。

词汇对等指的是一个词真正的意义在于它在语言中的用法。在翻译实践中，译者面临的一个问题就是如何在目的语中找到与源语词汇意义相等的词汇表达。尽管在两种语言之间，没有两个词的意义是完全相同的，但可以使用不同的表达形式来表达相同的意义。

句法对等指的是在翻译过程中应当注意源语和目的语的句子结构和语法。译者不仅要清楚目的语中是否有和源语一致的句子结构，还要明白上述句子结构在目的语和源语中的使用频率。同时，译者还需要注意词性、名词的单复数和句子时态等。

语篇对等指的是译者在进行语篇分析时不能只分析语言本身，而要看语言怎样在特定的语境中体现意义和功能。语篇对等包含三个层面：上下文语境，情景语境和文化语境。上下文语境指的是翻译时应对原文上下文进行分析，这有助于判断语义单位在原文中的含义，从而实现原文意思在源语和目的语之间的转换。情景语境指的是语言内容中具体参与的人和发生的事。某些语言现象无法通过上下文来明确其具体含义，必须参考语言使用时发生的事件和参与者等因素才能明确其具体意义。文化语境指的是语言运用的社会文化背景、历史文化传统及社会心理等。由于各门语言背后的文化历史背景、发展过程和社会发展阶段等的不同，各民族的价值观念、宗教信仰和风土人情等存在或大或小的差异，语言文化具有多样性。翻译的内容不仅仅是语言符号的转换，还是语言符号背后所承载的文化的再次呈现。

文体对等指的是语言风格的对等。不同文体的翻译作品有着各自独特的语言特征。只有在同时掌握源语和目的语两种语言的特征，且能熟练运用两种语言的情况下，译者才能创造出真实体现源语风格的翻译作品。

基于以上四个方面，奈达认为翻译出原文所要表达的意义是最重要的，其次才是风格上的对等。

此外，奈达认为，译者可以遵循以下的三个步骤以最大化再现源语所要传达的意思及源语背后承载的文化：第一，最大限度地创造出既与原文意思相一致又体现原文文化特色的译作以最大限度地再现源语文化。第二，如果意义和文化不能兼顾，译者只有舍弃形式对等，通过在译文中改变原文的形式达到再现原文意思和源语文化的目的。第三，如果形式的改变仍然不能够传达原文的意思和源语背后承载的文化，可以采用"重创"这一翻译技巧来解决文化差异带来的问题，使源语和目的语达到意义上的对等。

二、经济合同相关法律法规翻译原则

经济合同相关法律法规的翻译是法律语言翻译的一部分。法律语言要求准确、规范、严谨，要在两种语言间达成功能上的对等。经济合同相关法律法规翻译应当遵循以下翻译原则：

（一）确保译文准确无误

根据翻译功能对等理论，翻译出原文所要表达的意思是最重要的，其次才是风格上的对等。经济合同相关法律法规的主要内容是明确权利和义务，措辞规范严谨，因此在翻译经济合同相关法律法规时应该遵循确保译文准确无误原则。遵循该原则主要从两方面着手：一方面是措辞的严谨性，另一方面是语法的准确性。

第一，措辞的严谨性。需要注意以下两点：

(1) 根据翻译功能对等理论，词汇真正的意思体现在其实际用法中，要明确一个词汇的意思需要对原文上下文进行分析并判断语义单位在原文中的含义，从而更好地传达原文意思。

例 13

原文：第三十八条　**承兑**是指汇票付款人承诺在汇票到期日支付汇票金额的票据行为。

（《中华人民共和国票据法》）

译文：Article 38　**Acceptance** refers to a promise of a draft payer to pay the actual amount of draft when the draft is due.

例 14

原文：The goods which form the subject of a contract of sale may be either existing goods, owned or possessed by the seller, or goods to be manufactured or acquired by him after the making of the contract of sale, in this Act called future goods.

（《英国货物买卖法》*Sale of Goods Act* 1979 ［*England*］ 5.）

译文：成为买卖合同标的的货物既可以是卖方所有或持有的**现货**，也可以是买卖合同达成后卖方生产或取得的货物，本法称之为期货。

分析：在上述例子中，例 13 中的"承兑"是一个常见的术语，字面意思即"承诺到期兑现承诺"，而英文单词"acceptance"的本意为"接受；认可；相信"，根据《新牛津英汉双解大词典》，该单词还有"a draft or bill so accepted"的意思，即"承兑"。因此，译文中将"承兑"译为"acceptance"有一定的根据，用词合理，且符合票据法文本的语境。在例14中，"existing goods"和"future goods"这两个表达在贸易行业中分别被称为"现货"和"期货"，如果按字面意思将其分别翻译成"存在的货物"和"未来的货物"，则无法传达出原文的意思，且容易给译文读者带来阅读和理解上的障碍，甚至会因此带来一定的后果。

（2）两个看似意思相近的词在不同语境下可能代表着完全不同的权利和义务。

例 15

原文：第十七条　要约可以**撤回**。撤回要约的通知应当在要约到达受要约人之前或者与要约同时到达受要约人。

（《中华人民共和国合同法》）

译文：Article 17　An offer may be withdrawn. The withdrawal notice shall reach the offeree before or at the same time when the offer arrives.

例 16

原文：第十八条　要约可以**撤销**。撤销要约的通知应当在受要约人发出承诺通知之前到达受要约人。

（《中华人民共和国合同法》）

译文：Article 18　An offer may be revoked. The revocation notice shall reach the offeree before it has dispatched a notice of acceptance.

分析：从上述例子中可以知道，《中华人民共和国合同法》将要约的撤回与撤销分别列出，因此要约的撤回与撤销是有一定区别的。首先，两者表现形式不同。要约撤回发生在要约到达（或刚刚到达）受要约人之前；而要约撤销则发生在要约已经到达受要约人，受要约人尚未发出承诺通知之前。其次，两者发生的时间不同。要约撤回是在要约尚未生效（或刚刚生效）时发生的；要约撤销则是在要约生效后，受要约人发出承诺通知前。最后，两者要求的条件不同。要约撤销关于不可撤销的规定，特别是要求受要约人不仅得"有理由认为要约不可撤销"，而且要求"已经为履行合同作了准备工作"；而要约撤回没有这样的规定，只要要约撤回的通知先于或同时与要约到达受要约人，就可产生撤回的效力。因此，在翻译经济合同相关法律法规时应当对平常意思相近的术语或其他表达加以区分，确保措辞严谨，译文准确有据。

第二，语法的准确性。在经济合同相关法律法规中，中文明显表现时态的词或句子相对较少，英文中则会出现大量表现时态的标志性单词。同时，经济合同相关法律法规通常用于明确相关权利和义务，内容以相关当事人将来从事相关法律法规内容可能出现的情况为前提，因此中文经济合同相关法律法规多表达将来可能发生的相关内容。但是，英文经济合同相关法律法规多用一般现在时表现将来可能发生的相关内容。因此在翻译过程中应当注意中英双语语法的准确性。

例 17

原文：第五十二条　保证人清偿汇票债务后，可以行使持票人对被保证人及其前手的追索权。

(《中华人民共和国票据法》)

译文：Article 52　After the draft debt is cleared, the guarantor may exercise the right of recourse of the holder against the guaranteed and the prior holder.

例 18

原文：Unless a different intention appears, the following are rules for ascertaining the intention of the parties as to the time at which the property in the goods is to pass to the buyer.

(《英国货物买卖法》 *Sale of Goods Act* 1979 [*England*] 18.)

译文：除非有相反的意思出现，下列规则用来确定货物所有权转移给买方时双方当事人的意图。

分析：在上述两个例子中，例 17 原文中出现了"……后"，由此可知这条法律法规有一定的预见性，说明的是在某些活动完成后应该履行的权利和义务，在译文中用的是一般现在时和被动语态来表现原文的内容。类似地，例 18 中原文的时态是一般现在时，译文中没有明显的表现时态的表达。译者要准确地表达出原文的意思，则需要注意中英双语的语法规则和语言背后所承载的文化知识。

(二) 确保译文忠于原文

根据翻译功能对等理论，翻译不是单纯追求字面上的对等，而是语言功能的对等，功能对等的评判标准之一就是原文读者和译文读者反应的一致程度。因此，在翻译经济合同相关法律法规时，译者应做到原文信息的等值处理，优先考虑译文的准确度和真实还原度。遵循该原则主要从两方面着手：一是谨慎使用易混淆的词语；二是谨慎翻译关键细目。

第一，谨慎翻译易混淆的词语。在翻译经济合同相关法律法规时，中文经济合同相关法律法规中两个近义词可能代表着不同的权利和义务，如例 15 和例 16；英文经济合同相关法律法规中的内容可能因为介词或冠词等小词的不同而有所不同。

第二，谨慎翻译关键细目，明确当事方责任，明确交易数量等细致内容。经济合同相关法律法规内容相对详细具体，对于各种可能出现的情况都会尽可能地考虑到。因此，译者在翻译时应格外注意关键的细目，如明确当事各方和明确数据、金额和比例等。

(三) 维护文化的差异性

根据翻译功能对等理论，原文读者和译文读者的反应应尽可能保持一致。中文和英文是两种不同的语言，两者的语言表达方式和中英背景下人们的思维方式都存在一定的差异。因此，在翻译经济合同相关法律法规时，译者应尽可能维护好文化的差异性以避免出现理解偏差。

例 19

原文： 第一百六十六条　出卖人分批交付标的物的，出卖人对其中一批标的物不交付或者交付不符合约定，致使该批标的物不能实现合同目的的，买受人可以就该批标的物解除。

出卖人不交付其中一批标的物或者交付不符合约定，致使今后其他各批标的物的交付不能实现合同目的的，买受人可以就该批以及今后其他各批标的物解除。

买受人如果就其中一批标的物解除，该批标的物与其他各批标的物相互依存的，可以就已经交付和未交付的各批标的物解除。

(《中华人民共和国合同法》)

译文： Article 166　Where the seller is to deliver the subject matter in installments, if the seller fails to deliver one installment of the subject matter or the delivery fails to satisfy the terms of the contract so that the said installment cannot realize the contract purpose, the buyer may terminate the portion of the contract in respect thereof.

If the seller fails to deliver one installment of the subject matter or the delivery fails to satisfy the terms of the contract so that the delivery of the subsequent installments of subject matter can not realize the contract purpose, the buyer may terminate the portion of the contract in respect of such installment as well as any subsequent installment.

If the buyer is to terminate the portion of the contract in respect of a particular installment which is interdependent with all other installments, it may terminate the contract in respect of all delivered and undelivered installments.

例 20

原文： Instalment deliveries

Unless otherwise agreed, the buyer of goods is not bound to accept delivery of them by instalments.

Where there is a contract for the sale of goods to be delivered by stated instalments, which are to be separately paid for, and the seller makes defective deliveries in respect of one or more instalments or the buyer neglects or refuses to take delivery of or pay for one or more instalments, it is a question in each case depending on the terms of the contract and the circumstances of the case whether the breach of contract is a repudiation of the whole contract or whether it is a severable breach giving rise to a claim for compensation but not to a right to treat the whole contract as repudiated.

(《英国货物买卖法》 *Sale of Goods Act* 1979 [*England*] 23.)

译文： 分期交付

除非另有约定，买方没有通过分期交付的方式接受货物的义务。

货物买卖合同如果采用定期的分期交货、分期付款的方式,而卖方交付的货物有一批或数批存在瑕疵,或买方遗忘或拒绝提取一次或多次分期交货,或者遗忘或拒绝支付一次或多次分期付款,则应依据合同条款及具体案情决定买方能否以违反合同为由拒绝履行整个合同,但如果属于可分开的合同,则买方只能请求赔偿而不能拒绝履行全部合同。

分析:上述两个例句的内容都是和货物的分期交付相关,例 19 的原文来自中文经济合同,对于卖方的其中一批货物不符合规定导致合同目的不能达到时,买方有权根据情况解除标的物。例 20 的原文来自英文经济合同,卖方的其中一批货物不符合规定导致合同目的不能达到时,买方能否以违反合同为由拒绝履行整个合同应依据合同条款及具体案情决定,对于可分开的合同,买方只能请求赔偿而不能拒绝履行全部合同。由此可见,中英文经济合同相关法律法规的内容存在一定的差异性,译者在翻译时应维护好文化的差异性。

三、经济合同相关法律法规翻译方法与技巧

经济合同相关法律法规表达严谨规范,本节主要讨论其词汇和句子的翻译方法和技巧。

(一) 词汇翻译

根据翻译功能对等理论,奈达认为翻译的第一个步骤就是最大限度地创造出既符合原文语义又体现原文文化特色的译作以最大限度地再现原文。在经济合同相关法律法规中,译文的选词显得尤为重要。中英词汇有一定的差异,如中文中名词复数没有明显的语言标志,而在英文中,名词的单数和复数有着明显的区别。同时,中英词汇的表达对等又存在不同的情况,共包含了字词对等、多词同义、一词多义、词义交织和无对等词语五种对应情况,其中字词的完全对等情况主要是专用名和技术词汇。因此,经济合同相关法律法规的词汇翻译有以下技巧和方法:

第一,明确词汇的通用含义和特殊含义,并根据文本语境选择相对应的含义。

例 21

原文:When the seller of goods has a voidable **title** to them, but his **title** has not been avoided at the time of the sale, the buyer acquires a good **title** to the goods, provided he buys them in good faith and without notice of the seller's defect of **title**.

(《英国货物买卖法》*Sale of Goods Act* 1979 [England] 23.)

译文:如果卖方对货物的所有权可被撤销,但卖方在所有权被撤销之前将货物出售,只要买方不知道卖方权利的瑕疵,并且是出于善意而购买,就可取得货物完好的所有权。

分析:在上述例句中,"title"一词出现了 4 次,该单词通常为"标题"和"头衔"的意

思，但是将这两个意思放在例 21 中都不合适。在《新牛津英汉双解大词典》中，该词在法律领域中还有一个意思，即 "a right or claim to the ownership of property or to a rank or throne"，也就是"所有权"的意思。显然，在《英国货物买卖法》中，原文中的"title"指的就是"货物的所有权"。

第二，由于历史因素以及语言表达习惯，在经济合同相关法律法规中，尤其是英文经济合同相关法律法规中，会出现少量的非英文表达，这些表达相对正式规范，多为书面语，体现了法律的保守性和契约性。面对这类词汇时，译者应明确其具体意思，再根据原文的上下文选择最合适的意思表达。

例 22

原文：Where goods are shipped and by the bill of lading the goods are deliverable to the order of the seller or his agent, the seller is **prima facie** to be taken to reserve the right of disposal.

(《英国货物买卖法》*Sale of Goods Act* 1979 [*England*] 19.)

译文：货物已装船，货物处于提单持有人即卖方或其代理人指令交付时，则**初步**认为卖方保留有货物处分权。

分析：在上述例句中，"prima facie"来源于拉丁语，最早使用于 15 世纪。根据《柯林斯英汉双解大词典》英文释义可知，"Prima facie is used to describe something that appears to be true when you first consider it"，中文意思即"初步印象的；乍看的"。根据原文内容，将该表达译为"初步"相对合理通顺。

第三，翻译经济合同相关法律法规时，应选择理性客观的表达方式，切忌词藻华而不实。如果一个单词出现多次，且该词有不同的状语或定语成分修饰，译者应谨慎选词，准确、客观且理性地传达原文内容。

例 23

原文：Where a **person** having sold goods continues or is in possession of the goods, or of the documents of title to the goods, the delivery or transfer by that **person**, or by a mercantile agent acting for him, of the goods or documents of title under any sale, pledge, or other disposition thereof, to any **person** receiving the same in good faith and without notice of the previous sale, has the same effect as if the **person** making the delivery or transfer were expressly authorised by the owner of the goods to make the same.

(《英国货物买卖法》*Sale of Goods Act* 1979 [*England*] 24.)

译文：如果卖方将货物出售后继续占有货物或货物所有权凭证，并由其或其商务代理人将货物或货物所有权凭证以任何出卖、质押或其他方式处分并交付或转移给买方之外的第三人，只要该第三人是善意的，并对前一交易行为不知情，则卖方或其商务代理人所实施之交付或转移行为可被视为与得到货主明示授权后的行为具有同等效力。

分析：在上述例句中，原文中的"person"出现了 4 次，该词原意指"人"。在经济合同相关法律法规原文例句中则代表着当事方。"a person having sold goods"意思是卖东西的一方，即"卖方"。"that person"指的是"a person having sold goods"，即"卖方"。"any person receiving the same in good faiths"意思是善意接受货物的任何一方，即"第三方"。"the person making the delivery or transfer"意思是实施交付或转移行为的一方，即"卖方或商务代理人"。因此，翻译经济合同相关法律法规中的词汇时应注意译文表达准确、理性且客观。

（二）句子翻译

根据翻译功能对等理论，句法对等也是功能对等非常重要的一方面。经济合同相关法律法规句子结构严谨，语言简洁。除了部分短句，还有着大量的长句。这些长句根据句子结构可以分为简单长句、并列长句和复合长句。本节将主要介绍以上三种长句的翻译方法和技巧。

第一，简单长句的翻译。简单长句的主要特点为句子长，句子结构简单，句子有明确主语和谓语，句子内容是由一系列动作铺开或者按时间顺序或逻辑顺序等展开。翻译简单长句时，首先划分句子的主干，然后用原文中的定语或状语等成分内容补充句子主干，最后根据原文内容对译文进行调整。值得注意的是，由于中英两种语言的表达习惯和思维方式存在差异，内容调整是翻译经济合同相关法律法规长句时一个必不可少的环节。例如，中文的定语在名词前，英语的定语位置则相对灵活。而且，中文没有关系代词，这就意味着英汉翻译时需要考虑定语从句的顺序和组合等。

例 24

原文：第八条　招标人是依照本法规定提出招标项目、进行招标的法人或者其他组织。

(《中华人民共和国投标招标法》)

译文：Article 8　A tenderer is a legal person or any other organization that, in accordance with the provisions of this Law, puts forth a project subject to tender and carries out the tender.

例 25

原文：Nothing in this section affects the duties or liabilities of either seller or buyer as a bailee or custodier of the goods of the other party.

(《英国货物买卖法》*Sale of Goods Act* 1979 [*England*] 20.)

译文：本条的规定不影响买卖双方作为另一方之受托人或保管人的义务或责任。

分析：在上述例句中，例24的句子主干为"招标人是法人或者其他组织"，定语为"依照本法规定提出招标项目、进行招标的"。译文则首先译出主干"A tenderer is a legal person or any other organization"，然后将定语部分处理为定语从句"…（organization）that puts forth a project subject to tender and carries out the tender"，并将"依法（in accordance with the provisions of this Law）"处理为插入语放在译文中。例25的句子主干为"Nothing affects the duties or liabilities of either seller or buyer"，定语"in this section"修饰"nothing"，状语"as a bailee or custodier of the goods of the other party"修饰"either seller or buyer"。译文将其整合成一句话，逻辑清晰，表达顺畅易懂。

第二，并列长句的翻译。并列长句的主要特点为有着明显表示并列的符号、词、短语或从句，句中多平行结构。翻译并列长句时，为了减少句子成分缺失的可能性，适合使用分译法，即将两个句子单独成句。

例26

原文：第一百一十四条　……约定的违约金低于造成的损失的，当事人可以请求人民法院或者仲裁机构予以增加；约定的违约金过分高于造成的损失的，当事人可以请求人民法院或者仲裁机构予以适当减少。

（《中华人民共和国合同法》）

译文：Article 114　…Where the amount of liquidated damages agreed upon is lower than the damages incurred, a party may petition the People's Court or an arbitration institution to make an increase. Where the amount of liquidated damages agreed upon are significantly higher than the damages incurred, a party may petition the People's Court or an arbitration institution to make an appropriate reduction.

例27

原文：Unless otherwise agreed, delivery of the goods and payment of the price are concurrent conditions, that is to say, the seller must be ready and willing to give possession of the goods to the buyer in exchange for the price and the buyer must be ready and willing to pay the price in exchange for possession of the goods.

（《英国货物买卖法》*Sale of Goods Act* 1979 [*England*] 28.）

译文：除非另有协议，货物的交付和价款的支付应是同时履行的条件。换言之，卖方必须乐意让出对货物的占有以交换价款；同时买方须乐意支付价款以交换对货物的占有。

分析：在上述例句中，例26中分号表明这是一个并列句，分号前后分别讲的是约定的违约金低于造成的损失和约定的违约金过分高于造成的损失两种情况下当事人可以采取的措施。译文将分号前后的句子以单独的句子形式列出，原文和译文的意思和形式达到了最大化对等。例27中出现了"that is to say"和"and"，说明原文中有三个并列的句子，译文将三个句子单独译出并添加适当的连接词使句子之间的衔接更加自然。

第三，复合长句的翻译。复合长句的主要特点为句子长，语法结构复杂，思路清晰有条理，逻辑严密。翻译复合长句时，应首先划分出句子的主干和支干，然后理清句子内容的逻辑关系，再进行初步翻译，必要时对句子进行拆分和重组，最后适度润色句子。

例28

原文： 第一百零五条　票据的付款人对见票即付或者到期的票据，故意压票，拖延支付的，由金融行政管理部门处以罚款，对直接责任人员给予处分。

(《中华人民共和国票据法》)

译文： Article 105　In cases when the payer deliberately detain negotiable instruments payable at sight or negotiable instruments due in order to delay payment, the payer shall be fined and the person or persons directly responsible shall be punished by the financial administrative departments.

例29

原文： Where there is a contract for the sale of specific goods or where goods are subsequently appropriated to the contract, the seller may, by the terms of the contract or appropriation, reserve the right of disposal of the goods until certain conditions are fulfilled; and in such a case, notwithstanding the delivery of the goods to the buyer, or to the carrier or other bailee or custodier for the purpose of transmission to the buyer, the property in the goods does not pass to the buyer until the conditions imposed by the seller are fulfilled.

(《英国货物买卖法》 *Sale of Goods Act* 1979 [*England*] 19.)

译文： 特定物买卖合同中或货物被划拨合同项下时，卖方可以依据合同或划拨条款，将货物的处分权一直保留直到特定条件成就；在这种情形下，尽管货物已交付至买方，或出于转送买方的目的而将货物交付承运人或其他受托人或保管人，在由卖方施加的条件成就之前，货物所有权并不转移至买方。

分析： 在上述例句中，例28原文句子偏长，多短句，内容多而杂。首先，对例28进行初步的分析之后可知，句子主干是"(在一定情况下)金融行政管理部门对票据付款人处以罚款和对直接责任人员给予处分"，该句主干可以看作一个并列句。然后，主句内容发生效力的条件是"票据的付款人对见票即付或者到期的票据，故意压票，拖延支付"，因此支干部分可以以条件状语从句的形式出现。最后，句子主干部分宜使用被动语态来体现原文内容的客观性，对整句加以润色即可。例29原文句子主干和支干明确，由两个并列句组成，两个并列句主语和谓语明确，因此，例 29 的译文在形式上与原文大致保持对等，并且传达意思明确清晰。

此外，译者翻译经济合同相关法律法规时，首先要掌握相关背景知识和语言特点。其次，应熟知专业知识和文化背景并具有一定的常识判断能力。再次，译者应培养翻译责任意识，要有正确的立场和原则、很强的责任心和职业道德素养，忠实于原文，不能改变原意。最后，在必要时应虚心向专业人士请教。

第三节　常用词汇与表达

原文	译文
sales contracts	买卖合同
actor	行为人
statutory representative	法定代表人
arbitration institution	仲裁机构
natural person	自然人
deposit	定金
force majeure	不可抗力
subject matter	标的物
installment payment	分期付款
sale by sample	样品买卖
sale by trial	试用买卖
sale by auction	拍卖
sale by tender	招标投标买卖
tenderer	招标人
bidder	投标人
contracts for supply of power, water, gas, or heat	供用电、水、气、热力合同
suspend the power supply	中断供电
gift contracts	赠与合同
contracts for loan of money	借款合同
technical performance	技术性能
contracts for work	承揽合同
contracts for construction projects	建设工程合同
transportation contracts	运输合同

续表

原文	译文
passenger transportation contracts	客运合同
carrier	承运人
consignor	托运人
cargo transportation contracts	货运合同
multi-modal transportation contract	多式联运合同
technology contracts	技术合同
technology transfer contracts	技术转让合同
patent licensing contract	专利实施许可合同
technical consulting contracts and technical service contracts	技术咨询合同和技术服务合同
storage contracts	保管合同
depositor	寄存人
depository	保管人
warehouse receipt	仓单
commission contracts	委托合同
contracts of commission agency	行纪合同
commission agent	行纪人
intermediation contracts	居间合同
drafts	汇票
drawing of a draft	出票
endorsement	背书
acceptance	承兑
guarantee	保证
right of recourse	追索权
check	支票
foreign-related negotiable instruments	涉外票据
public tender	公开招标
procuratorial agency	招标代理机构
consortium	联合体
bid opening	开标
bid winning	中标

第四节 译 文 赏 析

一、汉译英

原文	译文
第十四章　融资租赁合同	**Chapter 14　Financial Leasing Contracts**
第二百三十七条　【定义】融资租赁合同是出租人根据承租人对出卖人、租赁物的选择，向出卖人购买租赁物，提供给承租人使用，承租人支付租金的合同。	Article 237　A financial leasing contract is a contract whereby the lessor, upon purchase of the lessee-selected lease item from a lessee-selected seller, provides the lease item to the lessee for its use, and the lessee pays the rent[1].
第二百三十八条　【合同的主要条款及形式】融资租赁合同的内容包括租赁物名称、数量、规格、技术性能、检验方法、租赁期限、租金构成及其支付期限和方式、币种、租赁期间届满租赁物的归属等条款。 融资租赁合同应当采用书面形式。	Article 238　The contents of a financial leasing contract include terms such as the name, quantity, specifications, technical performance, and method of inspection of the lease item, the lease term, the rental components and the time, method and currency of payment, as well as the ownership of the lease item at the end of the lease term, etc. A financial leasing contract shall be concluded in writing[2].
第二百三十九条　【租赁物的购买】出租人根据承租人对出卖人、租赁物的选择订立的买卖合同，出卖人应当按照约定向承租人交付标的物，承租人享有与受领标的物有关的买受人的权利。	Article 239　Under the sales contract concluded by the lessor according to the lessee's selection of the seller and the lease item, the seller shall deliver the subject matter to the lessee in accordance with the contract, and the lessee enjoys the rights of the buyer in respect of taking delivery of the subject matter.
第二百四十条　【索赔权】出租人、出卖人、承租人可以约定，出卖人不履行买卖合同义务的，由承租人行使索赔的权利。承租人行使索赔权利的，出租人应当协助。	Article 240　The lessor, the seller and the lessee may agree that any claim arising from the seller's failure in the performance of its obligations under the sales contract will be made by the lessee. Where the lessee makes such a claim, the lessor shall provide assistance[3].
第二百四十一条　【买卖合同的变更】出租人根据承租人对出卖人、租赁物的选择订立的买卖合同，未经承租人同意，出租人不得变更与承租人有关的合同内容。	Article 241　Without the consent of the lessee, the lessor may not amend any lessee-related term in the sales contract concluded by it according to the lessee's selection of the seller and the lease item[4].

续表

原文	译文
第二百四十二条 【租赁物所有权】出租人享有租赁物的所有权。承租人破产的，租赁物不属于破产财产。	Article 242　The lessor shall be entitled to the ownership of the lease item[5]. In case the lessee goes bankruptcy, the lease item is not part of its bankruptcy assets.
第二百四十三条 【租金的确定】融资租赁合同的租金，除当事人另有约定的以外，应当根据购买租赁物的大部分或者全部成本以及出租人的合理利润确定。	Article 243　Unless otherwise agreed by the parties, the rent under a financial leasing contract shall be determined based on the major portion of or full costs of purchasing the lease item and the lessor's reasonable profit.
第二百四十四条 【租赁物的瑕疵担保责任】租赁物不符合约定或者不符合使用目的的，出租人不承担责任，但承租人依赖出租人的技能确定租赁物或者出租人干预选择租赁物的除外。	Article 244　Where the lease item does not comply with the contract or is not fit for the intended purpose, the lessor is not liable, except where the lessee relies on the skills of the lessor in selecting the lease item or the lessor interferes with the selection thereof[6].
第二百四十五条 【租赁物的占有和使用】出租人应当保证承租人对租赁物的占有和使用。	Article 245　The lessor shall give warranty in respect of the lessee's possession and use of the lease item.
第二百四十六条 【租赁物造成的损害责任】承租人占有租赁物期间，租赁物造成第三人的人身伤害或者财产损害的，出租人不承担责任。	Article 246　If in the possession of the lessee, the lease item causes personal injury or property damage to a third party, the lessor is not liable[7].
第二百四十七条 【租赁物的保管、使用、维修】承租人应当妥善保管、使用租赁物。 承租人应当履行占有租赁物期间的维修义务。	Article 247　The lessee shall keep and use the lease item with due care. While in possession of the lease item, the lessee shall perform the obligations of maintenance and repair thereof.
第二百四十八条 【承租人拒付租金责任】承租人应当按照约定支付租金。承租人经催告后在合理期限内仍不支付租金的，出租人可以要求支付全部租金；也可以解除合同，收回租赁物。	Article 248　The lessee shall pay the rent in accordance with the contract. Where the lessee fails to pay the rent within a reasonable time limit after receiving the demand for payment from the lessor, the lessor may require payment of the full rent; or it may terminate the contract and take back the lease item[8].

续表

原文	译文
第二百四十九条 【租赁物价值的部分返还权】当事人约定租赁期间届满租赁物归承租人所有，承租人已经支付大部分租金，但无力支付剩余租金，出租人因此解除合同收回租赁物的，收回的租赁物的价值超过承租人欠付的租金以及其他费用的，承租人可以要求部分返还。	Article 249　Where the parties agree that the lease item shall belong to the lessee at the expiry of the lease term, the lessee has paid the majority of the rent but is unable to pay the remaining rent, and the lessor terminates the contract for this reason and takes back the lease item. If the value of the lease item taken back exceeds the rent and other expenses which the lessee owes to the lessor, the lessee may request the lessor to return a certain part[9].
第二百五十条 【租赁期满租赁物归属】出租人和承租人可以约定租赁期间届满租赁物的归属。对租赁物的归属没有约定或者约定不明确，依照本法第六十一条的规定仍不能确定的，租赁物的所有权归出租人。	Article 250　The lessor and the lessee may agree on the ownership of the lease item at the expiry of the lease term. Where ownership of the lease item is not agreed or the agreement is not clear, nor can it be determined in accordance with Article 61 of this law, the ownership of the lease item shall belong to the lessor.

（选自《中华人民共和国合同法》）

难点 1

原文：融资租赁合同是出租人根据承租人对出卖人、租赁物的选择，向出卖人购买租赁物，提供给承租人使用，承租人支付租金的合同。

译文：A financial leasing contract is a contract whereby the lessor, upon purchase of the lessee-selected lease item from a lessee-selected seller, provides the lease item to the lessee for its use, and the lessee pays the rent.

分析：古体词"whereby"的原意是"because of which; by which"（《新牛津英汉双解大词典》），即"凭此；借以；由于"。古体词的使用是法律语言的重要特征，体现了该经济合同法律法规的保守性和契约型。

难点 2

原文：融资租赁合同应当采用书面形式。

译文：A financial leasing contract shall be concluded in writing.

分析：英文经济合同相关法律法规中多使用情态动词。原文中的"应当"可以用情态动词"shall"来表达。

难点 3

原文：出租人、出卖人、承租人可以约定，出卖人不履行买卖合同义务的，由承租人行使索赔的权利。承租人行使索赔权利的,出租人应当协助。

译文:The lessor, the seller and the lessee may agree that any claim arising from the seller's failure in the performance of its obligations under the sales contract will be made by the lessee. Where the lessee makes such a claim, the lessor shall provide assistance.

分析:对经济合同相关法律法规中的当事方应明确。本例为融资租赁合同,因此会出现出租人、出卖人、承租人,即 the lessor, the seller and the lessee。

难点 4

原文:出租人根据承租人对出卖人、租赁物的选择订立的买卖合同,未经承租人同意,出租人不得变更与承租人有关的合同内容。

译文:Without the consent of the lessee, the lessor may not amend any lessee-related term in the sales contract concluded by it according to the lessee's selection of the seller and the lease item.

分析:原文是典型的条件句,即原文的权利和义务是发生在一定条件之上的。由于中英文语言表达习惯存在差异,中文中的条件句"未经承租人同意"放在了原文的句中,英文可以将表条件的内容以状语的形式(without the consent of the lessee)放在句首。

难点 5

原文:出租人享有租赁物的所有权。

译文:The lessor shall be entitled to the ownership of the lease item.

分析:"出租人享有租赁物的所有权"即租赁物的所有权应该归属于或者被赋予于出租人,译文中使用被动语态以表现原文内容的客观性。

难点 6

原文:租赁物不符合约定或者不符合使用目的的,出租人不承担责任,但承租人依赖出租人的技能确定租赁物或者出租人干预选择租赁物的除外。

译文:Where the lease item does not comply with the contract or is not fit for the intended purpose, the lessor is not liable, except where the lessee relies on the skills of the lessor in selecting the lease item or the lessor interferes with the selection thereof.

分析:古体词"thereof"原意为"of the thing just mentioned; of that"(《新牛津英汉双解大词典》),即"在其中;其"。

难点 7

原文:承租人占有租赁物期间,租赁物造成第三人的人身伤害或者财产损害的,出租人不承担责任。

译文:If in the possession of the lessee, the lease item causes personal injury or property damage to a third party, the lessor is not liable.

分析：原文为一个简单长句，句子内容按照逻辑顺序展开，先说明情况发生时间和发生的情况，再说明最后的结果。译文理清了原文内容之间的逻辑关系，将原文处理为主句和条件状语从句，原文和译文在意思和形式上达到了功能对等最大化。

难点 8

原文：承租人经催告后在合理期限内仍不支付租金的，出租人可以要求支付全部租金；也可以解除合同，收回租赁物。

译文：Where the lessee fails to pay the rent within a reasonable time limit after receiving the demand for payment from the lessor, the lessor may require payment of the full rent; or it may terminate the contract and take back the lease item.

分析：原文为一个并列长句，原文内容讲的是在承租人经催告后在合理期限内仍不支付租金的情况下，承租人可以作出的两个不同的选择。译文将其处理为用连词连接的两个单独句子，并在第二个句子中使用了形式主语。

难点 9

原文：收回的租赁物的价值超过承租人欠付的租金以及其他费用的，承租人可以要求部分返还。

译文：If the value of the lease item taken back exceeds the rent and other expenses which the lessee owes to the lessor, the lessee may request the lessor to return a certain part.

分析：原文是一个复杂长句，前提条件相对较多，信息量大。译文将其处理成两个单独的句子。第一句说明事情发生的原因及结果，保障出租人的权益，即当事人约定租赁物租期届满归承租人所有，承租人支付部分租金但是无力支付剩余租金，出租人因此解除合同并收回租赁物。第二句表现了对承租人利益的维护，说明出租人收回租赁物时可能发生的情况，当承租人利益受到损害时，可以要求部分价值返还。译文一方面清晰地传达了原文意思，另一方面也清晰地表现了原文内容的内在逻辑层次。

二、英译汉

原文	译文
§ 2-319 F. O. B. and F. A. S. Terms.	第 2-319 条 船上交货条件和发运港船边交货条件[1]
(1) Unless otherwise agreed, the term F. O. B. (which means "free on board") at a named place, even though used only in connection with the stated price, is a delivery term under which	(1)除非另有协议，特定地点船上交货条件，即使仅用来规定价格，仍构成交货条件，其中[2]：

续表

原文	译文
(a) when the term is F. O. B. the place of shipment, the seller must at that place ship the goods in the manner provided in this Article (Section 2-504) and bear the expense and risk of putting them into the possession of the carrier; or	a. 当条件是发运港船上交货时，卖方必须[3]按本篇规定的方式(第2-504条)在该地发运货物，并承担将货物交付给承运人的费用和风险[4]；或
(b) when the term is F. O. B. the place of destination, the seller must at his own expense and risk transport the goods to that place and there tender delivery of them in the manner provided in this Article (Section 2-503);	b. 当条件是目的港船上交货时，卖方必须自行承担费用和风险把货物运输到目的地，并按本篇规定的方式提示交货(第2-503条);
(c) when under either (a) or (b) the term is also F. O. B. vessel, car or other vehicle, the seller must in addition at his own expense and risk load the goods on board. If the term is F. O. B. vessel the buyer must name the vessel, and in an appropriate case the seller must comply with the provisions of this Article on the form of bill of lading (Section 2-323).	c. 不论使用第a项或第b项条件，如果另外规定需要在船舶上、汽车上或其他运输工具上交货，卖方必须另外自行承担费用和风险把货物装上相应的运输工具。如果规定的是在船舶上交货，买方必须提供船舶的名称。在适当情况下，卖方必须遵守本篇有关提单形式的条款(第2-323条)[5]。
(2) Unless otherwise agreed the term F. A. S. vessel (which means "free alongside") at a named port, even though used only in connection with the stated price, is a delivery term under which the seller must	(2)除非另有协议，特定发运港船边交货条件，即使仅用来规定价格，仍构成交货条件，其中卖方必须：
(a) at his own expense and risk deliver the goods alongside the vessel in the manner usual in that port or on a dock designated and provided by the buyer; and	a. 自行承担费用和风险，将货物以惯常的方式运至船边，或运至买方指定或者提供的码头；并且
(b) obtain and tender a receipt for the goods in exchange for which the carrier is under a duty to issue a bill of lading.	b. 取得并交付使承运人承担开立提单义务的货物依据[6]。
(3) Unless otherwise agreed, in any case falling within subsection (1)(a) or (c) or subsection (2) the buyer must seasonably give any needed instructions for making delivery, including when the term is F. A. S. or F. O. B. the loading berth of the vessel and in an appropriate case its name and sailing date. The seller may treat the failure of needed instructions as a failure of cooperation under this Article (Section 2-311). He may also at his option move the goods in any reasonable manner preparatory to delivery or shipment.	(3)除非另有协议，涉及第1款第a项、第c项或第2款所规定的情况时，卖方必须及时提供交货所需的指示。在使用发运港船边交货或船上交货条件时，此种指示包括船舶的装运舱位，在适当情况下，还包括船舶的名称和启航日期[7]。如果卖方未得到所需的指示，他可以认为买方未按本篇规定进行合作(第2-311条)。卖方为了就交付或发运货物作准备，还有权决定是否将货物合理移放。

续表

原文	译文
(4) Under the term F. O. B. vessel or F. A. S. unless otherwise agreed, the buyer must make payment against tender of the required documents and the seller may not tender nor the buyer demand delivery of the goods in substitution for the documents.	(4) 在使用船舶上交货条件或者发运港船边交货条件时，除非另有协议，卖方一旦提示交付所需的单据，买方就必须付款。卖方不得提示交付货物以替代交付单据，买方也不得做此要求[8]。

(选自《美国统一商法典》U. C. C. -ARTICLE 2-SALES (2002))

难点 1

原文：§ 2-319 F. O. B. and F. A. S. Terms

译文：第 2-319 条 船上交货条件和发运港船边交货条件

分析：国际贸易术语知识拓展：

第一类国际贸易术语适用于任何运输方式：

CIP (Carriage and Insurance Paid)	运费/保险费付至目的地
CPT (Carriage Paid To)	运费付至目的地
DAP (Delivered At Place)	目的地交货
DAT (Delivered At Terminal)	目的地或目的港的集散站交货
DDP (Delivered Duty Paid)	完税后交货
EXW (Ex Works)	工厂交货
FCA (Free Carrier)	货交承运人

第二类国际贸易术语适用于海运和内河运输：

CFR (Cost and Freight)	成本加运费
CIF (Cost, Insurance and Freight)	成本保险费加运费
FAS (Free Alongside Ship)	装运港船边交货
FOB (Free On Board)	装运港船上交货

(选自香港国际采购网)

难点 2

原文：Unless otherwise agreed, the term F. O. B. (which means "free on board") at a named place, even though used only in connection with the stated price, is a delivery term under which…

译文：除非另有协议，特定地点船上交货条件，即使仅用来规定价格，仍构成交货条件，其中……

分析：原文是一个简单长句，句子主干成分(the term F. O. B. (which means "free on board") at a named place is a delivery term)明确清晰。此外，还有一个条件状语从句和一个插入语。译文根据原文的句法结构翻译，并根据上下文语境添加了"仍(然)"表明该条法律法规的可行性和严谨性。

难点 3

原文：…when the term is F. O. B. the place of shipment, the seller must…

译文：……当条件是发运港船上交货时，卖方必须……

分析：原文中出现了情态动词"must"表明该条法律法规下所规定的义务的强制性，译文应根据原文所用情态动词的不同而在对译文处理上有所调整。通常情况下，"must"需翻译成"必须"，"may"可以处理为"可以"或者"可能"，"shall"一般翻译成"应(该)"，译文中所采用的具体词义还要根据上下文内容做出适当的调整。

难点 4

原文：…when the term is F. O. B. the place of shipment, the seller must at that place ship the goods in the manner provided in this Article (Section 2-504) and bear the expense and risk of putting them into the possession of the carrier…

译文：……当条件是发运港船上交货时，卖方必须按本篇规定的方式(第 2-504 条)在该地发运货物，并承担将货物交付给承运人的费用和风险……

分析：原文是并列长句，两个并列谓语成分的主语相同(the seller)。因此，译文在处理两个并列成分时沿用原文的句法结构，明确说明了当条件是发运港船上交货时卖方的义务。

难点 5

原文：If the term is F. O. B. vessel the buyer must name the vessel, and in an appropriate case the seller must comply with the provisions of this Article on the form of bill of lading (Section 2-323).

译文：如果规定的是在船舶上交货，买方必须提供船舶的名称。在适当情况下，卖方必须遵守本篇有关提单形式的条款(第 2-323 条)。

分析：原文由一个简单长句和一个并列长句组成，且原文的内容均围绕装运港特定地点交货条件下另外规定在运输工具上交货时卖方的义务。第一个简单长句主干部分清晰明确，可以直接根据原文的句法结构翻译，译文和原文意思上和形式上取得最大的对等。第二个并列长句说明特定地点船舶上交货时买卖双方的义务。并列的成分为两个单独的句子,所以译文在处理该句时将两个句子单独成句以分别明确买方和卖方的义务。

难点 6

原文:…obtain and tender a receipt for the goods in exchange for which the carrier is under a duty to issue a bill of lading.

译文:……取得并交付使承运人承担开立提单义务的货物依据。

分析:"issue a bill of lading"的意思是"开立提单"。提单是指用以证明海上货物运输合同和货物已经由承运人接收或者装船,以及承运人保证据以交付货物的单证。提单有三项主要功能,提单是货物凭证、物权凭证和合同成立的证明文件。

难点 7

原文:…when the term is F. A. S. or F. O. B. the loading berth of the vessel and in an appropriate case its name and sailing date.

译文:……在使用发运港船边交货或船上交货条件时,此种指示包括船舶的装运舱位,在适当情况下,还包括船舶的名称和启航日期。

分析:原文第一句是复杂长句,句子总体偏长,句子主干成分相对模糊,包含了两个状语从句。译文将原文的意思划分为两个层次,将原文处理成两个独立的句子。此外,为了增强句子之间的衔接,第二句使用了表达"此种指示"来指代前一句所说的情况。

难点 8

原文:Under the term F. O. B. vessel or F. A. S. unless otherwise agreed, the buyer must make payment against tender of the required documents and the seller may not tender nor the buyer demand delivery of the goods in substitution for the documents.

译文:在使用船舶上交货条件或者发运港船边交货条件时,除非另有协议,卖方一旦提示交付所需的单据,买方就必须付款。卖方不得提示交付货物以替代交付单据,买方也不得做此要求。

分析:原文是并列长句,译文将原文处理成两个单独的句子以说明在使用船舶上交货条件或者发运港船边交货条件时买卖双方的义务。

翻 译 练 习

一、词组翻译

perform one's obligations
liability for breach of contract

conclude a contract
barter transaction
method of repayment
corresponding price
payable at sight
criminal responsibility
technology development contract
dishonourable check
承担责任
遵循公开、公平、公正和诚实信用的原则
招标公告
一般规定
融资租赁合同
利率
邀请招标
评标
本票
仓储合同

二、句子翻译

(一) 汉译英

1. 背书人在汇票上记载"不得转让"字样，其后手再背书转让的，原背书人对后手的被背书人不承担保证责任。

2. 多式联运经营人负责履行或者组织履行多式联运合同，对全程运输享有承运人的权利，承担承运人的义务。

3. 订立借款合同，借款人应当按照贷款人的要求提供与借款有关的业务活动和财务状况的真实情况。

4. 本票是出票人签发的，承诺自己在见票时无条件支付确定的金额给收款人或者持票人的票据。

5. 评标委员会成员应当客观、公正地履行职务，遵守职业道德，对所提出的评审意见承担个人责任。

(二) 英译汉

1. Unless otherwise agreed, the goods remain at the seller's risk until the property in them is transferred to the buyer, but when the property in them is transferred to the buyer the goods are at the buyer's risk whether delivery has been made or not.

2. In the event that a contractual obligation is not performed or is performed defectively in a

non-trivial fashion, Singapore law provides for a variety of legal responses and remedies, depending on the nature of the failure of performance.

3. Where the technology which is the subject matter of a technology development contract is made public by a third party, thereby making the performance of the technology development contract meaningless, the parties may terminate the contract.

4. There is no clear definition as to when a person is/is not privy to a contract. Generally, a party who is an offeror or offeree will be privy to the contract. However, it seems that merely being mentioned in the contract is not enough.

5. Unless otherwise agreed, where goods are delivered to the buyer, and he refuses to accept them, having the right to do so, he is not bound to return them to the seller, but it is sufficient if he intimates to the seller that he refuses to accept them.

三、语篇翻译

第五章 法律责任

第四十九条 违反本法规定，必须进行招标的项目而不招标的，将必须进行招标的项目化整为零或者以其他任何方式规避招标的，责令限期改正，可以处项目合同金额千分之五以上千分之十以下的罚款；对全部或者部分使用国有资金的项目，可以暂停项目执行或者暂停资金拨付；对单位直接负责的主管人员和其他直接责任人员依法给予处分。

第五十条 招标代理机构违反本法规定，泄露应当保密的与招标投标活动有关的情况和资料的，或者与招标人、投标人串通损害国家利益、社会公共利益或者他人合法权益的，处五万元以上二十五万元以下的罚款，对单位直接负责的主管人员和其他直接责任人员处单位罚款数额百分之五以上百分之十以下的罚款；有违法所得的，并处没收违法所得；情节严重的，暂停直至取消招标代理资格；构成犯罪的，依法追究刑事责任。给他人造成损失的，依法承担赔偿责任。前款所列行为影响中标结果的，中标无效。

第五十一条 招标人以不合理的条件限制或者排斥潜在投标人的，对潜在投标人实行歧视待遇的，强制要求投标人组成联合体共同投标的，或者限制投标人之间竞争的，责令改正，可以处一万元以上五万元以下的罚款。

第五十二条 依法必须进行招标的项目的招标人向他人透露已获取招标文件的潜在投标人的名称、数量或者可能影响公平竞争的有关招标投标的其他情况的，或者泄露标底的，给予警告，可以并处一万元以上十万元以下的罚款；对单位直接负责的主管人员和其他直接责任人员依法给予处分；构成犯罪的，依法追究刑事责任。前款所列行为影响中标结果的，中标无效。

第五十三条 投标人相互串通投标或者与招标人串通投标的，投标人以向招标人或者评标委员会成员行贿的手段谋取中标的，中标无效，处中标项目金额千分之五以上千分之十以下的罚款，对单位直接负责的主管人员和其他直接责任人员处单位罚款数额百分之五以上百分之十以下的罚款；有违法所得的，并处没收违法所得；情节严重的，取消其一年至二年内参加依法必须进行招标的项目的投标资格并予以公告，直至由工商行政管理机关吊销营业执照；构成犯罪的，依法追究刑事责任。给他人造成损失的，依法承担赔偿责任。

第五十四条　投标人以他人名义投标或者以其他方式弄虚作假，骗取中标的，中标无效，给招标人造成损失的，依法承担赔偿责任；构成犯罪的，依法追究刑事责任。依法必须进行招标的项目的投标人有前款所列行为尚未构成犯罪的，处中标项目金额千分之五以上千分之十以下的罚款，对单位直接负责的主管人员和其他直接责任人员处单位罚款数额百分之五以上百分之十以下的罚款；有违法所得的，并处没收违法所得；情节严重的，取消其一年至三年内参加依法必须进行招标的项目的投标资格并予以公告，直至由工商行政管理机关吊销营业执照。

第五十五条　依法必须进行招标的项目，招标人违反本法规定，与投标人就投标价格、投标方案等实质性内容进行谈判的，给予警告，对单位直接负责的主管人员和其他直接责任人员依法给予处分。前款所列行为影响中标结果的，中标无效。

第五十六条　评标委员会成员收受投标人的财物或者其他好处的，评标委员会成员或者参加评标的有关工作人员向他人透露对投标文件的评审和比较、中标候选人的推荐以及与评标有关的其他情况的，给予警告，没收收受的财物，可以并处三千元以上五万元以下的罚款，对有所列违法行为的评标委员会成员取消担任评标委员会成员的资格，不得再参加任何依法必须进行招标的项目的评标；构成犯罪的，依法追究刑事责任。

（选自《中华人民共和国招标投标法》）

◎ 参考文献

[1] Eugene, A. Nida. *Toward a Science of Translating* [M]. Leiden：E. J. Brill, 1964.

[2] 柯林斯 COBUILD 高阶英汉双解学习词典[Z]. 北京：外语教学与研究出版社，2011.

[3] 潘琪，译. 美国统一商法典（中英双语）[M]. 北京：法律出版社，2020.

[4] 新加坡合同法. *The Law of Contract*.

[5] 新牛津英汉双解大词典(第 2 版)[Z]. 上海：上海外语教育出版社，2013.

[6] 英国货物买卖法. *Sale of Goods Act* 1979 [*England*].

[7] 中华人民共和国合同法.

[8] 中华人民共和国票据法.

[9] 中华人民共和国招标投标法.

翻译练习参考译文

第一章 经济文本翻译导论

一、词组翻译

原文	译文
环境友好型社会	environment-friendly society
南水北调工程	the South-to-North Water Diversion Project
西气东输工程	the West-to-East Natural Gas Transmission Project
最低生活保障金	subsistence allowance
经济适用房	economically affordable housing
外汇储备	foreign exchange reserve
金融衍生工具	financial derivatives
带薪休假	paid vocation
龙头企业	leading enterprise
技术密集型产业	technology-intensive industries
catering culture	饮食文化
trade barrier	贸易壁垒
investment portfolio	投资组合
emerging economies	新兴经济体
economies of scale	规模经济
disposable income	可支配收入
credit rating	信用评级
listed company	上市公司
urbanization	城镇化
regional economic integration	区域经济一体化

二、句子翻译

(一) 汉译英

1. In accordance with the requirement for establishing a socialist market economy, we will continue to open to the outside world in all directions. We should correctly handle the relations between and among reform, development and stability and cultivate a unified and open market system with orderly competition.

2. Many Chinese companies believe in the strategy of low profit margin and volume sales based on the assumption that lower price will increase the speed of turnover and eventually generate higher profit. While the low-price strategy is widely adopted, some companies use a high-price strategy, taking advantage of the conventional wisdom of China that "pian yi wu hao huo" (cheap is no good) and "yi fen qian yi fen huo" (each additional cent paid is associated with additional value).

3. Agriculture is important for expanding domestic demand and making structural adjustment, and it is a sector vital for ensuring China's stability and maintaining public confidence. We must make doing a good job in our work relating to agriculture, rural areas, and farmers the number one priority in all our endeavors and accelerate agricultural modernization in order to ensure China's food security and increase farmers' incomes.

4. For some time to come, we will focus on three tasks, each concerning 100 million people: granting urban residency to around 100 million rural people who have moved to cities, rebuilding rundown city areas and villages inside cities where around 100 million people live, and guiding the urbanization of around 100 million rural residents of the central and western regions in cities there.

5. We must improve the system and mechanisms for integrating rural and urban development and embark on a new path of urbanization. This new type of urbanization should have the following features: putting people first; integrating the development of industrialization, IT application, urbanization and agricultural modernization; improving the spatial layout; protecting the ecological environment; and carrying forward Chinese culture.

(二) 英译汉

1. 外国直接投资继续涌入中国,经常账户与贸易的平衡仍将在可预期的未来继续带来顺差。

2. 虽然经济控制的松绑以及对国有企业体制的改革即将展开,中央政府在未来几年里还将继续承受补贴国有公司、粮食价格以及各种公共事业的压力。

3. 国内储蓄和外国直接投资对建设必要的基础设施将起着关键的作用,而基础设施的建设反过来又可推动经济的持续增长。

4. 从长期来看,我们预计中国将通过降低关税、向外国人开放服务业和金融部门以及减少其在国有银行和企业中的存在,进一步实现经济自由化。

5. 经济的继续解放加上国内的大量储蓄,稳定的外国直接投资以及强有力的出口,可以使经济增长保持在8%到9%的范围内。

三、语篇翻译

(一)汉译英

With the development of economy and improvement of civilization, broadcasting will undoubtedly play a more and more important role in propaganda. Under the background of the globalization in world media industry, China's broadcasting industry has developed rapidly in recent years. Satellite TV and terrestrial channels have been multiplied. Media's initiative is undergoing a change from the seller's market to the buyer's market. Media managers are faced with increasingly fierce competition which is inevitable. How to make good programs and expand space of development are urgent tasks for Hubei Broadcasting Corporation now. How to adopt scientific marketing methods, increase attractiveness, become more vigorous and competitive is an acid test for radio and television broadcasters. Despite of the 2008 Wenchuan Earthquake, global economic crisis and other unfavorable issues, Chinese media industry is growing at a surprisingly high speed. The total income of China's broadcasting industry (including government's subsidies) is 166.721 billion, up 20.49% from a year earlier, growing faster than the last two years. The income of radio and television industry was 135.004 billion yuan, an increase of 19.54% over the previous year. And the growth rate was higher than that of the previous two years. The radio and broadcasting industry of all areas also develop steadily. Hubei is a big province with rich culture has jurisdiction over 16 cities or regions and more than 70 counties with different styles. There are 18 provincial radio and TV broadcasting institutions in Wuhan which cover a wide range such as entertainment, economy, movie and TV, sports and education. Located in Wuhan with convenient transportation, how we can make full use of our advantages is a question for us. It is strategic work for us to do good in marketing.

(二)英译汉

世界上不存在"平价的战争"这么一说。首先,人力成本。战争必然导致死亡,同时会对健康之人的身心造成伤害。当个人损失惨重至极、无法计量时,我们却可以估算出整个社会的经济损失,这一算法由法国经济学家让·巴蒂斯特·萨伊于1803年首次提出。让·巴蒂斯特·萨伊认为,由于战争成本包含伤亡人口(士兵和平民)如未参战时终生可以创造的收入,所以战争成本远远不止直接成本。

其次,经济成本。战争的经济成本包括毁坏建筑、耕地、森林、公共服务设施(如自来水厂、发电配电系统等)、公路、桥梁、港口、机场造成的损失,以及毁坏住宅、所有物、工厂、机器、交通工具、飞机等任何形式的个人及集体财产造成的损失。因此,战争还会破坏先前经济活动创造的实体资本。

翻译练习参考译文

战后重建是一种特殊的经济负担,其所动用的资金、进口资本货物以及人力只能弥补一个国家遭受的损失,却无法增加该国资本存量。所以战后重建即使可以弥补所有实体损失,也依然消耗了原本能够用以扩大和增强经济活动的稀缺资源。自1945年以来,大多数战争发生在第三世界国家,世界上最贫穷的国家反而在战争中承担着最惨重的经济损失。

战争同样消耗了大量商品和服务,用以制造战争武器以及为参战人员提供物资。从制造武器的金属和化学药品,到食物、服装和军营,投入战争的诸多商品和服务减少了现有的民用消费,降低了人们的生活水平。用来制造坦克的金属无法用来搭建桥梁,用来运输军用物资的燃料无法驱动校车,用来修建弹药库的水泥无法用来修建房屋。这就构成了战争的机会成本。也就是说,参战国家放弃了将这些资源投入和平使用的机会。

战争的机会成本将在未来得以显现。国家经济除了把资源分配给消费领域(满足现在的需求),还会分配给投资领域(新工厂和新机器将生产未来所需的商品和服务)。投入战争的资源无法用于创造未来消费所需的生产力,使得人们日后的生活水平低于不参战的情况。

总而言之,战争总成本包含各种战争所耗经济资源的预先使用成本:战争中死亡人员的终生收入,战争中永久性伤残人员的医疗成本,战争中摧毁或损坏实体资本的更新成本,为武装部队提供战争武器的成本,维系武装部队及后勤部门(包括其工资及抚恤金)的成本,以及将原本可以用作未来经济实力和平建设的诸多资源投入战争造成的经济损失。

第二章 经济新闻报道翻译

一、词组翻译

原文	译文
市场份额	market share
跳水	to dive
黄金地段	prime location
电子商务	e-business
贸易战	trade war
软着陆	soft landing
泡沫经济	bubble economy
资本市场	capital market
摩根士丹利中国指数	Morgan Stanley Chinese Index

续表

原文	译文
投资热	invest rash
外向型经济	export oriented economy
牛市	bull
deflation	通货紧缩
brick and mortar	实体店
Nasdaq Industrial Average	纳斯达克指数
non-performing	不良资产率
repay	偿还
cross border money	跨境资金
IMF	国际货币基金组织
in stock	库存
the Dow Jones Industrial Average	道琼斯工业平均指数

二、句子翻译

(一) 汉译英

1. China cuts US Treasury holdings for 5th month.

2. The purchasing managers index (PMI) of the non-manufacturing sector posted at 54 percent last month, down 0.4 percentage points from August, 2014, according to a report released by the National Bureau of Statistics.

3. Consumption, already responsible for 60% of growth, keeps going strong and up-market.

4. Despite moderation in growth, the Chinese economy is moving in the desired direction of stronger domestic demand and innovation.

5. We are creating over 10 million jobs a year and disposable-income growth is outstripping that of GDP.

(二) 英译汉

1. 这些机构表示它们将保证借款者有机会获得偿还贷款所需的信息，获得公平待遇的庇佑，并且保证服务机构会为自身行为负责。

2. 商业巨头沃尔玛星期二表示，由于员工工资上涨增加了成本，并投入资金发展了电商业务，所以最近一季度的营业额下降了8.8%。

3. 有一篇报告说第二季度的 GDP 比预期增长得快，美国经济发出的这个乐观信号让投资者镇定了下来。

263

4. 亚行九月预测中国经济今年或增长6.8%，明年或增长6.7%。

5. 我们正处在一个新的宏观经济时代，其中通货紧缩风险高于通货膨胀，我们不能依赖市场经济的自我修复功能。

三、语篇翻译

（一）汉译英

Special Economic Zones

The special economic zones were the first locations in China to open to the outside world. Their dynamic economic exchanges with the rest of the world make them the best regions of China's reform and opening-up. Special economic zones were initiated by Deng Xiaoping, and established in the late 1970s and early 1980s. This was a far-reaching decision by the CPC Central Committee and the State Council to promote reform, opening-up and socialist modernization. In April 1979 the central leadership took up Deng Xiaoping's suggestion and decided to designate certain areas in Guangdong and Fujian Provinces as "special export zones" that would open first by exploiting their geographical locations near Hong Kong, Macao and Taiwan and their close ties with overseas Chinese. In May 1980 the name "special export zones" was changed to "special economic zones", and in August the Standing Committee of the Fifth NPC decided to build special economic zones in Guangdong's Shenzhen, Zhuhai and Shantou, and Fujian's Xiamen. In April 1988 Hainan Special Economic Zone was established, and in May 2010 Xinjiang's Khorgas and Kashi were added to the list. Special economic zones practice special economic policies and management systems to develop an export-oriented economy. They are major channels for China to boost its own economy by utilizing overseas capital, technology, personnel and management expertise, and are windows on and models of China's reform and opening-up.

（二）英译汉

摩根大通：降息不会让房地产业重获生机

摩根大通（JP Morgan）表示，澳大利亚储备银行（Reserve Bank of Australia）预计，降息行为既不会将拍卖清除率提高到50%以上，也不会阻止今年房价进一步下跌五个百分点。

摩根大通的经济学家汤姆·肯尼迪（Tom Kennedy）表示，上周低于预期的经济增长数据促使许多经济学家作出央行（即澳大利亚储备银行）今年将下调而非上调基准贷款利率的预计，尽管如此，但由于降息空间较小，这一次进一步下调利率带来的影响没有上一次的大。

肯尼迪先生表示，摩根大通目前预计今年将下调50个基点，7月和8月将采取降息措施，但这并不会激活房地产市场，房产供应商已经把心理预期下调到"更现实"的水平，并减少对市场的期望。

经济学家预计,尽管降息将会产生积极影响,但并不能彻底激活房地产市场。

"尽管这有利于房地产市场,但我认为,即使澳大利亚储备银行重启宽松周期,房价也不会像2014年至2016年期间那样疯狂上涨,"肯尼迪先生表示。"因为现金利率的变动幅度不够大。"

由于一系列降息措施,澳大利亚出现了长达五年的房地产繁荣期。这些措施从2011年11月开始实施,当时储备银行第一次降低现金利率,从4.75%下降到4.5%。即使在2015年和2016年,基准利率也从2.5%下降到1.5%,这一降幅远远低于澳大利亚储备银行目前可能做出的降幅。

摩根大通的评论与澳大利亚储备银行在周一发表的研究结果是一致的。该研究称,尽管利率是房价变动的主要驱动力,但关键因素是利率的变化幅度,而不是利率的水平。肯尼迪在《澳大利亚房产拍卖:季节性变化》的研究报告中表示,拍卖成交率的明显企稳(上周末初步恢复到了52%),不太可能会像过去一样促使价格趋稳,因为供应商的折扣可能会压低房价。

他表示:"起初,这表明房价下跌过度,并有望在未来几个月企稳或走高。"

"鉴于清仓率和价格增长之间出现的分歧很可能与房产供应商调整预期时的卖方贴现有关,因此我们将对这一做法发出警告。随着住宅建设规划的继续发展以及房贷的增长放缓,我们预计现状将持续下去,2019年的房价增长仍将面临压力。"

第三章 经济研究与调查报告翻译

一、词组翻译

原文	译文
复工复产	work resumption
援企稳岗	provide assistance to enterprises to stabilize employment
大众创业 万众创新	mass entrepreneurship and innovation
供给侧结构性改革	supply-side structural reform
自贸试验区	pilot free trade zones
综合保税区	integrated free trade zone
减税降费	cut taxes and fees
excess capacity	产能过剩
economies of scale	规模经济
comparative advantage	比较优势
alternative cost	选择成本

续表

原文	译文
non-performing loans	不良贷款
risk exposure	风险敞口
tariff concessions	关税减免
financial repression	金融抑制

二、句子翻译

(一) 汉译英

1. Domestically, consumption, investment, and exports have declined. Pressure on employment has risen significantly. Enterprises, especially micro, small, and medium businesses, face growing difficulties. There are increasing risks in the financial sector and other areas. The budgetary imbalances of primary-level governments have intensified.

2. The shock of the covid-19 pandemic has sent the world economy into severe recession, disrupted industrial and supply chains, and caused a contraction in international trade and investment and volatility in commodity markets.

3. We need to pursue reform and opening-up as a means to stabilize employment, ensure people's well-being, stimulate consumption, energize the market, and achieve stable growth. We need to blaze a new path that enables us to respond effectively to shocks and sustain a positive growth cycle.

4. We should tighten regulation and prevent funds from simply circulating in the financial sector for the sake of arbitrage. As financial institutions and the businesses that borrow from them share a common stake, we encourage banks to make appropriate interest concessions.

5. We will support enterprises of all sizes in pursuing development through collaboration with each other. We will conduct impartial regulation to ensure fair competition, and make sustained efforts to create a market-oriented, law-based, and internationalized business environment.

(二) 英译汉

1. 目前，国债期货市场参与者仍以机构投资者为主，主要是证券公司、证券投资基金、期货公司资管计划及私募机构等。

2. 受访银行的贷款与垫款总额延续了往年的增势，增长了 6.4%，增速显著高于 2018 年的 3.5%。

3. 十大受访银行的总经营收入增长了 4.7%，而与此同时，总经营支出上升了 6.8%，抵消了经营收入的增长。十大银行的加权平均成本收入比率从 2018 年的 40.4% 小幅增至 2019 年的 41.2%。

4. 随着中国多层次证券市场的发展,并购重组、财务顾问等一系列增值服务仍有可观的增长空间。

5. 随着股票价格的快速上升,投资者纷纷涌入A股市场,市场成交量快速增加,日成交金额屡创新高。

三、语篇翻译

新冠疫情对香港银行业的影响

新冠疫情的爆发给香港银行业带来了严重的破坏和巨大的挑战。我们预计在2020年及以后年度,疫情将对香港银行业的财务业绩以及业务和运营模式产生重大影响。

我们当前正面临前所未有之变局,在这样的时期预测财务业绩并非易事。但是,香港银行业的收入很大一部分来自净利息收入。我们预计香港银行业将面临一系列影响其净息差的挑战。例如,美国的利率目前维持在低水平,这反过来将影响香港的利率以及香港银行业维持资产收益和存款利差所产生的收入水平的能力。与此同时,2020年,香港将有八家虚拟银行进入市场,预计将与传统银行开展价格竞争,以吸引客户和存款,从而推高资金成本。尽管如此,我们预计虚拟银行的存款在总存款余额中所占的比例将相对较小,至少在短期内大约占总存款余额的2%至3%。这预示着虚拟银行造成的特殊压力在短期内不会太大。

我们还需要记住,银行可以反映基本经济活动。在当前的宏观环境下,经济预计将发生萎缩,而且企业面临倒闭的风险,香港企业出于业务扩张而产生的贷款融资需求势必将会减少,这将对银行的收入产生影响。

当然,银行的收入还包括非利息收入。在这方面,我们认为情况会稍微乐观一些。坊间证据显示,无论是权益产品还是固定收益产品,金融市场业务在2020年上半年实际上都相当强劲,尽管我们并不认为这种情况在下半年一定会持续下去。香港的股市已经上涨,收复了三月份的大部分失地。这种波动性对投资管理公司和财富管理公司而言是喜闻乐见的。我们认为,中央银行实施的货币政策措施(例如增加量化宽松规模)以及公司债券的低利率意味着人们更有可能投资于股票市场,以获得更高的收益。这种情况可能会持续一段时间,但重要的问题在于,股市的回升是否可以持续并且得到经济基本面的支撑。

此外,我们预计信贷成本和贷款减值准备将会上升,这也将对香港银行业在2020年的业绩产生重大影响。在过去15年左右,香港银行业的贷款减值比率非常低。未来不良贷款或减值贷款的增加将推升贷款减值比率,并且随着信用风险上升,贷款减值准备的计提依据从12个月内的预期信用损失转变为整个存续期内的预期信用损失,从而推高银行的贷款减值准备。此外,由于业绩下滑,用于计算预期信用损失的基本参数(如违约概率和违约损失率)将上升,这反过来又将导致减值费用增加。

第四章　经济学论文翻译

一、词组翻译

原文	译文
difference-in-differences	双差分模型
quantitative equilibrium	定量平衡
global sourcing	全球采购
expenditure switching	支出转换
joint taxation	联合税收
fundamental surplus	基本盈余
trade-off	权衡
supplemental security income	社会生活补助金
边际收益	marginal income
异质性	heterogeneity
最优配置	optimal allocation
影子价格	shadow pricing
空头支票	blank checks
储备货币	reserve currencies
逆向选择	adverse selection

二、句子翻译

（一）英译汉

1. 全球采购的利润研究——以美国公司为例
2. 驾驶电动汽车对环境是否有好处取决于本地因素
3. 随着20世纪80年代利率互换市场的发展，伦敦同业拆利借率被当作一项基准，因其能够最恰当反映同业交易融资成本，因此被用作"无风险"利率的代理。
4. 隔夜指数掉期（OIS）是一种固定浮动利率掉期，其浮线数值参考每天在具体的掉期期限内清零的隔夜指数。按照每日隔夜指数的复利计算浮动线的利息。浮动利率指数通常是银行之间的隔夜抵押贷款利率。
5. 市场参与者通常将单一利率曲线向流动性市场产品调整，例如保证金、远期利率协议、短期利率期货（如欧洲美元期货）和/或利率互换。

(二) 汉译英

1. The effects of credit risk, liquidity risk, collateral agreements and funding costs were largely ignored.

2. The price of the replicating portfolio is identical to all agents in the market, and is therefore independent of any assumptions of risk preferences, either averse or seeking.

3. Overtreatment or Higher Diagnostic

4. WTO Accession and Performance of Chinese Manufacturing Firms

5. A shift in final spending away from tradable sectors, largely caused by declines in durable investment efficiency, accounts for most of the collapse in trade relative to GDP.

三、语篇翻译

The thesis presents the background, significance and innovation points of the subject and a brief introduction between informal institutions and China's economy development. Starting with theoretical research of informal institutions influencing China's economy development. First, four aspects are selected as the transmission medium to illustrate the impact and demonstrates the transmission route of informal institutions on China's economic development. Representing four dimensions of informal institutions, cultural tradition, ideology, manners and customs and moral principles give argument and analysis on the internal mechanism and conduction way of China's economic development relations. In this way, the theoretical basis of informal institutions and China's economy development has been built. In the second place, based on theoretical basis, this study discusses the informal institutions and the development of China's economy from the perspective of the measurement standard, index selection and index trend of different dimensions. The argumentation and analysis in this thesis are strictly in accordance with the character and content of informal institutions and the course of China's economic development to measure each dimension and select measurable indexes that conform to the informal institutions and have economic characteristics according to the national economic development standard, measurements, and Fishbone Diagram. The unification of data selection, screening and optimization process are used to ultimately determine 16 measure indexes of informal institutions and 22 measure indexes of China's economic development to constitute the initial sequence panel data set respectively, and draw smooth curves and trend charts of the 16 and 22 indexes in turn, with the aid of data and abnormal distribution of critical point, and combining with the historical process and characteristics of China's economic development to present the cause of the more basic explanation. Third, build and correlate the comprehensive evaluation function of informal institutions and China's economic development through confirming analytical method. Then, according to the 22 indexes selected for China's economic development, establish the data panel of four large regions in China and the functions of informal system and the economic development of four regions in China respectively, demonstrate the impact relationship between informal institutions and regional economic development, and further illustrate the impact of informal institutions on China's economy. Meanwhile, the measurement index system of the transmission medium between the informal institutions and China's economic development is constructed, and the functional relationship between the informal institutions and the transmission medium, as well as between the China's economy and the transmission medium is established, which verifies the transmission path between the informal institutions and China's economic development. Finally, based on the above theoretical analysis, using the empirical data as a result, respectively from the "correct guiding ideology and efficient change" "accelerate the construction of market economy and culture" "attaches great importance to the customs, habits are effective change" "to accelerate the promotion of a new era of socialist morality" "we will accelerate reform of the system of effective formal, pull to rise the informal system combines the development" "increasing the financial input in education, improve the cultural value of human capital" and "adhere to the Party and the government lead new concept, expanding the effective supply increase consumer demand" seven aspects related to informal institutional content is put forward to promote China to the high quality and economic development of countermeasures and suggestions.

第五章　经济学教材翻译

一、词组翻译

原文	译文
exogenous variable	外生变量
endogenous variable	内生变量
the Optimization Principle	最优化原理
economic agents	经济人
reservation price	保留价格
competitive market	竞争性市场
comparative statics	比较静态
monopoly	垄断
discriminating monopolist	歧视性的垄断者
excess demand	超额需求
Pareto efficiency	帕累托效率
consumption bundle	消费束

续表

原文	译文
budget set	预算集
numeracies price	本位价格
budget line	预算线
opportunity cost	机会成本
strict preference	严格偏好
indifferent	无差异的
value tax	从价税
quantity tax	从量税

二、句子翻译

(一)英译汉

1. 在这个均衡价格上,愿意至少支付 p* 租金的每个消费者都能够找到公寓租住,每个房东都愿意按照现行的市场价格出租公寓。

2. 供给冲击是指可能直接引起企业生产成本和价格变化的事件;它改变了企业总供给曲线,从而影响到菲利普斯曲线。

3. 想打怪兽吗?外包给中国人吧

4. 如果牧场主只生产牛肉,而农场主只能生产土豆,那么,贸易的好处是显而易见的。在一种情况下,农场主和牧场主可能选择"老死不相往来"。

5. 补贴(subsidy)正好和税收相反。在从量补贴(quantity subsidy)的情形下,政府根据消费者购买某种商品的数量,给与他一定金额的补助。

(二)汉译英

1. Such a curve is an example of a demand curve—a curve that relates the quantity demanded to price.

2. Economists call a person's maximum willingness to pay for something that person's reservation price.

3. If there are many people and their reservation prices differ only slightly from person to person, it is reasonable to think of the demand curve as sloping smoothly downward, as in Figure 1.2.

4. The situation we will consider is where there are many independent landlords who are each out to rent their apartments for the highest price the market will bear. We will refer to this as the case of a competitive market.

5. Whatever price is being charged, the same number of apartments will be rented namely,

all apartments that are available at that time.

三、语篇翻译

(一) 英译汉

所有政府——从华盛顿特区的联邦政府到小镇的地方政府——都用税收为公路、学校和国防这类公共项目筹资。由于税收是一种非常重要的政策工具,而且,由于税收在许多方面影响着我们的生活,所以我们在全书中经常要研究税收这个话题。在这一节,我们的研究从税收如何影响经济开始。

为了设定一个分析的范围,设想一个地方政府决定举办一个年度冰淇淋节,节日期间将有游行、烟火以及本镇官员的讲话。为了筹到这项活动的经费,该镇决定对每个冰淇淋蛋卷的销售征收0.5美元的税收。当这项计划公布时,我们的两个游说集团立即采取行动。全国冰淇淋消费者协会声称,冰淇淋消费者无力支付,并认为,冰淇淋的卖者应该支付此项税收。全国冰淇淋制造商组织声称,它的成员在竞争市场上为生存而挣扎,并建议,冰淇淋的买者应该支付此项税收。市长希望双方达成妥协,建议买者支付一半税收,卖者支付一半税收。

为了分析这些建议,我们需要解决一个简单而敏感的问题:当政府对一种物品征税时,谁实际上承担了税收负担?是购买此物品的人,还是出售此物品的人?或者,如果买者与卖者分摊税收负担,什么因素决定如何分配税收负担?政府能像这位市长建议的一样,简单地通过立法来分配税收负担吗?还是要由更基本的市场力量来决定税收负担的分配?税收归宿(tax incidence)这个术语是指税收负担如何在组成市场的不同人之间分配。正如我们将看到的,通过运用供求工具,我们可以得到一些有关税收归宿的令人惊讶的结论。

向卖者征税如何影响市场结果

我们首先考虑向一种物品的卖者征税。假设当地政府通过了一项法律,要求冰淇淋的卖者每卖一个冰淇淋蛋卷向政府支付0.5美元的税收。这项法律将如何影响冰淇淋的买者和卖者呢?为了回答这个问题,我们可以遵循第4章中分析供给与需求时的三个步骤:(1)确定该法律影响供给曲线,还是需求曲线。(2)确定曲线移动的方向。(3)考察这种移动如何影响均衡价格和数量。

第一步:在这种情况下,税收对冰淇淋的卖者产生了直接影响。由于并不向买者征税,在任何一种既定价格下,冰淇淋的需求量是相同的,所以,需求曲线不变。与此相反,对卖者征税使冰淇淋经营者在每一价格水平下的获利能力减少了,因此将使供给曲线移动。

第二步:由于对卖者征税提高了生产和销售冰淇淋的成本,因此,税收减少了每一种价格下的供给量。供给曲线向左移动(也可以说是向上移动)。

除了确定供给曲线移动的方向之外,我们还要准确地知道该曲线移动的幅度。在任何一种冰淇淋的市场价格下,卖者的有效价格——他们在纳税之后得到的数量——要降低 0.5 美元。例如，如果一个冰淇淋蛋卷的市场价格正好是 2 美元，卖者得到的有效价格将是 1.5 美元。无论市场价格是多少，卖者就如同在比市场价格低 0.5 美元的价格水平上来确定冰淇淋的供给量。换言之，为了促使卖者供给任何一种既定的数量，现在市场价格必须高 0.5 美元，以便弥补税收的影响。因此，如图 6 所示，供给曲线从 S1 向上移动到 S2，移动幅度正好是税收量（0.5 美元）。

第三步：在确定了供给曲线如何移动之后，我们现在可以比较原来的均衡与新均衡。图 6 表明，冰淇淋蛋卷的均衡价格从 3 美元上升到 3.3 美元，而均衡数量从 100 个减少为 90 个。由于在新均衡下，卖者的销售量减少了，买者的购买量也减少了，因此税收缩小了冰淇淋市场的规模。

含义：现在我们回到税收归宿问题：谁支付了税收？虽然卖者向政府支付了全部税收，但买者与卖者分摊了税收负担。由于在引进税收后，冰淇淋蛋卷的市场价格从 3 美元上涨为 3.3 美元，买者购买一个冰淇淋蛋卷的支出比没有税收时增加了 0.3 美元。因此，税收使买者的状况变坏了。卖者从买者那里得到了一个更高的价格（3.3 美元），但交税后的有效价格从征税前的 3 美元下降为 2.8 美元（3.3 美元 − 0.5 美元 = 2.8 美元）。因此，税收使卖者的状况也变坏了。

（二）汉译英

Pareto Efficiency

One useful criterion for comparing the outcomes of different economic institutions is a concept known as Pareto efficiency or economic efficiency. We start with the following definition: if we can find a way to make some people better off without making anybody else worse off, we have a Pareto improvement. If an allocation allows for a Pareto improvement, it is called Pareto inefficient; if an allocation is such that no Pareto improvements are possible, it is called Pareto efficient.

A Pareto inefficient allocation has the undesirable feature that there is some way to make somebody better off without hurting anyone else. There may be other positive things about the allocation, but the fact that it is Pareto inefficient is certainly one strike against it. If there is a way to make someone better off without hurting anyone else, why not do it?

The idea of Pareto efficiency is an important one in economics and we will examine it in some detail later on. It has many subtle implications that we will have to investigate more slowly, but we can get an inkling of what is involved even now.

Here is a useful way to think about the idea of Pareto efficiency. Suppose that we assigned the renters to the inner-and outer-ring apartments randomly, but then allowed them to sublet their apartments to each other. Some people who really wanted to live close in might, through bad luck, end up with an outer-ring apartment. But then they could sublet an inner-ring apartment from someone who was assigned to such an apartment but who didn't value it as highly as the other person. If individuals were assigned randomly to apartments, there would generally be some who would want to trade apartments, if they were sufficiently compensated for doing so.

For example, suppose that person A is assigned an apartment in the inner ring that he feels is worth $200, and that there is some person B in the outer ring who would be willing to pay $300 for A's apartment. Then there is a "gain from trade" if these two agents swap apartments and arrange a side payment from B to A of some amount of money between $200 and $300. The exact amount of the transaction isn't important. What is important is that the people who are willing to pay the most for the apartments get them—otherwise, there would be an incentive for someone who attached a low value to an inner-ring apartment to make a trade with someone who placed a high value on an inner-ring apartment.

Suppose that we think of all voluntary trades as being carried out so that all gains from trade are exhausted. The resulting allocation must be Pareto efficient. If not, there would be some trade that would make two people better off without hurting anyone else—but this would contradict the assumption that all voluntary trades had been carried out. An allocation in which all voluntary trades have been carried out is a Pareto efficient allocation.

To see the answer, just note that anyone who has an apartment in the inner ring must have a higher reservation price than anyone who has an apartment in the outer ring—otherwise, they could make a trade and make both people better off. Thus if there are S apartments to be rented, then the S people with the highest reservation prices end up getting apartments in the inner ring. This allocation is Pareto efficient—anything else is not, since any other assignment of apartments to people would allow for some trade that would make at least two of the people better off without hurting anyone else.

第六章 经济学经典文献翻译

一、词组翻译

原文	译文
二次探底	double dip
恩格尔系数	Engle coefficient
反垄断调查	anti-monopoly probe
点心债券	dim sum bond
次级债务	subordinate debt
不完全信息	incomplete information
"使用财产就要付费"体制	"buy-him-in" system

续表

原文	译文
"let-him-buy-his-way out" system	"付费他人不使用财产"体制
personal income tax	个人所得税
Purchasing Managers Index of non-manufacturing sector	非制造业采购经理人指数
employment discrimination	就业歧视
scarcity of resource	资源的稀缺性
equilibrium price	均衡价格
Indifference Curve	无差异曲线
Ability-to-pay Principle	支付能力原则

二、句子翻译

(一)英译汉

1. 相反,地主的资本固定在其土地的改良上,它的安全性就和人事活动在本质上所能达到的极限一样高。

2. 就持续的高失业率和失业时间而言,经济仍在为此付出代价。

3. 只要认为制度不打压人类天性,那么在城镇土地完全开垦和改良以前,它们的发展规模绝不能超过当时土地开垦和改良的水平。

4. 如果在同一地区内,某一用途比其他用途明显有利或不利,那么许多人就会舍弃比较不利的用途,转而去拥护比较有利的用途。如此一来,这种用途的利益不久便会回归到与其他用途利益相等的水平。

5. 以倾销的价格销售的商品的数量与价格、需求减少或消费模式的变量、各种技术的不断发展以及国内相关产业的出口都是这方面有关的原因。

(二)汉译英

1. Better supplied with the amenities of life as he is, he sooner reaches the point at which he looks upon any further increment in the disutility of labor as an evil which is no longer outweighed by the expected further increment in labor's mediate gratification.

2. The employers would be in a position enabling them to lower wage rates by concerted action only if they were to monopolize a factor indispensable for every kind of production and to restrict the employment of this factor in a monopolistic way.

3. One thousand men working with the traditional old-fashioned tools in small artisan shops somewhere in the backward countries of Asia produce over the same period of time, even when working much longer than forty hours weekly, many fewer than m pairs.

4. From this angle, the main character of the first transition was to advance step by step like

across the river by touching stones.

5. It should be noted that under the lure of industry interests, there is still a long way to go to realize separation of government administration from enterprise management and capital, and finally to realize the public welfare of the state-owned assets.

三、语篇翻译

(一) 英译汉

Ⅰ. 有待分析的问题

本文涉及对他人产生有害影响的那些工商业企业的行为。一个典型的例子就是,某工厂的烟尘给邻近的财产所有者带来的有害影响。对此类情况,经济学的分析通常是从工厂的私人产品与社会产品之间的矛盾这方面展开的。在这一方面,许多经济学家都因袭了庇古在《福利经济学》中提出的观点。他们的分析结论无非是要求工厂主对烟尘所引起的损害负责赔偿,或者根据工厂排出烟尘的不同容量及其所致损害的相应金额标准对工厂主征税,或者最终责令该厂迁出居民区(当然也指烟尘排放对他人产生有害影响的地区)。以我之见,这些解决办法并不合适,因为它们所导致的结果不是人们所需要的,甚至通常也不是人们所满意的。

Ⅱ. 问题的相互性

传统的方法掩盖了不得不作出的选择的实质。人们一般将该问题视为甲给乙造成损害,因而所要决定的是:如何制止甲?但这是错误的。我们正在分析的问题具有相互性,即避免对乙的损害将会使甲遭受损害。必须决定的真正问题是,是允许甲损害乙,还是允许乙损害甲?关键在于避免较严重的损害。我在前文中列举了糖果制造商的机器引起的噪声和震动干扰了某医生的工作的事例。为了避免损害医生,糖果制造商将遭受损害。此事例提出的问题实质上是,是否值得去限制糖果制造商采用的生产方法,并以减少其产品供给的代价来保证医生的正常工作。另一事例是走失的牛损坏邻近土地里的谷物所产生的问题。倘若有些牛难免要走失,那么只有以减少谷物的供给这一代价来换取肉类供给的增加。这种选择的实质是显而易见的:是要肉类,还是要谷物?当然,我们不能贸然回答,除非我们知道所得到的价值是什么,以及为此所牺牲的价值是什么。再举一例:乔治·J. 施蒂格勒教授提到的河流污染问题。如果我们假定污染的有害后果是鱼类的死亡,要决定的问题则是:鱼类损失的价值究竟大于还是小于可能污染河流的产品的价值。不言而喻,必须从总体的和边际的角度来看待这一问题。

(二) 汉译英

The growth factors of rural economy will fall on the distinctive towns in the future. At present, there are about 18,000 organic towns and 20,000 towns at scale nationwide, and the economic development issues of nearly 40,000 towns need to be solved in the second urbanization. Following the plan, China will build 1,000 distinctive towns by 2020 and the administrative division of each town covers generally from tens to hundreds of square kilometers with a core town area presenting urban form of about 2-3 kilometers, which requires an investment of 5 billion yuan in three years, and the total investment of 1,000 characteristic towns will reach 5 trillion yuan. In the next two or three decades, the similarly significant changes will fall on the 40,000 towns, which will be a pillar to China's GDP development. As a consequence, the distinctive towns will play a significant role in killing development disparity between urban and rural as a pivot. None of the typical distinctive town has nothing to do with the urban economy. Instead, the more successful the towns are, the more they make full use of the gradient dividend and innovation dividend of the integration of urban and rural economy. Meanwhile, it's accepted that the new space for development and the new economy model with friendly environment are interdependent when the old economy model has declined in the first round of urbanization and industrialization. Therefore, the development of distinctive towns becomes the commanding height of the new economy model. In addition, the business investment may exactly find new opportunities on the distinctive town for its integration of may experience economic elements such as industry, tourism, leisure, consumption and so on.

第七章 经济会议演讲发言翻译

一、词组翻译

原文	译文
global financial architecture	全球金融体系
stagnant trade	贸易停滞
financial system	金融体系
energy economy	能源经济
International monetary fund	国际货币基金组织
industrial subsidies	产业补贴
bilateral trade agreements	双边贸易协定
transfer payment from the exchequer	财政转移支付
关税壁垒	tariff barrier
国内投资	domestic investment
反倾销	anti-dumping
休会	adjourn
第三产业	tertiary industry
高层会谈	high-level talks
自由贸易区	FTZ(free trade zone)

二、句子翻译

(一) 英译汉

1. 历史表明：如果政府之间不仅进行货物自由流通，而且能够进行思想自由交流，经济将更加繁荣；在开放的经济社会中，繁荣发展的创新之路将越走越宽。

2. 面对各种挑战，我们寻求新的解决办法，我们充满自信地捕捉新机遇，收获甚丰。

3. 但我也警告过会有市场不稳定的危险，而在经济复苏时，新货币政策委员会能进行前瞻性指导，有效引导预期。

4. 其中有些人还表示，他们从中得到启发，可以将经验带回本国，为恢复国内制造业城市的活力提供借鉴。

5. 不妨回顾一下，我们6个月前面临的局势——经济萎缩，失业剧增，贸易停滞，金融系统几乎停止运行。

(二) 汉译英

1. We, as the leaders of major economies, are duty bound to recalibrate the direction of the world economy and global governance at this critical juncture, work together to boost market confidence, and bring hope to our people.

2. Let me conclude by saying that China has full confidence in following its path and running its own affairs well. At the same time, China will work in the spirit of peaceful co-existence and win-win cooperation with all other countries to build a community with a shared future for mankind and to tirelessly pursue a brighter future of the global economy.

3. It is a great pleasure to be with you here, to discuss ways of building a bridge of cooperation to advance our shared prosperity.

4. We must remain committed to openness and mutual benefit for all so as to increase the size of the global economic "pie".

5. Let us work together to promote interconnected growth for shared prosperity and build toward a global community with a shared future.

三、语篇翻译

Look Beyond the Horizon and Steer the World Economy in the Right Direction
— Remarks at Session I of the G20 Summit

President Mauricio Macri,

Dear Colleagues,

It's been ten years since the global financial crisis broke out and the first G20 Summit was convened. Today, the global economy, while maintaining growth on the whole, is still not free from the underlying impacts of the crisis. Old growth drivers are yet to be replaced by new ones. Various risks are rapidly building up. The new round of technological revolution and industrial transformation are triggering profound changes, the wealth gap keeps widening, and social contradictions are growing. The world economy is facing another historical choice.

An ancient Chinese philosopher observed that "Reviewing the past enables us to learn about the law governing the evolution of history." We G20 members must closely follow the underlying historical trend so as to chart the course for the future. In mankind's relentless quest for development and progress, the trend toward openness and integration among countries is unstoppable despite ups and downs in the global economy. The ever growing and expanding industrial chain, value chain and supply chain have boosted the flow of production factors across the world and led several billion people out of poverty and toward prosperity. Greater coordination and complementarity among countries meet the need of productivity growth. They will also shape the future of relations of production. In this process, countries are increasingly becoming a community with shared interests, shared responsibilities and a shared future. Going forward, win-win cooperation is the only choice for us, be it in good times or bad. This is dictated by the law of economics, and it is in keeping with the development of human history. Facing various challenges, we must have a stronger sense of urgency, be rational in approach and look beyond the horizon. We must fulfill our responsibility and steer the global economy in the right direction.

The G20 was born out of the international community's need to maintain stable growth of the global economy. Over the past decade, we have braced difficulties together, navigated the global economy out of recession and brought it back to the track of recovery and growth. Ten years later, let us work with the same courage and strategic vision and ensure that the global economy grows on the right track.

First, we should stay committed to openness and cooperation and uphold the multilateral trading system. Five years ago, when I attended the G20 Summit for the first time, I called for joint efforts to uphold and build an open world economy. Five years on, this has obviously become an even more urgent task for us. The number of new trade restrictive measures applied on a monthly basis among G20 members has doubled compared with six months ago. In 2018, the growth of trade in goods may decline by 0.3 percent globally. We should firmly uphold free trade and the rules-based multilateral trading system. China supports necessary reform of the World Trade Organization, and believes that it is critical to uphold the WTO's core values and fundamental principles such as openness, inclusiveness and non-discrimination and ensure the development interests and policy space of developing countries. We need to conduct extensive consultation to achieve gradual progress instead of imposing one's position on others.

Second, we should forge strong partnership and step up macro policy coordination. Partnership is the most valuable asset of the G20. We G20 members should work together to surmount whatever difficulty that lies ahead. We should employ the three tools of fiscal and monetary policies and structural reform in a holistic way to ensure strong, balanced, sustainable and inclusive growth of the global economy. Strengthening policy coordination, which is essential for global growth, is also the due responsibility of major economies. Developed economies, when adopting monetary and fiscal policies, should give more consideration to and work to minimize the impact such policies may exert on emerging markets and developing economies. The IMF's 15th General Quota Review should be concluded on schedule. The international monetary system should become more diversified, and the global financial safety net should continue to be strengthened.

Third, we should stay committed to innovation and create new momentum for growth. The global economy is embracing the trend of digital transformation, and the new round of industrial revolution will reshape human society in profound ways. We should encourage innovation and leverage the role of the digital economy in growing the real economy. We need to watch out for risks and challenges brought by the application of new technologies, and strengthen the legal and regulatory framework. And we need to do more to boost education and vocational training. We should give priority to achieving development through fully tapping our innovation potential. At the same time, we also need to keep our doors open and encourage the spread of new technologies and knowledge so that innovation will benefit more countries and peoples. To better adapt to and guide technological innovation, I propose that the G20 carry out an in-depth study on the application and impact of new technologies on a priority basis to explore new thinking and new ways of cooperation in this area.

第八章　经济会议联合公报翻译

一、词组翻译

原文	译文
制度	system
治理	governance
完善	improved
健全	improving
优势	superior dominant
联动增长	interconnected growth
基础设施互联互通	connectivity
精简	streamlining

续表

原文	译文
lending capacity	贷款能力
regional financing arrangements	区域融资安排
swift disbursements	迅速付款
the Flexible Credit Line (FCL)	灵活信贷额度(FCL)
the Precautionary and Liquidity Line (PLL)	预防和流动性额度(PLL)
Debt Limit Policy (DLP)	债务限额政策(DLP)
non-concessional borrowing	非优惠借款

二、句子翻译

(一) 汉译英

1. We are determined to foster an innovative, invigorated, interconnected and inclusive world economy to usher in a new era of global growth and sustainable development, taking into account the *2030 Agenda for Sustainable Development*, the *Addis Ababa Action Agenda* and the *Paris Agreement*.

(*G20 Leaders' Communiqué*: Hangzhou Summit)

2. Our growth, to be dynamic and create more jobs, must be powered by new driving forces. While reaffirming the importance of addressing shortfalls in global demand to support short-term growth, we believe it is also imperative to address supply side constraints so as to raise productivity sustainably, expand the frontier of production and unleash mid-to long-term growth potential.

(*G20 Leaders' Communiqué*: Hangzhou Summit)

3. Looking into the future, we envisage high-quality "Belt and Road" cooperation in enhancing connectivity by promoting development policy synergy, infrastructure development, unimpeded trade, financial cooperation and people-to-people bond, thereby enhancing practical cooperation for the well-being of our peoples. In this context, we look forward to more efforts by cooperation partners.

(*Joint Communiqué of the Leaders' Roundtable of the 2nd "Belt and Road" Forum for International Cooperation*)

4. We will strive to build high-quality, reliable, resilient and sustainable infrastructure. We emphasize that high-quality infrastructure should be viable, affordable, accessible, inclusive and broadly beneficial over its entire life-cycle, contributing to sustainable development of participating countries and the industrialization of developing countries.

(*Joint Communiqué of the Leaders' Roundtable of the 2nd "Belt and Road" Forum for International Cooperation*)

5. We call for the swift, effective and universal implementation of the FATF standards and of the provisions of the UN Security Council resolution 2253 worldwide.

(*G20 Leaders' Communiqué*: *Hangzhou Summit*)

(二) 英译汉

1. 我们重申，我们致力于建立更强大的全球金融安全网，并以强大的、以配额为基础且资源充足的国际货币基金组织为其中心，密切审查其资源需求。

（G20各国财政部长及央行行长会议）

2. 我们二十国集团领导人将致力于保护生命，保障人民的就业和收入，重振信心，保持金融稳定与恢复增长，最大限度减少对全球供应链的干扰，帮助全部有需要的国家，以及协调公共卫生和财务措施。

（G20各国财政部长及央行行长会议）

3. 我们同意，如确有必要，采取的应对新冠肺炎紧急贸易措施必须有针对性、成比例、透明且暂时。并且它们不会对贸易造成不必要的障碍或破坏全球供应链，且符合世界贸易组织规则。

（G20各国财政部长及央行行长会议）

4. 根据贸易和投资部长的协议，我们将继续共同努力，创造一个自由、公平、非歧视性、透明、可预测和稳定的贸易投资环境，并保持我们的市场开放。

（G20各国财政部长及央行行长会议）

5. 我们将分享关于COVID-19遏制措施、其实施和随后的消除的最新信息和国家经验，以尽量减少负面溢出和第二波影响，包括增加继发感染波的风险。

（G20各国财政部长及央行行长会议）

三、语篇翻译

《行动计划》附件——向有需要的国家提供COVID-19国际支持

需要采取全球行动，防治新冠肺炎及其对卫生和经济的影响。

我们欢迎国际货币基金组织、世界银行、区域开发银行和中央银行已经采取的包括部署和扩大双边互换额度在内的重要举措。

这种财政对策应包括：提供一套全面的国际货币基金组织一揽子支助方案，并利用区域筹资安排的现有工具；迅速执行世界银行和区域开发银行提议的支助；向最贫穷国家提供暂停偿债；确保效率和业务协调，以优化资源使用。我们欢迎各国央行为支持金融稳定而采取的行动。

1. 提供一套全面的国际货币基金组织一揽子支助方案，并利用区域筹资安排的现有工具

我们欢迎国际货币基金组织紧急设施（快速融资工具/快速信贷工具）的年度准入限制

暂时翻一番，为有紧急国际收支需要的国家提供融资。我们支持充分利用现有的工具和贷款能力，包括诸如灵活信贷额度（FCL）和预防和流动性额度（PLL）等预防性手段，以及 IMF 准备动员其 1 万亿美元的贷款能力来满足通过增加现有计划或新计划来满足会员的需求。我们还支持简化和加快内部程序，以便迅速付款。

此外，我们支持通过短期流动资金线，包括对 2022 年进行审查，通过可预测和可再生的方式帮助具有非常强大的基础和政策的国家获得国际货币基金组织的资源。我们还呼吁国际货币基金组织借鉴以往危机的相关经验，探索其他工具，在危机演变时满足其成员的需要。

我们重申，我们致力于在全球金融安全网（GFSN）的中心建立一个强大、以配额为基础、资源充足的国际货币基金组织。我们欢迎各国为采取必要的国内措施而采取的措施，以维持国际货币基金组织目前的资源规模，并敦促其他国家迅速采取行动。我们将继续致力于在 2023 年 12 月 15 日之前重新审视配额的充分性，并继续根据第 16 次配额总审查，包括新的配额公式作为指导，继续开展国际货币基金组织的治理改革进程。

我们欢迎区域融资安排提供的工具，并呼吁在深化国际货币基金组织和区域融资安排之间的合作方面取得进一步进展。

2. 迅速执行世界银行和区域开发银行提议的支助

我们欢迎多边开发银行通过其董事会及时作出决定，根据各自的任务和地域范围，确定和通过全面的应急一揽子计划。多边开发银行提供的财政支助共达 2000 亿美元，用于新兴和低收入国家。这包括①与世卫组织等专门机构协调，在卫生部门实施有针对性的投资方案；②通过安全网和现金转移方案向最贫穷者提供支助；③向受影响国家提供紧急财政支持，特别是通过符合国际货币基金组织方案的一般和部门预算支助；④向私营部门，包括公司和金融机构，特别是通过贸易融资、流动性和流动资金计划提供支助。多边开发银行贷款机构将继续增加承诺，最大限度地提高其贷款能力，并调动所有资源。我们期待着这一资金迅速落实。

我们鼓励多边开发银行与国家一级的发展伙伴密切合作，确保一致性，优化资源使用，确保债务保持可持续，并最大程度地促进发展。我们期待着多边开发银行就进一步实施国家拥有的平台提供最新情况。

我们期待进一步讨论多边开发银行在大流行病危机之后的作用，因为它们将为发展中国家从危机中复苏，恢复强劲、可持续、平衡和包容的增长发挥关键作用。

3. 向最贫穷国家提供暂停偿债

我们欢迎已经宣布的捐款，我们呼吁提供更多捐款，补充减贫与增长信托基金（PRGT）和灾难遏制与救济信托基金（CCRT），帮助最贫穷国家减少其对国际货币基金组织的债务义务。

我们支持向要求延期的最贫穷国家实行有时限的偿还债务。我们商定了一个协调办法，并商定了一份共同期限表，该表提供了该债务偿还暂停计划的主要特征，巴黎俱乐部也对此表示同意。所有双边官方债权人都将按照本国法律和内部程序参与这一举措。

我们呼吁通过国际金融研究所工作的私人债权人以可比条件参加该倡议。我们要求多边开发银行进一步探索在暂停期内暂停偿还债务的选择,同时保持其当前的评级和较低的融资成本。我们呼吁债权人在该倡议的执行阶段继续密切协调。

第九章 经济发展计划翻译

一、词组翻译

原文	译文
精准扶贫	targeted poverty alleviation
高质量发展	high-quality development
共有产权住房	homes with shared ownership
新型城镇化	new model / type of urbanization
党的领导、人民当家作主、依法治国	the Party as leaders, the people as masters, law-based governance
党的基本理论、基本路线、基本纲领、基本经验	Party's basic theory, line, program and experience
纠正"四风"(形式主义、官僚主义、享乐主义、奢靡之风)	take action to address formalism, bureaucratism, hedonism, and extravagance
西电东输、西气东送	transporting natural gas and electricity from the west to the east
shared development	共享发展
macro regulation	宏观调控
commodity	大宗商品
ecological conservation redline	生态保护红线
negative list	负面清单
overcapacity	产能过剩
spirit of craftsmanship	工匠精神

二、句子翻译

(一)汉译英

1. All Party members should fully understand the practical and historical significance of this change, align their thinking, act in unison, work to deepen reform, break new ground, and

thereby drive China's development to the next level.

2. Innovation should be placed at the heart of China's development and promoted in every field, from theory to institutions, science, technology, and culture.

3. We will protect legitimate income and regulate invisible income. We will prevent the use of non-market means to earn income, such as the abuse of power and administrative monopolies, and clamp down on all methods for ilegal gains.

4. The growth rates of the average disposable incomes of both urban and rural residents have reached 11.3% and 10.5% respectively.

5. We will implement a more proactive employment policy, create more job opportunities, work to solve problems of structural unemployment, and encourage business startups that create employment, so as to ensure relatively full and high quality employment.

(二)英译汉

1. 在商业方面,要协力打造适合可持续产品的框架,在欧盟乃至欧盟以外地区提供新的机遇。

2. 以更密切的客户关系、大规模定制化服务、分享与协作经济为基础,以物联网、大数据、区块链和人工智能等数字技术为助力,创新的模式不仅会加速循环,还能加快经济的减物质化,降低欧洲对初次原材料的依赖。

3. 可以预见,随着合理的监管框架的进一步发展,衡量民生福祉的因素将不再局限于国内生产总值。

4. 受到老龄化和人口下降的影响,日本的实际国内生产总值长期增长缓慢,可能会出现负增长。

5. 美国原本计划将对从中国进口的价值2000亿美元的商品征收的关税从10%提升至25%,但在谈判期间,美国同意将关税生效时间从2019年1月1日延迟至2019年3月1日。

三、语篇翻译

(一)汉译英

We will persist in putting job enlargement in the prior position of economic and social development, combine promoting development of industry with expanding employment, create equal employment opportunity and strive to achieve full employment.

We will implement more active employment policy. We will vigorously develop service industry as well as labour intensive industry, adopt the policies of credit and tax preference to support the development of small enterprise and create jobs by various forms and channels. We should establish and improve the mechanism of the construction of major projects to create more employment opportunities. We should improve policies on tax break as well as subsidy on job, training, social insurance and skills recognition, and encourage enterprises to absorb more workers to obtain jobs. We will thoroughly promote nation-wide entrepreneurship, improve and implement policies of small guaranteed loan, financial discount and arrangements of workplace to encourage self-employment, perfect the system of services for start-up business, and strive to carry out start-up business training programmes for 500,000 people in 5 years. We will encourage migrant workers to return home to start their own business.

We will give priority to the employment of key groups. We will strengthen the employment service and policy support of college graduates, open channels of employment to encourage college graduates to work in urban and rural organizations at the grassroots level as well as small and medium-sized enterprises and start their own business. We will vigorously develop export of labour services. Meanwhile, we will accelerate the construction of industry cluster districts and professional industrial parks, develop rural secondary and tertiary industries, push forward processing industry of the agricultural by-products to be centralized distribution in producing areas, promote rural labour force to get employed in local area or in the vicinity, and strive to transfer agricultural labor force to a total of 5,000,000 in five years. We will do a good job to promote the employment of urban residents with difficulty finding jobs and veterans, strengthen service and assistance of employment, implement placement programs of public welfare positions and strive to develop about 100,000 of public service jobs every year.

We will vigorously carry out labor skills training. We should improve vocational training system for the labor force, move closely around the demands of industrial structure adjustment and undertaking industrial transfer in our province, make emphasis on cultivating industry skilled talents with high quality, carry out vocational skills training extensively, comprehensively improve the employability and entrepreneurial abilities of laborers. We will carry out practical skills training free of charge for laid-off workers, migrant workers, and generally implement prejob training courses for secondary-school graduates who have failed to gain higher education. We will implement the basic skills revitalization project for the whole people. By 2013, we will accomplish employment skills training of rural labor transfer for 10 million people, skills upgrading training for 2 million on-post staff in enterprises, 1.5 million people for vocational skills training for unemployed personnals to transfer jobs, and 0.1 million for newly trained technicians and senior technicians.

We will strengthen public employment service. We will improve the unified, standardized and flexible human resources market, strengthen the construction of employment service facilities at the basic level of county and township, and build up public employment service system covering urban and rural areas. We will improve monitoring system of labor employment, perfect system of unemployment monitoring and early warning, comprehensively carry out labor contract system, strengthen management of labor quota standard, intensify mediation and arbitration on labor disputes, reinforce the law enforcement of labor security supervision, and practically protect the lawful rights and interests of laborers. We should give full play to the role of government, labour union and enterprises, strive to form benefit sharing mechanism of enterprise and employees, and construct harmonious labor relations.

（二）英译汉

赋能消费者，为他们提供节约成本的机会，是可持续产品政策框架的关键组成部分。为了加强消费者在循环经济中的参与度，欧洲委员会将提议修改欧盟消费者法律，以确保消费者在购买产品时能够获得与产品相关的可靠信息，包括关于产品生命周期以及维修服务、备件和维修手册可获得性的信息。欧洲委员会还将考虑进一步加强消费者保护，避免"漂绿"和过早报废，设定关于可持续标识/标志及信息工具的最低要求。

此外，欧洲委员会还将努力确立新的"维修权"，例如，针对备件的可获得性或者获取维修权，考虑为消费者提供新的横向材料权，以及针对信息通信技术和电子产品，提供获得升级服务的权利。在提供更具循环性的产品时，担保可能发挥一定作用，欧洲委员会也将结合对指令2019/771的评审，探索此方面的可能变化。

欧洲委员会还提议公司采用产品和组织环境足迹的方法，落实其环境主张。欧洲委员会将尝试在欧盟生态标签中融合此类方法，更系统性地在欧盟生态标签规范中加入耐久性、可循环使用性和可再生成分含量等内容。公共机构的购买力占到欧盟GDP的14%，因此可以将之作为强大的驱动力，推动对可持续产品的需求。为发挥此种潜力，欧洲委员会将建议在部门立法中纳入最低的强制性绿色公共采购（GPP）规范与目标，分阶段引入强制性申报程序，以监督绿色公共采购的应用情况，同时避免让公共买家承担不合理的行政负担。此外，欧洲委员会将继续通过指导、培训以及宣传良好实践等措施，支持能力建设，鼓励公共买家参与"公共买家气候与环境"倡议，此倡议旨在促进致力于实施"绿色公共采购"的买家之间的交流。

要更广泛地推动产业转型，实现气候中和及长期竞争力，就离不开可循环性。可循环性可以大幅缩减整个价值链和生产流程中的原材料消耗，创造附加价值，发掘经济机遇。结合工业战略中规定的目标，欧洲委员会将通过以下措施实现更高的循环性：

• 结合对工业排放指令的评审，评估在工业流程中进一步推广循环性的选择，包括在即将发布的"最佳可用技术"参考文件中融入循环经济的做法；

• 通过制定产业主导的申报与认证制度，促进产业共生，推动产业共生的贯彻落实；

• 通过落实生物经济行动计划，支持具有可持续性及可循环性的生物部门；

• 推广使用数字技术追踪、追查资源，绘制资源分布图；

• 通过一个可靠的认证系统，将欧盟环境技术认证制度登记为欧盟认证标志，以推广绿色技术的应用。

新的中小企业战略将依托培训、欧洲企业网络（Enterprise Europe Network）就集群协作提供的建议以及通过欧洲资源效率知识中心(European Resource Efficiency Knowledge Centre)完成的知识传递，促进中小企业之间的循环产业协作。

第十章　经济合同相关法律法规翻译

一、词组翻译

原文	译文
perform one's obligations	履行某人的义务
liability for breach of contract	违约责任
conclude a contract	订立合同
barter transaction	互易合同
method of repayment	还款方式
corresponding price	对价
payable at sight	见票即付
criminal responsibility	刑事责任
technology development contract	技术开发合同
dishonourable check	空头支票
承担责任	undertake liability / bear the responsibility
遵循公开、公平、公正和诚实信用的原则	conform to the principles of openness, fairness, impartiality and good faith
招标公告	tender announcement
一般规定	General Provisions
融资租赁合同	Financial Leasing Contracts
利率	interest rate
邀请招标	invitational tender
评标	bid assessment
本票	promissory note
仓储合同	Warehousing Contracts

二、句子翻译

（一）汉译英

1. If an endorser writes the words "Not Transferable" on a draft and the draft is transferred by the subsequent endorser, the original endorser shall not bear the liability of guarantee to the

subsequent endorsee.

2. A multi-modal carriage operator is responsible for performing, or arranging for performance of, the multi-modal transportation contract, and it enjoys the rights and assumes the obligations of a carrier throughout the course of carriage.

3. In entering into a contract for loan of money, the borrower shall provide true information concerning its business operation and financial condition in connection with the loan as required by the lender.

4. A promissory note is an instrument written and issued by a drawer, promising to pay unconditionally a fixed amount of money to a payee or holder at the sight of the instrument.

5. Members of the bid assessment committees shall objectively and impartially perform their duties, comply with the code of ethics and be personally liable for their assessment opinions.

(二) 英译汉

1. 除非另有协议，货物的风险直到货物所有权转移至买方才从卖方转移至买方；但如果货物所有权转移至买方时，无论是否作出交付行为，风险均转移至买方。

2. 如果未履行合同义务或不适当履行合同义务，新加坡法律规定了各种法律对策和补救措施，具体取决于履约失败的性质。

3. 因作为技术开发合同标的的技术已经由他人公开，致使技术开发合同的履行没有意义的，当事人可以解除合同。

4. 关于某个人何时是或者不是相对人没有清晰的法律定义。一般而言，要约人或受要约人会成为合同的相对人。但是，仅仅是在合同中被提到名字尚不足以使该人成为相对人。

5. 除非另有约定，货物在交付到买方且买方拒绝接受货物并有权这样做时，买方无义务将货物送还卖方，买方只需向卖方宣称其拒绝接受货物。

三、语篇翻译

Chapter V　Legal Liabilities

Article 49　If a unit, in violation of the provisions of this Law, fails to carry out a tender for a project subject to tender or breaks a project subject to tender into parts or resorts to any other form to dodge tender, the unit shall be ordered to make corrections within a given period of time and may be imposed a fine exceeding 0.5 per cent and not exceeding 1 per cent of the contracted sum of the winning project; if the project uses, completely or partly, the State-owned fund, the project may be suspended or the allocation of fund may be suspended; and the person-in-charge directly responsible and other persons directly responsible of the unit shall be given sanctions according to law.

Article 50　If a procuratorial agency, in violation of the provisions of this Law, divulges confidential information and materials related to the tender and bid activity or colludes with a tender or bidder to prejudice the State's interests, the social and public interests or the legitimate rights and interests of other persons, the agency shall be imposed a fine exceeding 50,000 yuan and not exceeding 250,000 yuan and the person-in-charge directly responsible and other persons directly responsible of the agency shall be imposed a fine exceeding 5 per cent and not exceeding 10 per cent of the fine imposed on the agency; the illegal gains therefrom, if any, shall be confiscated of; if the circumstance is serious, its qualifications for procuratorial agency shall be suspended or revoked; and if a crime is constituted, criminal responsibility shall be demanded for according to law. If any loss is caused to other persons, the agency shall be liable therefor according to law.

If an act set forth in the preceding paragraph affects the bidding result, the result shall be void and invalid.

Article 51 A tenderer who restricts or excludes an intended bidder with unreasonable requirements, applies discriminate treatment to an intended bidder, compels bidders to form a consortium to jointly submit their bids, or restricts competition among the bidders, shall be ordered to make corrections and may be imposed a fine exceeding 10,000 yuan and not exceeding 50,000 yuan.

Article 52 If a tenderer for a project subject to tender according to law discloses to another person the names and numbers of intended bidders who have already acquired his tender documents or any other information related to the tender and bid which likely affects fair competition, or leaks the base bid price, the tenderer shall be given a warning and concurrently, may be imposed a fine exceeding 10,000 yuan and not exceeding 100,000 yuan; the person-in-charge directly responsible and other persons directly responsible of the tenderer shall be given sanctions according to law; and if a crime is constituted, criminal responsibility shall be demanded for according to law. If an act set forth in the preceding paragraph affects the bidding result, the result shall be void and invalid.

Article 53 If a bidder colludes with another bidder in submitting their bids or colludes with the tenderer in submitting his bid, or if a bidder resorts to the manner of offering bribes to the tenderer or members of the bid assessment committee to win the bid, his winning of the bid shall be void and invalid, the said bidder shall be imposed a fine exceeding 0.5 per cent and not exceeding 1 per cent of the sum of the winning project, the person-in-charge directly responsible and other persons directly responsible of the bidder shall be imposed a fine exceeding 5 per cent and not exceeding 10 per cent of the fine imposed on the bidder; the illegal gains therefrom, if any, shall be confiscated of concurrently; if the circumstance is serious, his qualifications to take part in bidding of projects subject to tender shall be cancelled for one to two years and the cancellation shall be announced or even his business license shall be revoked by the administrative department for industry and commerce; and if a crime is constituted, criminal responsibility shall be demanded for according to law. If any loss is caused to other persons, the said bidder shall be liable therefor according to law.

Article 54　If a bidder submits his bid in the name of another person or resorts to deception to win the bid, his winning of the bid shall be void and invalid, if a loss is caused to the tenderer, the said bidder shall be liable therefor according to law; and if a crime is constituted, criminal responsibility shall be demanded for according to law. If a bidder of a project subject to tender according to law commits an act set forth in the preceding paragraph and does not commits a crime, the said bidder shall be imposed a fine exceeding 0.5 per cent and not exceeding 1 per cent of the sum of the winning project, the person-in-charge directly responsible and other persons directly responsible of the bidder shall be imposed a fine exceeding 5 per cent and not exceeding 10 per cent of the fine imposed on the bidder; the illegal gains therefrom, if any, shall be confiscated of concurrently; and if the circumstance is serious, his qualifications for taking part in bidding for projects subject to tender according to law for one to three years shall be cancelled and the cancellation shall be announced, or even his business license shall be revoked by the administrative department for industry and commerce.

Article 55　If a tenderer for a project subject to tender according to law, in violation of the provisions of this Law, negotiates with a bidder on such substantial contents as the bid price or bidding plan, the said tenderer shall be given a warning and the person-in-charge directly responsible and other persons directly responsible of the said tenderer shall be given sanctions according to law. If an act set forth in the preceding paragraph affects the bidding result, the result shall be void and invalid.

Article 56　If a member of a bid assessment committee accepts property or other benefits from a bidder or if a member of a bid assessment committee or a working personnel taking part in the bid assessment discloses to another person the assessment and comparison of bid documents, recommendation of candidate winning bidders or any other information related to bid assessment, the member or the personnel shall be given a warning, be confiscated of the property accepted and may concurrently be imposed a fine exceeding 3,000 yuan and not exceeding 50,000 yuan, the member of the bid assessment committee committing any of the illegal acts set forth shall be revoked his qualifications as a member of the committee and may no longer take part in bid assessment of projects subject to tender according to law; and if a crime is constituted, criminal responsibility shall be demanded for according to law.